The Indus Civilization

To the memory of Margaret M. Pugh
who helped me get this far

The Indus Civilization

A Contemporary Perspective

GREGORY L. POSSEHL

ALTAMIRA
PRESS

A Division of
ROWMAN & LITTLEFIELD PUBLISHERS, INC.
Lanham • Boulder • New York • Toronto • Plymouth, UK

ALTAMIRA PRESS
A division of Rowman & Littlefield Publishers, Inc.
A wholly owned subsidiary of The Rowman & Littlefield Publishing Group, Inc.
4501 Forbes Boulevard, Suite 200
Lanham, MD 20706
www.altamirapress.com

Estover Road
Plymouth PL6 7PY
United Kingdom

British Library Cataloguing in Publication Information Available

Library of Congress Cataloging-in-Publication Data

Possehl, Gregory L.
   The indus civilization : a contemporary perspective / Gregory L. Possehl.
      p.   cm.
   Includes bibliographical references and index.
   ISBN 0-7591-0171-X (cloth : alk. paper)—ISBN 0-7591-0172-8 (pbk. : alk. paper)
   1. Indus civilization.   I. Title.

   DS425 .P64   2003
   934—dc21   2002001960

Printed in the United States of America

♾™ The paper used in this publication meets the minimum requirements of American National Standard for Information
Sciences—Permanence of Paper for Printed Library Materials, ANSI/NISO Z39.48–1992.

Contents

Figures

Tables

Preface

THIS IS A BOOK ON THE INDUS CIVILIZATION FOR A MORE general audience than the other books I have authored and edited. It will fit into the larger series I am doing, entitled the Indus Age, as a kind of summary statement.

The material for *The Indus Civilization: A Contemporary Perspective* has been assembled from other work, some of it published, some of it manuscript. But the configuration of the book, and the presentation of Ancient India's earliest urban landscape, is new, especially in my attempts to begin to deal with the ideology of the Indus peoples.

I want to thank my new colleagues at AltaMira Press for taking on the Indus Age series, especially Mitch Allen. He and his associates have been a pleasure to work with.

I should also thank those colleagues who read my work in progress and/or provided me with the kind of scintillating discussion that continues my education. I list them here in the order in which I became actively engaged with them as a part of my intellectual life: Bridget and Raymond Allchin, M. Rafique Mughal, V. N. Misra, Kenneth A. R. Kennedy, Louis Flam, Jim G. Shaffer, Richard Meadow, Maurizio Tosi, Rita Wright, Mark Kenoyer, Vasant Shinde. I also want to acknowledge the fact that my views on the Indus Civilization continue to bear influences from my early training with Walter A. Fairservis Jr.

There are many illustrations in this work. The preface gives me a chance to thank those who helped me here: Catherine and Jean-François Jarrige for imagery from Mehrgarh, Michael Jansen for architectural images and some from Mohenjo-daro, Alexandra Ardeleanu-Jansen for images relating to Indus sculpture, the Archaeological Survey of India (especially my friend and colleague R. S. Bisht) for its assistance, *Man and Environment*, Cambridge University Press, the American Museum of Natural History, *Puratattva*, Ferozsons (Lahore), the American Oriental Society, Istituto Italiano per l'Africa e l'Oriente (formerly IsMEO), *Arabian Art and Archaeology*, the Peabody Museum of Harvard University, the University of California Archaeological Research Facility, *The New Yorker* magazine, and finally my own institution, the University of Pennsylvania Museum. Without the collegiality and cooperation of these individuals and institutions, *The Indus Civilization* would be a very plain book.

Finally, my appointment as an Overseas Fellow of Churchill College, the University of Cambridge, has given me the freedom to bring this book to completion. Churchill College has been extremely generous in this regard, something I thank them for as well.

Ancient Indian Civilization

One cannot expect to build great edifices of theory on archaeological evidence without also anticipating their collapse.

—Walter A. Fairservis Jr.,
The Roots of Ancient India

ANCIENT INDIAN CIVILIZATION

This is a book about an ancient civilization in India and Pakistan. It was christened the "Indus Civilization" by one of British India's great Directors General of Archaeology, Sir John Marshall.[1] The term *Harappan Civilization* has also been applied to these peoples since their remains were first reported from the city of Harappa on the left bank of the Ravi River in the Punjab (figure 1.1 and figure 1.2).

The Indus Civilization, or alternatively the Mature Harappan (2500–1900 B.C.), is a time of cities, developed social classes, craft and career specialists, writing and long-distance trade with Mesopotamia, Central Asia, and even the countries at the mouth of the Red Sea. The foundations for this extraordinary civilization are deep in time, going back to the transition from hunting and gathering to agriculture and pastoralism early in the Holocene, 9,000 to 10,000 years ago. The productive power of food production played a critical role in the growth and differentiation of peoples of ancient India and Pakistan that led by processes still only dimly illuminated to urbanization and the sociocultural differentiation that characterizes it. I use the notion of an "Indus Age" for the period from the

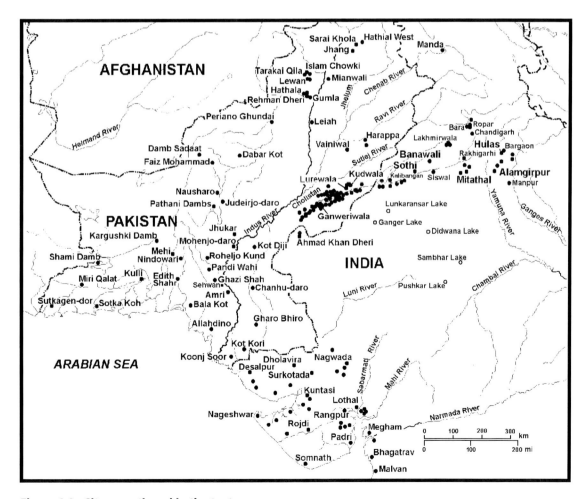

Figure 1.1 Sites mentioned in the text

1

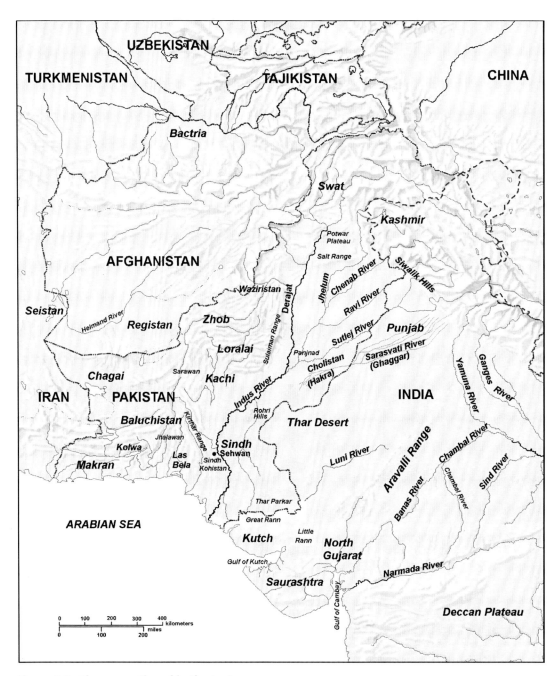

Figure 1.2   Places mentioned in the text

beginnings of agriculture and pastoralism through the Indus Civilization to the widespread use of iron technology
at about 1000 B.C.

Early in the second millennium B.C., by about 1900 B.C.,
the city of Harappa and its counterpart in Sindh,
Mohenjo-daro, were no longer functioning urban centers.
The Indus Civilization came to an end as a complex sociocultural system. Human life continued on the plains and
in the hills and mountains of Pakistan and northwestern
India, but the people were no longer organized by class

and occupational specialization. While there was continuity of life, there was also much change. The ideology of the
Indus Civilization was largely abandoned and the peoples
of the region adopted new customs and beliefs. The
change was not complete; older cultural patterns persisted,
especially in the affairs of these peoples that were closely
tied to the natural world, their use of plants and animals,
of the land itself.

By about 1000 B.C. a new technology appeared across
the Subcontinent. Smelted iron, the first metal of the peo-

ple at large, made its first widespread appearance. The use of this metal was made possible more through the control of pyrotechnology than anything else. It did bring new efficiencies and technologies to the lives of the ancient Indians. And, at about the same time, a new ideology manifested based on the beliefs expressed in the Vedas, the texts on which modern Hinduism is based. The formulation of the Vedic beliefs in the Early Iron Age is a convenient historical marker at which to end the Indus Age, or, more probably, it is an historical transition point at which the cultural traditions of the Subcontinent begin to be more clearly associated with the modern world.

Taken together, I have termed the 6,000 to 7,000 years from the beginnings of food production to the Early Iron Age in Pakistan and northwestern India the "Indus Age." It is the story of this long *durée* that unfolds through the pages of this book.

WHY IS THE INDUS AGE WORTH STUDYING?
Anthropology informs us that all peoples and places are worthy of study, since the collectivity of humankind, in all our historical depth and geographical spread, is the only complete documentation of human diversity, cultural and biological—and that is what anthropology is all about. This is the first and most fundamental reason that the study of the Indus Age is important. Over the past eighty years or so, a number of interesting observations have been made concerning the peoples of the Indus Age and their sociocultural systems. These observations emerge as themes that set the Indus Age and the Indus Civilization apart in quite specific ways from other peoples and places. These themes are used to provide structure and coherence for the story told here.

The Indus Age Was an Archaeological Discovery
In the first weeks of September 1924 the earliest reliable date in Indian history was 326 B.C., the year of Alexander the Great's raid into Gandhara, the Achaemenid Province of South Asia. Nowhere in South Asian history was there a reference to a great civilization of the Bronze Age, not even in the Vedas, the earliest of the Subcontinent's texts. Then, on September 24, 1924, Sir John Marshall announced in the *Illustrated London News* the discovery of Mohenjo-daro and Harappa, and a week later the Assyriologist A. H. Sayce firmly placed the remains in the Bronze Age by citing the occurrence of Mohenjo-daro-type seals in Mesopotamia and Iran.[2]

As we look back, it is clear that remains of the Indus Civilization had been collected and published prior to 1924. Seals from Harappa were published in the nineteenth century.[3] Such places as Dabar Kot, Sutkagen-dor,

and Kalibangan were known, with pottery and other finds published in reputable journals—but no one knew how old the artifacts were because there was no historical context in which to place them and no reliable dating methods known. So, the notices of these sites sat as unknown curiosities.

Unlike ancient Mesopotamia, Dynastic Egypt, and ancient Chinese civilization, for which historical records informed us of the antiquity of urban life, nowhere in the records of ancient India was there even a hint of the Indus Civilization, save in the mounds of the Greater Indus region.

The Peoples of the Indus Age Lived Their Own Lives and Had Their Own Cultural Traditions, But Were a Part of a Larger World
The Greater Indus region is the easternmost portion of a large cultural and natural area of antiquity, stretching from the Mediterranean Sea to the Thar Desert of India, and from the Arabian Gulf to the plains of Central Asia. There is today a vast number of different peoples there. Characteristically, each of these peoples has their own language (or dialect) and distinctive way of life, or culture. The archaeological record and later textual materials indicate that there was also a diversity of peoples in this region in antiquity, at least since the beginning of the Holocene, about 10,000 years ago, following the retreat of the continental glaciers.[4]

Within the Greater Indus region, similarities among archaeological assemblages inform us about communication and interaction among the people who created them. This communication and interaction was undoubtedly made manifest in many ways, both directly and indirectly, through third, fourth, fifth, *n*th . . . parties. Individual innovations in culture that had value to these peoples were spread in these ways throughout this region; for the most part, this communication probably happened very quickly, over a matter of a few years (even weeks and months, in some cases), but the acceptance and implementation of change may have taken longer. Such change may have been accepted within the variable sociocultural systems of the Greater Indus region because, most likely, there were close underlying sociocultural similarities among these diverse peoples.

There is evidence of variation in the frequency and intensity of the forms of communication and interaction throughout the Indus Age. But communication never dropped to nil, or even close to it. The region was always alive—sometimes it was more alive than others— with activity linking the diverse peoples there.

While the forms of communication and interaction are not known in detail, or even with much certainty, we have some hints of the range of activities that took place. This knowledge comes from the study of the archaeology, the historical and ethnographic records, and a reading of the cultural geography. Based on the observation that the early history of the Indus Age is one of success and growth, it is reasonable to believe that balanced, symbiotic relationships favorable to this end were in place. Anthropologists have used the term *exchange systems* to describe relationships that serve to share risk so that if disaster befalls one people in one place, their neighbors can be called on to assist them. Such relationships enhance survivability. They also imply interaction, not only in the time of need, but over protracted periods of time. The mechanism here is exchange, for which the regular and predictable interchange of "gifts" is used to sustain a relationship that is in part used to mollify the hardship of periodic but unpredictable events—flood, crop failure, pestilence, warfare, and other disasters.

Seasonality in the lives of farmers and herders is based in part on geography and the fact that adjacent regions can be complementary. The symbiosis of the highlands of Baluchistan and the Northwest Frontier with the Indus lowlands is one of the timeless facts of life within the Greater Indus region. Migration of pastoralists from the mountains in the winter, and back again for the summer, is one of those constant, enduring patterns of movement and interaction that were present during the Indus Age and beyond, into modern times. These nomads are frequently also craftspeople, traders, tinkers, transporters, bards, and messengers. They bring news from afar and bring along their children—potential marriage partners for the people with whom they stay in the course of their yearly round.

It is clear that the peoples of the Indus Age had a heavy dependence on animals, especially cattle and to a lesser extent sheep and goats. In this sense they were pastoralists, whether settled or nomadic. Seasonal nomadism must have been common. Some individuals may have been settled for a part of their lives and nomadic at other times. This leads unmistakably to the proposition that the constant search for pastureland may well have been one of the most important of the great engines driving the interaction and communication within the Greater Indus region. But it should also be clear that not all of the mobile craftspeople, traders, tinkers, transporters, bards, and messengers were involved in the pastoral component of the subsistence economy. Some must have been sustained in other ways, outside of this subsistence regime. The nature of their integration into their own society and the sociocultural system of those around them, however, led to movement, travel, and the spread of products and ideas.

It is in the nature of people to contemplate what I call the "thrill of travel": crossing a river just because it is there; visiting a "foreign" place just because it sounds interesting and the journey is challenging; going to an island that can be seen only from a mountaintop just because no one has ever done it. This is very human stuff and another in the range of human attitudes and activities that shapes the distribution of artifacts across a landscape such as the Greater Indus region. It implies the movement of people and their possessions as well as their skills.

Another related activity has to do with bards and people who carry news. These are "professional" wanderers who tell tales, keep an oral folk literature alive, and carry to new localities information of happenings in the places they have visited. They tell of famines and plagues; war and peace; marriages and deaths; the comings and goings of the great, near great, and even those who only presume such status.

We have little grasp of the details of the social structure of the peoples of the Indus Age; this is another challenge to those of us who deal with these ancient peoples. But, with the dawn of the Indus Civilization, we begin to have a sense of social hierarchy and craft and career specialists. From the disparate archaeological remains dated to a single stage or phase of the history of the Indus Age, as well as from some considerations of physical anthropology, we also get a sense that there was considerable ethnic and social diversity throughout this period.

This serious gap in our knowledge is, in reality, simply another of the major challenges for future archaeologists. But we can say that the life of families everywhere does imply the movement of people. Bringing new men or women into families after marriage is one source of mobility. Near the end of their productive lives, persons of the elder generation may take up residence with the young. Children are often shared among dispersed segments of a family or lineage. There are also the shorter-term gatherings for marriages, births, rights of passage, and "holidays." We clearly do not know the social forms of the peoples of the Indus Age and therefore cannot talk about patrilocal postmarriage residence, or the form of their lineages and/or clans, or even whether they had them. But what we can say is that the social life of humans everywhere in every age implies some degree of movement of people and their possessions. This distribution of artifacts also implies the movement of skilled persons, who, for short or long periods, took up residence in varying locations. Thus, when we look at the geographical spread of artifacts, we see that it is not all trade and commerce, transportation specialists, and pastoral nomads moving in their search for pastureland. Some of it is the ordinary stuff of family business: acquiring a mate, caring for the elderly, sharing happy or socially important occasions with relatives and friends.

These and related activities are the forces of diffusion and migration, whether direct or indirect. The word *diffusion* is not used much in this book, but the study of the Indus Age is certainly concerned with the distribution of artifacts. Since we know that the artifacts themselves did not move in some self-propelled way across the Greater Indus region, we must surmise that human mechanisms were involved. While we have little grasp of the specifics of the ancient world in terms of which of these activities or customs was responsible for this or that distributional pattern, we do have an understanding of the range of mechanisms used.

The flip side to this interaction and movement of peoples and things is that we also see cultural and biological diversity among the peoples both today and, in a less precise way, in deep antiquity. The interaction has not now, or ever, led to cultural and biological homogenization. Geography, distance, the forces of human parochialism, strong senses of group identity, and the need for protection and solidarity have combined to yield a diversity of peoples and cultures.

Sometimes, perhaps most often, this diversity is expressed in hierarchies of affiliation, sometimes nested. In Pakistan, for example, the national identity combines with regional affiliations of peoples: Sindhis, Punjabis, Baluchis, Pathans, and the like. Within each of these regional sociocultural populations there are divisions by subregion, occupation, lineage,and so forth, down to the family and individual.

The forces of intercommunication, diffusion, homogenization, and regional unity are in constant, dynamic tension with local forces of parochialism and the need for group identity and solidarity. All of these forces are real and in some ways contradictory. Over the long *durée* of the Indus Age, they led to a kind of "unity of diversity" from the Mediterranean to the Indus.[5] They also make telling the story of the Indus Age a difficult task, as one tries to seek and explain the roles of autochthonous and interregional culture processes.

There are two large issues addressed in this book that are influenced by the point of view just expressed: the nature of the food-producing revolution and the rise of urbanization.

A Food-Producing Subsistence System Very Much at Home in the Subcontinent

It is virtual archaeological dogma that the domestication of wheat, barley, sheep, goats, and cattle took place in the Near East in the early millennia of the Holocene, 8,000 to 10,000 years ago. There are new perspectives on this important transition in human history, and the borderlands of the Subcontinent may have played a pivotal role in this transformation, giving the region a more central place in human history. More is said of this complex matter in chapter 2.

The Indus Civilization Arose and Flourished by Processes of Change That Are Essentially Local, and Yet It Participated in a Much Larger World of Trade, Commerce, and Culture History

On the eve of its discovery the Indus Civilization was called the "Indo-Sumerian Civilization," by Sir John Marshall, so close was the historical relation thought to be.[6] This was a suggestion that was based mostly on the presence of Indus-style seals in Mesopotamia and southwestern Iran, as well as a few other artifacts. It was soon seen to be a mistaken notion and dropped, the individual character of the Indus remains having come through. It is now clear that the process of urbanization in ancient India was an autochthonous one, recalling that the Greater Indus region was never isolated from the larger region to the west, or for that matter to the north, south, and east as well. The ancient cities of the Indus did not arise in an historical vacuum—but then, neither did the ancient cities of Mesopotamia, but that is another story. This part of the Indus Age story is told in chapter 3.

We know that for virtually all of the second half of the third millennium (2500–2000 B.C.) at least some of the peoples of the Indus Civilization were engaged in trade, exchange, and what appears to have been quite intense, regular intercourse with peoples in the Arabian Gulf, Mesopotamia, Central Asia, and the Iranian plateau. This interaction moved significant amounts of material culture all over the mega-region, and there was a certain amount of ideological iconography involved as well. But still, the Indus, Mesopotamia, the Gulf, and Central Asia remained distinctive cultural entities. This part of the story is outlined in chapter 12.

The Indus Civilization Is an Example of Archaic Sociocultural Complexity, But Without the State

There is no real consensus among archaeologists on the definition of the archaic *state*, although there seems to be some agreement on a few points. The ancient state was a form of political organization. It developed among civilizations with large-scale economies and considerable specialization in craft and career tracks. The administration of the state was a prominent feature of this form of political organization, and some portion of the career specialists formed the bureaucracy of the state. The craft and career specialists, and the other peoples of their society, were arranged in a hierarchy of classes. The state monopolized the use of force as a means of social control and as an agency to protect, if not expand, the sovereignty of the people it encompassed. The state form of organization placed the management of diplomacy and warfare within the domain of a strong, forceful leader. States focused power on individual leaders, usually called kings.

The Indus Civilization is something of a faceless sociocultural system. Individuals, even prominent ones, do not readily emerge from the archaeological record, as they do in Mesopotamia and Dynastic Egypt, for example. There are no clear signs of kingship in the form of sculpture or palaces. There is no evidence for a state bureaucracy or the other trappings of "stateness." Nor is there evidence for a state religion in the form of large temples or other monumental public works.

It is clear that the Indus Civilization is an example of archaic sociocultural complexity, just as complex in its own way as the archaic civilizations of Mesopotamia and Dynastic Egypt or the Maya and Inca of the New World. But the Indus Civilization was not organized as a state, if by *state* we adhere to the criteria previously outlined.

It is its marked deviance from the norm of ancient sociocultural complexity that makes the Indus Civilization so fascinating, at least to me. To my knowledge, there is, for example, no close parallel to it in either the archaeological or ethnographic record. In that sense, the Indus Civilization comes across as a kind of counterintuitive civilization, possibly "strange" because there are no existing examples that we can point to as comparative.

The sociocultural form that the Indus polity took is not known, and more clearly characterizing it is one of the most important challenges to archaeologists interested in South Asia and archaic sociocultural complexity.

Whatever the reason(s) for the emergence of the Indus Civilization, its peoples were deeply rooted in the South Asian landscape. They were masters of food production and the extraction of raw materials from a bountiful environment.

GEOGRAPHY OF THE INDUS AGE

In this section, the cultural/natural regions of the Indus Civilization, called Domains, are presented, along with the nature and history of the two principal rivers: the Indus and Sarasvati. Climatic change is discussed, and, finally, a short review of Indus Civilization settlement patterns and subsistence regimes is offered.

Geography

The Indus Civilization covered an area of approximately one million square kilometers. The westernmost Indus site is Sutkagen-dor, near the modern border separating Pakistan and Iran. The principal regions are Baluchistan and the Northwest Frontier, the mountainous eastern end of the Iranian plateau. The plains of the Indus Valley, the Pakistani and Indian Punjabs, Haryana and Ganga-Yamuna Doab are included. The northern and western tracks of the Thar Desert in Rajasthan were occupied by the Indus peoples, as were the sandy North Gujarat plain, Kutch, and the hilly savanna of Saurashtra.

Rainfall for the western domains came from the winter westerlies, which brought snow to the mountains of Baluchistan and the Northwest Frontier and rain to the Punjab and northwestern India. The summer rain of the southwest monsoon brought moisture to Saurashtra, North Gujarat, the Punjab, and northwestern India, and sometimes even to the western domains.

Domains

Sometime ago I proposed a scheme of subregions that could be used in the study of the Indus Civilization.[7] These turned out to be quite like those proposed by J. P. Joshi.[8] I developed this scheme in an attempt to break up the Indus "monolith" and challenge the "sameness" principle that had been invoked by Wheeler and Piggott. This scheme has been further developed.[9] I have come to call these subregions *Domains* (figure 1.3).

This approach to defining the Domains of the Mature Harappan was based on geography and Mature Harappan settlement patterns. G. Smith has examined them from the perspective of locational geography.[10] He undertook two statistical analyses of Mature Harappan sites larger than 10 hectares. The first analysis used a gravity model; the second was a cluster analysis. Both of these analyses produced subregional geographical units that closely match the Domains I have proposed, providing an independent confirmation that there is something important in the study of Mature Harappan Domains as such.[11] Smith thinks of the units that his analyses produced as "Harappan polities," which just might be the case.

The Indus River

The most ancient name of the greatest of rivers in Pakistan is "Sindhu." In the Rgveda, this may mean simply "stream," but in most cases it clearly refers to the Indus itself.

> Flashing and whitely gleaming in her mightiness she
> moves along her ample volumes through the realms.

Figure 1.3   Domains of the Indus Civilization

Most active of the active Sindhu unrestrained,
like a dappled mare, beautiful, fair to see.[12]

Within the plains of modern Sindh, the Indus River is a fully mature stream. It has a reputation for being a powerful, violent, unpredictable river. But Sindh would be a desert without the Indus. Table 1.1 lists statistics on the characteristics of the Indus.

Table 1.1   Figures on the flow of the Indus River

Total length	2900 km
Length in Sindh, with meanders	Approximately 1000 km
Discharge, maximum	885,165 cu ft/second
Discharge, minimum	17,568 cu ft/second
Maximum high water at Sukkur	+5.40 m
Total silt per year carried past Sukkur (average for 29 years)	9,937,000,000 cu ft
Average silt carried	1,000,000 tons/day
Maximum velocity in Sindh	3.2 m/s

The Indus floods during the summer because of the Himalayan snow melt—not so much because of rain. The upper course of the river is deep in the mountains, and it is often blocked by ice dams and landslides. The release of these impounded waters is the source of the most devastating of the Indus floods. The alluvium from the Indus is very fertile and is renewed each year. Sindh is, therefore, a proverbial "green machine," and famine is unknown there.

An outline of the channel history of the Indus River is available from the works of several scholars.[13] By identifying paleochannels, studying their shape, direction, and preservation, it has been possible to suggest that the earliest course seen today flowed through the Kachi Plain, well to the west of the modern course. The second course, which may be of the third millennium B.C., flowed just to the west (not east) of Mohenjo-daro (figure 1.4). The Indus was captured by a gap in the Rohri Hills, a limestone formation rich in chert, sometime after the voyage down

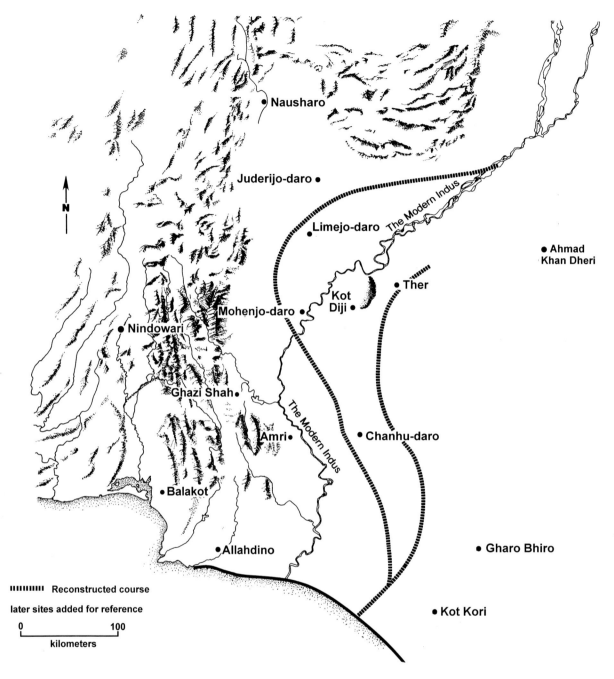

Figure 1.4 The best estimate of the course of the Indus River during the Indus Age

the river of Alexander the Great in the fourth century B.C. and prior to the thirteenth century A.D.

The Sarasvati River

There is a river in the Great Indian Desert that is mostly dry. Today it is generally called Ghaggar in India and Hakra in Pakistan. In ancient times it was called Sarasvati and appears in the Rgveda in many places. It was a holy river, the "foremost of rivers," in the Vedas:

Foremost mother, foremost of rivers, foremost of goddesses, Sarasvati, We are, as 'twer, of no repute and dear Mother, give thou us renown.

In thee, Sarasvati, divine, all generations have their stars. Be, glad with Sunahotra's sons:

O Goddess grant us progeny.[14]

Linguistic, archaeological, and historical data show that the Sarasvati of the Vedas is the modern Ghaggar or Hakra. During its early (Plio-Pleistocene?) history, the

Sarasvati flowed south out of the Siwalik Hills through Rajasthan. A series of shifts took place in its channel, and the course moved steadily in a clockwise direction, eventually flowing east-southeast rather than south. Stream capture by the emerging Yamuna River compromised its watershed, and the Sarasvati began to dry up. By Mature Harappan times, it terminated in an inland delta near the modern Pakistani city of Fort Derawar.[15] There is a large number of Mature Harappan sites there, which seem to have taken advantage of the inland delta as a place that had its soils renewed by flood and was naturally irrigated.

The Sarasvati seems to have never reached the sea, at least in the third millennium when it was in the vicinity of Fort Derawar. Its early history, when it probably did reach the sea through Kutch, is to the south. In spite of its orientation and the presence of fossil riverbeds near the northern Rohri Hills, from Fort Derawar, for about 150 kilometers in a southwesterly direction, there is nothing that resembles the remains of an ancient river—just sand dunes and old alluvium.[16]

Climatic Change

During the Indus Age, there is no sound evidence for climatic change that had an effect pronounced enough to be picked up by archaeological methods. Marshall proposes that there was more rainfall in the Greater Indus region during the Mature Harappan.[17] He notes that the high density of prehistoric villages in Baluchistan can be accounted for only by the existence of a more productive environment. He also notes that elephants, tigers, and rhinoceroses are all depicted on Indus stamp seals and are animals that prefer a wet habitat. The lion, a dryland animal, is conspicuous in its absence from Indus imagery. Baked bricks were used for shelters that provided protection from the rains rather than the sun-dried variety, which is susceptible to erosion in climates with heavy rainfall. Moreover, the elaborate civic drainage system at Mohenjo-daro must have been created to handle something more than today's scanty rainfall. The acceptance of this position seems to be one of the few points of agreement shared by Sir Mortimer Wheeler and Marshall.[18] Their "higher rainfall hypothesis" was thoroughly critiqued in the 1960s.[19]

In 1971 G. Singh published a paper reviewing the findings from an investigation of pollen cores from three salt lakes in Rajasthan: Sambhar, Didwana, and Lunkaransar (see figure 1.2).[20] The pollen cores were also associated with several radiocarbon dates, and Singh notes an increase in the salinity of the lakes in the early second millennium B.C. He proposes that this increase in salinity was due to increased aridity and that this climatic change could have been the root cause for the eclipse of the Indus Civilization. There has been additional palynological research at these lakes and others in Rajasthan.[21] There are two critiques of this work and its findings, concluding that the salt lakes of Rajasthan do not provide sound evidence for climatic change.[22]

The changing salinity of these lakes, which appears to be well documented, need not be attributed to changes in rainfall. The geology of Rajasthan is complex. The three lakes investigated are hypersaline today, but there are also freshwater lakes in this same region (Lakes Pushkar and Ganger; see figure 1.2). This observation leads to the conclusion that under one climatic regime in Rajasthan, there can be both freshwater and hypersaline lakes, calling into question the Singh hypothesis.

There is some evidence that the salinity of the lakes is controlled by underground drainage, which in turn is controlled by tectonics. When the underground drains are tightly squeezed together, plugged, the only way water can leave the basins is through evaporation, resulting in a buildup of salts. When the subterranean drains are open, there is a regular flow of water, and the salts accumulated during evaporation are carried off in groundwater. Tectonics resulting from continental drift and the Subcontinent's collision with the rest of Asia control the underground drains. Tectonics may also have an important, even controlling, effect on surface drainage and the capture of the Sarasvati's waters by the Yamuna, as previously noted.

Whatever the climate of the Indus Age, the weather was not exactly the same from year to year. But it does not appear that over the long run any period was markedly different from any other or that there were long-term trends of increasing or decreasing precipitation or temperature or dramatic shifts in the weather from season to season. During the whole of the Holocene, virtually all of the Greater Indus region had two principal seasons: one hot and wet, the other cold and dry.

That is the way it was in, say, 1902 B.C., and that is the way it was in A.D. 1902, when the Viceroy of India, Lord Curzon, made an important appointment. It was cool but comfortable in Calcutta on February 21, 1902, when the government of India announced the appointment of John Hubert Marshall as the new Director General of the Archaeological Survey of India (ASI). Marshall is the man with whom the discovery of the Indus Age and the Indus Civilization can be most closely associated, and it is to that story that I now turn.

THE DISCOVERY OF THE INDUS AGE

Lord Curzon of Kedleston, who became Viceroy of India in 1899, was disgusted with the manner in which his colonial

Figure 1.5   Sir John Marshall

government was handling the cultural heritage of its dominions in India. He developed a plan to change this negligence, a major part of which called for the rejuvenation of the ASI. This meant assigning a new person to the post of Director General, and Curzon wanted someone young and vigorous. He found John Marshall (figure 1.5).

Marshall was then a twenty-six-year-old student of Greek archaeology from Cambridge University. He had been trained in field archaeology at Knossos by Sir Arthur Evans, from whom he had learned the best and most recent methods of excavation.[23] Marshall was also a brilliant young scholar, full of promise.

In 1902 nothing was known of the truly ancient periods of Indian life, and the discovery of the Indus Age is a story of archaeological exploration on a grand scale. Prior to the excavations at Harappa and Mohenjo-daro in the 1920s, the earliest secure date in the history of India and Pakistan was the spring of 326 B.C., when Alexander the Great made his raid into the northwestern provinces of the Subcontinent. There was no hint, even in the earliest Indian texts, that during the Bronze Age there had been a period of urbanization of the Greater Indus Valley and Baluchistan, including the fertile plains of Sindh, Gujarat, Punjab, Haryana, northern Rajasthan, and western Uttar Pradesh, and extending as far west as the Dasht River on the modern border between Pakistan and Iran.

THE FIRST VISIT TO AN HARAPPAN SITE[24]

The story of discovery actually begins in March or April 1829 when a man known as Charles Masson visited the huge mounds adjacent to the modern village of Harappa, near an abandoned course of the Ravi River in Sahiwal District of the Punjab (figure 1.6).[25] Masson traveled in the western borderlands of British India in the 1820s and

1830s as an antiquarian from the state of Kentucky in America, but he was in fact a deserter from the British Army of Bengal. He confused Harappa with the city of Sangala, the capital of King Porus, who Alexander the Great defeated in his last great battle. Masson's was a good enough guess for the times.

We do not know what *Harappa* means. T. G. Aravamuthan has proposed that the name was derived from Mesopotamia, a place called "Arrapha" or "Arrapkha" on the site of the modern town of Kirkuk. This is surely fanciful, probably just as fanciful as the notion that the Harappa of today is the "Hariyupiya" of the Rgveda.[26]

In 1831 Lieutenant Alexander Burnes made an historic journey up the Indus River. In the course of the journey, Burnes visited the site of Amri and was the first man to publish it as an archaeological site. While in the Punjab, Burnes went to Harappa, just two years after Masson's visit. His observations on the site do not vary significantly from those of Masson.

The early notices of Harappa by Masson and Burnes have historical importance primarily because they came to the attention of Sir Alexander Cunningham, the first Director General of the Archaeological Survey. In 1875 Cunningham reported that at Harappa "in 1853, and again in 1856, I traced the remains of flights of stairs on both the eastern and western faces of the high mound to the northwest, as well as the basement of a large square building."[27] In this report he noted the size of the site (4 kilometers in circuit) and the height of the mounds (12 to 18 meters). He also noted, with considerable regret, that many of the features he had seen earlier had disappeared: "The whole have now been removed to form ballast for the railway. Perhaps the best idea of the extent of the ruined brick mounds of Harapa [sic] may be formed from the fact that they have more than sufficed to furnish brick ballast for about 100 miles of Lahor [sic] and Multan railway."[28] Cunningham acquired a stamp seal from one Major Clark, which today can be identified as a typical Indus type, although Cunningham thought that it was not "Indian" since the bull did not have the hump of the zebu (figure 1.7).

In 1886 M. Longworth Dames published a second seal from Harappa that had been acquired by an education inspector by the name of J. Harvey. In his one-page note, Dames discusses and illustrates Cunningham's (or rather Major Clark's) seal and the new find, as well as some interesting but obscure bibliography.

J. F. Fleet published a third seal from Harappa in 1912 that had been acquired by Mr. T. A. O'Connor, then the District Superintendent of Police. O'Connor excavated at the site in 1886, and this seal came from his work there. The Fleet paper is important for two reasons: (1) He reveals that

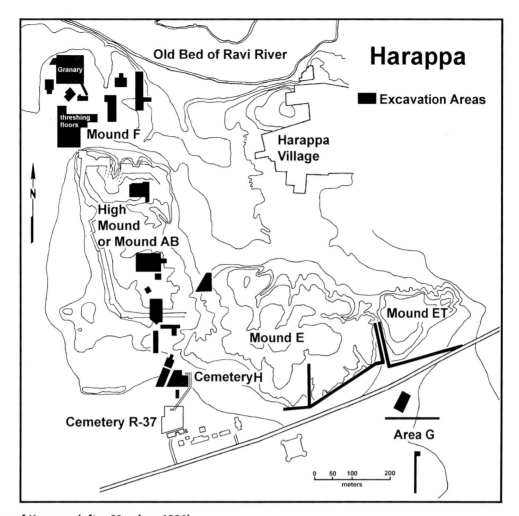

Figure 1.6　Plan of Harappa (after Meadow 1991)

all three seals were in the British Museum, where they remain today; and (2) the Cunningham–Clark seal is published accurately as a photograph of the impression and not as Cunningham's rather crude drawing.

Marshall was on home leave in 1906 and examined the

Figure 1.7　The first seal from Harappa (after Cunningham 1875)

three published seals in the British Museum during this visit. Not long after his return to India he had two of his associates in the ASI visit Harappa to report on the scale and condition of the site. In 1920 Marshall instructed his colleague in the ASI, the Rai Bahadur Daya Ram Sahni, to conduct an excavation at Harappa. He opened trenches on the mound labeled "A-B" on Cunningham's plan as well as on the northernmost mound, now labeled "F." Sahni found more stamp seals in stratigraphic context, and by the end of the season Marshall felt that the results proved that the Harappa seals belonged to a time prior to Alexander the Great, or, in Indian terms, the pre-Mauryan epoch—a real breakthrough in ancient history.

Sahni spent three consecutive field seasons at Harappa. He helped archaeologists solve the "mystery of the seals." But neither he nor Marshall understood that there was an entire civilization waiting for them. This insight was to come from the south, in Sindh, at a place called Mohenjo-daro.

Mohenjo-daro was first visited by Superintendent Archaeologist Devadatta Ramkrishna Bhandarkar in 1911–1912. He thought the site was not old because the bricks looked modern to him—a real miss there.

Bhandarkar's successor was Rakal Das Banerji, a gifted and energetic man. During the field season of 1919–1920, one year prior to Sahni's initial probing of Harappa, Banerji visited Mohenjo-daro. He correctly identified the Buddhist stupa, which dates to the early centuries of the common era (c. a.d. 150–500), on the summit of the site and noted the double-mound layout. Banerji picked up a flint scraper from the surface of Mohenjo-daro, and, concluding that Mohenjo-daro was a very ancient site, he decided to excavate. During this work, two more stamp seals were found in a trench near the stupa below the level of the Buddhist structures.

By summer of 1924 Marshall knew that there was something important at the two sites, Mohenjo-daro and Harappa. He had his staff bring material from the excavations to his headquarters where they could be compared.

So impressed indeed was I by their novel character that I lost no time in publishing an account of them in the *Illustrated London News,* my hope being that through the medium of that widely read journal I might succeed in getting some light thrown on their age and character by archaeologists in other countries. . . . In the following issue of the *Illustrated London News* appeared a letter from Professor Sayce pointing out the close resemblance between these objects from the Indus Valley and certain Sumerian antiquities from southern Mesopotamia, and a week later there appeared in the same journal a longer article from the pens of Messrs. Gadd and Sidney Smith giving a more detailed comparison of the pictographic script and other antiquities found in the two countries . . . there can now no longer be any doubt that the Punjab and Sind . . . [sites are] roughly contemporary with the Sumerian antiquities of Mesopotamia. . . . Simultaneously also the same conclusion was reached by Dr. E. Mackay, director of the American expedition at Kish, who in an unpublished letter to me pointed out the similarity between the ceramic wares found at Mohenjo-daro and at Kish.[29]

FURTHER EXCAVATIONS AT MOHENJO-DARO AND HARAPPA

Marshall and his colleagues knew that they were now onto something very big—an entirely new civilization of the Bronze Age, dating to the time of the Sumerians and Dynastic Egypt. The ASI was spurred to action. Brick robbing had destroyed much of the architecture at Harappa, so their main efforts were in Sindh, where Rao Bahadur Kashinath Narayana Dikshit took charge of the excava-

tions at Mohenjo-daro in 1924–1925 (figure 1.8). He published the first site plan of Mohenjo-daro with his substantial preliminary report.[30] We can see from this plan that Dikshit did a great deal during this season, opening up trenches all over Mohenjo-daro. Dikshit's "Site E" is a trench approximately 450 meters long that yielded a series of striking and important antiquities as well as what he (incorrectly) called a "temple" or "shrine" (figure 1.9). The small finds poured in during this season: "The quantitative results of the operations were no less striking than the character of the remains disclosed. The total number of small finds registered during the season was 7,152, far exceeding the number of antiquities recorded during a single season at any other ancient site in India."[31] The next field season (1925–1926) at Mohenjo-daro was a huge undertaking, directed by Marshall himself.

Indo-Sumerian Civilization: The First Name

In the preliminary reports on the excavations at Mohenjo-daro and Harappa prior to 1926 the term *Indo-Sumerian Civilization* was used to describe the remains. It was clear that the peoples of the Indus Valley and Mesopotamia were in contact, and that might have shaped ancient Indian civilization. In 1926 Marshall dropped the term in favor of *Indus Civilization* (never *Indus Valley Civilization*), noting that the previously used "term ('Indo-Sumerian') is likely to imply a closer connection with Sumer than seems now justified."[32]

Mohenjo-daro 1925–1926: The Big Season

Marshall had proper staff quarters and facilities, including a site museum, built at Mohenjo-daro, and in December 1925 he began a very large-scale excavation at the site. Vir-

Figure 1.8 Rao Bahadur Kashinath Narayana Dikshit

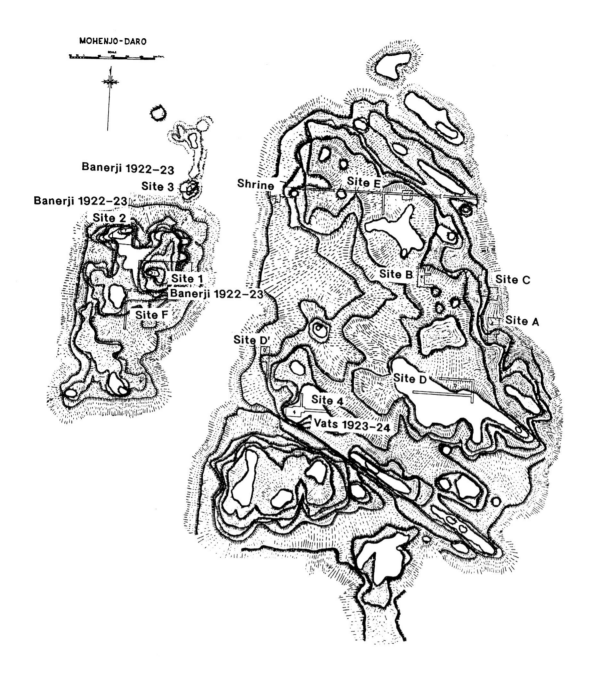

MOHENJO-DARO

Banerji 1922–23
Site 3
Banerji 1922–23
Site 2
Site 1
Banerji 1922–23
Site F

Shrine
Site E

Site B
Site C

Site A

Site D'

Site D

Site 4
Vats 1923–24

Figure 1.9   The first site plan of Mohenjo-daro (after Dikshit 1924–25)

tually everyone who was anyone in the ASI was there. Marshall's financial resources for this season allowed him to hire as many as twelve hundred laborers. By the end of the season significant portions of the Lower Town had been opened, plans of many buildings drawn, and numerous artifacts discovered. For example, they found the so-called priest-king. It was Marshall's only season of excavation at the site, but he discovered the Great Bath, surely one of the most significant finds in all of the digging at Indus sites.

The Need for New Leadership at Mohenjo-daro

No matter what the importance, or success, of the Mohenjo-daro program, Sir John Marshall had many other things to do. His senior staff members were busy with their duties as well. It was also clear that the work at Mohenjo-daro needed someone familiar with Mesopotamian archaeology, so on two accounts Marshall needed a new man. He selected Ernest John Henry Mackay (figure 1.10).

Mackay was a veteran archaeologist when he joined the

Figure 1.10   Ernest John Henry Mackay (from a photograph in the Field Museum, Chicago)

ASI in 1926. He had been trained in field archaeology by Sir Flinders Petrie in Egypt, where he worked until 1916. Mackay then moved on to excavate tumuli in the Arabian Gulf. He served in the army in Palestine during the First World War and from 1919 to 1922 was Custodian of Antiquities for the government there. In 1922 Mackay became field director of the Field Museum–Oxford University Archaeological Expedition to Mesopotamia, where he excavated Jamdat Nasr and the important Sumerian city of Kish. Mackay demonstrated an interest in the Harappan Civilization in early correspondence with Marshall and in a paper on Indo-Sumerian connections.[33] He arrived at Mohenjo-daro in time for the 1926–1927 field season.

Mohenjo-daro 1926–1931: The Final Five Large Seasons of Work

Mackay jumped right into the work and began excavating in L Area, south of the stupa on the Mound of the Great Bath. He uncovered the so-called Assembly Hall and other architectural remains that are not well understood, even today. He also found three pieces of sculpture: the Seated Man (L-950); a reasonably well preserved bust called the Stern Man (L-898); and a very poor, abraded head, possibly of a woman, called the Lady of L Area (L-127).

Mackay was partnered with Daya Ram Sahni, who went to work on the lower city and succeeded in opening a total area of approximately 140 by 120 meters, most in HR Area, but including part of the adjacent VS Area. Sahni made good progress in linking roads and lanes between these parts of the city. It was during this season that the beautiful bronze "dancing girl" was found as well as one of the exquisite jewelry hoards in HR Area.

The remaining four major seasons of work during the early period of excavation at Mohenjo-daro were completely in Mackay's charge. His labor force was 600 men, about one-half that of the 1925–1926 season. They were mostly Sindhis from surrounding villages, who returned home following their work at the site. But some Brahuis from Kalat joined and were well regarded by Mackay for their strength and intelligence.

Mackay was on a long leash. He went to the northwestern quarter of Mohenjo-daro, the rich DK Area, and expanded Dikshit's operation. He also did the first deep digging of any scale at the site, thereby gaining some sense of the stratigraphy of the northern part of the lower city. N. G. Majumdar assisted him in 1927–1928 and part of 1928–1929, but Majumdar left the work at Mohenjo-daro to excavate Jhukar, 25 kilometers away.

Mackay succeeded in clearing a vast architectural complex in DK Area, which gives the visitor to Mohenjo-daro a real sense of walking through an ancient city. The splendidly preserved baked-brick buildings stand today much as they did over 4,000 years ago, all published by Mackay himself.[34]

In 1931 financial problems put an end to the large-scale excavations at Mohenjo-daro. The final field season started on November 3, 1931, with Mackay planning to investigate remains to the northeast of Mound of the Great Bath. He thought there might be a part of the city wall there. On the morning of November 6, he put four gangs of men to work there, but a telegram arrived from the headquarters of the ASI informing him that a budget crisis demanded he cease all excavations immediately. This brought an end to the major excavations at Mohenjo-daro. Some small-scale work continued there, but the big campaigns were over.

CONTINUED EXCAVATION AT HARAPPA

Harappa was far from forgotten. Sahni had undertaken three seasons of independent excavation at Harappa between 1920–1921 and 1924–1925. He had made a good start at the site, but there was a lot left to do, in spite of the ravages of the railroad brick robbers. There was no excavation there in 1925–1926, presumably because of the very large scale of the program at Mohenjo-daro, when Marshall directed the field team and brought so many of his colleagues with him. Sometime in 1925–1926 Madho Sarup Vats became the Superintendent Archaeologist for the northern circle and settled in to address the task of excavating Harappa. At this site, he undertook eight seasons of work, which extended through the end of the 1933–1934 field season. He exposed structures on Mound F, investigated the cemeteries, and defined the "Cemetery H Culture." A number of important artifacts came to light, including a magnificent red jasper torso and a male dancer.

Mound F was the best preserved of the excavation areas probed in the early years. This part of the site has a complex set of remains that Sahni and his successor chose to call "the area of the parallel walls." In 1926–1927, Marshall resolved this issue. He notes in the annual report on the activities of the survey that this architectural complex seems to have been a storage facility since it could be favorably compared to storage rooms associated with Cretan palaces.[35] Marshall's training at Knossos with Sir Arthur Evans gave him the necessary experience to make this connection, one of the clearest examples of how experience in archaeology shapes an archaeologist's interpretation of remains. From the day of Sir John's judgment until the present, this building has been called the Granary, despite the fact that there is almost nothing to support his conclusion except the probably fanciful comparison to Knossos.

When Vats retired from excavation at Harappa, some work continued. K. N. Sastri discovered an Indus cemetery at Harappa in excavation square R-37. This cemetery is, in fact, an extension of the Posturban Cemetery H, excavated by Vats. R-37 dates to the middle to later portions of the Mature Harappan, but it was the first Mature Harappan cemetery to have been discovered and is still the largest. There is no cemetery known at Mohenjo-daro, although stray burials and other interesting human skeletal finds are known.

SIR JOHN MARSHALL AND THE INDUS CIVILIZATION

By 1931 there was a paradigm for this extraordinary body of material and the two cities, Mohenjo-daro and Harappa, from which it had been derived. This early synthesis was largely the creation of Sir John himself, but was expanded by both Mackay and V. Gordon Childe.

Marshall's Paradigm for the Indus Civilization

Marshall put forth his synthesis of the Harappan Civilization in the opening chapters of his monumental work, *Mohenjo-daro and the Indus Civilization*.[36] His first concern was for the physical environment, and he proposed that the climate was different during the Bronze Age in Pakistan and northwestern India. Marshall supported this with the following evidence: (1) Baked bricks were used as protection against heavier rainfall; (2) street drains were used to carry off the rainwater and would not be needed under today's dry conditions; (3) the lion, a dry-country animal, may be completely absent in the representations of animals. Finally, the great archaeological explorer Sir Aurel Stein found the remains of flourishing Bronze Age communities in Baluchistan, leading him to conclude that there was a substantially larger population in this region during those times. Stein attributed this in large part to a wetter climate. V. Gordon Childe supported Stein's position with this observation: "The lavish use of baked brick in prehistoric cities would seem a needless extravagance under modern rainless conditions."[37]

The hypothesis that the climate in the Greater Indus Valley was remarkably wetter in the third millennium is no longer accepted.[38] The view presented in this book is that the climate of this region was not markedly different in the third millennium B.C. from the one we have today.

On the cultural side, Marshall saw a striking uniformity at Mohenjo-daro and Harappa. "Though these two cities are some 400 miles apart, their monuments and antiquities are to all intents and purposes identical."[39] Once again, Childe concurs, noting how the two sites were "astonishingly homogenous . . . the agreement is so complete that every remark in the subsequent description would apply equally to either site."[40]

Marshall went on to say that the Harappans were just as individual (interestingly, he used the term *national* in this context) as the other civilizations, shown by the character of the domestic architecture and such monuments as the Great Bath. The "remarkably naturalistic quality" of Indus art is another feature, as is the painted pottery. The use of cotton instead of flax and the quality of the writing system were also seen as unique, national markers for the Indus. "But behind these and manifold other traits that are peculiar to the Indus Civilization and give it its national character is a tissue of ideas, inventions and discoveries which were common property of the then civilized world and cannot be traced to their respective sources."[41] These shared features included domestication of animals; cultivation of wheat, barley, and other grains; growing of fruits; building of houses; organization of society in cities; spinning and weaving of textiles and dyeing them various colors; the use of the potter's wheel and the decoration of wares; river navigation; the use of wheeled vehicles; the working of metals; writing; fashioning of ornaments from faience, ivory, bone, shell, and semiprecious stones.

The Indus Civilization was centered in Sindh and the Punjab, but Marshall did not think of the two metropolitan centers as "twin capitals." There was already some evidence for an extension of the civilization into Saurashtra (Kathiawar, for him), although there was sparse evidence available from the east, since little work was done there. It is interesting to see that he thought in terms of a diffusion of the civilization from Sindh to the west, into Baluchistan.[42]

The script was much like other quasi-pictographic scripts of the era, but its similarity had misled those who wished to decipher it. Four attempts, each using another of the scripts (Sumerian, proto-Elamite, Minoan, and Hittite) as a model, had failed by 1931, and Marshall cautioned against the use of this methodology.[43]

He found no reason to connect the language of the Indus people with Sanskrit, or its culture with the Aryans. In fact, he argued forcefully, and correctly, that the Indus Civilization was earlier than the Vedic period and that these cultures were the products of different peoples. Marshall, speaking on the Harappan language, said that so vast an area probably contained the native speakers of more than one language but that it was likely that these were within the Dravidian group.[44]

Marshall's discussion of Indus religion was the longest and most complex of all his statements on these ancient peoples. Briefly, he found evidence for a great male god, a female deity, cults associated with sexual symbols, and the beginnings of Shaktism.[45] Childe, the preeminent interpreter of ancient civilizations, joined the Marshall paradigm in 1934.[46]

There are three theoretical positions that come through in Marshall's essays. First, the Harappan Civilization was a member of a class of civilizations, most closely related to Sumer and the proto-Elamites. It was "natural" that parallels between these civilizations would be found because of geography and this close relationship. While it was not sufficiently close for the Harappans to be termed "Indo-Sumerian," the connection was real and important. He even included a simple list of finds that indicated close contact between the Indus and the Tigris-Euphrates regions.[47] There was continuity between the twentieth century and these distant peoples, and he was justified in using historical and ethnographic observations to further his understanding of the Indus peoples. It also helped him to interpret the language and ethnic or biological diversity of the Indus population. Finally, Marshall was a scholar with a commitment to the epistemology of his field. We are not presented with a fait accompli in terms of his propositions concerning the Harappans, but rather a reasoned argument, backed by a sophisticated use of other people's works and insights. Even when he is wrong, as in the case for a wetter climate, Marshall offers his reasons for believing as he does, and this is a trait of considerable scholarly merit—certainly not found in all discourse on this civilization, even today.

In spite of Marshall's greatness, archaeology did not prosper upon his retirement. There was only one major excavation of note conducted in British India in the mid-1930s. This was the inspiration of Professor W. Norman Brown of the University of Pennsylvania.

W. NORMAN BROWN ENTERS THE FIELD AT CHANHU-DARO

The spectacular finds at Mohenjo-daro generated interest in fieldwork in a number of scholars and institutions concerned with Indian archaeology. In 1932 the government of India decided to test these waters and to allow "outsiders" to excavate. The door was not thrown open but was left slightly ajar, and an American team managed to slip through.

One of the great institution builders in the study of Indology in America was Professor W. Norman Brown of the University of Pennsylvania. He was determined to further American involvement in the archaeology of the Subcontinent (figure 1.11).

Brown hired Mackay to be the field director of an excavation and raised money from the Museum of Fine Arts in Boston to fund it. After some searching, and a misstart or two, they settled on Chanhu-daro as the site to excavate. The work took place in 1935–1936, the publication appearing shortly before Mackay's death in 1943.[48] The Chanhu-daro excavations are important for two reasons. First, the recovery of bead- and seal-making workshops gives us important insights into Mature Harappan technology. The excavation also recovered the Posturban Phase, Jhukar material, in context, even though Mackay did not do as good a job of excavating and recording this material as he might have.

A young student of Indian archaeology, H. D. Sankalia, was at Chanhu-daro for almost a month during the excavation (figure 1.12). Sankalia was to emerge as

Figure 1.11 W. Norman Brown

Figure 1.12   Hasmukh Dhirajlal Sankalia

one of the giants of this field, but he departed from this project well before its conclusion.[49] In his autobiography Sankalia discusses his time there, which was not much to his liking.[50] He had attended classes given by Wheeler at the University of London and had toured sites in England with him. This thoroughly imbued him with the necessity of three-dimensional recording and stratigraphic excavation. Since Mackay understood none of this, Sankalia was put off by the field methods he saw being employed at Chanhu-daro. Moreover, Sankalia was still quite young, and he once admitted to me that he did not take full advantage of this special opportunity. It is also interesting that Brown and Sankalia should come together at this point because they ended up being close colleagues, working together in the 1950s and 1960s on various projects connected with the American Institute of Indian Studies and Deccan College.

Between January 19 and 28, 1936, Mackay had an American visitor at Chanhu-daro. He was the young linguist, Murray B. Emeneau, whose work with Dravidian, especially the etymological dictionary he compiled with Thomas Borrow, would contribute to efforts to decipher the Indus script. Emeneau wanted to hear Brahui, and because many of Mackay's laborers spoke the language, Emeneau took this as a convenient opportunity to see an excavation in progress and to conduct his linguistic fieldwork.[51]

Excavation was the early focus in the discovery of the Indus Age. The most important exploration was that undertaken by Majumdar. There was more done by Stein in the 1920s and 1930s.

The years between Marshall's retirement and 1944 were not good ones for the ASI due to many factors that culminated in a crisis in leadership.[52] In June 1943, the Viceroy, Lord Wavell, tried to improve things by appointing a new Director General.

Sir Mortimer Wheeler at Harappa

A rejuvenation of Indus archaeology had to wait for World War II to be almost over and for the arrival of a Brigadier General from the North African front. In 1944 Robert Eric Mortimer "Rick" Wheeler, a giant of Roman archaeology in Britain, was called away from active military duty to become the Director General of the ASI (figure 1.13). Without skipping a beat, Wheeler went to his new office in Simla. His first day on the job revealed his sometimes theatrical behavior. Wheeler recounts:

> On the top floor of the gaunt railway board building where the Archaeological Survey was then housed at Simla, I stepped over the recumbent forms of peons, past office windows revealing little clusters of idle clerks and hangers-on, to the office which I had taken over that morning from my Indian predecessor. As I opened my door I turned and looked back. The sleepers had not stirred, and only a wavering murmur like the distant drone of bees indicated the presence of drowsy human organisms within. I emitted a bull-like roar, and the place leapt to anxious life . . . one after another my headquarters staff was ushered in, and within an hour the purge was complete. Bowed shoulders and apprehensive glances showed an office working as it had not worked for many a long day. That evening one of the peons (who later became my most admirable headquarters Jemadar) said tremulously to my deputy's Irish wife, "Oh, memsahib, a terrible thing has happened to us this day.[53]

Wheeler lost little time in setting the Archaeological Survey straight. He had his plan to implement. He recon-

Figure 1.13   Sir Mortimer Wheeler

stituted the excavations branch, closed since 1932, and created a new prehistory branch to study the stone ages of the Subcontinent. *Ancient India,* the journal of the Archaeological Survey of India was begun. But most important, there was the Wheeler persona: self-confident, even bold, energetic, and powerful as a bull, ready to seize the survey and create a new future for archaeology in the Subcontinent.

One of Wheeler's first stops was at Harappa. The day in May 1944 was hot there, so hot that Wheeler was advised to be on the site only between the hours of 5:30 and 7:30 A.M.[54] As he approached the looming AB Mound, promptly at dawn, he was astounded by its size and was immediately struck by the fact that it must have been a citadel, put in place to protect the inhabitants of the city from attack. The presence of a citadel at Harappa would be revolutionary if true, since the prevailing opinion was that the Harappans were a remarkably peaceful people, energetically engaged in commerce. The lack of palaces, or anything even approaching this kind of social isolation for any class, suggested quite a different social structure from the contemporary peoples of Egypt, Mesopotamia, or even Crete. A few minutes of scraping at the surface of the AB Mound revealed the presence of brick lines, and Wheeler felt that his initial impression was probably right. As he said in his autobiography: "A few minutes' observation had radically changed the social character of the Indus Civilization and put it at last into an acceptable focus."[55]

Wheeler's Training Excavations

Wheeler worked in many directions to bring the survey along the path he had laid out, but the keystone of the plan was a series of training excavations. These were the forums within which he tutored new leaders, and his personal supervision of the schools allowed him to spot talent and bring it along. The schools were held at Taxila (1944–1945), Arikamedu (1945), Harappa (1946), and Brahmagiri and Chandravalli (1947).

Wheeler went back to Taxila as his first venture into the field. He was, after all, the preeminent excavator of Roman sites in England, and Taxila would produce materials with which he was familiar.

These intensive training excavations produced a cadre of competent field archaeologists, which fanned out into government service and universities. The only significant person who was not part of the training schools was H. D. Sankalia, who, in a different context, was trained as a fieldworker by Wheeler, not Mackay, as has been suggested.[56] South Asian archaeology owes a great debt to Wheeler. These training excavations instilled in a generation of fieldworkers the need for clear problem orientation, discipline, and sound recording.

Figure 1.14   Stuart Piggott

The Wheeler–Piggott Paradigm

Stuart Piggott did not join Wheeler in the ASI, but he did study archaeology while in British India during World War II (figure 1.14). He and Wheeler set about creating a new paradigm for the Harappan Civilization that differed substantially from the one that had been put forward by Marshall, Mackay, and Childe.

The new paradigm had begun at Harappa on Wheeler's first visit to the site, before he had even begun to excavate there. He saw in the AB Mound a citadel to defend the inhabitants of the city from attack. During times of peace, the city's priests and godhead were proposed to have been there. Based on what Wheeler knew of Mesopotamian civilization, the times "produced in India a social organization not altogether unlike those of the contemporary west";[57] and "in Sumer, the wealth and discipline of the city-state were vested in the chief deity, i.e. in the priesthood or a Priest-King. The civic focus was the exalted temple, centre of an elaborate and carefully ordered secular administration under divine sanction."[58] This led Wheeler to think of the Harappan Civilization in a similar way:

> It can no longer be doubted that, whatever the source of their authority—and a dominant religious element may fairly be assumed—the lords of Harappa administered their city in a fashion not remote from that of the Priest-Kings or governors of Sumer and Akkad. In other words, the social structure of Harappa conformed in principle with that of the other great riverine civilizations of the day.[59]

Here, we have returned very close to something that Marshall wisely abandoned in 1926: Indo-Sumerian civilization.

Piggott follows this line of thought, but is more subtle

in his treatment of Sumerian matters. His version of the paradigm is found in his book *Prehistoric India:* "A state ruled by priest-kings, wielding autocratic and absolute power from two main seats of government, and with the main artery of communication between the capital cities provided by a great navigable river, seems, then, to be the reasonable deduction from the archaeological evidence of the civilization of Harappa."[60]

Wheeler pursues this theme in a book meant for a wide audience. In this work he uses such phrases as the following to characterize his understanding of the Harappan Civilization: "All is orderly and regulated . . . dull, a trifle lacking in the stimulus of individuality"; the "absence or suppression of personality in its details from street to street"; and "this sense of regimentation"; and in another place he refers to the "astonishing *sameness* of the civilization . . . another quality of it is its *isolation.*"[61]

The presence of citadels and the lack of evidence for warfare posed a problem for Wheeler and Piggott. Without evidence for arms and warfare, where was the enemy—from whom were the priest-kings protecting themselves? Wheeler addresses this problem in the first edition of *The Indus Civilization.*

> The Indus Civilization inevitably derived its wealth from a combination of agriculture and trade. How far these sources were supplemented and enlarged by military conquest is at present beyond conjecture, but it is to be supposed that the wide extent of the civilization was initially the product of something more forcible than peaceful penetration. True, the military element does not loom large amongst the extant remains, but it must be remembered that at present we know almost nothing of the earliest phase of the civilization.
>
> As at present known, fortifications at the two major cities are confined to the citadels; it is not apparent that the lower city was in either case fenced. This in itself suggests that the function of the armed citadel may have been as much the affirmation of domestic authority as a safeguard against external aggression. Until, however, the negative evidence in respect of the lower city is stronger than it is at present, too much stress may not be laid upon this interpretation.[62]

The problem with envisioning the high mounds at Mohenjo-daro and Harappa as citadels has not improved since 1953, and the concept has been dropped by most modern interpreters of the Harappan Civilization. Since it is not known what kind of architecture was on the summit of the AB Mound at Harappa, it is difficult to be definitive there. But the Mound of the Great Bath at Mohenjo-daro seems to have been a place of ritual, the elevation being a symbol of the auspicious, rather than a safeguard against attack. It was also a place of storage, and this does bring an important economic function into the domain of the religious establishment.

Some prominent features of the Marshall paradigm were carried forward in the Wheeler–Piggott interpretation. Analogy, not likeness, with Sumer and Egypt is a feature of both, and the same justification for its use is given: The three civilizations were all members of a larger class of historical phenomena. A wetter climate was also postulated, and the sameness of the remains was highlighted in both views. There is little difference between these interpretations in their treatment of Harappan craft production and "science."

Many of the elements of these two syntheses are radically different. With Marshall, we learn of Harappan trade, commerce, and shared ideology; with Wheeler and Piggott, we are informed about priest-kings, temple complexes, state granaries, and the nature of theocratic power. Marshall's effective use of his knowledge of the Indian tradition and ethnographic analogy disappears from later reasoning, being replaced by a comparative method and such notions as Indo-Sumerian civilization. The Wheeler–Piggott paradigm changed Marshall's Harappans from austere, peaceful, perhaps even boring, urban merchant burghers, whose beliefs were harbingers of Indian ideologies, into a people victimized by despotic priest-kings who wielded absolute power from remote citadels, where they safeguarded themselves and the gods who justified their authority.

PARTITION, INDEPENDENCE, AND MORE RECENT DIGGING

The description of the discovery of the Indus Age would be incomplete without some recognition of more recent projects that have played a role in shaping our perceptions of the Harappan Civilization. This research is not so distant from us that it can be considered historical, yet it is very much a part of the substance of this book. There are, however, several undertakings that deserve special attention because of their overall impact on our understanding of the Indus Age. They are enumerated more or less in the order in which they were initiated.

At partition, the archaeologists in the new Indian nation were isolated from the Indus Civilization. Most of the sites and the two great metropolitan centers were in equally new Pakistan. This led Indian archaeologists to begin an intensive period of exploration followed by excavation of key sites. The following contains a minimum of documentation, better coverage of which is available.[63]

The first of the key projects was undertaken by S. R. Rao of the ASI, who began intensive exploration in Gujarat. This led to the excavation of Rangpur and Lothal.[64]

These two bodies of work, which were multiyear programs, brought to light important new material that redefined the borderlands of the Harappan Civilization. Rao's explorations and excavations set protohistoric archaeology in this region on a new course, and his site of Lothal has proven to be an extremely important place in terms of understanding the Mature Harappan. Rao's work in Gujarat has been carried forward by J. P. Joshi and his explorations and excavations in Kutch, especially at Surkotada, my own work at Rojdi and in the Ghelo and Kalubhar Valleys, and more recently by R. S. Bisht at Dholavira.

In 1955, a year after Rao began his excavations at Lothal, his colleague in Pakistan, F. A. Khan, initiated a project at Kot Diji.[65] The Kot Diji project defined this aspect of the Early Harappan and documented the relationship between the Kot Dijian assemblage and the Mature Harappan. Work was also undertaken by the Pakistan Department of Archaeology at the Neolithic, Early Harappan, and Iron Age site of Sarai Khola.[66]

Kalibangan was taken under excavation for nine seasons (1960–1961 to 1968–1969) by B. B. Lal and B. K. Thapar, both of whom had participated in the Wheeler field schools.[67] This was the first horizontal excavation of an Early Harappan settlement and informed us of the nature of both the Early and Mature Harappan in the Sarasvati valley.

There are two current excavations in India at Indus cities. The first of these is at Dholavira, on the island of Kadir in Kutch. This is a massive settlement of about 60 hectares, built largely of stone, with large public spaces and huge cisterns and a magnificent water management system.[68]

The other excavation is at Rakhigarhi in Hissar District of Haryana, just to the west of Delhi. The ASI excavations there are only in their third year, and not much is known of them. But, there seems to be a Mature Harappan cemetery there, and an impressive number of stamp seals have been found at this site, which is at least 80 hectares in size.[69]

CONCLUSIONS

The discovery of the Indus Age was an act of pure archaeological adventure. The pioneers in this effort were Marshall, Sahni, Banerji, Vats, and Dikshit, who knew early literature on the archaeology of the Indus region and would not let slip their knowledge of the enigmatic seals from Harappa. This awareness and their curiosity led them to Harappa and Mohenjo-daro and on to "First Light on a Long Forgotten Civilization," to use Marshall's words. The early work at Harappa and Mohenjo-daro was soon expanded to other sites, eventually including the 206 excavated sites of the Indus Age, including 96 excavated Mature Harappan settlements.

A part of the research that began with the excavations at Harappa and Mohenjo-daro led to the discovery that the rise of urbanization in the Greater Indus region rests on a long history of food-producing peoples. This is the topic to which we turn next.

NOTES
1. Marshall 1931i.
2. Marshall 1924; Sayce 1924.
3. Cunningham 1875.
4. The following paragraphs have been taken and edited from the introduction to Possehl 1999b.
5. This is a cliché, I know, but nonetheless true.
6. Marshall 1925–26: 75.
7. Possehl 1982.
8. Joshi 1984.
9. Possehl 1992 and 1997c.
10. Smith 1997.
11. Possehl 1997c.
12. Rgveda book X, hymn 75, verse 7; Griffith 1896.
13. Lambrick 1964; Holmes 1968; Flam 1999; Possehl 1999b: 298–302.
14. Rgveda book II, hymn 41, verses 16–17, modified after Griffith 1896.
15. Lambrick 1964: 31.
16. Possehl 1999b: 372–84.
17. Marshall 1931b: 2–4.
18. Wheeler 1953: 4–8; Piggott 1950: 135.
19. Raikes and Dyson 1961.
20. Singh 1971, see also Singh et al. 1974.
21. Singh, Wasson, and Agrawal 1990.
22. Possehl 1996b; Misra 1984.
23. Ghosh 1953b: 31.
24. There are several good sources for the history of Indian archaeology, some of which also focus on the discovery of the Harappan Civilization and related prehistoric remains in the Subcontinent. These sources can be used to provide the documentation for this story, which has been abbreviated in this account; Ghosh 1953b; Roy 1961; Chakrabarti 1988; Jansen 1986; Possehl 1999b: 38–154.
25. Possehl 1999b: 44–45.
26. Possehl 1999b: 45; Dani 1950.
27. Cunningham 1875: 106.
28. Cunningham 1875: 106–7.
29. Marshall 1923–24: 48.
30. Dikshit 1924–25: pl. XVI; Possehl 1999b: 71.
31. Dikshit 1924–25: 71.
32. Marshall 1925–26: 75.
33. Mackay 1925b.
34. Mackay 1937–38.
35. Marshall 1926–27: 53; see also Possehl 1999b: 89.
36. Marshall 1931i.
37. Childe 1934: 205.

38. Raikes and Dyson 1961.
39. Marshall 1931g: 91, cf. 102–3.
40. Childe 1934: 205–6.
41. Marshall 1931g: 95.
42. Marshall 1931a: 2, 1931g: 96.
43. Marshall 1931d: 41.
44. Marshall 1931d: 42.
45. Marshall 1931e.
46. Childe 1934: 207–8.
47. Marshall 1931h: 103–5.
48. Mackay 1943.
49. Mackay 1943: vii.
50. Sankalia 1978: 21–24.
51. Mackay 1943: vii; Emeneau, personal communication 1988.
52. Possehl 1999b: 115–28.
53. Wheeler 1955: 186.
54. Wheeler 1955: 190.
55. Wheeler 1955: 192.
56. Chakrabarti 1988: 177.
57. Wheeler 1947: 74.
58. Wheeler 1947: 74.
59. Wheeler 1947: 76.
60. Piggott 1950: 153.
61. Wheeler 1950: 28–29, original emphasis.
62. Wheeler 1953: 52–53.
63. Possehl 1999b: 139–41.
64. Rao 1963a, 1979, 1985.
65. Khan 1965.
66. Halim 1972a, 1972b.
67. Lal 1981; Thapar 1975.
68. Bisht 1991.
69. Nath 1998.

CHAPTER 2

The Beginnings of the Indus Age

SETTING THE SCENE

The mastery of agriculture and management of domesticated animals was one of the great revolutions in human history. It involved the combined arts of food production and domestication, which led to significant changes in human society, increases in population, and immense human biological change, not all of which was positive. The beginnings of village life and the symbiosis between agriculturalists and pastoralists, so important in understanding ancient India and Pakistan, originate here. The revolution ultimately set the scene for the rise of urbanization in South Asia and the Old World in general.

The potency and vigor inherent in food production and domestication were critical in sustaining the large populations implied by urbanization. There is a link, a deep causality, between the development of food production, village farming communities, and the rise of city life, with a single unbroken historical narrative involving the development of early villages and pastoral camps and the transition to urbanization in the Greater Indus region.

DEVELOPMENT OF FOOD PRODUCTION AND DOMESTICATION

The "Neolithic": An Outdated Term

In well-established but outmoded terminology, the beginnings of food production and domestication define the Neolithic period. The *Neolithic* was originally defined as the era within which ground-stone tools and pottery made their first appearance in local archaeological sequences. The great synthesizer of Old World archaeology, V. Gordon Childe, revised this definition when he proposed the Neolithic as the period within which humans first used domesticated plants and animals for food production and settled into villages and pastoral camps. This shifted the definition from a technological stage to one relating to the settlement and subsistence system of a people.

We know that ground stone and pottery appear in local archaeological sequences quite independently from food production, sometimes much earlier, as with the Jomon ceramics in Japan. While the study of ground stone and pottery is interesting and has its own importance, archaeologists know that these technologies did not have the tremendous impact on human societies that food production did. Therefore, Childe's shift in definition is a very

good one; one more meaningful to the human condition and career than just stones and pots. It is a good enough idea, in fact, that it calls for new terminology to assist in the prevention of misunderstanding; something attempted by the American archaeologist Robert J. Braidwood.[1] Following Braidwood's lead, I think in terms of an era of primary village farming communities and pastoral camps, rather than a Neolithic period.

Early Domesticates: Near East and South Asia

The logical place to look for the early domestication of plants and animals is within the habitats of their wild forms. In the case of the Near Eastern civilizations and the Indus, this involves the wild forms of barley, wheat, cattle, sheep, and goats. Botanical surveys in the twentieth century have indicated that wild barley is present in the Indo-Iranian borderlands, as are the wild cattle, sheep, and goats that were domesticated just after the end of the great Ice Age, about 10,000 years ago. But wild wheat has not been documented on the Indo-Iranian borderlands, and this fact calls for some discussion.[2]

A South Asian center for the domestication of plants and animals is an old concept, going back to the famous Russian botanist Nicoli Vavilov.[3] A number of scholars have observed that the Afghan-Baluch region is environmentally and ecologically very much akin to the entire Iranian Plateau and the uplands of the regions bordering the Mediterranean: It has a steppe-like quality with pistachio, juniper, and almond tree cover, along with the hard, cold winters in which wheat and barley evolved.[4] It is also within the range of the winter westerlies, which bring moisture, often in the form of snow, to the Near East on across the Iranian Plateau to the Punjab and western Sindh.[5] What this tells us is that the Afghan-Baluch region is a perfectly reasonable place for both wild barley (which is documented) and wild wheat to have been found. The absence of wild wheat there today may mean that the modern distribution of the wild ancestors of early domesticates may not reflect the late glacial or early Holocene distribution of the same species. In other words, the absence of wild wheat in the Afghan-Baluch region in modern times does not mean that it was not there in deep antiquity. Given the approximately 10,000 years of intensive land use in this region, wild wheat could have been on the regional "endangered species list" many thousands of years ago and may have ended up extinct in the region. This observation clearly needs serious research before it is accepted, but it is an attractive hypothesis because of (1) the general nature of the Afghan-Baluch environment, and (2) the presence of wild barely as well as other early domesticates, especially the animals.

The presence or absence of wild wheat in the Afghan-Baluch region is important because without wheat the case for an indigenous process of domestication in the region is difficult to make. As the story of early domestication in western South Asia unfolds, particular attention is paid to this grain.

Early Food Production and Domestication

It has been virtual archaeological dogma for decades that Braidwood's constellation of potentially domesticable plants and animals (wheat, barley, sheep, goats, cattle, pigs) were first domesticated in the Near East (Israel, Lebanon, Syria, southwestern Turkey, Iraq, western Iran) early in the Holocene (c. 8,000 to 10,000 years ago). The most coherent story has been told for the Greater Jordan Valley and the sequence from the sophisticated Natufian hunter-gatherers through "Pre-Pottery Neolithic A" (PPNA) and "Pre-Pottery Neolithic B" (PPNB). The chronology is given in table 2.1.

Table 2.1 A chronology for food production in the Greater Jordan Valley

PPNB		7300/7200 to c. 5800 B.C.
PPNA	Sultanian	8300/100 to 7300/200 B.C.
PPNA	Khiamain	8500/8300 to 8100 B.C.
Natufian	Late	c. 9000 to 8500/8300 B.C.
Natufian	Early	10,800/10,500 B.C. to c. 9000 B.C.
Geometric Kebaran		12,000 to 10,800/10,500 B.C.

After Bar-Yosef and Belfer-Cohen 1989:455.

The sequence can be briefly summarized. The Natufians were advanced hunter-gatherers, some of whom were sedentary for most, perhaps all, of the year. Domesticated plants are associated with PPNA villages, such as Jericho. Domesticated animals, at least the biological features that allow archaeozoologists to identify them, come later, in PPNB villages.[6]

The usual story is that domesticated plants and animals, and the techniques of food production, then somehow "diffused" to other parts of the Old World, including South Asia. Some scholars are quite explicit about this matter.[7] Those who hold to this view can point to the early dates from Near Eastern sites and the robust archaeological data sets that backstop their position. There is no doubt that

there are early dates for food-producing sites in the Near East and that the substantial amount of excavation there has yielded a coherent culture historical sequence, but it has led to a kind of self-fulfilling prophesy. Convinced that the Near East was *the* early center, archaeologists have turned their attention to the investigation of this region, at the expense of others.

It is now possible to mount a challenge to this archaeological dogma about the domestication of plants and animals. The data come from Afghanistan and Mehrgarh on the Kachi Plain of Pakistan.

THE ORIGINS AND DEVELOPMENT OF FOOD-PRODUCING PEOPLES IN SOUTH ASIA

The western borderlands of southern Asia are an excellent environment in which to conduct archaeological research on food production and domestication. The raw materials are there in the form of wild ancestors of early domesticates. Moreover, this region has an abundance of archaeological remains that have barely begun to be exploited. That there are thousands of unrecorded sites is a probability.

Experiments with Food Production and Domestication in Afghanistan

In the late 1960s and early 1970s A. Vinogradov conducted a survey bordering the Amu Darya.[8] This survey produced masses of microlithic stone tools, implying the significant presence of early Holocene hunter-gatherers within a zone that has potentially domesticable resources. This provides a tie to two sites on the Balkh River in the northern hills of Afghanistan at the town of Aq Kupruk (figure 2.1).

L. Dupree conducted small-scale excavations at the sites of Horse Cave (Aq Kupruk II) and Snake Cave (Aq Kupruk I) on the Balkh River in Afghanistan.[9] Horse Cave has evidence for domesticated sheep and goats at circa 10,000 B.C. This follows an Upper Paleolithic occupation. This date is somewhat corroborated by the evidence from Snake Cave across the Balkh River, where there is evidence for domesticated sheep and goats at circa 7500 B.C.[10]

The materials from these two extraordinary sites were never fully analyzed, so these observations must be considered preliminary in nature. But they may be a telltale sign of something important and should not be dismissed simply because they challenge the dogma of the Near Eastern center for the domestication of barley, wheat, cattle, sheep, and goats. The Aq Kupruk caves may give us reason to believe that important innovations leading to the domestication of plants and animals in human subsistence practices were taking place in areas other than the Near East. More

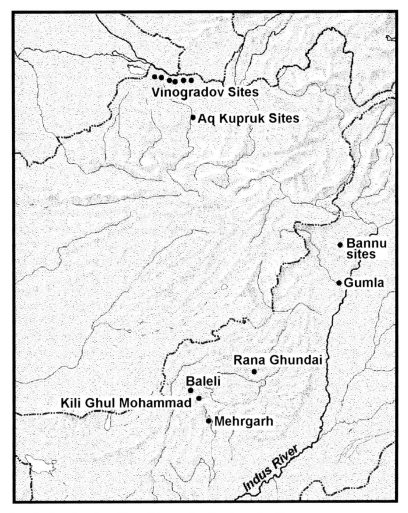

Figure 2.1 Some early sites in South Asia with evidence for food production

and better data on the early domestication of plants and animals come from Mehrgarh in Pakistan.

Mehrgarh: An Early Village Farming Community

The early food-producing village of Mehrgarh is located on the Kachi Plain of the Indus Valley. Kachi is an extension of the Indus plain into an anomalous "nick" in the eastern edge of the Iranian Plateau. It is thought that the Pleistocene Indus River flowed in this area, well to the west of its present course, so the alluvium is quite deep.[11] The Bolan River provides a major route of communication between the Indus Valley and Baluchistan. It is the principal hydrological feature of the Kachi Plain today where it runs along the eastern edge of Mehrgarh. The Bolan Pass is a relatively easy route to the Quetta Valley and central Baluchistan. Mehrgarh sits at a strategic place, at the base of this route, just off the central plain of the Indus River. This is a very important, special location; a hub of communication, a place where peoples met and mixed.

Mehrgarh Period I

There is an excellent book on Mehrgarh that is well illustrated and tells the story of the first eleven seasons of excavation there.[12] Period I was found in the northeastern corner of the site in excavation area MR 3 (figure 2.2). It can be seen from the plan that Mehrgarh is not a "tell" with levels stacked one on the other. Instead, the settlers here occupied one portion of the bank of the Bolan River for some centuries and then shifted their settlement pretty consistently to the south. So, Mehrgrah is a linear site, more than 2 kilometers long and over 1 kilometer wide in places. The stratigraphy of the site also is immensely complex, but it seems that Period I is aceramic, with pottery first appearing in Period II. Dwellings, frequently subdivided into four or even six rooms, were found made of simple mud brick (figure 2.3). The floors of these houses occasionally have the impression of reeds. Ovens and hearths were usually found in the corners of rooms, and signs of their use can be seen as traces of

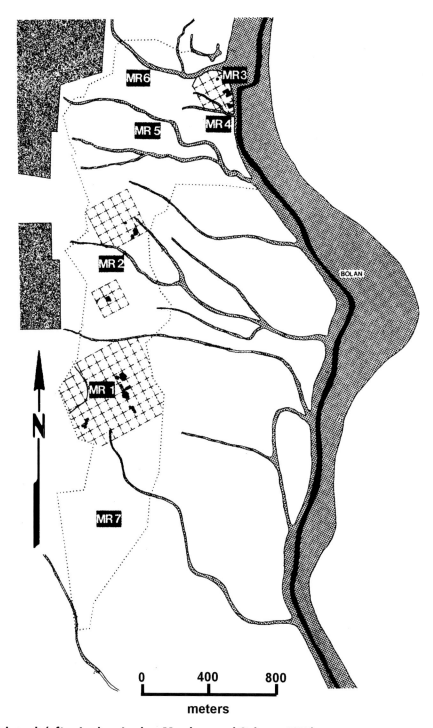

Figure 2.2 Plan of Mehrgarh (after Jarrige, Jarrige, Meadow, and Quivron 1995)

smoke on the plastered walls. One circular oven was lined with bricks and had a dome.

Bricks of regular size were the standard. They are generally bun-shaped and have finger impressions on their tops. Some house walls were thin, with only one course of bricks; others were wider, with two or three. There were also compartmentalized storage structures (figure 2.4). These buildings may have been entered through the roof since no doors have been found and some walls are preserved to a substantial height; one to a distance of 3 meters.

The technology of Mehrgarh I was relatively simple. There is native copper. The bed of the Bolan River carries cobbles of light brown flint, from which tools were fash-

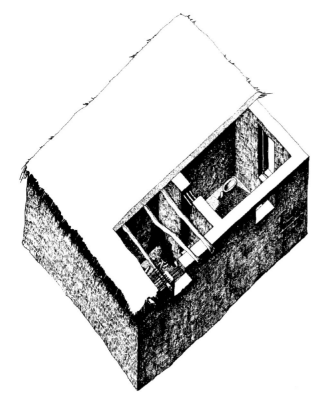

Figure 2.3   House of Mehrgarh Period I (after Jarrige, Jarrige, Meadow, and Quivron 1995)

ioned: Some were made into sickle blades. A profusion of ground-stone food-processing tools was found, including a large number of quern and grinding-stone fragments. Baskets are in evidence, some of which were lined with bitumen to strengthen and waterproof them. There is evidence for the manufacture of calcite beads. Shell bangles and clay figurines were also present.

A great deal of information on the paleobotany of Mehrgarh is available. The collection from Period I is especially rich. The dominant plant of Period I is domesticated, naked six-row barley. There are two other varieties of domesticated barley as well. Domesticated wheat is present in the form of einkorn, emmer, and a free-threshing hard durum, but in amounts much smaller than the barley sample. The noncereals so far identified for the period include the Indian jujube and dates, represented by stones in Periods I and II. Richard Meadow has observed: "While there is a possibility that local wild barleys could have been brought under cultivation in the Mehrgarh area, this is much less likely for wheat."[13] On the other hand there are some hints of a process that could be pursued. The free-threshing durum wheat can be seen as arising from a cross between emmer and goat face grass, which is found in Baluchistan. Thus, the conditions for the emmer–goat face grass cross existed locally, and free-threshing durum wheat

"could have originated as easily in the Pakistan area as in northwestern Iran."[14]

The animal economy is dominated by twelve species of what can be termed "wild big game": gazelle, swamp deer, nilgai, blackbuck, onager, spotted deer, water buffalo, sheep, goats, cattle, pigs, and elephants. These are animals that would have lived on the Kachi Plain itself and the hills that surround it. "The lack of substantial numbers of fish and bird remains suggests that the Bolan Pass and the lake/swampy environments associated with it were of little importance to them,"[15] but no screening was undertaken at Mehrgarh, and the recovery of fish and bird bone was therefore somewhat compromised.

Meadow has noted that it is now clear that cattle (the humped South Asian zebu) were locally domesticated at Mehrgarh.[16] He goes on to note:

1. Sheep are likely to have been domesticated from local wild stock during Period I.
2. Goats were kept from the time of the first occupation of the site.
3. Size diminution in goats was largely complete by late Period I, in cattle by Period II, and in sheep perhaps not until Period III.
4. The contribution of domestic or "pro-domestic" stock to the faunal assemblages came to surpass that of other animals early in the aceramic, but not in the earliest levels.
6. The development of animal keeping by the ancient inhabitants of Mehrgarh took place in the context of

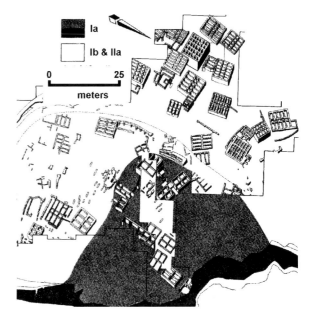

Figure 2.4   Compartmented buildings of Mehrgarh I and II (after Jarrige, Jarrige, Meadow, and Quivron 1995)

cereal crop cultivation, the building of substantial mud-brick structures, and the existence of social differentiation and long-distance trade networks as attested by the presence of marine shells, lapis lazuli, and turquoise in even the earliest graves.[17]

The View Taken Here: Expanding the Geographical Dimensions of the Nuclear Zone

Most (perhaps all) of the wild progenitors of the plants and animals on which premodern western and southern Asian civilizations are founded are native to the uplands of the Near East, Iran, and the Afghan-Baluch region. From the point of view of soil, water, and climate, these regions are suitable for growing wheat and barley and raising cattle, sheep, and goats on a significant scale. Thus, the environment is right for the early domestication of these plants and animals, and Meadow has carefully documented the fact that zebu cattle were a product of local domestication.

One of the physical changes that took place as cattle, sheep, and goats were domesticated was size reduction. This was a progressive change that took centuries. Meadow documents progressive size reduction and, therefore, what seems to be the process of domestication for not only cattle, but sheep and goats as well. This is nicely seen in graphs he has prepared and implies that the inhabitants of Mehrgarh were manipulating these animals in the same way that their neighbors all across the Iranian Plateau to the Mediterranean Sea were.[18] Since this is a gradual process involving centuries, the fact that Meadow can document it at Mehrgarh is good evidence that the domestication process was a local one.

There are two pieces of evidence that inform us that domesticated cattle, sheep, and goats probably were not imported to Mehrgarh. First, the cattle are the local zebu breed, not the taurine cattle of the west. Second, the cattle, sheep, and goats at Mehrgarh start out as wild beasts and are gradually brought under domestication. The case is so strong for the local domestication of cattle that this part of the discussion can be set aside. There is a chance, one might suppose, that partially domesticated sheep and goats were continuously migrating to Mehrgarh from the west, somehow replacing or gradually interbreeding with the local stock not disrupting the size reduction documentation. This would have had to be a rather steady process, always unidirectional, west to east, from the culturally advanced Near East into "primitive" South Asia. Such a model is intellectually quite inefficient and filled with old-fashioned notions about the cultural "supremacy" on the Near East and the unidirectional flow of ideas out of this center to southern and Central Asia.

If cattle were domesticated in Pakistan, why not sheep and goats along with them? The wild forms of all three animals were a part of the Mehrgarh environment. The efficiency of scientific reasoning, Occam's razor, is best served by accepting a model indicating that local processes were at work.

Barley and wheat are another matter. The case for the local domestication of barley is not so much an issue as that of wheat, since wild wheat has never been documented in the Afghan-Baluch region. But the region is a suitable habitat for wild wheat, and intensive botanical survey might change that observation. So, too, might paleobotanical/paleoenvironmental research demonstrate that wild wheat was present in the early Holocene and then became extinct. Both of these approaches represent serious research challenges, and both are testable.

If the cattle, sheep, and goats were locally domesticated, something I take to be true for cattle and likely for sheep and goats, then it makes sense for us to think that the ancient peoples of the Afghan-Baluch region were also engaged in the domestication of plants. The sensible thing to do is to treat this statement and others like it as testable archaeological hypotheses and to not continue along, at the expense of all other ideas, with the old dogma advocating a culturally advanced Near Eastern "hearth" and the diffusion of domestication from it.

There are indications that the development of food production and the domestication of all early plants and animals did not come to the Subcontinent by diffusion from the west. What is emerging is a notion that the old Near Eastern hearth of domestication was simply much larger than older hypotheses assumed. Rather than ending in the Zagros Mountains of Iraq/Iran, it spread all the way across the Iranian Plateau to the Indus Valley. The early Holocene peoples across this vast region, from the Mediterranean to the Indus, were engaged in the development of food-producing practices at that time. This area can be seen as a large interaction sphere in prehistoric times. This is the expanded nuclear zone for Near Eastern, Iranian, Central and South Asian domestication. The domestication of those plants and animals on which Near Eastern, South, and Central Asian civilizations were founded seems to have taken place in this nuclear zone. Interaction within it may have been so intense and regular that future excavations will find no predominant early center of innovation within it, but that the ideas and products of early experiments with plants and animals were rapidly disseminated within the interaction sphere. The forces of cultural change and adaptation were regional, rather than local (Near Eastern, South Asian, Iranian, Afghan, etc.). Rich communication and sharing of ideas and products were essential ingredients in this process of cultural change. A useful, productive, successful innovation in one place may have been quickly adopted elsewhere, with no single region emerging as a clear and consistent "leader" in the process, at least not over the time scale used in prehistoric archaeology. (The means and mechanisms of these communications are outlined in other sections of this book.)

There are two other points that should be made about Mehrgarh I. First, Mehrgarh is on the edge of the natural distribution of the potentially domesticable plants and animals, not within it. The inhabitants of this site had already gained sufficient control over their subsistence system that the plants and animals could be removed from their wild habitats and still survive. Second, without doubting the importance of Mehrgarh, and the very high quality of the French excavations there, we should recall that the earliest inhabitants of the site came there with a broad suite of fully domesticated food grains, including both wheat and barley. In this sense, Mehrgarh I is not a place where we have evidence of the earliest experiments with domestication. Mehrgarh might be compared to an early Pre-Pottery Neolithic B site in the Near East, with its mud-brick buildings and domesticated food grains. The really early experiments with food production on the Indo-Iranian borderlands are found closer to, even embedded within, the habitats of Braidwood's constellation of potentially domesticable plants and animals. This is the mountains of Baluchistan, the Northwest Frontier, and Afghanistan, at such places as Aq Kupruk.

The beginning of the Indus Age is marked by the existence of village farming communities and pastoral camps. The chronology of the Indus Age is discussed in the next section.

THE BEGINNINGS OF A CHRONOLOGY

The date of the Indus Civilization, the times during which Mohenjo-daro and Harappa were functioning urban centers, is based on both comparative analysis with the well-documented Mesopotamian chronology and a growing number of radiocarbon determinations. The most important Indus materials in Mesopotamia are the stamp seals with Indus script and the etched carnelian beads, reviewed later in this book. These materials allow us to tie the Mature Harappan to the Mesopotamian sequence as early as the "Royal Graves of Ur" (c. 2300 B.C.) through the Akkadian Period and just beyond (c. 2000 B.C.).[19] The radiocarbon determinations for the Indus Civilization are largely in agreement with these dates.[20]

Terminology and Chronology

If one thinks of time in anthropological terms, the notion of "periods" with hard boundaries disappears in favor of looser notions of "phases" with "fuzzy" transitions. The use of the term *phase* in the chronology of the Indus Age is found in the first attempts to define an internal chronology for Mohenjo-daro.[21] It reemerges quite clearly in my own work as well as that of Jim Shaffer.[22] The scheme of stages and phases used for the Indus Age is shown in table 2.2.

Defining Phases and Stages

The *phase* of the Indus Age is an archaeological construct based on an assemblage of material culture, which can be

Table 2.2 Chronology for the Indus Age

Stage One: Beginnings of Village Farming Communities and Pastoral Camps	
Kili Ghul Mohammad Phase	7000–5000 B.C.
Burj Basket-marked Phase	5000–4300 B.C.

Stage Two: Developed Village Farming Communities and Pastoral Societies	
Togau Phase	4300–3800 B.C.
Kechi Beg/Hakra Wares Phase	3800–3200 B.C.

Stage Three: Early Harappan *Four phases thought to have been generally contemporaneous*	
Amri-Nal Phase	3200–2600 B.C.
Kot Diji Phase	3200–2600 B.C.
Sothi-Siswal Phase	3200–2600 B.C.
Damb Sadaat Phase	3200–2600 B.C.

Stage Four: The Early Harappan–Mature Harappan Transition	
Early Harappan–Mature Harappan Transition	2600–2500 B.C.

Stage Five: Mature Harappan *Five phases thought to have been generally contemporaneous*	
Sindhi Harappan Phase	2500–1900 B.C.
Kulli Harappan Phase	2500–1900 B.C.
Sorath Harappan Phase	2500–1900 B.C.
Punjabi Harappan Phase	2500–1900 B.C.
Eastern Harappan Phase	2500–1900 B.C.
Two related phases in adjacent regions thought to be generally contemporaneous with the Mature Harappan	
Quetta Phase	2500–1900 B.C.
Late Kot Diji Phase	2500–1900 B.C.

Stage Six: Posturban Harappan	
Jhukar Phase	1900–1700 B.C.
Early Pirak Phase	1800–1000 B.C.
Late Sorath Harappan Phase	1900–1600 B.C.
Lustrous Red Ware Phase	1600–1300 B.C.
Cemetery H Phase	1900–1500 B.C.
Swat Valley Period IV	1650–1300 B.C.
Late Harappan Phase in Haryana and Western Uttar Pradesh	1900–1300 B.C.
Late Harappan–Painted Gray Ware Overlap Phase	1300–1000 B.C.
Early Gandhara Grave Culture Phase	1700–1000 B.C.

Stage Seven: Early Iron Age of Northern India and Pakistan	
Late Pirak Phase	1000–700 B.C.
Painted Gray Ware Phase	1100–500 B.C.
Late Gandharan Grave Culture Phase	1000–600 B.C.

associated with a subsistence regime(s), patterns of trade and communication, sociocultural institutions, and a geographic area. In some ways the phase is like the old notion of an archaeological *culture,* a term used rarely in today's anthropological archaeology, due to the fact that we now realize that there is a significant difference between the reality of culture, as it is dealt with in contemporary life, and archaeological reconstructions of culture. Phases are not defined by a chronology, either relative or absolute; but a chronology can be ascribed to them. The independent variables in this equation are the artifacts and activities of ancient peoples. The dependent variables are the relative and absolute chronological facts that archaeologists gather as part of their research on these activities and peoples.

Contending with change within a phase, especially one that is over a thousand years long, is difficult. Anthropological theory says that no culture could be stable for such a protracted period of time. Still, the present level of sophistication available to handle the phases of the Indus Age does not really allow us to define just what might be changing in most phases. Long chronological units also make the analysis of settlement data difficult since not all of the sites assigned to any given unit are likely to have been occupied for the entire span of a phase or its equivalent.

The phase and stage terminology focuses attention on the relative and absolute chronological beginnings and endings of these constructs. The dates for the beginning and end of a phase are given on the chronological table in a rather hard and fast way. But in creating an archaeological norm, or "type fossil," for the phase, the construct is actually best defined toward its center or mean than at the edges, that is, the beginning or end.

Linear Culture Historical Sequences

The chronological scheme presented in table 2.2 is basically linear, with patterns of change presented as though they took place simultaneously over vast areas of the northwestern region of the Subcontinent. This is not an historical reality. For example, it seems unlikely that the Early Harappan–Mature Harappan Transition began at precisely the same time in all regions of the Early Harappan area, or that the transition from the Togau to the Kechi Beg Phase took place at the same instant wherever these peoples were found. Archaeologists do not really know, for example, when the Kechi Beg Phase or the one called Togau began. Even the notion that stages and phases have something called a beginning and an end is debatable. In the first place, the archaeological assemblages themselves are not defined with sufficient breadth or precision for them to be endowed with meaning that goes beyond a kind of crude approximation. They are archae-

ological devices that must be invoked in the absence of chronological precision.

As chronological control and precision are developed to the point where we are really in control of the dates of the phases and stages of the Indus Age, the discussion of chronology will have to move to a new conceptual level. Then we will begin to see what is already sensed: that the phases and stages do not have crisp beginnings and endings and some areas will be seen to be more conservative and retain older styles in their artifactual assemblages. The subtleties, vagaries, and complexities of the historical record will begin to emerge and defeat the simplistic conceptual schemes of past scholarship. This will demand intellectual innovation, probably the abandonment of phases and stages altogether, as we move to handle data sets that are far more particularistic in their detail but still need to be integrated and synthesized.

Shaffer's 1992 chronology for the Indus Valley, Baluchistan, and Helmand Traditions is presented in a way that seems to be somewhat nonlinear with much overlap between phases as seen in his figure 2.2.[23] As Shaffer knows, it is not clear whether this overlap is because of the inherent weakness of the radiocarbon method or an artifact of history.

STAGE ONE: THE BEGINNINGS OF THE VILLAGE FARMING COMMUNITY AND PASTORAL CAMP

Kili Ghul Mohammad Phase	7000–5000 B.C.
Burj Basket-marked Phase	5000–4300 B.C.

Early food-producing peoples are not yet well documented in the western borderlands of the Greater Indus region. The earliest phase has been called Kili Ghul Mohammad after the site in the Quetta Valley of Baluchistan where this phase was first identified.[24] For many years, there was room for doubt about the aceramic status of Kili Ghul Mohammad I. Excavations at Mehrgarh have done much to ease the situation. A similar archaeological assemblage may also be present at Gumla in Dera Ismail Khan.[25]

Mehrgarh Period II: Burj Basket-Marked Phase

There are strong signs of continuity between Periods I and II, but change is present as well. Pottery is introduced in Period II. It is a soft, chaff-tempered ware, handmade with simple shapes. This soft ware was not found at Kili Ghul Mohammad, but has a wide distribution across the Iranian Plateau into the Zagros Mountains (Tepe Yahya, Belt and Hotu Caves, Tepe Sialk, Sarab, Jarmo, Hajji Firuz). In these contexts it comes in the middle of the sixth millennium B.C. (5500 B.C.), a date acceptable to the Mehrgarh sequence.

The same basic kind of architecture is present in Period II as in Period I. Twenty-three compartmented buildings can be attributed to Period II. Various retaining walls and terracing features are assigned to these times. Domestic structures are also known.

Among these structures of Period II are various flat, hard clay surfaces, some of which were paved with bricks and/or associated with fireplaces. In one of these areas there were deposits of trash with burnt pebbles, ash, animal bones, bone tools, hammer stones, polishers colored with red ocher, and a very large collection of blades, cores, and flint debitage. This looks very much like the suite of artifacts one would expect from a shop for leather working, basket making, or weaving.

Cotton seeds may have been found in Period II. Costantini remains cautious about this identification, but woven cotton cloth was found at Mohenjo-daro so the presence of cotton seeds at Mehrgarh may indicate that the use of this plant reaches the very beginnings of food production in Pakistan.[26]

Subsistence Activities of Mehrgarh II

The dependence on domesticated animals continued to grow through this period, as did the reliance on cultivated plants. An interesting observation on the subsistence regime of these times comes from the paleobotanical remains of Period II (Burj Basket-marked times): "The charred seeds of wheat and barley . . . that, according to L. Costantini, grow only on irrigated fields, also were collected from the ashy layers of Period II."[27] This is important documentation for the beginnings of local irrigation.

An Aside on the South Asian Mesolithic

The different contexts of microlithic technology in India are important since each has some chronological and cultural significance. *Microlith, microlithic,* and *Mesolithic* are terms that are somewhat abused in South Asian archaeology. They can be employed to cover a very wide range of human adaptations as well as a chronological range from circa 30,000 B.C. through medieval (perhaps even modern) times in the Subcontinent and Sri Lanka.[28] A discussion of this can begin with a consideration of three different forms of settlement and subsistence that have an association with a microlithic stone-working technology: the Mesolithic Aspect, the Early Food-Producing Aspect, and the Interactive Trade and Barter Aspect.

Mesolithic Aspect   Sites of the Mesolithic Aspect are found over much of the Subcontinent. They frequently occur in small caves and open settings. Tools are often abundant and associated with the remains of wild mam-

mals, shells, and an occasional ground-stone implement. Ring stones or "mace heads" are the most common of the latter type.

The *Mesolithic* is a term properly used to refer to Old World archaeological assemblages that fall within the Holocene and lack evidence for food production or an accommodation with food-producing peoples. In Sri Lanka in the caves of Fa Hien, Batadomba Lena, and Beli Lena Kituigala have Mesolithic occupations at circa 33,000–28,000 B.P. Mesolithic peoples in South Asia made proper microliths: lunates, crescents, triangles, microblades, and the like. But it is also true that many archaeological assemblages there ought not to be called Mesolithic and yet have an abundance of such tools. There is no necessary correlation between these tools and a particular form of settlement and subsistence. Confusion over the definition of the Mesolithic—settlement and subsistence versus typology—has muddled much writing on Indian sites with microlithic technology. Some authors seem to imply, or even state, that if a tool assemblage contains microliths, it is thereby Mesolithic. This equation has little utility since it raises such questions as to what percentage of microliths present is necessary to classify a body of material as Mesolithic. Is the Mature Harappan village of Allahdino a Mesolithic site because it has a few microlithic tools? Third, and most important, a focus on typology may actually mask the rich, historically significant aspects of the peoples who made and used these tools. As I discuss later, these folk were involved in a diversity of sociocultural settings and economic activities. They were, in fact, playing key roles in regional economies. Dwelling on tool typologies is not likely to be the most profitable way to understand these aspects of the human career.

Early Food-Producing Aspect   Microlithic tool technology was employed by many peoples involved in development of food production in India. This can be seen at such places as Koldihwa or the Mahagara Neolithic, where there is evidence for some attention being devoted to cultivation.[29] However, another process, especially in western India, involved the integration of domesticated animals, principally sheep and/or goats, into economies that would otherwise be classed as hunting and gathering. The later history of these peoples seems to have involved increasing sedentariness in some cases, leading to the establishment of village farming communities. A certain amount of indigenous "experimentation" with the control and increased productivity of local flora and fauna may also be a part of this story.

Interactive Trade and Barter Aspect   Sites of the Interactive Trade and Barter Aspect have the classic microlithic technology associated with variable faunal and floral assemblages. At times, domesticated plants and animals are a part of the picture, although this is not exclusively the case. Of interest in sites of this aspect is the presence of technologically sophisticated materials such as copper/bronze, iron, and glass. Other materials such as carnelian beads, seashells, and steatite also occur. Coins are known from some of these sites. Pottery is generally present and usually can be tied to the ceramics of surrounding village farming communities. Trade and interaction between these sites and surrounding communities, at times some distance away, can be inferred from these ceramics and the known source areas for the "exotic" materials found at these small settlements. A relationship of this sort seems to have existed between the Mature Harappan site of Lothal, in Gujarat, and peoples on the North Gujarat Plain, at sites like Langhnaj.

Chronological Significance of the Three Aspects of the Microlithic Something has already been said of the long period of time in which true microlithic tools (lunates, crescents, trapezoids, triangles, and the like) were made in the Subcontinent. They go back to circa 33,000 B.P. in Sri Lanka and may even have been made in the early twentieth century A.D. Tool kits of this sort are certainly associated with iron tools and coins.

Sites with microlithic tool kits conforming to one or more of the aspects just outlined are noted from time to time in this book. One of the most interesting, called Bagor, is reviewed in a later section.

Settlement Patterns of Stage One
Archaeological exploration in Baluchistan, the Northwest Frontier, Kachi, and Sindh has revealed a total of twenty sites that can be attributed to the Kili Ghul Mohammad Phase.[30] The sites of Stage One are small (generally 2 to 3 hectares) and seem to cluster in the hills and piedmont of Baluchistan and the Northwest Frontier, the "old Neolithic homeland" of farming and pastoral peoples in the Subcontinent (figure 2.5). Settlement data for Stage One are given in tables 2.3 and 2.4.[31]

Table 2.3 Settlement data for the Kili Ghul Mohammad Phase

Total sites known	20
Sites with size estimate	9
Settled area of sites with known sizes	23.85 hectares
Sites with size unknown	11
Average site size	2.651 hectares
Estimated settled area of sites without size	29.15 hectares
Estimated total settled area	53 hectares

Table 2.4 Settlement data for the Burj Basket-marked Phase

Total sites known	33
Sites with size estimate	19
Settled area of sites with known sizes	48.95 hectares
Sites with size unknown	14
Average site size	2.58 hectares
Estimated settled area of sites without size	36.12 hectares
Estimated total settled area	85.07 hectares

Since the settlement record for the ancient times considered here will never be complete, my position is that the absolute numbers and sizes of sites is a portion of what was actually a part of the historical record. Second, archaeological exploration has proceeded in a way that has led, more or less, to the same proportion of sites reported from each phase. Thus, looking not at the absolute numbers and sizes of sites but at the relative magnitude of change between phases can offer us a hint in seeing trends in population growth and settlement size.

Pastoral and Camp Sites
It is apparent that pastoralism emerged as an adaptation at the very beginning of the food-producing era in South Asia. The evidence for this comes from small encampments with a relative abundance of pottery, a nonmicrolithic tool kit, and without signs of permanent architecture.[32]

Bagor: Another Kind of Camp
There is an important campsite in southeastern Rajasthan known as Bagor.[33] It is small, about 80 meters by 80 meters. There are three phases of occupation at Bagor. The chronology presented here is based on the calibration of radiocarbon dates. Phase I at Bagor would be part of the Burj Basket-marked Phase.

Phase III	c. 600 B.C.– A.D. 200
Phase II	c. 2800–600 B.C.
Phase I	c. 5500–2800 B.C.

The significance of Bagor I stems from its microlithic tool industry associated with the remains of animals that might be domesticated. The same species, zebu, sheep, goats, and pigs, are basically represented in all three periods, but they vary in frequency and density. The inhabitants of Bagor were also hunters and the remains of many wild animals were found there, including water buffalo, blackbuck, Indian gazelle, chital, sambar, fish, tortoises, and frogs. Meadow has cautioned that the analysis of the Bagor faunal remains was done at a time when many of the current methods used in archaeology were still being developed, and this important data set

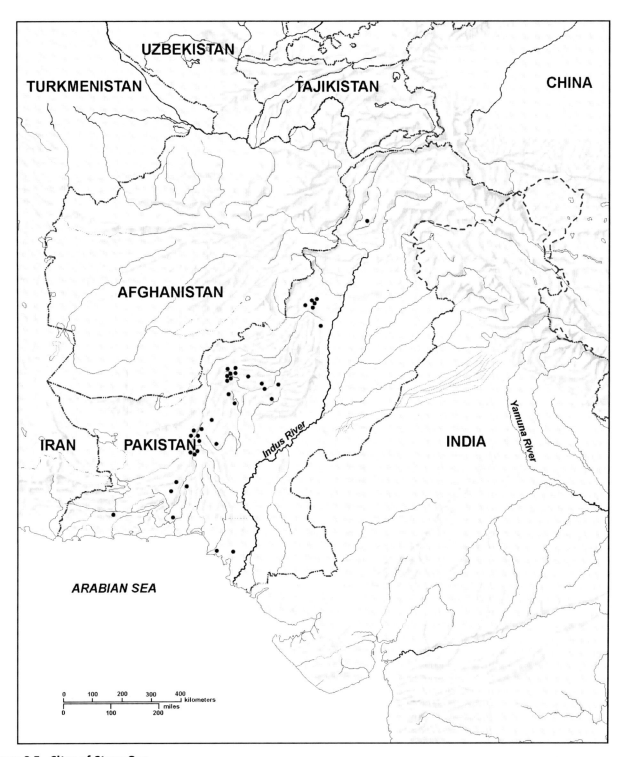

Figure 2.5 Sites of Stage One

may need to be revisited (Meadow, personal communication, 1999).

This mix of domesticated and wild animals associated with the camp of a people with a microlithic tool industry is indicative of the range of adaptations of people in pro-

tohistoric times in the Subcontinent. The most important domesticated animals at Bagor were sheep and goats, with sheep more prevalent. Recall that wild sheep and goats are found in Baluchistan and the Northwestern Frontier and are not a part of the environment in eastern Rajasthan.

Thus, it seems that the inhabitants of Bagor acquired these animals from the west. This probably happened in a number of ways: collecting strays, stealing animals, or taking animals as compensation for work. The integration of these domesticates into an otherwise hunting and gathering subsistence regime is an important development in the history of subsistence strategies in South Asia and can be seen as an indication of the flexibility and adaptability of these ancient peoples. Bagor is not a unique site, as this form of adaptation is documented at Adamgarh Cave, near Hoshangabad on the central Narmada River[34] as well as in Europe.[35]

The Interactive Trade and Barter Aspect is also documented at Bagor. Copper arrowheads appear in Period II and are similar to those found at a number of Mature Harappan sites. A spearhead of copper/bronze has a midrib, not a feature of Indus metallurgy, and could be later. The beads of the period were made of several stones, including banded agate, carnelian, and garnet. The carnelian is particularly interesting because of its special association with the Mature Harappan. But this aspect is properly of another part of the Indus Age, and I return to it again in this book.

STAGE TWO: THE DEVELOPED VILLAGE FARMING COMMUNITY AND PASTORAL SOCIETIES

Togau Phase	4300–3800 B.C.
Kechi Beg Phase	3800–3200 B.C.
Hakra Wares Phase	3800–3200 B.C.

Some of the most remarkable findings of the last forty years of archaeology in the Subcontinent are the strong lines of continuity in prehistoric life, from the very beginnings of village farming communities to the present. The Subcontinent has been raided and invaded, conquered and colonized on many occasions throughout the 9,000 years of history involved here, but the strength of the established cultural traditions has always proved to be as powerful and enduring as the customs brought by new peoples.

The Nature of Stage Two

This stage of developed village farming communities and pastoral societies is a special time in the prelude to the Mature Harappan. Three themes characterize this age: growth, continuity, and geographical expansion. There is increasing sophistication of the potter's art, and the introduction of the Togau, Kechi Beg, and Hakra Wares ceramic assemblages is widespread and easily recognized. Some form of potter's wheel makes its appearance at this time. Togau Phase sites are found in Baluchistan and adjacent regions. The Kechi Beg Phase is later in time, with

the site distribution overlapping that of the Togau Phase settlements.

Settlement Data for the Togau Phase

It is apparent from the study of settlement patterns that there was a vast growth of settled life in this region. The expansion is documented by an increase in the number of sites and by the spread of food-producing peoples into the western delta of the ancient Sarasvati River near Fort Derawar in Cholistan. There are 84 Togau settlements and 279 attributed to the time period of the combined Kechi Beg–Hakra Wares Phases (see tables 2.5 through 2.8).

Table 2.5 Settlement data for the Togau Phase

Total sites known	84
Sites with size estimate	48
Settled area of sites with known sizes	168.27 hectares
Sites with size unknown	36
Average site size	3.51 hectares
Estimated settled area of sites without size	126.36 hectares
Estimated total settled area	294.63 hectares

Table 2.6 Estimates of settled area for the Kechi Beg Phase

Total sites known	153
Sites with size estimate	84
Settled area of sites with known sizes	304.52 hectares
Sites with size unknown	69
Average site size	3.63 hectares
Estimated settled area of sites without size	250.47 hectares
Estimated total settled area	554.99 hectares

Table 2.7 Estimates of settled area for the Hakra Wares Phase

Total sites known	126
Sites with size estimate	123
Settled area of sites with known sizes	822.40 hectares
Sites with size unknown	3
Average site size	6.69 hectares
Estimated settled area of sites without size	20.07 hectares
Estimated total settled area	842.47 hectares

Table 2.8 Estimates of settled area for the combined Kechi Beg–Hakra Wares Phases

Total sites with size estimate sites	279
Sites with size estimate	207
Settled area of sites with known sizes	1126.57 hectares
Sites with size unknown	72
Average site size	5.44 hectares
Estimated settled area of sites without size	391.68 hectares
Estimated total settled area	1518.25 hectares

The Togau Phase at Mehrgarh Is a Period of Significant Change

Mehrgarh III, the Togau Phase, saw significant change. This is the only known Togau Phase site with human funerary remains. One hundred and twenty-five interments were found in an area reserved as a cemetery.[36] Of these, ninety-nine were excavated. There is a change in the burial customs. Gone are the grave structures of Period I, and the practice of using red ocher in a lavish way was discontinued. There are also burials arranged in a manner that suggests collective graves. These were aligned in an east-west orientation, with the head always to the east and the bodies lying on their sides in a flexed position. Disarticulated secondary inhumations were also found.

Hemphill, Lukacs, and Kennedy have found skeletal evidence for a discontinuity between the Stage One and the Mehrgarh III (Togau) inhabitants. The Togau population shares important affinities with the individuals in the Mature Harappan Cemetery R-37 at Harappa, which, taken together, "bear close affinities to populations from the west, that is, from the Iranian Plateau and the Near East."[37] Lukacs feels that the Stage One population at Mehrgarh shared little with this western population, but had features pointing to a biological heritage to the east of the Subcontinent.

Shifts are reflected in other parts of the archaeological record as well. Mehrgarh III has evidence for the mass production of pottery, with more or less standardized shapes, a shift in the chipped stone tool industry away from true microliths to larger, bulkier types based on different technological principles.[38] There are also signs of technological innovation and an upsurge in craft production, including copper metallurgy (with crucibles), the use of gold, the manufacture of compartmented seals, glazed steatite, and beads.

There also is continuity between Stage One (Periods I and II) and Stage Two (Period III) at Mehrgarh, and it should not be imagined that this theme is any weaker than the one just noted. The architecture remains the same with two kinds of buildings, including the compartmentalized storage structures. The Togau Ware repertory of ceramics, while new in itself, draws heavily on past ceramic technology, and there is continuity in the subsistence regime of the site.

The Later Phases of the Developed Village Farming Community and Pastoral Societies

The later part of Stage Two, the Kechi Beg and Hakra Wares Phases, represent continued growth with consolidation, rather than development, of technology. These phases also mark the beginnings of regionalism in the Indus Age, with the first evidence for the movement of significant numbers of farmers and herders out of the old Neolithic homeland of Baluchistan and its eastern piedmonts, across the Indus River, and into the Punjab. This expansion was anticipated by the appearance of herders on the eastern fringes of the Thar Desert, possibly as early

as Kili Ghul Mohammad and Burj Basket-marked times, as noted at Bagor.

Kechi Beg settlements are found in the Kulli and Northwestern Domains, as well as the plains of the Indus Valley. But at the same time a large number of farmers and herders appear to have settled the eastern drainage of the ancient Sarasvati River, well away from the Kechi Beg zone. M. R. Mughal first found the remains of these people during his remarkable exploration of Cholistan, and he has given the name "Hakra Wares" to this phase.[39] None of Mughal's Hakra Wares sites in Cholistan have been excavated, but this material has been found in stratigraphic excavations at Jalilpur[40] and Harappa.[41]

Lifeways during the Kechi Beg Phase

We know comparatively little about the lifeways of the Kechi Beg Phase. Curiously, it is the most poorly known of the periods at Mehrgarh, where Periods IV and V have traces of this assemblage (figure 2.6). It is clear that there was continuity in metallurgy and some interesting changes in the subsistence regime. For example, at Mehrgarh, grape pips occur and persist through all subsequent periods until the abandonment of the site. The continued ascendancy of barley over wheat is documented, and barley continues to be the predominant grain through the Mature Harappan. It is widely believed that this is a reflection of barley's greater tolerance of salty soils, possibly an early reflection of poor management of irrigation. An irrigation canal on the Kachi Plain may date to Kechi Beg times.

Hakra Wares and the Beginnings of Regionalism

I have previously noted that this phase marks the beginnings of regional archaeological assemblages in the Greater Indus region with the colonization of Cholistan (figure 2.7). The Hakra Wares consist of an entire assemblage of different pottery types (figure 2.8).[42] The historical roots of the Hakra Wares are found at Mehrgarh and Sheri Khan Tarakai in Bannu. A black-slipped red ware is somewhat distinctive, but this technique is present at Anjira, although the forms there are different from the Hakra examples. A wide-shouldered vessel that is important at Kot Diji and later in the Mature Harappan also occurs.[43] Pottery shapes found in the Kot Diji suite of ceramic types are also found in the Hakra Wares assemblage (e.g., flanged rims). Some of the ceramics from Sheri Khan Tarakai have been compared to the Hakra Wares.[44]

Microlithic tools are typically abundant on Hakra Wares sites, especially the camps. Mughal also collected bits and pieces of copper, beads of shell, stone mace heads or ring stones, unworked carnelian, pestles along with terra-cotta animal figurines, bangles, and beads.

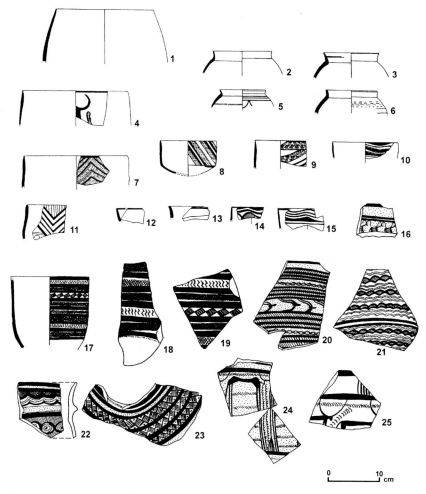

Figure 2.6 Ceramics of the Kechi Beg Phase (after Fairservis 1956)

Fifty-four of the Hakra Wares sites can be classified as camps. Camps are sites represented by a light scatter of pottery without a buildup of an archaeological midden. These settlements were located on the old alluvium of Cholistan as well as in stabilized sandy areas.[45] These sites seem to represent the seasonal monsoon abodes of pastoralists who came into Cholistan to maintain their animals. This is a provisional interpretation, of course, but if it is true, the presence of so many camps testifies to the importance of pastoralism in the time of the Hakra Wares. There are also forty-nine village farming communities. Mughal notes that many sites in Cholistan are buried under moving dunes or have been significantly altered or erased by wind.

THE NORTHERN NEOLITHIC: FOOD-PRODUCING COMMUNITIES ON THE NORTHERN FRONTIER OF THE INDUS REGION

A cultural tradition of farmers and herders separate from the type found at Mehrgarh has been found in the northern regions of Pakistan and western India. These peoples lived in the Vale of Kashmir and surrounding valleys extending into Swat and the northern plains of the Greater Indus Valley, at such places as Sarai Khola. They represent a cultural tradition whose origin is outside of South Asia. Archaeologists refer to this material as the "Northern Neolithic." Sites of this type begin just after the end of Stage Two.

Burzahom and Gufkral

Burzahom and Gufkral were both prehistoric villages (figure 2.9). Many of their dwellings were semisubterranean, with hearths and a central pole supporting the roof. The people were cultivators of wheat and barley and cared for domesticated animals: sheep, goats, and dogs. They also engaged in some hunting.

Northern Neolithic pottery is soft and gray to brown with mat and cord impressions. These people made a rich bone tool industry with points, needles, harpoons, and serrated points. The stone tools are mostly ground, with oval

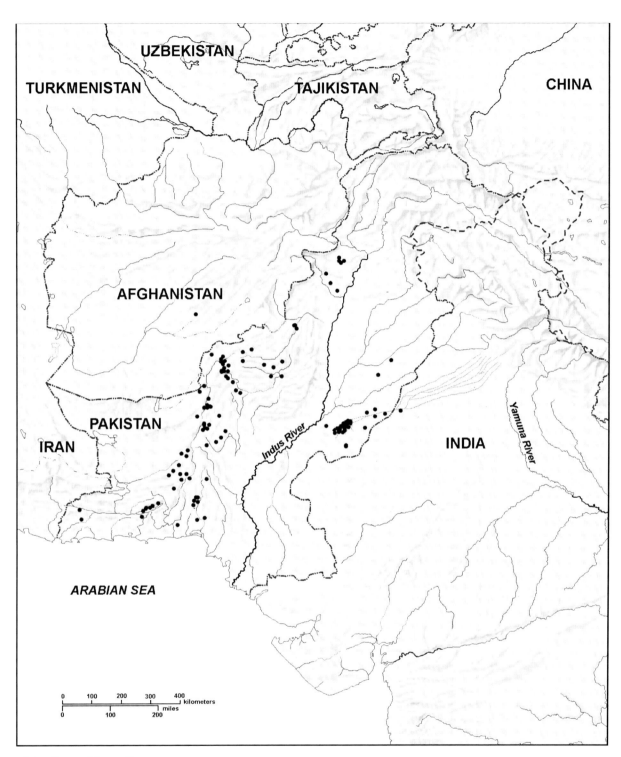

Figure 2.7 Sites of Stage Two

pointed butt axes, flat ring stones of jadeite, and a small knife. Many of the artifacts are illustrated in the preliminary reports on the excavation.[46] The small knife is quite specific in type. It is rectangular, generally with two perforations on the long side opposite the cutting edge. These were used to fasten a wooden handle. In northern Asia, where they are widespread, they are called *ulus* and are used as harvesting implements. *Ulus* have been found at other South Asian sites, most notably Kalako-deray in Swat. The chronology for these two sites is summarized in table 2.9.

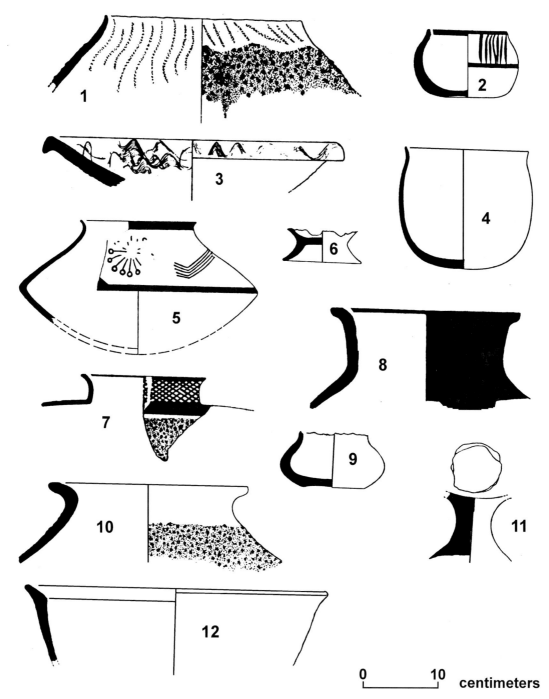

Figure 2.8 Hakra Wares from surface collections at sites in Cholistan (after Mughal 1997)

0   10 centimeters

Table 2.9 Chronology for the Northern Neolithic

Site	Period at site	Date	Indus stage
Gufkral Ic Burzahom Ib	Late Neolithic	2000–1500 B.C.	Posturban Harappan
Gufkral Ib Burzahom Ia	Early Neolithic	2500–2000 B.C.	Mature Harappan
Gufkral Ia	Aceramic Neolithic	2800–2500 B.C.	Early Harappan

Two Late Kot Diji–type pots were found at Burzahom in Period Ib. One of them contained approximately 950 beads of carnelian and agate and was decorated with the horned deity (Mahisha; figure 2.10).[47]

Cultural Roots of the Northern Neolithic

The cultural and historical affinities of the Northern Neolithic are clearly north Asian. The principal parallels are

Figure 2.9   Sites of the Northern Neolithic

the semisubterranean dwellings, mat-impressed pottery, rich bone industry, form of the ground-stone tools, and dog burials. Fairservis notes the significance of the Northern Neolithic:

> Burzahom represents the southernmost expression of a widespread north Asian complex. It represents a move-

ment that may well have started with the Mesolithic of Europe and which survived in the fertile valleys of Kashmir and perhaps Nepal, Tibet, Hunza, Baltistan and Ladakh. It is so clearly Inner Asian that one finds difficulty in including it as a part of Subcontinental archaeology except for the fact that it is in the river system of the Subcontinent. It is also a less important but nonetheless definitive manifestation of one of the cultural streams which were through time directed toward India. In this one is reminded of the historical travels of the Chinese monks Fa Hien and Hsuen Tsang.[48]

F. Southworth found some evidence for a language(s) of the Sino-Tibetan family in ancient South Asia.[49] The Northern Neolithic may be a concrete archaeological expression of this hypothesis. Settlement data for the Northern Neolithic are given in table 2.10.

Table 2.10   Estimates of settled area for the Northern Neolithic

Total sites known	25
Sites with size estimate	3
Settled area of sites with known sizes	23.6 hectares
Sites with size unknown	22
Average site size	7.87 hectares
Estimated settled area of sites without size	173.14 hectares
Estimated total settled area	196.74 hectares

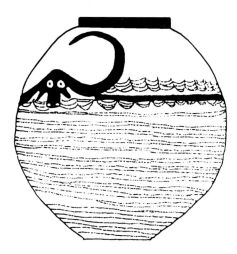

Figure 2.10 Kot Diji–type pot from Burzahom

Northern Neolithic: Summary

The Northern Neolithic is important for understanding the mechanism through which the Early and Mature Harappan peoples gained access to mountain resources: timber, stone, possibly metal. Many products found at Mohenjo-daro are found in Kashmir, timber among them.

There are four approximately contemporaneous, interrelated archaeological assemblages that make up the Early Harappan. While we do not know what these archaeological assemblages represent in terms of ethnicity, their existence does suggest that there was a diversity of peoples in the Greater Indus region at the time and that the Mature Harappan emerges from the interaction and fusion of these groups.

STAGE THREE: THE EARLY HARAPPAN

The themes that have been developed in Stages One and Two continue to be important in the Early Harappan: cultural continuity and change, growth, geographical expansion, and regionalism. There is a minimum of technological change, and the paradigm already established for the subsistence regime was expanded rather than modified.

The Early Harappan (c. 3200–2600 B.C.) is made up of four regional phases that are thought to be generally contemporary: the Amri-Nal, Kot Diji, Damb Sadaat, and Sothi-Siswal (figure 2.11). There is pronounced geographical expansion during the Early Harappan on to the Potwar Plateau and into the Indian Punjab, Haryana, northern Rajasthan, and western Uttar Pradesh as well as Gujarat. The chronology of the Early Harappan has been determined from a long series of radiocarbon dates. I have presented a discussion of this complex chronology elsewhere.[50]

The Amri-Nal Phase of Sindh, Baluchistan, and North Gujarat

The Amri-Nal Phase was first defined by Majumdar at the type site of Amri following his excavations there in December 1929–January 1930;[51] however, the definitive excavation at this site was conducted by J.-M. Casal between 1959 and 1962.[52] Exploration by Stein and B. de Cardi in southern Baluchistan has shown that assemblages sharing some features of period I at Amri are also found in the mountains there. While Nal material is found in both southern Baluchistan and Sindh, it is perhaps more at home in the highlands than the riverine plains. The two assemblages have been merged into a single regional phase; in Sindh, the Amri side tends to predominate, and in Baluchistan, the assemblage is more Nal-like (figure 2.12).

The Amri ceramic assemblage is made up of extremely well made fine wares, generally fired light red or buff. Red and buff slips are also found, often with black paint. At the beginning of the phase the designs are exclusively geometric, developing into more curvilinear motifs toward the end. Typical of Amri ware are open bowls and jars and tall vases with simple, featureless rims.

Nal ceramics are among the best-made and most attractive wares of prehistoric times in South Asia. They, too, are fine wares, and tend to have been fired buff to pink. The slips have a tendency to be very light, buff or weak red, giving a tint to the surface, rather than a dense overall color. The characteristic vessel forms are canisters and straight-sided bowls, with simple, knife-edge rims. Polychrome infilling of these designs includes the use of red, pink, blue, and yellow. Painting in white over a black slip is also known and is one of the features shared with Amri. In fact, the use of white paint is a hallmark of the Early Harappan (figure 2.13).

The Expansion of Food-Producing Peoples into Gujarat

Evidence for the early expansion of farmers and herders into Gujarat appears at a number of sites, the most prominent of which are Dholavira, Surkotada in Kutch and Moti Pipli, the Santhli sites, and Nagwada in North Gujarat (figure 2.14).

The sites in North Gujarat have ceramics suggesting a combination of Amri-Nal and Kot Diji stylistic features. Padri, Somnath, and Loteshwar have ceramics that are quite different from those of the Early Harappan and suggest an even earlier presence of pottery-making peoples in the region—a good example of one of the problems on which important, productive archaeology can be done in India.

Period I at Dholavira has ceramics that have typologi-

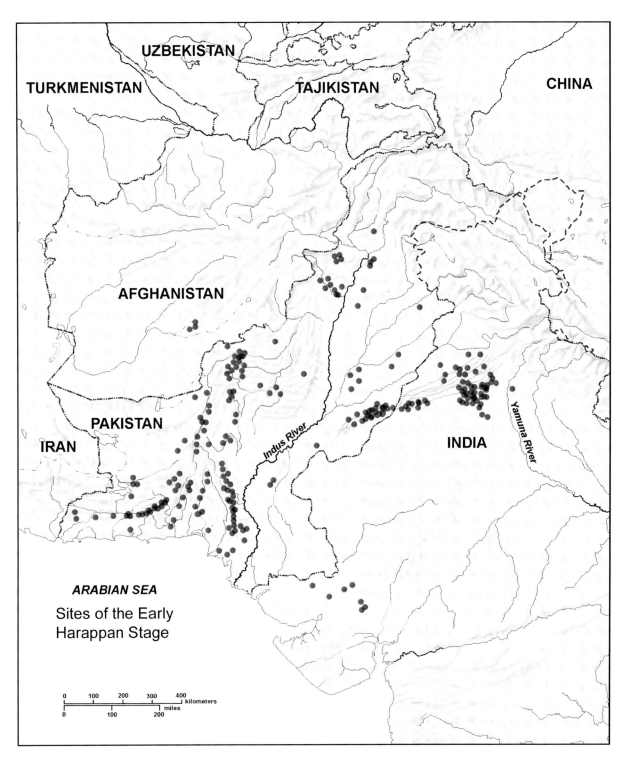

Figure 2.11 All Early Indus sites

cal similarities with Amri Period II (Transitional Stage).[53] Surkotada is on this list since a reanalysis of the ceramics from the small cemetery, 300 meters north of the habitation site, has shown that this was a place of interment for Amri-Nal peoples.[54]

The General Model of Expansion

Diffusion and the spread of peoples and their cultures is one of the oldest and most intractable topics in archaeology. The general hypothesis used here is that prehistoric pastoral peoples were usually the lead element in explor-

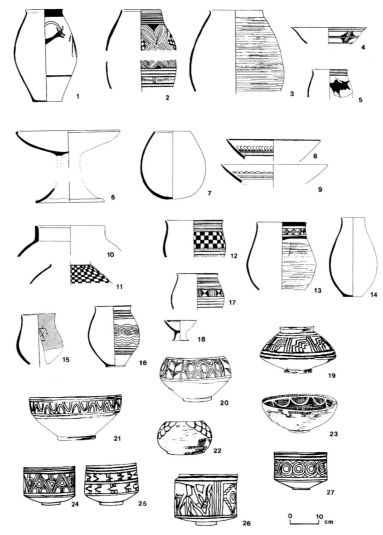

Figure 2.12   Amri-Nal ceramics (Amri 1–18; Nal 19–27) (after Hargreaves 1929)

ing new territory in the Greater Indus region. The reasoning behind this has to do with ecology and the mobility of these people and their need for new pasturelands, plus the economic rewards and prestige that would come with the discovery of new resources. But we cannot discount other motivations in ancient exploration: the pleasure and adventure of travel and exploration of new territory, the opportunity to meet new people even if possible conflict might be involved.

Settlement Pattern Data on the Amri-Nal Phase
The settlement pattern data for the Amri-Nal Phase (shown in table 2.11) document the continuation of a pattern of village farming communities and pastoralism. The presence of Nal ceramics in Sindh and Amri Wares in Baluchistan seems to indicate that groups of people who kept sheep, goats, and cattle spent summers in the high-

Table 2.11   Estimates of settled area for the Amri-Nal Phase

Total sites known	164
Sites with size estimate	88
Settled area of sites with known sizes	322.64 hectares
Sites with size unknown	76
Average site size	3.67 hectares
Estimated settled area of sites without size	278.92 hectares
Estimated total settled area	610.56 hectares

lands, had winter abodes in the Indus Valley, and ventured into the seasonally quiescent floodplains of the Indus Valley to gain access to resources there. This pattern of archaeological evidence may not signal the earliest pioneering of this environment, but it does seem to mark a time when it would have been a significant part of the subsistence pattern.

The penetration of the deeper riverine zones of Sindh

Figure 2.13 Ceramics from Nal (after Hargreaves 1929)

by pastoralists during the dry season might also mark the beginning of the process of burning, clearing, and perhaps draining this landscape. The search for grass and browse, cutting wood for temporary shelters, campfires and firing ceramics, along with the possibility of large-scale burning to create a more efficient, productive landscape for humans and animals would constitute a kind of "softening up" of this difficult terrain, preparing it for farming in Mature Harappan times. The use of fire for clearing land is not well documented in the archaeological record. But regional, manmade landscapes almost certainly began to emerge from the millennia of intensive use by domesticated animals as well as clearing land for cultivation.

The villages along the piedmont of Baluchistan were placed to take advantage of the hill torrents or *nais* and the natural springs that dot the outer face of the mountain front. Lake Manchar, the natural inundation basin of the Indus, was extensively utilized as an environment to be directly exploited for food (fish and shellfish, seasonally for birds) and as a huge, naturally irrigated farming tract, resulting from the seasonal expansion and contraction of the lake waters, as at the site of Lohri.[55]

Amri-Nal Site Size
Some Amri-Nal sites were very small camps, such as Jebri Damb One or Kuki Damb in Kalat, at one-tenth of a hectare, or Santhli Four in Gujarat at one-hundredth of a hectare. The largest Amri-Nal site in the "Gazetteer of Settlements of the Indus Age"[56] might be Dholavira, on Kadir Island in Kutch if it comes close to the size of the Mature Harappan settlement at 60 hectares. There is also some evidence that the first occupation there took place during the Transitional Stage, not the Early Harappan.

Sites of the Amri-Nal Phase cover the southern tier of the Indus Valley and Baluchistan. During this phase, the continued maturation of the subsistence system and a spread of farming and herding peoples to the seacoast and southeast into Gujarat is seen. Modest attempts at fortification may also characterize some Amri-Nal settlements.

The Kot Diji Phase of Northern Sindh and Elsewhere
Kot Diji is a splendid small site on the national highway linking Karachi and Hyderabad to Sukkur. It is situated on the old alluvium of the Indus Valley, below a huge Talpur Dynasty fortress of the nineteenth century A.D., which looms over it from the escarpment of the Rohri Hills.[57]

The Kot Diji archaeological assemblage is distinct from the Amri-Nal, although there is some overlap in ceramics, with some common vessel forms and decorative motifs especially among the simpler pots (figure 2.15). Both assemblages present us with extremely fine examples of the potter's art with well-fired red and buff wares. The tall jars and vases with featureless rims of the Amri-Nal assemblage are not a part of the Kot Diji ceramic corpus and

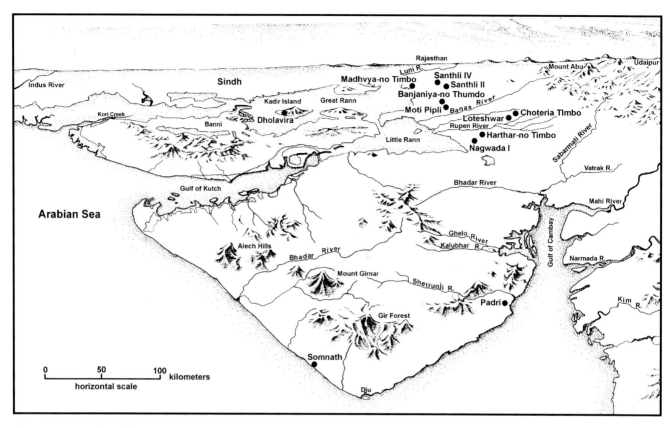

Figure 2.14 Early Indus and early third millennium sites in Gujarat

neither are the Nal canisters and fat-bodied pots. If anything like the distinctive Nal painting was found at a Kot Diji site, it would be dubbed an import. Settlement data for the Kot Diji Phase are given in table 2.12.

Table 2.12 Estimates of settled area for the Kot Diji Phase

Total sites known	111
Sites settled area of sites with known	83
Sizes with size estimate	523.38 hectares
Sites with size unknown	28
Average site size	6.31 hectares
Estimated settled area of sites without size	176.68 hectares
Estimated total settled area	700.06 hectares

The Damb Sadaat Phase of Central Baluchistan

Contemporary with the Kot Diji and Amri-Nal Phases is a smaller, more localized cultural phase of the Early Harappan, centered on the Quetta Valley. It rests on a long history of occupation in this fertile, well-watered valley. Quetta-Pishin is blessed with substantial subsurface water resources, available even to relatively primitive cultivators in the form of artesian wells. This valley is also the center of a natural corridor linking southern Afghanistan to the Indus Valley via the Bolan and Khojak Passes. Historically, these factors have made it a regional hub of settlement,

trade, travel, and administration. In prehistoric times a distinctive set of archaeological assemblages developed in Quetta-Pishin and the valleys to the immediate north, south, and beyond into Afghanistan, as at the famous site of Mundigak, and even reaching Shahr-i Sokhta in Seistan.

Damb Sadaat Phase Sites

There are thirty-seven Damb Sadaat sites, twenty-nine of which have data on size. They average 2.64 hectares. The largest site is the Quetta Miri (23 hectares), located at the one spot in the Quetta Valley that has been occupied continuously from prehistoric to modern times. The next largest site, Mundigak, is 18.75 hectares and is in the Kushk-i Nakhud Valley of the Helmand River drainage, over 200 kilometers to the northwest of the Miri. Mundigak was a town during Early Harappan times. It is entirely possible that the settlement was smaller than the 18-plus hectares estimated here. Settlement figures are given in table 2.13.

Pottery of the Damb Sadaat Phase was often slipped to create a uniform surface, even if it was not painted (figure 2.16). Paring was often done to thin the walls of vessels and the stems of goblets. A painted ceramic called Quetta Ware is the most characteristic type of pottery.[58] Short-

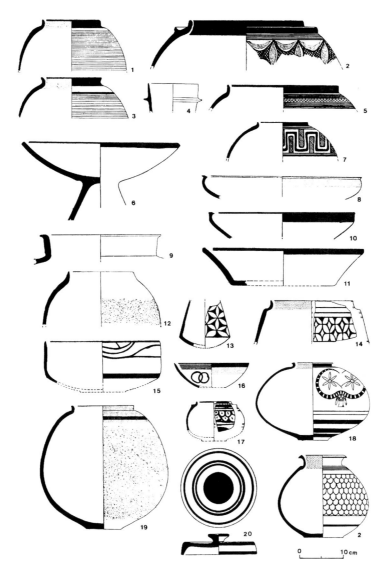

Figure 2.15   Kot Diji ceramics from various sites

neck, globular jars of Kot Dijian type also occur. A ceramic known as Faiz Mohammad Grey Ware was also manufactured. It is a fine ware ceramic, generally a plate, decorated with Quetta Ware designs. The technology used in its manufacture is somewhat complicated since it

took place in two stages of firing: first baked as a red-buff ware in an oxidizing atmosphere, then refired under reducing conditions to obtain the finished gray color.[59] The designs in black paint (sometimes red) are closely paralleled in the Quetta Ware repertory of motifs.

The Sothi-Siswal Phase of the Eastern Region

To the east, on the other side of the Greater Indus region, there were also important developments taking place during the Early Harappan Stage. These began along the natural route of the Sarasvati River and its Indian tributaries, especially the Drishadvati or Chautung, but it spread into Punjab, Haryana, with one lone site (Nawanbans) in the Ganga-Yamuna doab of western Uttar Pradesh. The name of this phase, "Sothi-Siswal," is

Table 2.13   Estimates of settled area for the Damb Sadaat Phase

Total sites known	37
Sites with size estimate	29
Settled area of sites with known sizes	76.42 hectares
Sites with size unknown	8
Average site size	2.64 hectares
Estimated settled area of sites without size	21.12 hectares
Estimated total settled area	97.54 hectares

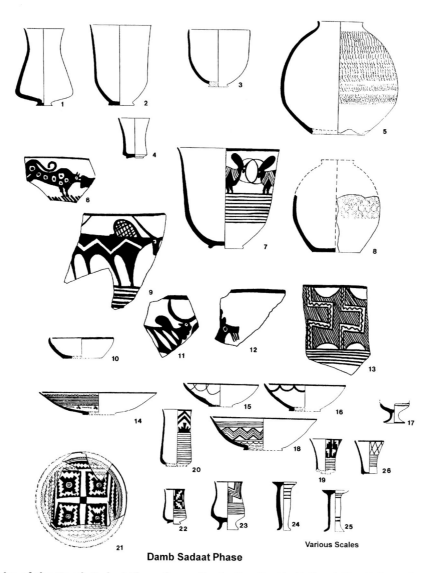

Figure 2.16   Ceramics of the Damb Sadaat Phase from sites in the Quetta Valley (after Fairservis 1956)

Damb Sadaat Phase

Various Scales

derived from the names of two excavated sites (figure 2.17).

Sothi-Siswal Settlement Patterns
There are 165 Sothi-Siswal sites, 91 of which have information on site size. The average settlement size is 4.28 hectares. There are two Sothi-Siswal settlements larger than 20 hectares. Settlement data are given in table 2.14.

Conclusions for the Early Harappan
The Early Harappan has little evidence for a significant degree of social differentiation, craft and career specialization, and little evolution of the political and ideological institutions that produce public architecture.[60] These sociocultural features are in marked contrast to levels of developments inferred for the Mature Harappan and must be

used to shape perceptions of the nature of Mature Harappan society, its institutions, and the historical, developmental process that took it from the Early Harappan Stage to urbanization. There is, however, good evidence for a growing population from the beginnings of food production to the threshold of civilization, as seen in table 2.15.

Table 2.14   Estimates of settled area for the Sothi-Siswal Phase

Total sites known	165
Sites with size estimate	91
Settled area of sites with known sizes	389.15 hectares
Sites with size unknown	74
Average site size	4.28 hectares
Estimated settled area of sites without size	316.72 hectares
Estimated total settled area	705.87 hectares

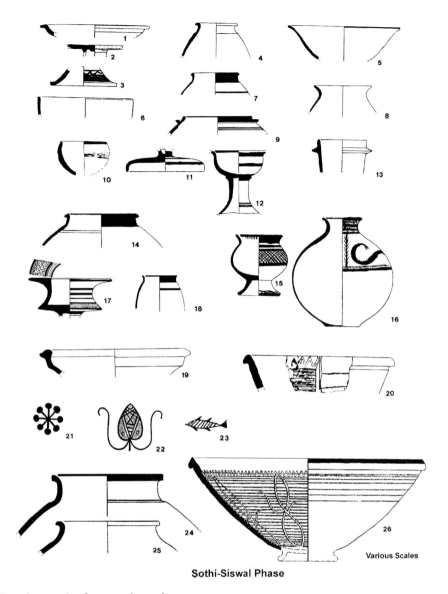

Sothi-Siswal Phase

Figure 2.17   Sothi Siswal ceramics from various sites

The graph of Early Harappan settlement size by phase gives a sense of the size distribution of sites. It suggests that the geographical center of cultural dynamics was to the north, with the Kot Dijian and Sothi-Siswal Phases (figure

Table 2.15   Settlement data on the Indus Age through the Mature Harappan

Phase/Stage	Number of settlements	Settlements with size	Average size (hectares)
Mature Harappan	1,019	537	7.25
Early Harappan	477	281	4.51
Kechi Beg and Hakra Wares	256	184	5.22
Togau	84	48	3.51
Burj Basket-marked	33	19	2.58
Kili Ghul Mohammad	20	9	2.65

2.18). It also documents the relatively small size of even the largest Early Harappan sites, as compared to those of the Indus Civilization (figure 2.19).

Disruptions at the End of the Early Harappan
The disruption and/or abandonment of sites toward the end of the Early Harappan is an important part of the record for this phase. Sites of central concern are Balakot, Kot Diji, Gumla and Kalibangan, Amri, and Nausharo.

Balakot Period I at Balakot, termed "Balakotian" by the excavator, appears to be a regional variant on the Amri-Nal theme. The radiocarbon dates for Periods I and II (Mature Harappan) suggest "a hiatus of several centuries between the Balakotian and the Harappan periods at Balakot."[61]

Early Harappan Sites

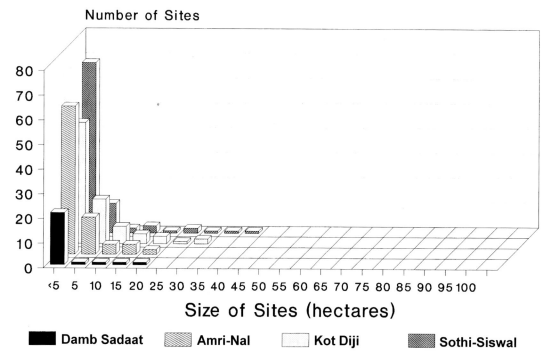

Number of Sites

Size of Sites (hectares)

■ **Damb Sadaat** ▨ **Amri-Nal** ▢ **Kot Diji** ▨ **Sothi-Siswal**

Figure 2.18   Graph of the site size distribution for the four phases of the Early Indus

Kot Diji The stratigraphy of Kot Diji is complex and in some ways not yet completely understood. There are obvious signs of massive burning over the entire site, including both the lower habitation area and the high mound. As F. A. Khan has observed:

> A thick deposit of burned and charred material, on top of layer (4), spreading over the entire site, completely sealed the lower levels (Kot Diji) from the upper ones (Mature Harappans). This prominent and clearly marked burnt layer strongly suggests that the last occupation level of the early settlers (that is the Kot Diji) was violently disturbed, and probably totally burnt and destroyed.[62]

Gumla Period III at Gumla, the Kot Diji occupation, seems to have come to a fiery end, with an ash layer separating this occupation from the succeeding Late Kot Diji. "The end of their period appears to be violent. There is a thick layer of ash, charcoal, bones, pot-sherds, etc. which all belong to period III."[63]

Amri Period II at Amri, the Transitional Stage, ended with signs of a significant amount of burning. Casal has observed: "The upper levels are blackish and ashy, but they are mostly so near the surface that it is difficult to say whether this occurrence should be interpreted as ev-

idence of some sort of violence or of fire."[64] A large fire was also evident in Period ID at the site, associated with a building that Casal believes was a godown, or storage facility.

Nausharo The excavations at Nausharo produced evidence of extensive burning associated with Period ID, a Transitional Stage occupation: "The two architectural complexes of Period ID . . . have been heavily burnt and the walls have turned red due to heat. At Kot Diji too, the final phase of the pre-Indus period has been destroyed by fire."[65]

Kalibangan There is an abandonment of Kalibangan between Periods I (Early Harappan) and II (Mature Harappan). The excavators detected signs of cleavage and displacement of strata in the Early Harappan levels, which might have been caused by an earthquake.[66] According to B. K. Thapar:

> This occupation continued through five structural phases, rising to a height of some 1.6 m, when it was brought to a close by a catastrophe (perhaps seismic), as evidenced by the occurrence of displaced (faulted?) deposits and subsided walls in different parts of the excavated area. There-

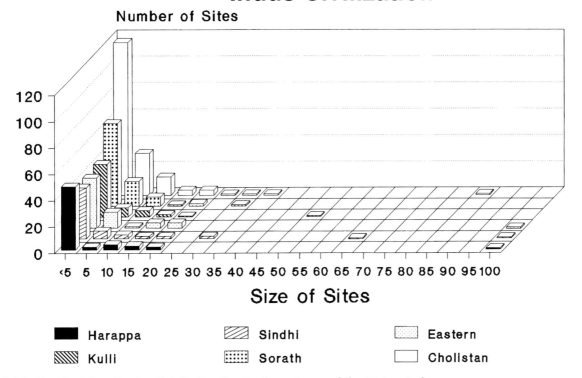

Indus Civilization

Number of Sites

120
100
80
60
40
20
0

<5 5 10 15 20 25 30 35 40 45 50 55 60 65 70 75 80 85 90 95 100

Size of Sites

■ Harappa   ▨ Sindhi   ▦ Eastern

▧ Kulli   ▤ Sorath   □ Cholistan

Figure 2.19   Graph of the site size distribution for the four phases of the Mature Indus

after the site seems to have been abandoned, though only temporarily and a thin layer of sand, largely infertile, accumulated over the ruins.[67]

An Evaluation of These Disruptions at the End of the Early Harappan

It is difficult to evaluate this kind of archaeological evidence. Fires, after all, can be accidental. Attributing burning to warfare or raiding is also outmoded in archaeological explanation, no matter how prevalent these activities were in the historical accounts of life in the Near East and South Asia. The disruption has also been noted by S. P. Gupta, who thinks of it in terms of natural calamities,[68] which might well be true for Kalibangan.[69] A disruptive or traumatic event at Balakot at the end of Period I is not suggested by the evidence there. Still, there is unmistakable evidence for burning in the Transitional Stage, the historical junction where the Early Harappan meets the Mature. This is a contrast to earlier times, when there is little evidence for large-scale burning at any of the sites of Stages One or Two. In fact, there is no evidence for large-scale fires in earlier levels at Amri, Gumla, or Nausharo, and no such evidence is found at Kalibangan, Balakot, or other sites in the Greater Indus region.

If fires are only accidental, one would expect a random or haphazard pattern to their occurrence, an occasional "blip" in the archaeological record resulting from the careless handling of flames or hot coals. It is significant that there is so little evidence for this kind of day-to-day tragedy in the lives of the ancient inhabitants of the region. It leads one to think that much evidence for the little fires, the kind that destroy one or two buildings and are the unhappy grist of daily life, is considerably erased by the process of cleaning up the mess and rebuilding. This evidence is probably still there in most cases, but it is a detail of the archaeological record: It does not jump out at the excavator as a significant enough catastrophe to make it into the site report. It follows then that when signs of large-scale burning are noted in an excavation, as at Kot Diji, Gumla, Nausharo, and to some degree Amri, it is likely to have been a large conflagration, the damage from which is so massive that it cannot be diffused by cleanup and rebuilding.

Following this line of reasoning, several points seem to be evident: The fires at these sites were large; this large-scale burning is associated with the Early Harappan–Mature Harappan junction; there is little, if any, evidence for such conflagrations at these or other sites in the region prior to or after the Early Harappan–Mature Harappan junction. These observations point to a pattern in the conflagrations, and, while it is true that fires begin for many reasons, a pattern like this might be telling us that they have a common cause.

Other Suggestions of Disruption

It is commonplace to observe that many Mature Harappan sites were founded on virgin soil. Related to this is the observation that many Early Harappan sites were abandoned and not reoccupied during the Mature Harappan, which might be considered just another form of destruction in the settlement history of the Greater Indus region. Quantifying this for the entire Indus region is possible, but would be misleading without some critical observations. First, Sindh and Cholistan have deep settlement histories and relatively dense occupation, but Saurashtra, for example, was a Domain that was apparently only sparsely settled during Early Harappan times. We know little of the settlement history of the Eastern Domain until the Early Harappan Stage, and even then there are significant chronological problems that remain unresolved. Mughal found a number of camps and purely industrial sites in his survey that are not used in the site counts. They do not have equivalents in Sindh. Table 2.16 presents some site counts from Sindh and Cholistan to illustrate the abandonment of Early Harappan sites and the founding of Mature Harappan settlements.

Table 2.16   Changes in settlement occupation: Sindh and Cholistan

	Sindh	Cholistan
Total number of sites	106	239
Total Early Harappan sites	52	37
Total Mature Harappan sites	65	136
Early and Mature occupations	22	2
Mature Harappan occupations on virgin soil	43	132
Early Harappan sites abandoned	29	33

These are striking numbers. In Cholistan, 33 of the 37 Kot Diji Phase sites were abandoned. For the Mature Harappan, 132 of the 136 sites were established as new settlements on virgin soil. A similar if less dramatic pattern is evident in Sindh. There seems to be an unmistakable conclusion to be drawn from this: The Mature Harappans liked to find new places to live. This observation presents another important discontinuity between these two stages in the cultural history of the Indus Age, complementing the signs of burning. It strengthens the feeling that the beginning of the Mature Harappan has qualities of renewal, of the people cutting their ties with older Early Harappan settlements and seeking fresh, different places to establish themselves and their new way of life and civilization.

THE EARLY HARAPPAN–MATURE HARAPPAN TRANSITION

The Transitional Stage between the Early Harappan and Mature Harappan was defined at Amri by Jean-Marie Casal.[70] Since that time the Transitional Stage has been found in excavations at Ghazi Shah,[71] Naushero,[72] Kunal,[73] Banawali,[74] Dholavira,[75] and Harappa,[76] although the recent revisions to the Harappa periodization do not specifically delineate this stage.

The Chronology of the Transitional Stage

A study of radiocarbon dates suggests that the Transitional Stage is circa 2600–2500 B.C.[77] This fits reasonably well with the two building levels in Period II at Amri. Thus, the Transitional Stage is thought to have been three or four generations long—anything but instantaneous.[78]

Jim G. Shaffer and Diane Lichtenstein: Another Anthropological View

Shaffer and Lichtenstein's contribution to understanding the Early Harappan and ethnic diversity in the early Indus region is a key one. In 1989 they proposed that the Mature Harappan is a fusion of their Bagor, Hakra, and Kot Diji ethnic groups in the Ghaggar/Hakra Valley.

> Fusion appears to have been very rapid, reinforced no doubt by its own success. The earliest set of Harappan dates are from Kalibangan, in the northern Ghaggar/Hakra Valley at ca. 2600 B.C.; while dates from Allahdino, Balakot and sites in Saurashtra indicate Harappan settlements were established in the southern Indus Valley by ca. 2400 B.C. Possehl and Rissman suggest a rapid origin of 150 years for the Harappan. We suggest it was even less, or 100 years, ca. 2600–2500 B.C. Within the next 100 years, the Harappan became the largest ethnic group within the Indus Valley. This rapid distribution rate was matched only by Harappan abandonment of large sections in the Indus Valley which was under way by ca. 2000 B.C., a process intensified by later hydrological changes. Whatever the Harappan ethnic group's organizational complexity, it was a cultural system promoting rapid territorial expansion.[79]

A number of other scholars have pointed to the rather short period of change that separates the Early Harappan from the Mature Harappan.

Sir Mortimer Wheeler

According to Sir Mortimer Wheeler, the Harappan Civilization was "a society strong in heart, disciplined, numerous and imaginatively led grasped the problem and, we may be sure, simultaneously solved it; else it had per-ished. Here if anywhere may we fairly discern in human affairs an example of that swift adaptation and progression which biologists know as 'explosive evolution.' "[80]

A. Ghosh

Ghosh notes that "at present, the nucleus of the Indus civilization appears to spring into being fully shaped. . . . Like other revolutions, the Indus civilization may in origin best be visualized as the sudden offspring of opportunity and genius."[81] In a discussion of the development of the Harappan Civilization he observed that "all such changes, vast as they are, could easily take place within a generation or two."[82]

S. P. Gupta

"The trouble is, as Wheeler has rightly observed, that urban growth of the Indus kind is usually so sudden and quick that within a generation or two, it may spread over a vast area, but the archaeological tool as applied to our protohistoric sites is too blunt to bring out the evidence of this kind."[83]

J.-F. Jarrige

In a discussion of his excavations at Naushaho, Jean-François Jarrige observed, "The elements of continuity between the end of Period I and the beginning of Period II are such that they leave little room for a time gap between them. This suggests that the emergence of the Mature Harappan civilization has been very rapid."[84]

M. Jansen

Michael Jansen holds the following view of Mohenjo-daro:

> If it was—during its urban phase—a planned platform-based city, then it would indicate an enormous step, not only politically, but also financially and organizationally regarding the effort to construct it. This step would have coincided with the appearance of seals, script, burnt-brick technology, hydrological technology such as circular wells constructed with wedge-shaped bricks, drains and bathing platforms. . . . We are dealing with a rather small time gap of not more than 80 years around 2400 B.C. where all of these elements must have been developed.[85]

Jansen's colleague M. Cucarzi notes:

> Jansen's thesis therefore, is that Mohenjo-daro represents the moment in which the urban phase explodes in the Indus civilization and, that in order to build Mohenjo-daro they constructed gigantic clay and/or mud platforms to raise its base level, mainly to protect themselves from the recurrent flooding of the Indus.[86]

The Look of the Transitional Stage

We do not know very much about the Early Harappan–Mature Harappan Transition. The Mature Harappan has a suite of artifacts and new technologies that are quite different from the Early Harappan. The entire "look" of the Mature Harappan is new, with a new style of pottery, including clay fabrics, vessel forms, and painting. There is some continuity in ceramics, but the differences between Early Harappan and Mature Harappan pottery are clear. There are new metal forms: pots, pans, copper tablets, blades, fishhooks, a razor, and the like. Bronze is introduced on a broad scale. Baked-brick architecture and the town planning that accompanies it are characteristic Mature Harappan features. Brick-lined well technology is also a feature of the Mature Harappan, the one example in earlier contexts probably being in the Early Harappan–Mature Harappan Transition. Bead-making technology is much expanded, along with the widespread use of carnelian, etching, and the complex technology of drilling very long, hard stone beads. Terra-cotta carts and triangular terra-cotta cakes are also unique to the Mature Harappan, although the triangular cakes are also found in the Late Kot Dijian. The distinctive Harappan stamp seal is a feature of the Mature Harappan not present in the Early Harappan.

This list could go on, but what has been presented suffices to make the point: From the perspective of artifacts, the Early Harappan and Mature Harappan are quite different. Since such changes do not take place instantaneously, it would seem that these technologies were developed within the Early Harappan–Mature Harappan Transition. We have some grasp on the Transitional ceramics from Naushaho Ic and Id as well as Amri II (figure 2.20).

Another feature developed within the Early Harappan–Mature Harappan Transition is writing.

The Beginnings of Writing

There is little if any evidence for the beginnings of writing in the Early Harappan. Signs on pots, both pre- and postfiring, begin early, in Stage Two, but this is not writing, and some of it is probably simple potter's marks or marks of ownership. Logic suggests that the relatively developed writing of the Mature Harappan has its roots in the Early Harappan–Mature Harappan Transition.

Further digging at places like Harappa and Naushaho may well produce evidence for the beginnings of the writing system and a sense of evolution of the script if careful seriation of materials is undertaken. Prototypes of the square Indus stamp seal have been found in the Transitional Stage levels of Kunal.[87]

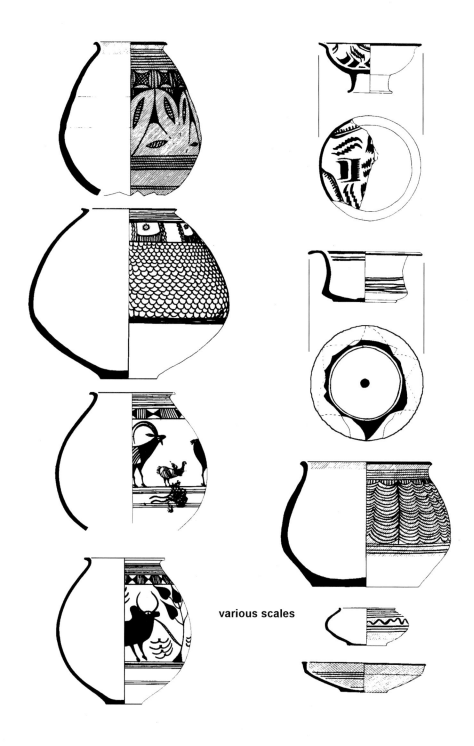

various scales

Figure 2.20 Ceramics from Nausharo ID showing the Early Indus–Indus Civilization Transition (after Jarrige 1988)

Changes in Social Structure

We do not have anything approaching even an outline of Mature Harappan social structure. A relatively simple "tribal" clan and/or lineage structure for the Early Harappan might be postulated. Several things in the Mature Harappan suggest that the society was quite different from and more complex than the Early Harappan, with more specialization of functional positions and a more developed social hierarchy. The scale of the cities suggests this, but so too does increased evidence of craft specialization, expansion of the economy, and the presence of what may well have been a single ideology synthesizing elements of the four phases of the Early Harappan Stage. There was a new ability to bring people together under a single civilizational rubric; to cause them to work together in new and more productive ways on projects dwarfed by the world of the Early Harappan.

The Foundations of the Indus Ideology

The Mature Harappan represents an ideology new to the Greater Indus region, and probably the world. Some new set of unifying ideas, or a single overarching idea, brought a new sense of unity to the Greater Indus region in the middle of the third millennium B.C. More is said of this later, but one suspects that the Indus ideology was also part of the cultural innovation that characterizes the Early Harappan–Mature Harappan Transition.

Summary

To define the Transitional Stage and outline some of the material objects that have been found there has been one of this chapter's objectives. I have also suggested some possible sociocultural implications of this phase as a link between the simple regional clans and lineages of the Early Harappan and the greater complexity of the Mature Harappan.

None of this should be elevated to the level of theory. The investigation of the Early Harappan–Mature Harappan Transition has only begun, and we know very little about it. But progress is made in archaeology and other sciences by setting up models, proposing hypotheses, and anticipating data, to speculate on what might be found and then "digging" for it. The archaeological record does not speak for itself and little in it is inherently obvious. None of the important issues such as the explanation of cultural change and the description of a prehistoric society in sociocultural terms will emerge from an approach free from theoretical speculation of this type.

NOTES

1. Braidwood 1975.
2. Zohary and Hopf 1988: 16–52.
3. Vavilov 1949–50.
4. Costantini and Biasini 1985: 16–17; Jarrige 1995: 64.
5. For further discussion, see Possehl 1999b: 407–12.
6. Bar-Yosef and Meadow 1995.
7. Zohary 1970; Zohary and Hopf 1988; Harlan 1971, 1977; Singh 1991; Willcox 1992: 292; Flannery 1995: 5; Lamberg-Karlovsky 1996: 173–74.
8. Vinogradov 1979.
9. Dupree 1972.
10. Possehl 1999b: 432–40.
11. Flam 1999.
12. Jarrige et al. 1995.
13. Meadow 1998: 13.
14. Meadow 1993: 301.
15. Meadow 1984: 35.
16. Meadow 1998: 12.
17. Meadow 1993: 311.
18. Meadow 1993: 307–8.
19. I have adopted the so-called low chronology proposed by J. Reade 2001.
20. See Possehl 1999b: 16–27 for a more detailed coverage of chronology.
21. Mackay 1937–38: xiv–xv.
22. Shaffer and Lichtenstein 1989; Shaffer 1992.
23. Shaffer 1992: vol. II, 426.
24. Fairservis 1956.
25. Dani 1970–71: 39, 41–42.
26. Jarrige et al. 1995: 318; Mackay 1937–38: 591–94.
27. Jarrige et al. 1995: 318.
28. Possehl and Rissman 1992: 469–78.
29. Possehl and Rissman 1992: 473–75.
30. See Possehl 1999b: 470–471 for a complete list of known sites of Stage One.
31. The evaluation of settlement data of the sort presented here is a difficult problem in archaeology. For a discussion, see Possehl 1999b: 562–67.
32. Possehl 1999b: 473–74.
33. Misra 1973.
34. Joshi 1978.
35. Geddes 1983.
36. Samzun and Sellier 1985: 96.
37. Hemphill, Lukacs, and Kennedy 1991: 174.
38. Lechevallier 1984.
39. Mughal 1997.
40. Mughal 1972.
41. Kenoyer and Meadow 2000; SAA 1997.
42. Mughal 1997: figs. 3–4 and pls. I–VI.
43. Mughal 1997: pl. 37 and fig. 9, no. 14.
44. Khan, Knox, and Thomas 1991: 39.
45. Mughal 1997: 40–44.
46. *Indian Archaeology, A Review* 1961–62: pls. XXXVII and XXXVIII.
47. *Indian Archaeology, A Review* 1964–65: 13.
48. Fairservis 1975: 317–18.
49. Southworth 1992.
50. Possehl 1999b: 576.
51. Majumdar 1934: 24–33.
52. Casal 1964.
53. R. S. Bisht 1992, personal communication.
54. Possehl 1997a.
55. Majumdar 1934: 65–67.
56. Possehl 1999b: 727–845.
57. Khan 1965.

58. Fairservis 1956.
59. Wright 1985
60. Possehl 1998; 1999b: 713–24.
61. Dales 1979: 47.
62. Khan 1965: 22.
63. Dani 1970–71: 39–40.
64. Casal 1964: 7.
65. Jarrige 1989: 64–65.
66. Lal 1979: 75.
67. Thapar 1973: 87.
68. Gupta 1978: 142.
69. Raikes 1968.
70. Casal 1964: 39–42.
71. Flam 1993.
72. Jarrige 1988, 1989.
73. Khatri and Acharya 1995.

74. Bisht 1982: 116.
75. Bisht 1991.
76. Meadow 1991.
77. Possehl 1986b: 96–98; Possehl 1993; Possehl and Rissman 1992.
78. Possehl 1990, 1993; Shaffer and Lichtenstein 1989.
79. Shaffer and Lichtenstein 1989: 123, citing Possehl 1986b: 96–98; Possehl and Rissman 1992.
80. Wheeler 1959: 108.
81. Ghosh 1965: 116.
82. Wheeler 1968: 24–25.
83. Gupta 1978: 144.
84. Jarrige 1988: 201.
85. Jansen 1987: 15.
86. Cucarzi 1987: 81.
87. Khatri and Acharya 1995.

CHAPTER 3

The Indus Civilization

INTRODUCTION

This chapter is devoted to an overview of the Indus Civilization and begins with a discussion of their ideology, followed with a perspective on the Indus political order, the diversity of its peoples, their settlement patterns, and the subsistence system. Finally, short reviews of some interesting sites are included.

THE IDEOLOGY OF THE INDUS CIVILIZATION

I have a strong sense that the defining characteristic of the Indus Civilization, as with most peoples, was their ideology. By *ideology* I am attempting to convey the notion that the Indus peoples had a well-defined set of concepts about human life and culture that they used to set themselves apart from other peoples. This was an Indus institution based on propositions that could be neither affirmed nor denied that set forth the social, especially political, aspirations of these peoples.

We can be sure that there was an Indus ideology, and this book gives me a chance to begin to grapple with it. I also want to open a subject matter that, if not new, is certainly not well developed in the writing on the Indus Civilization. Who were these Harappan peoples?—not biologically, or in the sense of their geographical home, but what were they like, what made them tick?

As my thoughts began to deal with the Indus ideology, I wondered what it could possibly be. I am still not sure, since finding "the" ideology of the Indus peoples was pretty clearly an impossible goal, at least at the moment. Therefore, I decided to accept a kind of proxy, or first approximation. Assuming that the ideology of the Indus peoples would be reflected (approximated) in the archaeological record, I decided to use as my proxies those traits of the Indus Civilization that come to mind as the most distinctive Harappan features—the important things I think of when I think of them. These are features of the Indus Civilization that define the civilization for me, give it character and substance, set it apart from other complex sociocultural systems of antiquity.

This led me to four aspects of the Indus ideology:

1. The Indus peoples were nihilists who sought to bring a new sociocultural order to the Greater Indus region.
2. Urbanization and city life were a part of this new ideology.

3. The physical and symbolic aspects of water formed a part of the Indus ideology. M. Jansen calls it *wasserluxus,* a term I have integrated into my position on Indus ideology.
4. The Indus ideology promoted technological prowess and innovation.

I have found that these aspects of ideology are expressed in visual and symbolic form in the Indus cities, towns, villages, and camps. They are found in the distinctive Indus artifacts—stamp seals, painted pottery, figurines, architecture, baked-brick buildings, brick-lined wells, bathing facilities, new or expanded technologies, and the like. The Early Harappan peoples were not seafarers; the Indus peoples were. Thus, the Indus maritime technology was also a part of, or resulted from, the Indus ideology.

In thinking about this ideology that I have "found," it became clear that it would be an excess to believe that it is "the" ideology of these peoples. Those things that I have used to define the "ideology of the Indus Civilization" may well be close to what the Indus peoples believed. Some of it might even be "spot on," but to think of this collection of observations as the genuine, complete ideology of the Indus Civilization would be wrong. It is an approximation of the deeper values of the Indus peoples that have been expressed to us archaeologically. My goal in this discussion is therefore quite modest. I want to pursue a theme in the study of the Indus Civilization that I believe to be important that has not yet received the attention it deserves.

The Indus Civilization and Nihilism

The immense differences between the Indus Civilization, as compared to the Early Harappan, can be seen as a replacement of the older Early Harappan symbolic system with a new order and way of life. The Indus peoples turned their backs on their own past and replaced it with this, a new order and way of life. Archaeologists see this new order, or ideology, expressed as new signs and symbols such as new artifact styles, architecture, town planning, innovations in technology, and the like.

The changes in settlement location that take place with the Mature Harappan can also be interpreted as an attempt to break with the past: stop living where the old traditions linger, build a new settlement where the new ideology will prosper. This is expressed in the archaeological record as abandoned Early Harappan sites and Indus sites founded on virgin soil. For example, Mohenjo-daro is thought to be a "founder's city," a place planned and built on virgin soil. Not all of the large Indus settlements were like this. Harappa, for example, has a very important Early Harappan occupation and a transitional occupation into the Mature Harappan. But there is a proclivity for Indus sites to be founded on virgin soil: 755 out of 1,058 sites, or 71 percent. Of the 523 Early Harappan sites we know of, 324 (62 percent) were abandoned prior to the Mature Harappan. This finding documents the observation that the Indus peoples tended to build new settlements, on fresh soil, abandoning their past in the form of the places that were home to their ancestors. The rate for the founding of Indus new settlements is significantly greater than that for the other stages of the Indus Age.[1]

I think of this kind of behavior as "nihilistic," a concept with many connotations. The one used here is as an ideology that espouses great, even revolutionary, change, in a sociocultural system whose past has come to be seen as vacuous, baseless, even corrupt, or perhaps just wrong. Nihilists are those who attempt to deny their heritage and replace it with a new order, or ideology. This resonates with my strong sense that the Indus Civilization brings with it a sense of originality, something new and fresh. Nihilistic movements may or may not be associated with violence. This is not the predominant theme that I see in the origins of the Indus Civilization, but I have already noted that the Early Harappan–Mature Harappan Transition was a period of unusual conflagrations, and that may be telltale of the fact that Indus nihilism was not free of aggression.

It is very difficult for a people to totally rid themselves of their past, so it is not surprising that there are lines of continuity, sometimes strong, between the Early Harappan and Mature Harappan. The most obvious of these is in food production and the fact that the Indus peoples were barley and wheat farmers and cattle pastoralists, just like their Early Harappan ancestors. This observation carries with it implications for continuities in symbiotic relations among regions, farming practices, knowledge of pastoralism, animal husbandry, and the like. Some of the vaunted Indus technology has its roots deep into the Indus Age, and there is much continuity in these fields. In this sense the Indus technologists built on a past rich in accomplishment, but this should not be used to lessen our sense of their prowess and the documentation of their spectacular achievements. The artifactual record has continuities as well with shared ceramic vessel forms and pottery motifs: intersecting circles, fish scales, and checkerboards come to mind.

While there is continuity between the Early Harappan and Mature Harappan, this is not the dominant theme. What is most apparent, and important to me, is that the Indus Civilization carries with it a sense of the new, of original creativity, to such a spectacular degree that it brings nihilism to mind.

Urbanization and Sociocultural Complexity in the Indus Civilization

Urbanization and sociocultural complexity are interrelated and defining features of the Indus Civilization. The cities of Mohenjo-daro and Harappa, now including Ganweriwala, Dholavira, and Rakhigarhi, both symbolize and define the Indus Civilization. The size and complexity of the Indus cities are distinctive features of the Mature Harappan, not clearly developed out of even the largest of the Early Harappan places.

The ancient cities of the Indus are interesting for many reasons. One of the most important is that they arose so rapidly from relatively undifferentiated Early Harappan communities. Mohenjo-daro and the Indus occupations of Harappa and Dholavira were different from the settlements that came before them. This is expressed in many ways: size, architectural elaboration, some sense of town planning, layout, water acquisition and management.

There is good evidence that the Indus Civilization was a well-developed, complex sociocultural form. This is best inferred from the large, complex Indus economy, the geographic scale of the civilization and implications of ethnic diversity, its technological achievements, and urbanization. There is evidence for so many complex jobs ("scribes," seal cutters, metalworkers, architects, and/or engineers, etc.) that one has to think in terms of a multiplicity of craft and career specialists. There are also differences between urban and rural settings in terms of wealth. This is documented by the richness of finds, especially the hoards, and speaks to the issue of sociocultural differentiation.

The sociocultural complexity of the Indus Civilization is distinctive in two important ways: the absence of temples or other monumental buildings serving the religious institution and the absence of monumental residences for kings and elites of this sort. The Indus ideology did not admit such sociocultural expressions. Just as this ideology inhibited such expressions, they were promoted in ancient Egypt and Mesopotamia. In fact, the religious and political institutions of the Indus Civilization expressed themselves in significantly different ways from all of the other civilizations of the ancient world.

There is no full consensus among archaeologists on the definition of the archaic state, although some agreement on a few points is at hand. The archaic state was a form of political organization. It is characteristic of peoples with large-scale economies, ethnic diversity, and considerable specialization in craft and career tracks. The administration of the archaic state was performed by a bureaucracy of career specialists. The craft and career specialists of an archaic state, along with other peoples of their society, were arranged in a hierarchy of classes. The archaic state monopolized the use of force as a means of social control and an agency to protect, if not expand, the sovereignty of the people it encompassed. The archaic state had a strong focus on kingship, or centralized leadership, that was in all likelihood given to the aggrandizement of the individuals who rose to this office. The economies of states tended to be somewhat centralized, controlled from the office of the king, so that they could effectively serve the diplomatic and military needs of the political apparatus. This implied staff functionaries (more bureaucrats) to implement and monitor the economic decision making as well as to collect revenue and produce for the center. Monumental religious architecture and a well-developed parallel hierarchy of the religious institution promoted allegiance and loyalty to the king and central administration of the archaic state. The notion of an archaic state carries with it a strong sense of elitism and exclusivity for relatively small numbers of powerful people. Key themes in understanding the archaic state are centralization and hierarchy.

It is increasingly apparent that not all archaic complex societies were organized as archaic states with their highly centralized, severely hierarchical sociocultural systems. Some archaic complex societies share with the archaic state key features such as urbanization, large political economies, vast territories, social classes, craft and career specialists, but the way these elements were expressed, the way they all fit together to form a working sociocultural system, was different from the archaic state.

R. Ehrenreich, C. Crumley, and J. Levy conceive of the archaic complex sociocultural systems that were not organized along the lines of the archaic state as "heterarchies."[2] They stress the decentralized nature of some archaic complex societies. This decentralization is linked to muted principles of centralization and hierarchy. It is not that centralization and hierarchy were absent from heterarchies, but differences among people were based on multiple criteria; there was an emphasis on shared power and the collective management of society. Institutions like kingship were either very weak, along the lines of "firsts among equals," or hardly present at all. Power was distributed, and accessed, differently in heterarchies as compared to archaic states.

R. Blanton and his associates contrast archaic complex sociocultural systems in terms of an emphasis on "exclusionary" versus "corporate" principles of organization.[3]

They emphasize that all complex societies incorporate elements of both "exclusivity" and "corporateness" in their makeup; but these principles can be expressed to very different degrees. The archaic state emphasized the exclusionary principle with centrality and well-developed principles of hierarchy. But corporate principles prevailed in other systems. They were heterarchical and less centralized, hierarchy was muted, and mechanisms such as joint rule and councils were used to govern and maintain social control.

Exclusionary and corporate sociocultural systems can be equally complex, both with large economies incorporating a multiplicity of ethnicities as well as craft and career specialists; rule vast territories; and build grand urban landscapes. But they are based on different sociocultural principles. Ancient Egypt and Mesopotamia were more exclusionary than corporate. The Indus Civilization was more corporate than exclusionary. The peoples of the Indus Civilization formed more of a heterarchy than they were a hierarchy.

Realizing that we do not know what the political form of the Indus Civilization was, but if it was more corporate than exclusionary, as hints in the archaeological record suggest, then I can imagine that the Indus peoples were ruled by a series of "councils" or gatherings of leaders, rather than a king. Age and gender probably counted for much in the determination of leadership, as did adherence to and practice of the Indus ideology. There may have been civic councils for individual settlements, regional councils for the Domains or the political unit above the civic, and possibly a supreme "Indus Council." I sense in the Indus peoples a marked distrust in government, per se, especially strong, centralized government.

In the absence of a strong, centralized religion and religious monuments, the Indus ideology emerges as of prime importance. The ideology lacks firm substance in terms of monumental buildings (gigantic pyramids, ziggurats, temples, etc.) and therefore may have been more in the mind of the Indus peoples than a physical reality that they gazed upon in awe and fear. Like being a "good Marxist" was valued in the former Soviet Union, being a "good Harappan" may have been what was valued by the peoples of the Indus Civilization. The ideology, like religion in the archaic state, thus emerges as the central force in Indus social control and allegiance.

The Indus Civilization and *Wasserluxus*

Water and its management played an interesting role in Indus life. This is probably clearest at Mohenjo-daro and Dholavira with the many wells, elaborate drainage systems, bathing facilities in virtually all of the houses, and the Great Bath itself. Water is such an important substance at Mohenjo-daro that M. Jansen has published a book titled *Mohenjo-daro: City of Wells and Drains, Water Splendor 4000 Years Ago.*[4] The translation of *wasserluxus* as "water splendor" from the original does not quite catch the word's meaning, so I use the German. The bathing facilities in each house inform us that washing and cleanliness were important to the Harappans. We have to anticipate, I think, that this involved both physical cleanliness, as well as something of a more symbolic nature. The many wells throughout the city were sources of new, pure water, essential for effective cleanliness. The drainage system served to move the effluent away from the houses, below ground, safely out of the way and safely out of sight, in brick-lined channels that prevented contamination of the earth and the city.

The Great Bath is a Mohenjo-daro bathing platform, raised to the civic level. It is larger and more complex than household facilities, but conforms to the proposition that cleanliness of both types was an important element in the Indus ideology. It is interesting, too, that the builders of the Great Bath used elevation and distance to symbolically set it apart from the rest of Mohenjo-daro. This was important ritual space, one that seems to have been reserved for the elites of the city, possibly the elites of the entire Indus world. As we shall see, the beginning of the end of the transformation of this great metropolis was at hand when the Great Bath was abandoned and no longer used.

Wheeler found *wasserluxus* an interesting and important feature of the Indus Civilization. He felt that the Great Bath and the "extravagant provision for bathing" in private homes were both testimonies to the importance of water in the life of the Indus peoples.[5]

The Indus Civilization and Technological Innovation

One of the most interesting features of the Indus Civilization is the range of new technologies associated with it. The craft specialists of the Indus Civilization were technological virtuosos. There was, for example, a significant increase in the ability of these peoples to control heat and direct it to pyrotechnology. This is best exemplified in their metal work and the development of bronze. But it is also apparent in the advancements they made with faience and stoneware, clear steps upward on the pyrotechnological ladder. Other significant technologies associated with the Indus are as follows:

City planning and the construction of large buildings from baked brick

The technology needed for the excavation of brick-lined wells

Urban drainage systems

Manufacture of very long, hard stone beads, including the sophisticated drilling technology

Spectacular pyrotechnological achievement along a number of fronts

Mastery of maritime sailing

Since these new technologies all appear in the Mature Harappan, or possibly the Transitional Stage, I have come to believe that a part of the Indus ideology promoted, even institutionalized, technological prowess and innovation.

Before we move on from this discussion of Indus ideology, I want to mention two interesting, but relatively less important, themes that "appear" with the Indus Civilization and would seem to be somehow woven into their ideology. There is also the issue of the cultural diversity of the Indus Civilization as well as the Indus identity.

Two New Iconographic Themes of the Indus Ideology

Horned human or humanoid figures are a motif frequently encountered in the iconography of the Indus Civilization (figure 3.1). These figures begin to appear in the Early Harappan–Mature Harappan Transition and continue into the Indus Civilization. The most famous of them is the so-called Proto-Siva or Mahayogi (figure 3.2). This seal is discussed in considerable detail in the chapter on religion. The motif combines the iconography of the water buffalo and ritual discipline, the beginnings of yoga. Given their "supernatural" appearance, they seem to be a part of the new Indus ideology or religion.

Another well-documented motif is the one with a human or humanoid inside a tree, usually a pipal tree (figure 3.3). Sometimes this motif is fronted by a kneeling human and a goat, with seven human "attendants." I have come to call this the seal of "Divine Adoration" as shown on seal 430 from Mohenjo-daro (figure 3.4). Once again, this is a scene with a narrative quality that seems to speak to the ideology of the Indus Civilization, but we do not know how to translate it. There is little doubt in my mind that this is the Indus peoples speaking to us of their world, of their stories about themselves, which probably aggrandize their lives, beliefs, culture, and history, which gave meaning to their way of life. In the old vocabulary of structural functionalism it contributed to Harappan self-esteem and to group solidarity by sharing experiences, both real and mythical.

THE DIVERSITY OF THE INDUS CIVILIZATION

It is clear that the Indus Civilization was an organization of diversity: diversity of culture, peoples, and geography. This

Figure 3.1　Horned figures in the Indus Civilization

diversity probably means that there were many ways to be a "good Harappan," just as there were many ways to be a "good Marxist" for those who valued Marxism. This diversity informs us of the many ways that the peoples of the Indus Civilization seem to have adopted and adapted this ideology to their own view of the world and way of going about creating a happy life. For example, the "Kullis" of ancient Baluchistan represent a major divergence from the Indus ideology as compared to the "Sindhis." I imagine the Kullis to have been a significant sectarian split of the Indus ideology, if *sectarianism* can be used in matters of this sort. The Sorath Harappans adapted the Indus ideology in their

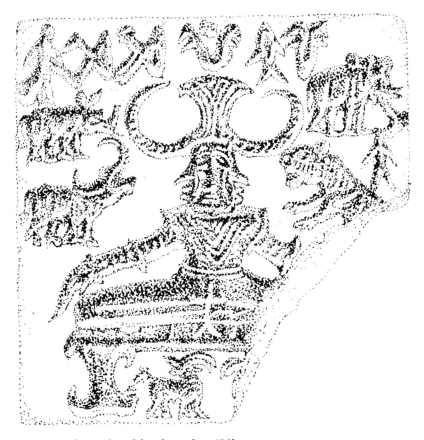

Figure 3.2　The "Proto-Siva" or Mahayogi seal (seal number 420)

Figure 3.3 Human in a tree motif

own way, to their own tastes, which gives a very special quality to their "Harappanness." They are quite different, to the point that some archaeologists wonder if the Sorath Harappans were Harappans at all.[6] They were Harappans, of course, since their cultural historical roots were in Sindh; it is just that their manner of expressing the Indus ideology is a regional one. In some ways, the Sorath Harappans were probably no less Harappan than any of the other Indus regional manifestations of the Indus ideology. In this sense they simply lend diversity to the character of the Indus Civilization, just as do the Kullis. There were just many ways of being Harappan.

There are some ways of "scaling" this notion of Harappanness if one turns to the regional archaeological indicators of the ways and degrees by which the Indus ideology was implemented or brought into reality. It seems to me that the Indus ideology is best and most clearly seen in Sindh, especially at Mohenjo-daro. I will not go into this in detail here because the rest of this book is in some ways intended to highlight this point among others. It is not that the ancient Sindhis were the "best Harappans"; it is just that their land is where it is most clearly exhibited. The Kullis diverge from this in significant ways. Possibly the most significant is found at Nindowari, where there may be a monumental platform with a drain in the top. This sort of structure is also seen in the Quetta Valley, at Damb Sadaat, although on a smaller scale. Such buildings seem to be deeply rooted in the Kulli regional history, and these peoples can be imagined to have somehow integrated it with the rest of the Indus ideology to produce the unique "Kulli-Harappan" expression.

I have already noted that the Sorath Harappan is its

own regional manifestation of Harappanness. Applying to them the scale on which the Indus ideology is apparent in the archaeological record reveals a relatively weak signature. There are no cities or much *wasserluxus,* and the technological component is not especially prominent, except for seafaring. There is a significant amount of Sorath Harappan pottery in the Arabian Gulf, especially on Bahrain Island, ancient Dilmun. But I detect much nihilistic vigor in these new settlers of Saurashtra, and their material culture has many of the "signs and symbols" of the Indus Civilization. Rojdi is a very well planned town, for example. Their ceramics are very Indus-like with dishes on stand, perforated ware, and the like. They used the Indus system of weights and the writing system, but not stamp seals. Nonetheless, the expression of the Indus ideology is attenuated in the Sorath Harappan, as it is in the Eastern Domain, but in a way different from the Sorath folk.

Recognizing this kind of cultural diversity is important as one investigates the world of the Indus Civilization. But by 1900 B.C. the world had changed, the Indus Civilization had undergone a transformation. This transformation was something that destroyed the original ideological basis of the civilization: The old nihilist paradigm was gone, of course, but so too were urbanization, *wasserluxus,* and the old technological prowess. M. Vidale and H. Miller very nicely highlight the key changes in technology with the emerging transformation of the Indus Civilization.[7]

The transformation in the Sindhi and Kulli Domains is the most pronounced. We just do not know enough about the Northwestern Domain in the early second millennium

Figure 3.4 Seal of Divine Adoration (seal number 430)

to know what went on there. In the Sorath and Eastern Domains there was much less change. This was due to the fact that transformation focused on the amendment of the heart of the civilization, its ideology. In the Sorath and Eastern Domains there was an attenuation of the ideology. This buffered and protected the peoples there from the changes that were quite profound in Sindhi, Kulli, Cholistan, and possibly in the Harappa Domains, where the Indus ideology was much more deeply seated in the lives of the people.

STAMP SEALS AND THE INDUS IDENTITY

The use of seal types in South Asia and the Middle East has been suggested to have significant symbolic value. C. C. Lamberg-Karlovsky has discussed the different seal types: for example, cylinders, "Persian Gulf" button, and square stamp seals. His position is this:

> A related matter of shared ideology and meaning can be derived from seals. The use of very distinctive, highly individualized styles and shapes of seals of the Indus (square), Persian Gulf (round), Mesopotamia (cylindrical), and Turkmenistan-Seistan (compartmented) in the middle of the third millennium is . . . far from accidental. The seals in all of the above areas are believed to have served a similar function. . . . [Among other things] the seals made it possible to identify the mother country of the merchant. . . . The seals, in short, provided an overt symbol of ethnic identity as well as a practical tool for trade regulation. It is interesting to note that coincidence in the distribution of distinctive seal types is overlapped by the distribution of equally distinctive ceramic types.[8]

The square Indus seal identified its holder as "Harappan," and the cylinder identified the holder as a Mesopotamian, all without anyone having to be literate.

The Character of the Indus Peoples

I want to say a few things to characterize the Indus peoples. Marshall noted a contradiction in this matter: "One of the most striking facts revealed by the excavations at Mohenjo-daro and Harappa is the complete uniformity of their culture. Though these two spots are some 400 miles apart, their monuments and antiquities are to all intents and purposes identical."[9] Then, in the same book, Marshall went on to say that the Indus is just as individual, just as national, as the other civilizations, as shown by the character of the domestic architecture and monuments like the Great Bath. The remarkably naturalistic quality of Indus art is another feature, and so is the painted pottery. The use of cotton instead of flax and the quality of the writing system were also seen as unique.

"But behind these and manifold other traits that are peculiar to the Indus Civilization and give it its national character, is a tissue of ideas, inventions and discoveries which were common property of the then civilized world and cannot be traced to their respective sources."[10]

The Indus Civilization is characterized by a sense of strict adherence to rules and thus a kind of internal isolation. This is shown in the painting of pottery, so carefully executed according to a plan, but also in the careful layout of the houses of Mohenjo-daro, not encroaching on one another or public space and streets, at least during the early and middle centuries of the city. Party walls are not an Indus trait, and each house is a self-sufficient entity.[11] A kind of privacy in life is shown by the fact that, by and large, Mohenjo-daro houses do not open onto major roads. Rather, the entrance is off a back lane, with a space for a *chowkidar* (watchman) on the ground level. As we will see, there is evidence that the ground floors of many houses were not used for living, at least not for the householder and family. Life took place up on the second floor and roof level, where there was light and air and where the family could find privacy and refuge from the hustle and bustle of street life in the city.

The Harappans had a sense of humor as well. One sees this especially in some of the terra-cotta puppet figurines of humans and animals. These have delightfulness that must have come from the maker, and not merely my biased, modern eye. It follows by inference that some of these puppets were intended as toys and were created by imaginative adults for children to enjoy.

Concluding Remarks on Indus Ideology and Related Matters

The fashioning of the Indus ideology drew on older cultural traditions of the Greater Indus region; but its development was also an act of creation, and there is much new within it. This nihilism was founded in urbanization and sociocultural complexity. Water and cleanliness were powerful forces in the Indus ideology. The Indus peoples were technological innovators.

The Mature Harappan was a time of some economic prosperity, with significant advances in technology, craft specialization, and long-distance trade. These activities did not begin with the Indus Civilization—their history is much deeper—but they were certainly expanded in the Mature Harappan, sometimes in an exponential way.

THE ETHNIC DIVERSITY OF THE INDUS PEOPLES

The Indus Civilization is a union of peoples of the four Early Harappan regional phases.[12] While we do not know where the ethnic boundaries are within the Early

Harappan, the presence of four distinctive phases very strongly suggests ethnic diversity. We cannot say that each of these phases was about one ethnic group. Nor can we say that any given ethnic group was confined to one of the regional phases, since it is quite possible that one or more ethnic groups were a part of, say, both the Kot Dijian and the Sothi-Siswal Phases. But the diversity of artifactual style does suggest (not prove) ethnic diversity, so I will proceed with this assumption.

Ethnic diversity in the Indus Civilization should be no surprise. Ancient India has always been known for its diversity of peoples, shown most clearly by the multitude of languages. The Vedas speak of different kinds of people and even have a word (*Mleccha*) for peoples who speak gibberish, or languages other than Sanskrit. Six hundred years after the appearance of the Vedas, Herodotus notes that "there are many Indian nations, none speaking the same language."[13]

Within the Mature Harappan there are themes of both cultural homogeneity and heterogeneity. There is an overarching sense of one civilization, but within this theme there is diversity, and that diversity of archaeological assemblages suggests ethnic diversity. Once again, no one knows how much diversity or where the boundaries were, and I am not equating ceramic pots or any other artifact or group of artifacts with "people." But the Sindhi Harappans stand out in contrast to peoples of the other domains, especially the Kullis and the peoples with whom I worked, the Sorath Harappans.[14] This comes through as not just different kinds of pots and other artifacts, but in terms of subsistence, adaptation, ways of life. I also speak of the peoples of the Sorath Harappan and those of the other domains as well, since there is no reason for us to believe that there was only one ethnic group per domain or that any given ethnic group was limited to any one domain.

The Indus religion emerges best at Mohenjo-daro, where there seems to be some evidence for an Indus "Great Tradition" as well as religious beliefs that are more folk or "Little Tradition" in nature.[15] When one looks at other sites, such as Harappa, Dholavira, Rakhigarhi, Kalibangan, and Lothal, for example, one gets the impression that there were a number of Indus Little Traditions, admitting considerable religious diversity within the Indus Civilization. Since religion along with language is so often a characteristic that defines a people, this dimension of Indus life also suggests ethnic diversity.

Physical anthropologists have also documented biological diversity in the Indus population. For example, Mohenjo-daro is somewhat different in its phenotypic traits from the population represented at northern sites, especially Harappa and Kalibangan.[16] Health profiles of individuals support the notion of biological heterogeneity since there are significant differences from region to region. The population at Mohenjo-daro has a high rate of anemia as compared to other Indus sites.[17] Thus, while the Mature Harappan as a whole can be seen as a population, if we look for diversity, it is there both culturally and biologically within the whole.[18]

The Late Kot Dijian of the Derajat and Potwar Plateau

The Kot Dijian ceramic assemblage has a late stage in the Derajat and Potwar Plateau, which takes a version of this assemblage into the second half of the third millennium, contemporary with the Harappan Civilization This was first suggested by A. H. Dani[19] and has been confirmed by a series of radiocarbon dates and description.[20] These sites, and the peoples who lived in them, are contemporary with the Indus Civilization (2500–1900 B.C.). A map and list of Late Kot Dijian sites is available in the references.[21]

The evidence documenting that the Late Kot Dijian and the Indus Civilization were contemporary is not based on radiocarbon dates alone. Some Indus painted motifs are found on Late Kot Dijian ceramics: pipal leaves, fish scales, intersecting circles, and peacocks. Indus perforated ware occurs at Gumla IV. Other Indus artifacts occur also in the Late Kot Dijian: Gumla IV produced an etched carnelian bead, a cubical stone weight, a faience button or seal, steatite (paste) disk beads, toy cart frames with wheels, triangular terra-cotta cakes, and "missiles."[22]

The Late Kot Dijians of the Derajat and Potwar Plateau seem to represent peoples outside the Indus ideology, peoples who chose to stay with the older ways of the Early Harappan and who preserved their suite of material culture, best represented by their ceramics, as symbolic representation of this decision. That their relationship with the Mature Harappan peoples was a peaceful one can perhaps be inferred from the recently discovered presence of Indus sites in among the Late Kot Dijian settlements of the Derajat.[23]

Thus, we see that the Indus ideology was not totally accepted everywhere. There were holdouts. The political, economic, and ideological relationships between the Indus and Late Kot Dijian peoples must have been both rich and complex, and it is therefore sad to say that we know so little about them.

Conclusion

The Indus Civilization had an identifiable archaeological assemblage. The differences between it and the Early Harappan testify to the immense changes that took place during the Early Harappan–Mature Harappan Transition.

This transition is hypothesized to have been the period when the Indus ideology developed and proliferated. There is evidence for the existence of a diversity of peoples in ancient India that were a part of this civilization. It is taken from the diversity found within the Indus archaeological assemblages, but also from the physical remains of the Harappans themselves. It is not surprising, after all, to find cultural and physical diversity in a civilization that covers over 1 million square kilometers.

INDUS SETTLEMENT PATTERNS AND SUBSISTENCE

Introduction

This section presents the environmental and human dimensions in the natural world of the Greater Indus region. In chapter 1, the cultural/natural regions of the Indus Civilization, called domains, were presented, along with the nature and history of the two principal rivers, the Indus and Sarasvati. What follows is a review of Indus settlement patterns and the subsistence practices of the Indus peoples.

Settlement Patterns

There are 1,052 settlements of the Indus Civilization known today.[24] They range from tiny places one-tenth of a hectare or less in size, to Mohenjo-daro and Harappa, both nearly 100 hectares. No one has successfully demonstrated that the settlements of these people can be rationalized into a three- or four-tier system that is hierarchically arranged. While there are cities and towns, some of the best-known places are actually quite small (e.g., Lothal at 4.8 hectares, Chanhu-daro at 4.7 hectares). There is very good evidence for village farming communities. Many of the small sites, with thin scatters of pottery and no signs of permanent architecture, are interpreted reasonably as pastoral camps.

The Indus "Breadbasket"

During the Mature Harappan, the Sarasvati (Ghaggar-Hakra) River terminated in an inland delta near Fort Derawar. There are about 140 Mature Harappan sites in the vicinity of this delta, making it the most densely settled area of the time. There is actually an interesting succession of settlements in the Cholistan Domain. Dense occupation during the Indus Age begins with 82 Hakra Wares sites. During the Early Harappan, occupation drops, with only 20 Kot Dijian settlements. This is followed by the final "bloom" during the Mature Harappan, with approximately 140 sites.

These data may indicate the variable flow of the Sarasvati. The flow would have been strong during the Hakra Wares Phase, dropped off during the Kot Dijian, and then strengthened again during the Mature Harappan. The final drying up may be documented by the progressive drop-off in settlement during the Posturban (Cemetery H, 40 sites) and Painted Gray Ware (14 sites) Phases.[25]

Concluding Observation

Indus settlements tend to cluster, with the open space between them occasionally filled with a few individual settlements. I have suggested that the open space was probably occupied by pastoralists, nomadic and otherwise.[26]

The nine Indus sites that measure 50 hectares or more are given in table 3.1. Table 3.1 omits some large sites in Saurashtra because of lateral (spreading) stratigraphy. This also might be the case at Nagoor and Tharo Waro Daro as well. Also excluded are the giant sites in Bhatinda District (Lakhmirwala, Gurnikalan One, and Hasanpur Two).[27] The raw data on their size indicate that they were 225 hectares, 144 hectares, and 100 hectares, respectively. Further investigation of these sites may illuminate why three cities developed so close together during the Mature Harappan. Perhaps lateral stratigraphy and/or the spreading of remains through agricultural activities is the explanation for the unusual sizes of these sites.

Table 3.1 Mature Harappan sites of 50 hectares or more

Site	Province/State	Estimated size (hectares)
Mohenjo-daro	Sindh	100
Harappa	West Punjab	100
Rakhigarhi	Haryana	80
Ganweriwala	West Punjab	80
Dholavira	Gujarat	60
Nagoor	Sindh	50
Tharo Waro Daro	Sindh	50
Lakhueenjo-daro	Sindh	50
Nindowari	Baluchistan	50

Note: See Possehl 1999b: 727–845 for documentation.

Subsistence

The Indus peoples were mostly farmers and herders. Barley seems to have been the principal food grain, except in the Sorath Domain, where the people were cattle keepers par excellence who also raised goats, sheep, water buffalo, and a variety of crops. Cattle remains are consistently one-half or more of the faunal remains from Indus sites, no matter how the remains are measured (e.g., by bone count, bone weight, minimum numbers of individuals). Pigs may not have been domesticated, but pig remains and figurines document their use. The Indus peoples domesticated the chicken and kept several breeds of dogs[28] and possibly house cats.[29] Camels may also have been domesticated. Camel remains that have been found may be either the dromedary or Bactrian species. There is a certain amount of controversy over the domestication of the horse, which I believe results from the misidentification of the remains of the Indian wild ass.[30] As far as I can tell, there are lots of asses documented at Indus settlements, but no domestic horses (*Equus caballus*).

Most Indus agricultural activities took place during the winter *rabi* season. The active floodplains and the areas directly adjacent to them were most intensely cultivated during the *rabi* season. Whether rice was a cultivar of significance during the Mature Harappan has yet to be determined.

They grew dates and grapes and collected the Indian jujube. They were also great fish eaters, exploiting the rivers and lakes, especially in Sindh. Large fish vertebrae have been found at some Kutch Harappan sites. Salted and/or dried fish were traded over large distances during the Mature Harappan as documented by the presence of a marine species of catfish at Harappa.[31]

Indus peoples apparently grew cotton for its fiber and perhaps for its oil. There is good evidence of the use of cotton cloth at Mohenjo-daro. Fibers were found in four contexts there (table 3.2). Additional information on cotton and a bibliography are also available in the references.[32]

Table 3.2 Cotton at Mohenjo-daro

Two silver vases, originally wrapped in a cotton bag	Sahni 1931a: 194
Cord wound around a copper blade	Mackay 1937–38: 441, DK 8376
Fabric adhering to razor	Mackay 1937–38: 441, pls. CXVIII, no. 7
Fine cord wrapped around a copper rod	Mackay 1937–38: 441, DK 5844

Gossypium-type pollen has been found at Balakot. This sample came from layer 4, which places it rather late in the Mature Harappan sequence. McKean argues as effectively as she can that this pollen resulted from cultivated cotton.[33]

Lorenzo Costantini has observed that cotton was used at Mehrgarh during Period II. Several hundred charred seeds were associated with a fireplace in one of the compartmented buildings there.[34] This was a provisional identification, included in the preliminary report for the 1978–1979 field season, and the work on these seeds needs further study. A single carbonized cottonseed was also found at Hulas, in the Late Harappan or Posturban Phase.[35]

African millets appear in the Indus Civilization. The plants, with their Hindi-Urdu names, are sorghum or *jowar*, pearl millet or *bajra*, and finger millet or *ragi*. The importance of these plants is that they are summer grasses

that prosper during the southwest monsoon, unlike wheat and barley, which are winter grasses that do not thrive as monsoon crops. The millets thus led to double or year-round cropping and were important, if not critical, additions to the prehistoric food supply.

The appearance of these plants coincides with the beginnings, or at least the expansion, of significant maritime activity in the Arabian Gulf and Indian Ocean. It is proposed that an extension of this maritime activity took Indus sailors at least as far as the southern end of the Red Sea and possibly farther south along the east coast of Africa. It is in this environment that they came in contact with the millets, integrated them into their food supply, and eventually carried them back home to the Subcontinent.

E. H. Aitken has noted that "famine is unknown in the Indus Valley";[36] however, scarcity does visit the desert areas. The productivity of the nineteenth-century agro-pastoral system produced so much grain that horses were fed with rice instead of grass. In Sindh, the traditional method of cultivation, prior to the large-scale canalization of the nineteenth century, was to find and plant, often without plowing, the fresh alluvium, especially in small side channels of the annual flood. The seeds of wheat and barley were often broadcast and left to mature on their own.[37] Barley and wheat were sown in November and December and harvested in April.

One of the unresolved issues is whether significant canal irrigation works were associated with the Indus agricultural regime. The question is not whether they were able to dig ditches to drain swamps and move small amounts of water to and from their fields, but rather the bigger problem of moving water from the active river course(s) to different, higher, riverine environments, outside of the valley that would have been flooded naturally. This is an important, twofold issue. It has to do with the question of the Indus population's capacity to gather and manage large labor forces, as well as the salinization of agricultural fields with its consequent drop in productivity.

There are some things that are known about irrigation in the Indus Age. At Mehrgarh, "The charred seeds of wheat and barley . . . grow only on irrigated fields, also were collected from the ashy layers" of Period II, according to L. Costantini.[38] This is followed with evidence for the existence of a ditch of significant size that was filled with Mehrgarh Period IV trash.[39] This seems to indicate a date of Togau or Kechi Beg Phase use.

L. Flam proposes that there were three different forms of irrigation in Sindh, Kohistan, and along the Kirthar front during the Early Harappan and Mature Harappan.[40] The first used the natural flooding of a hill stream to irrigate land. The second form, documented at the site of Kai Buthi, made use of small, shallow ditches to gently guide spring water out onto a flat area that was used for cultivation. The third irrigation practice used by the Sindhis involved check dams, either as low, linear mounds of earth across broad fields called "bunds" or as larger stone structures along streams called *gabarbands*. The *gabarbands* are proper dams made of stone and built about half way across hill torrents and small rivers. They are designed to capture both soil and water.[41]

There was some diversity in the Mature Harappan subsistence regime. The people of the Sorath Harappan in Gujarat were heavily dependent on pastoralism and relied on a suite of hardy, drought-resistant plants.

> In all, nearly 80 different plant species were identified from Rojdi. Of these taxa, only a small number were found in all phases of occupation (Rojdi A, B, and C) and in amounts or in densities which imply significant use of the plant. A general plant-based subsistence system can be identified at Rojdi, which is maintained throughout the Harappan portion of the occupation. In this system, Rojdi was a food-producing settlement occupied throughout the year where cultivation, the use of domesticates, and various pastoral activities were being performed locally, and where, to a lesser extent, plant gathering and hunting were also being practiced. The bulk of cultivation was centered on the summer monsoon and involved millets, although winter cultivation increased in importance during the occupation. In addition, the plants being exploited never needed intensive human involvement and were all hardy, drought resistant species.[42]

Baluchistan and the Northwest Frontier (the Kulli and Northwestern Domains) would have been places suitable for the cultivation of winter wheat and barley. The hills and valleys of this mountainous area are also good pastureland and would have been home to large numbers of domesticated animals, especially sheep, goats, and cattle. Transhuman pastoral nomadism would have linked the highlands to the lowlands in a symbiotic partnership.

The abundant remains of cattle and of cattle imagery generally seem to inform us that pastoralism, sometimes involving nomadism, was an important part of Indus life.[43] The Punjab, or Harappa Domain, would have been home to both pastoral nomads and farmers. The ethno-historical record informs us that life there prior to the excavation of canals during colonial times was a duality of pastoralism and agriculture. The pastoralists lived in the higher areas between the rivers, and the farmers settled in the river entrenchments,[44] as seen in this nineteenth-century account:

> Thus the district may be divided into two distinct portions—one the cultivated portion or *des,* and the other the grazing tract or *bar.* [*Des*] comprises . . . the land . . . on the banks of the rivers to the south. [*Bar*] contains that large, uncultivated tract which [is between the rivers]. . . . In the *des* we find agriculturists of settled habits, with rights and property in the soil, and deriving their chief support from their cultivation; whilst the people of the *bar* are graziers, leading a nomad life; possessing little or no landed property, and subsisting more on the profits derived from their cattle than their land.[45]

This account highlights a great pattern in the lives of the Indus peoples as well: the complementarity of settled agriculture and pastoralism. While there must have been a variety of occupations for the peoples of the Indus Civilization, most of them would have been farmers and/or pastoralists. They produced the food that sustained the nonagricultural people in the great cities and towns of this civilization.

A SELECTION OF THE PRINCIPAL SITES

Ninety-seven of the 1,052 known Mature Harappan sites have been examined by excavation. Most of the work has been done at the large places: Harappa, Mohenjo-daro, Dholavira. But at least one Indus city remains untouched: Ganweriwala in Cholistan. Mehrgarh, with its very long sequence of occupations, has been much deserving of the sustained work there. Table 3.3 gives a short account of those sites of the Indus Age with five or more seasons of excavation. Harappa is far and away the place that has been intensely excavated, largely due to the substantial work done there since 1986 by the joint American-Pakistani team. Moreover, excavation alone does not tell the entire story. Michael Jansen conducted intensive, rewarding research at Mohenjo-daro for eight years, but undertook no excavation.[46] It is also interesting to see that some of the best-known places of Indus life are missing from this list. Chanhu-daro, for example, famous as it is, has been subjected to only two seasons of excavation. Kulli and Mehi were barely scratched by Sir Aurel Stein when he was there in 1928. On the other hand, nine seasons of excavation have been devoted to the comparatively little known Sanghol.

Mohenjo-daro

For me, Mohenjo-daro is the epitome of all Mature Harappan settlements. It is about 100 hectares in size and I suspect that it was founded in the Early Harappan–Mature Harappan Transition by a group of Harappan "true believers." The activities occurring at Mohenjo-daro were the essence of Harappan life and ideology. While each Mature

Table 3.3 Sites of the Indus Age with five or more seasons of excavation

Site	Seasons of excavation
Harappa	36
Mehrgarh	17
Mohenjo-daro	15
Dholavira	12
Rojdi	11
Kalibangan	10
Sanghol	9
Lothal	8
Allahdino	6
Rangpur	6
Naushnaro	6
Amri	5
Banawali	5
Hulas	5
Prabhas Patan	5

Harappan settlement has its own character as a settlement or an urban center, Mohenjo-daro symbolically represents a good deal of what it meant to be Harappan.

There is an entire chapter on Mohenjo-daro in this book (see chapter 11). This testifies my sense of the city's importance in understanding the Harappan Civilization.

Harappa

Harappa is the old Mature Harappan city, with settlement reaching back into the Kechi Beg–Hakra Wares Phase (3800–3200 B.C.; see figure 1.6). The site is situated at a place where the entrenchment of the Ravi River broadens, not surprisingly, into an area where substantial agriculture is possible. Mohenjo-daro is 600 kilometers to the southwest. The apparent size of Harappa, taken from the mounded area and associated artifact scatter, is approximately 100 hectares.

Archaeological deposits dating to the Mature Harappan have been found under alluvium around the city, and no one is certain of the city's exact size—it may perhaps be as large as 200 hectares. With a population density of about 200 people per hectare, and 100 hectares settled at one time, total population would have been approximately 20,000.

There are five principal periods of occupation at Harappa, as shown in table 3.4. There is an imposing high area on the west at Harappa, surrounded by substantial brick walls. It is generally called Mound A-B. Wheeler labeled it a "citadel," just like the Mound of the Great Bath at Mohenjo-daro. The Mature Harappan citadel is another archaic thought about these cities; but not much is known of Mound A-B.

Mound F, to the north of A-B, has a series of interesting buildings. Construction here seems to have begun late in Period 3A or early 3B. The most imposing building on Mound F has sets of parallel walls laid precisely on either side of a central road or corridor and is thought of as a granary, although this has never been confirmed by charred grain, storage vessels, or other collateral evidence. The granary at Harappa seems to have been built late in Period 3B. There is a series of circular threshing platforms to the south of the building. Their function has been determined through careful excavation of the wooden mortars in their centers, which are associated with grain husks (figure 3.5).

Mounds E and ET, to the south, have what might be the remains of an outer city wall of substantial proportions. The configuration of this wall suggests that the valley between Mounds E and ET is an artifact of ancient city planning.

There are two cemeteries at Harappa designated R-37 and H. They are located in the same general part of the site. The one designated R-37 is the largest Mature Harappan cemetery known to us. The dead in this place were treated in a variety of ways. Some skeletons have been found in an extended, supine position inside wooden coffins, the way many contemporary Americans are buried. Cemetery H is a burial ground for Period 5 and contains pot burials and a variety of other interments in the earth (fractional, dismembered, and so forth).

Artifacts from Period 3 at Harappa include the usual square Indus stamp seals, black on red painted pottery, and carnelian beads, some of which were etched. There is considerable use of baked brick (not as much as at Mohenjo-daro). While the use of baked brick began in the Early Harappan–Mature Harappan Transition (possibly the Early Harappan), it can be thought of as a more or less distinctive feature of the Indus Civilization.

Harappa is an extraordinary place, and much more about the Indus Civilization can be learned from it. The continuing excavations there, by a team of excellent archaeologists, offer us new and important insights into the Harappans, their predecessors, and their successors.

Table 3.4 Phases of occupation at Harappa

Period 5	Cemetery H, Posturban Harappan	1800–1500 B.C.
Period 4	Transition from Mature Harappan to Posturban	1900–1800 B.C.
Period 3C	Final Mature Harappan	2200–1900 B.C.
Period 3B	Middle Mature Harappan	2450–2200 B.C.
Period 3A	Early Harappan–Mature Harappan Transition and Early Mature Harappan	2600–2450 B.C.
Period 2	Early Harappan (Kot Dijian Phase)	3200–2600 B.C.
Period 1	Ravi Aspect of the Hakra Wares Phase	3800–3200 B.C.

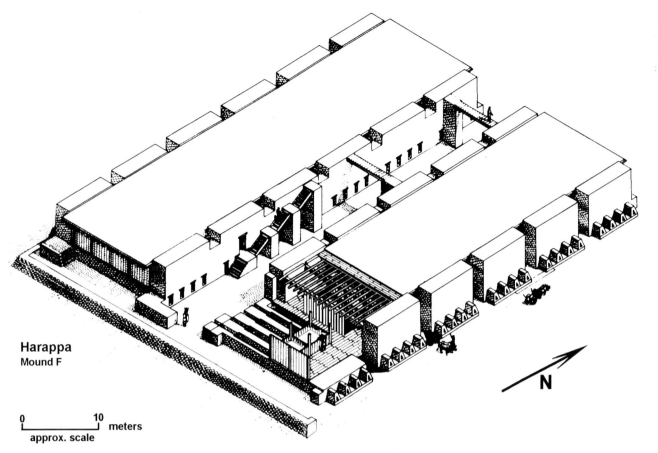

Harappa
Mound F

0   10   meters
approx. scale

N

Figure 3.5   Reconstruction of the "Granary" at Harappa (after Wheeler 1966)

Ganweriwala

A third, unexcavated Indus city, Ganweriwala, is located about 50 kilometers southwest of Fort Derawar in the Cholistan Desert. It was discovered by Mughal as a part of his great survey of the region. It is about 80 hectares in size and seems to have been founded on virgin soil, just as Mohenjo-daro probably was. We know that Ganweriwala is big, almost as big as Mohenjo-daro, and that it is almost exactly half way between Mohenjo-daro and Harappa. In terms of locational geography it is perfectly situated within the Mature Harappan settlement grid as an urban center. An excavation at this ancient metropolis can be anticipated as one of the truly rewarding experiences in Harappan archaeology.

Dholavira

The ASI has been excavating this important site of the Indus age since 1989.[47] Dholavira is large, spreading to 60 hectares. It was discovered by J. P. Joshi in 1967–1968 on Kadir Island in the central part of the Great Rann of Kutch (figure 3.6).

Continuous, large-scale excavation has revealed that Dholavira has a long sequence of habitation that seems to begin in the Early Harappan–Mature Harappan Transition

(c. 2600–2500 B.C.) and extends to the early centuries of the second millennium B.C. R. S. Bisht, the director of the Dholavira excavations, has defined seven periods of occupation, or stages, at the site. The first two fall within the Early Harappan–Mature Harappan Transition. Stages III, IV, and V are Mature Harappan, and the final two stages are Posturban Harappan.

The radiocarbon method does not seem to work well at Dholavira, so the chronology for the site is an estimate put together using a comparative method. An estimate for the dates for the seven stages is given in table 3.5. A variance of 100 to 150 years is possible for most stages.

Table 3.5   A chronology for Dholavira

Stage	Date
Stage VII Posturban Harappan B	1650–1450 B.C.
Period of desertion, apparently longer than the one between Stages V and VI	
Stage VI Posturban Harappan A	1850–1750 B.C.
Short period of desertion	
Stage V Mature Harappan C	2000–1900 B.C.
Stage IV Mature Harappan B	2200–2000 B.C.
Stage III Mature Harappan A	2500–2200 B.C.
Stage II Early Harappan–Mature Harappan Transition B	2550–2500 B.C.
Stage I Early Harappan–Mature Harappan Transition A	2650–2550 B.C.

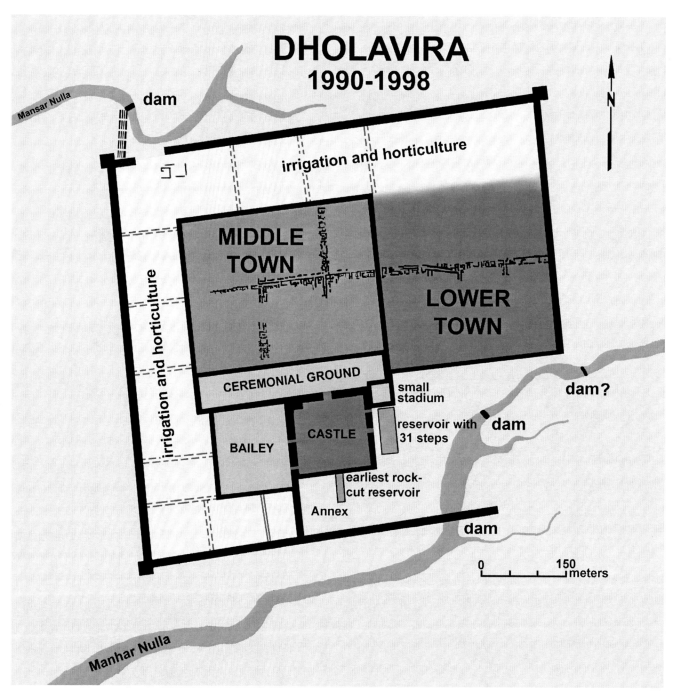

Figure 3.6 Plan of Dholavira (after *Indian Archaeology, A Review* 1991–92)

Stage I was founded on virgin soil. These pioneers knew the arts of copper working, bead making, and masonry and were careful planners of their architecture. The settlement of Stage I was located in the vicinity of the Citadel and was surrounded by a very substantial fortification, as thick as 11 meters at its base. The houses were built of molded mud bricks, with the Indus proportion of 4:2:1. The ceramics are a mix, but there are parallels to Amri Period II, Nausharo

ID, and Kot Diji during the Early Harappan–Mature Harappan Transition.

Stage II sees the widening and strengthening of the fortification wall and the enlargement of the settlement with construction to the north. The early fortification wall was found to be plastered on both sides, and parts of it were covered with a veneer of stone. At this time the inhabitants of Dholavira exhibited an affinity for bright plasters, white and reddish pink, that is still preserved in the fortification wall of Stage II. The use of this bright plaster continues through Stage III, then it is discontinued. The material culture of Stages I and II is similar, but there was an increase in the number of antiquities that were recovered in excavation. A boat-shaped crucible documents metalworking at the site.

During Stage III, Dholavira grew from a small settlement to a large town or city with two sets of fortifications, separate districts, and a water storage system of significant scale. This period marks the raising of the Citadel and Bailey, as seen in figure 3.6. Painted Indus black-on-redware pottery and small finds, including square Indus stamp seals, allow us to date this stage to the early Mature Harappan. Some of the stamp seals from Stage III at Dholavira do not bear Indus writing, but animal devices are present. They could represent the early conventions of Indus seal making.

Stage III saw the clearing, leveling, and paving of an old Stage II residential area. This created an expanse of open ground that Bisht believes was a ceremonial ground. To the north, a large residential area called the Middle Town was laid out, secured by the second fortification wall. This latter facility was provided with gates, bastions, and drains. The Middle Town was divided into residential areas, with streets and lanes laid out in a grid-iron pattern. These rectilinear houses are within the Mature Harappan mold and are equipped with sumps and jars in the streets, apparently for sanitary purposes. There are no street drains here or in the Lower Town, and no evidence of bathing facilities was found; all characteristics somewhat different from Mohenjo-daro.

During Stage III, the inhabitants of Dholavira invested heavily in several types of hydraulic facilities. Kutch is virtually a desert, and there is no large river like the Indus nearby, so they collected and stored water in the forms of both rain and runoff. At Dholavira, unlike Mohenjo-daro, the functional need for the inhabitants of the city to provide for themselves a guaranteed year-round supply of water was great. There is an abundance of *wasserluxus* at Dholavira, but it is intertwined with the kind of water symbolism we see at Mohenjo-daro and the functional need for water to be available to sustain life.

As one part of the water-harvesting system, the Castle was built with a network of connected drains and catchment surfaces. These collected rainwater and moved it to two interconnected chambers of stone. One part of this system is a remarkable water cascade, quite carefully fashioned of cut stone.

The seasonal stream that runs to the north and south of the site was dammed in several places. These bunds al-

lowed the inhabitants of Dholavira to direct and conserve runoff from the interior of Kadir Island.

The Dholavirites created sixteen or more reservoirs of varying size during Stage III. Some of these took advantage of the slope of the ground within the large settlement, a drop of 13 meters from northeast to southwest. Other reservoirs were excavated, some into living rock. Recent work has revealed and mostly emptied two large reservoirs, one to the east of the Castle, one to its south, near the Annex. The eastern reservoir has thirty-one steps from top to bottom and is a marvel of technology and effort. We know that this reservoir was 24 meters wide and varied between 7.5 and 5 meters in depth. The reservoir near the Annex, to the south of the Castle, has an exposed length of 95 meters and a width of approximately 10 meters. The depth varies from about 2 to 4 meters.

Dholavira in Stage III seems to have been a busy, prosperous city, with its citizens engaged in making substantial investments in their settlement. There is an abundance of small finds, metal, and other artifacts that sustain this observation, along with the architecture. They have different kinds of public space: the Bailey, Castle, ceremonial ground, and a small stadium. The investment in public facilities, meant for the general civic good, is also seen in the construction of the reservoirs and water-harvesting facilities.

Toward the end of Stage III Dholavira seems to have been struck by an earthquake of major magnitude. This is documented by slip faults in sections and the displacement of architectural features. This led to repairs within Stage III that are very large in scale. Parts of the Citadel and the residential areas were cleared of houses. Other residential areas were extended, especially to the east, necessitating the extension of the city wall. Monumental gateways were built on the Citadel (figure 3.7), and the settlement reached its largest, best-organized, perfected point.

Stage IV can be thought of as the middle Mature Harappan. The city was carefully maintained, including the monumental gateways, fortification walls, and the drainage system. Of special note in Stage IV is the now famous mosaic inscription of ten large signs of the Harappan script found facedown in a chamber of North Gate (figure 3.8).

All the classic Mature Harappan objects including pottery, seals with writing, tools, beads, weights, and other items of gold, copper, stone, shell, and clay are found in abundance in Stage IV. Perhaps the most impressive architectural elements are pillars and freestanding columns made of locally available limestone. At least some of the so-called Harappan ring stones were used in these constructions.

Stage V sees the beginnings of a general decline of the city. The urban core, the Citadel and Bailey, were not

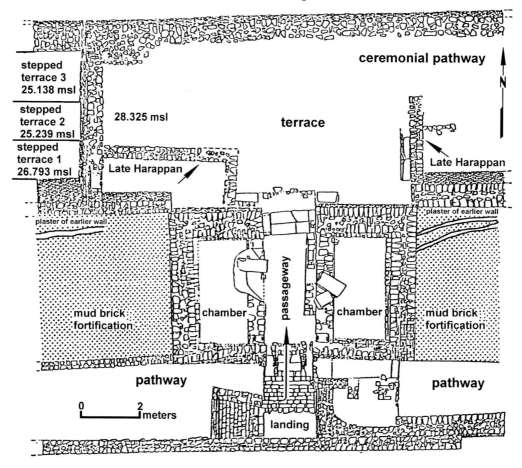

ceremonial ground

ceremonial pathway

stepped
terrace 3
25.138 msl

28.325 msl

terrace

stepped
terrace 2
25.239 msl

Late Harappan

stepped
terrace 1
26.793 msl

Late Harappan

plaster of earlier wall

plaster of earlier wall

passageway

mud brick
fortification

chamber

chamber

mud brick
fortification

pathway

pathway

0   2
└─────┘ meters

landing

N

Figure 3.7   Plan of the North Gate at Dholavira (after *Indian Archaeology, A Review* 1991–92)

maintained. In contrast to this, the material culture of Dholavira, ceramics and seals, for example, continue in their classic Mature Harappan forms and styles. We can think of this stage as a late Mature Harappan something like the Late I Period at Mohenjo-daro, the time after which the Great Bath had been abandoned.

Following Stage V there was a temporary desertion of the site apparently for a few decades. The following Stage VI presents the Harappan cultural tradition in a form that is widely seen in Saurashtra to the south. The once grand city shrank to a small settlement centered on the Bailey and Castle and the southern portion of the Middle Town, where a wall of inferior construction (if measured against earlier work at Dholavira) was built. The houses show no continuity with earlier buildings and are laid out on a different plan. This represents the transforma-

Figure 3.8   Sign board inscription from Dholavira (courtesy of R. S. Bisht)

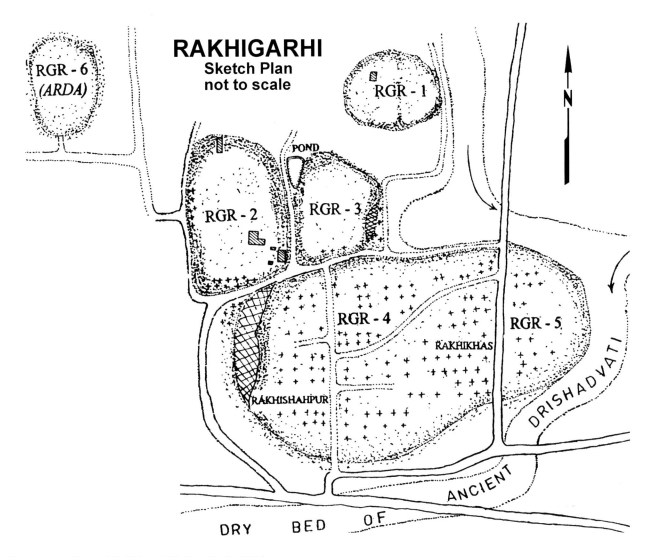

RAKHIGARHI
Sketch Plan
not to scale

RGR - 6
(ARDA)

RGR - 1

POND

RGR - 2

RGR - 3

RGR - 4

RAKHIKHAS

RGR - 5

RAKHISHAHPUR

DRISHADVATI

DRY   BED   OF   ANCIENT

N

Figure 3.9   Plan of Rakhigarhi (after Nath 1998)

tion and devolution of the Indus Civilization, with strong ties to the Late Sorath Harappan and little contact with Sindh. The distinctive Banas white painted black and red ware from southern Rajasthan occurs in some quantity. The once grand city of Dholavira was transformed into a place of minimal diversity without the trappings of urbanization. Stage VI comes to an end after about a century, with the second abandonment of the settlement.

The duration of the second abandonment is not known. The new settlers were much like their Stage VI predecessors, with clear ties to the Late Sorath Harappans. They built circular houses and engaged in limited craft activities. These interlopers left little impression on the site.

Dholavira is a splendid ancient city, filled with architectural achievements that were certainly not anticipated. The magnificent attention to water, its movement, and

storage are very much within the Indus ideology, but quite different from what we see at Mohenjo-daro or Harappa. I think of it as the central link in the Sindhi Harappan connection to Gujarat and the sea. It was a regional center of authority, a hub of communications, an ancient *caravansarai* for traders and travelers. There is another Indus city to the north at Rakhigarhi.

Rakhigarhi

Rakhigarhi (also known as Rakhishahpur) is a huge mound in Hisar District of Haryana, associated with the right, or northern, bank of the Drishadvati River. The site is large enough to have two named villages on it: Rakhishahpur and Rakhikhas. Suraj Bhan discovered Rakhigarhi in 1964.[48] There is both a Sothi-Siswal and a Mature Harappan occupation at the site (figure 3.9).[49]

The site is about 17 meters in height. The southern face

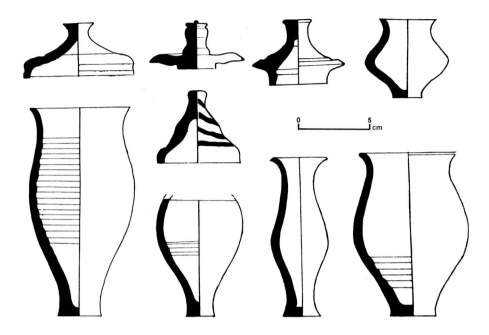

Figure 3.10   Indus Civilization ceramics from Rakhigarhi (after Nath 1998)

of the mounds is rather abrupt and steep. The northern side slopes down to the surrounding plain. The contours of the site have led the excavator to divide up the place into five mounds (RGR-1 through 5). RGR-6, a Sothi-Siswal site known as Arda, was probably a separate settlement. I have visited Rakhigarhi and believe that it is 80 hectares in size.

Occupation at Rakhigarhi begins during the Early Harappan, Sothi-Siswal Period, although some Hakra Wares are present.[50] The exposure of this period is still small, but it is 3 meters deep. Rectilinear houses, oriented to the cardinal directions, were found. Baked brick was extensively used in this period, very unusual for the Early Harappan; however, the length, width, thickness ratio is 1:2:3, not the Indus 1:2:4. The bricks had graffiti marks on them, some signs of which are said to be close to those in the Indus script. A baked-brick street drain was found, to which a house drain was connected. The street drain is in the vicinity of a floor made of brickbats with four circular pits, perhaps dyeing vats.

The Indus occupation saw the construction of a substantial mud-brick wall, possibly a fortification, exposed in the southeastern corner of RGR-2, the "acropolis" of the site. There is a public drain of baked brick. There are also household drains, some of which discharged into the street, others into soak jars pretty much along the pattern as at Mohenjo-daro.[51] "Fire altars" with similarities to those reported from Kalibangan are also reported.

The finds include standard Indus ceramics (figure 3.10).

Several "unicorn" seals have been found, along with a terracotta amulet with an elephant on the front. Of particular interest is a faience cylinder seal, with the long-snouted Indus crocodile, the gavial, along with Indus script.[52] Assorted objects of metal, including copper–bronze, gold, and silver have been recovered as well.

There is a Mature Harappan cemetery at Rakhigarhi. The new excavations uncovered eight interments. The grave pits were often brick-lined, with one wooden coffin, as in Cemetery R-37 at Harappa. We have so few human remains from Mature Harappan sites, and they can tell us so much about the people and their way of life; therefore, this cemetery is of exceptional importance.

There is much to be learned from long-term excavation at Rakhigarhi. The Early Harappan settlement with baked bricks, Mature Harappan–style drains, and graffiti signs that may be harbingers of the later Indus writing system would seem to be especially significant in our understanding of the genesis of the Indus Civilization.

Kot Diji

"Fort of the Daughter," or Kot Diji, is located high on the southern end of the Rohri Hills (figure 3.11). It is an imposing fortress of the Talpur Dynasty. On the plain below is the prehistoric mound of the same name. The location is a strategic one, given the junction of the Indus with the massif of the Rohri Hills. The Pakistan Department of Archaeology excavated at Kot Diji in 1955 and 1957.[53]

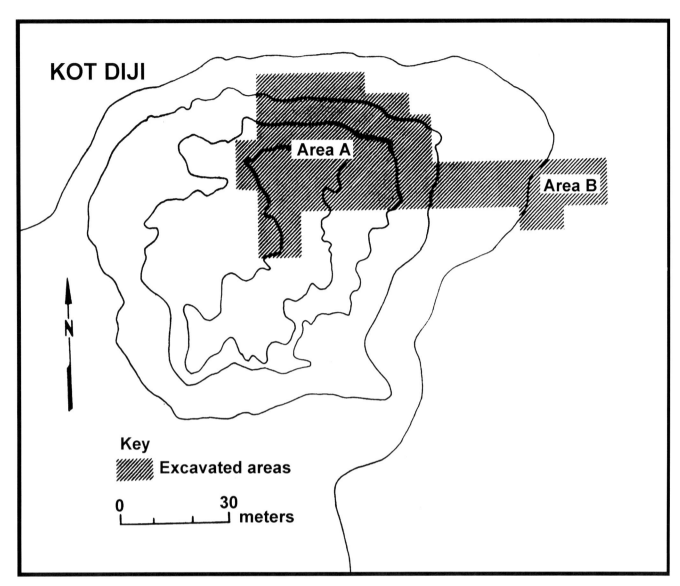

KOT DIJI

Area A

Area B

Key

Excavated areas

0   30 meters

Figure 3.11   Plan of Kot Diji (after Khan 1964)

The site has two parts: Area A, on the mound itself, some 12 meters high; and Area B, the Lower Town. Both places have a stratigraphic succession from Early Harappan to Mature Harappan. The Early Harappan is the distinctive Kot Dijian type, defined through these excavations.[54] There may be a fortification associated with this period. The end of the Kot Dijian occupation is coincident with signs of massive burning. It is followed by the Indus occupation. There may be a Transitional Stage occupation between them. A well-known pot, with a buffalo motif that seems to figure in the Indus Mahayogi seal (see chapter 8 on religion), is probably attributable to the Early Harappan–Mature Harappan Transition at Kot Diji (figure 3.12).

The Indus occupation held evidence for copper–bronze objects (including a fine example of an Harappan flat axe),

bangles, arrowheads, and two chisels. An etched carnelian bead also surfaced. Terra-cotta antiquities were numerous: bangles, cart frames and wheels, model plows, styli, beads of several types, large and small balls, cones, and triangular cakes. Faience disk beads also occurred. The figurines include bulls, humped and unhumped, and birds, painted and plain. Terra-cotta human figurines, which seem to conform to examples from Mohenjo-daro and Chanhu-daro, are also present.[55] The absence of lapis lazuli, turquoise, and other luxury raw materials is noteworthy. There is no report on either plant or animal remains.

Kot Diji is an extraordinary site. It occupies a strategic position on the Indus plains, on the more lightly settled eastern side of the valley. It superbly documents the Kot Dijian Phase in upper Sindh, and it played an important

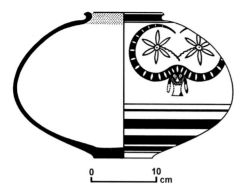

Figure 3.12 Pot with the buffalo motif from Kot Diji (after Khan 1964)

role in the definition of the Early Harappan.[56] Further work at the site would offer an opportunity to gain some information on the subsistence regime.

Chanhu-daro

Chanhu-daro is one of the best-known settlements of the Indus Civilization. Today it is a group of three low mounds that excavation has shown were parts of a single settlement estimated to have been approximately 5 hectares in size (about the same size as Lothal; see figure 3.13).

Chanhu-daro was excavated by Majumdar in March 1930[57] and again during the winter field season of 1935–1936 by Mackay.[58] The latter's excavations show that the occupation of Chanhu-daro was divided into four periods, with four occupational sublevels within the Mature Harappan (table 3.6).

Table 3.6   Periods of occupation at Chanhu-daro

Period IV	Jhangar (Late Bronze Age?)
Period III	Trihni
Period II	Jhukar (Posturban Harappan)
Period I A–D	Mature Harappan

The Indus occupation had buildings of baked brick, paved bathrooms, and a civic drainage system that "was as well thought out and doubtless quite as effective as that of the larger city (Mohenjo-daro)."[59] Some buildings were grouped along a wide street that ran northwest to southeast but was cut by at least one thoroughfare coming in at a right angle. This attention to town planning was not seen in the uppermost Indus levels.

A bead factory and furnace are the most interesting features of this occupation.[60] The center piece of the installation was a furnace that was used in several ways, including the glazing of steatite, providing heat to bring out the red color of carnelian, and preparing stone for better chipping, also a part of the bead-making process (figure 3.14).

There are two copper–bronze toy vehicles from Chanhu-

daro.[61] The human figurines are very much like those at Mohenjo-daro; however, the very elaborate females are not present. One interesting male figurine has a very close parallel from Nippur.[62] Chanhu-daro seems to have a larger number of bird figurines than other Mature Harappan sites. Perhaps the most interesting figurines are the bulls with single horns, true unicorns.[63]

Little is known of the upper periods at Chanhu-daro, and the exact relationship between the important Jhukar levels and the Mature Harappan has not yet been settled. Of Trihni and Jhangar almost nothing is known, and further exploration of these periods is a pressing problem in the regional archaeology of Sindh.

During Mature Harappan times, Chanhu-daro seems to have been a regional craft center for the Sindhi Harappans. This is seen in the bead- and seal-making area and was also confirmed by intensive surface exploration that found concentrations of pottery wasters, debris from the making of chalcedony/carnelian beads, faience work, and shell working.[64] These are much the same kinds of materials and craft activities that are found at Lothal 250 kilometers to the southeast, and one would suspect that there was an intimate connection between these two sites during the period of the Indus Civilization.

Kalibangan

Kalibangan, also known as Kala Vangu and Pilibangan, is another of the well-known Indus settlements. It is a two-period site, with a Sothi-Siswal and Mature Harappan occupation. The site is situated on the southern escarpment of the Sarasvati, near its confluence with the Drishadvati. The ASI undertook excavation there for nine seasons beginning in 1960–1961 and ending in 1968–1969 (figure 3.15).[65]

The Sothi-Siswal settlement is surrounded by a wall approximately 250 by 170 meters in extent. The first phase of the wall was made of mud bricks laid to a thickness of approximately 1.90 meters. A second phase of construction brought the thickness of this wall up to 3 or 4 meters, varying from place to place. The inner and outer faces of the "fortifications" were plastered with mud. Only one entrance, at the northwest corner, was excavated; other entrances were probably obscured by later Harappans.

Direct evidence for cultivation was found in the form of a preserved plowed field, about 100 meters to the south of the Period I settlement. It was covered by slump from the Sothi-Siswal occupation and consisted of alternating furrows and hummocks in the earth. These were oriented to the cardinal directions and have a close ethnographic parallel in modern Rajasthani agricultural practice.[66]

When the Indus peoples reoccupied Kalibangan, their

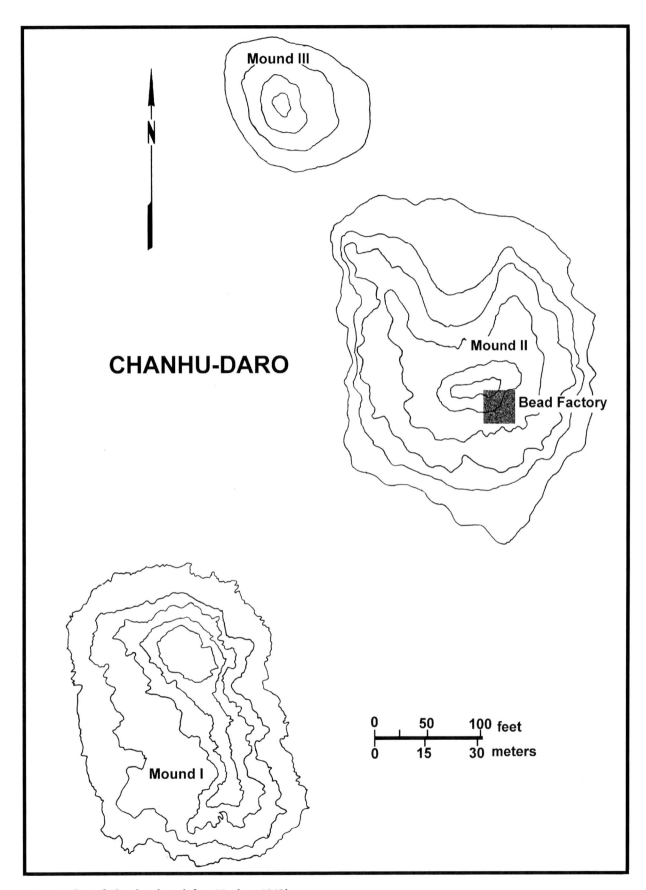

Figure 3.13   Plan of Chanhu-daro (after Mackay 1942)

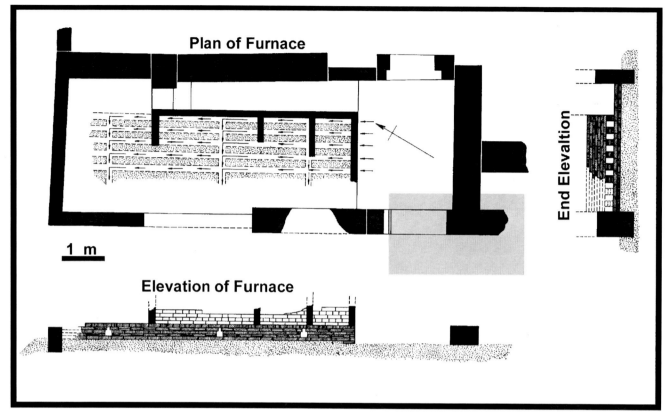

Figure 3.14 The furnace in the bead factory at Chanhu-daro (after Mackay 1942)

ceramics included many of the shapes and fabrics of the Period I occupation. This lasted for about one-half of Period II, when it gave way to a more purely Indus ceramic corpus.[67] Other sites in the northeastern region of the Indus Civilization share this mixture of ceramics as seen at Kalibangan. The Mature Harappan plan of Kalibangan is significantly different from the original. There are two parts: the High Mound (KLB-1) to the west, covering most of the abandoned Early Harappan settlement; and to the east is the Lower Town (KLB-2), most of which is on virgin soil. The old entrance in the northwestern corner of the High Mound was once again used.

During Period II, the High Mound was well fortified, although the southern half was stronger than the north. The southern half of the High Mound was equipped during Indus times with a series of mud-brick platforms on which "ritual structures," connected with the use of fire and possibly animal remains, were located. These have been called "fire altars." They are oval in plan, sunk in the ground, and lined with mud plaster or bricks.

Most of the people lived in the Lower Town of Kalibangan. It was surrounded by a fortification wall ranging in thickness from 3.5 to 9 meters. The wall had three or four phases of construction, and it, like the High Mound, was

plastered with mud and tapered from bottom to top. The fortifications protected the town, which was laid out in a gridiron plan, separating blocks of habitations. There were four streets running the full north-south distance of the settlement and three (possibly four) oriented east-west. It is interesting that the north-south streets do not run parallel to the fortifications, and two of them converge on the principal entrance to the Lower Town in the northwest corner of the settlement. The brickwork tells us that buildings at some intersections seem to have been equipped with wooden fenders to limit damage to, and done by, vehicular traffic. There is some indication of habitation extending outside the fortifications in the protected area to the south of the High Mound and to the west of the Lower Town.

A significant number of Indus stamp seals and sealings were found at Kalibangan, including examples of both unicorn and zebu motifs. A cylinder seal is of particular note (figure 3.16).

There is a small mound about 75 meters to the east of the Lower Town at Kalibangan. This has been designated KLB-3 and is called a "ritual structure." Excavation exposed a mud-brick structure enclosing fire altars much like the ones on the High Mound at the site.

A cemetery is located about 300 meters west-southwest

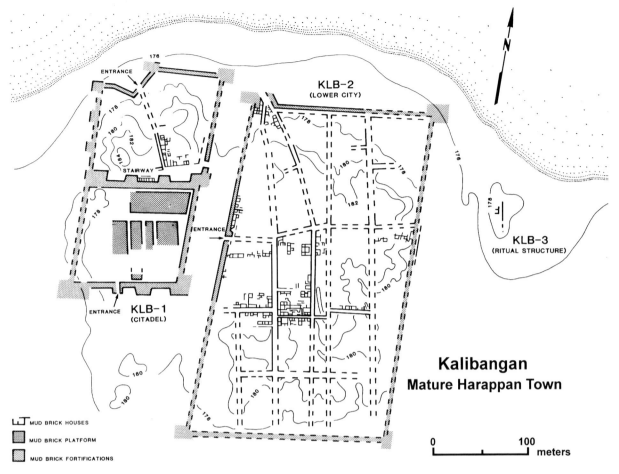

Figure 3.15 Plan of Kalibangan (after Thapar 1975)

of the habitation area.[68] This is both downwind and down-river from the settlement itself. There are three types of burials at Kalibangan, and they can all be assigned to the Mature Harappan:

1. Typical Harappan extended inhumation in a rectangular or oval pit
2. Pot burials in circular pits, but without skeletons
3. Cenotaphs in the form of pottery grave goods in pits but without skeletal material

Kalibangan is one of the few Mature Harappan sites with a true double-mound layout, as at Mohenjo-daro. It is strategically located at the confluence of the Sarasvati and Drishadvati Rivers and must have played a major role as a way station and monitor of the overland communications of the Harappan peoples.

Kulli

Kulli is a mound of about 11 hectares at the eastern end of the Kolwa Valley in southern Baluchistan. The mound rises

9 meters above the valley floor. Sir Aurel Stein conducted a small excavation at Kulli during his 1927–1928 exploration of Gedrosia.[69] There are no radiocarbon dates for this site, but dates from other sites with Kulli remains (Nindowari and Niai Buthi) indicate that it was contemporary with the Indus Civilization. This dating is sustained by similarities in Kulli material to that of the Mature Harappan (figure 3.17).

Figure 3.16 Impression of the Kalibangan cylinder seal (after Thapar 1975)

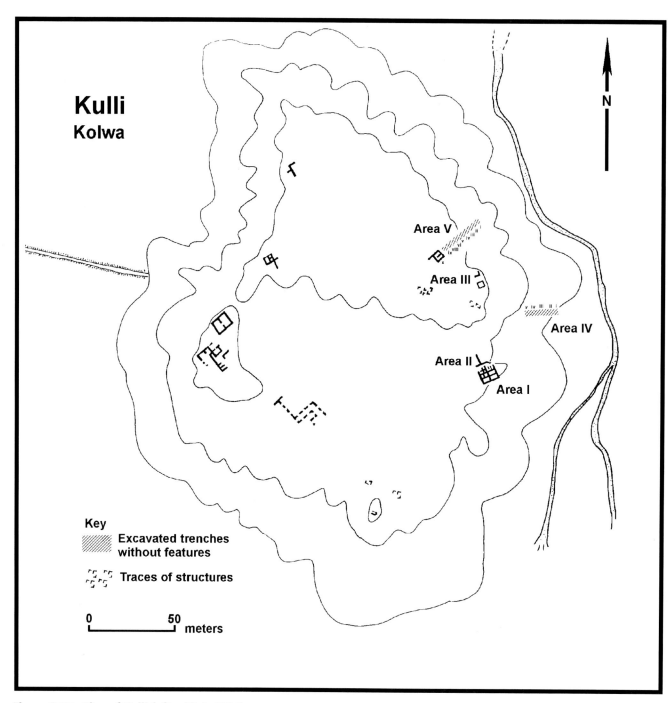

Figure 3.17   Plan of Kulli (after Stein 1931)

Kulli and the Indus Civilization

Kulli pottery includes many vessel forms identical to those of the Indus Civilization: dishes on stands, "graters," some jars, and large storage vessels. There is also a great deal of purely Mature Harappan plain red ware on Kulli sites. However, the Kulli painting style, especially with the wide-eyed animals and fish motifs, is distinctive (figure 3.18).

This figure contains some Mature Harappan–like pots from Kulli's sister site, Mehi.

Nindowari is also a very large site with monumental architecture and Harappan unicorn seals.[70] The geographic juxtaposition of the Kulli and Sindhi Domains, with ecological complementarity and these cultural dimensions, leads to the conclusion that the Kulli complex

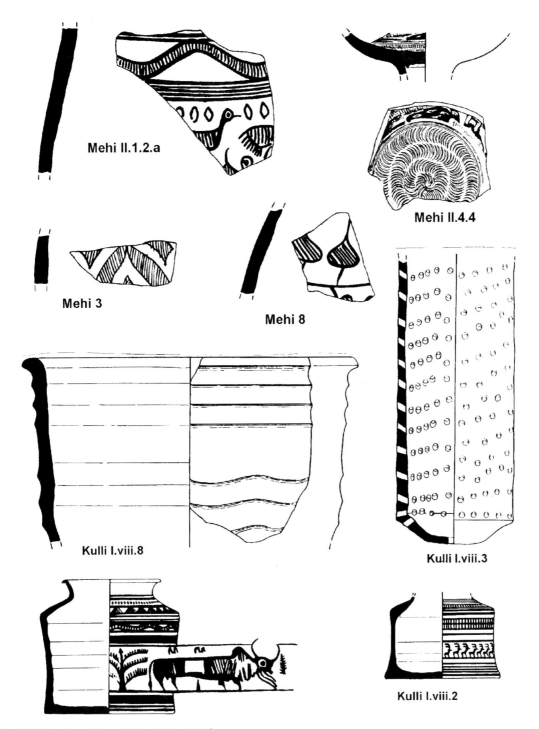

Figure 3.18   Kulli-style pottery (after Stein 1931)

Mehi II.1.2.a

Mehi II.4.4

Mehi 3

Mehi 8

Kulli I.viii.8

Kulli I.viii.3

Kulli I.viii.2

represents the highland expression of the Harappan Civilization.[71]

Sutkagen-dor

The westernmost Indus site is Sutkagen-dor, located in the Dasht Valley of the Makran (figure 3.19). It is near the western bank of the Dasht and its confluence with a smaller stream, known as the Gajo Kaur. This is 42 kilometers from the sea along the Dasht River route. Sutkagen-dor was discovered in 1875 by Major E. Mockler, who conducted a small excavation there. As a part of his Gedrosia tour, Stein came in 1928 and conducted a small excavation.[72] Dales was at Sutkagen-dor from October 7 through 20, 1960, as a part of his Makran survey.[73]

Figure 3.19   Reconstruction of Sutkagen-dor (after Dales and Lippo 1992)

Sutkagen-dor measures approximately 300 by 150 meters, or 4.5 hectares. Stein found structures outside the northern wall of the enclosure, and there are other remains on the eastern side of the site, possibly only to the north. He found "cinerary deposits . . . one above the other. . . . The uppermost deposit proved to consist of two pots, one stuck in the other."[74]

Dales unearthed a structure built against the western fortification wall. This was made of both stone and mud bricks, some of the latter being rather large (50 centimeters long) and made without straw. A trench across the eastern fortification wall demonstrated that the inner face of the wall was vertical. It is estimated that the outer wall at this point would have been about 7.5 meters thick at the base.[75]

Stein noted the high number of flint blades, 127 of them, up to 27.5 centimeters long, but no cores.[76] Stone vessels—one fine example in alabaster—were found. Arrowheads in both chipped stone and copper–bronze were also found. The copper–bronze examples have good parallels at Mohenjo-daro.[77] Stein also noted the abundance of worked-shell and a fine onyx bead. The Dales excavations recovered a complete copper–bronze disk of the type found at Mehi and probably associated with the Bactria-Margiana Archaeological Complex (BMAC).

The pottery is typical Indus red ware in the usual shapes, including the dish-on-stand and black-on-red painted ware. Dales and Lipo note the absence of square stamp seals of Mature Harappan type along with figurines, beads, faience, and clay balls.[78]

Sutkagen-dor is a more or less pure Sindhi Harappan site in the Kulli Domain. There is no Kulli pottery mentioned in the reports on the site. It was not a port, since it

is so far from the sea. Still, the place may have played a role in commerce between the Indus Civilization and the west, but further work at the site is needed to demonstrate this.

Lothal

The ancient site of Lothal was a town of the Indus Civilization. The name could be interpreted to mean "Mound of the Dead Men," the same as Mohenjo-daro. Lothal was discovered by S. R. Rao of the ASI in 1954. He excavated there from 1954–1955 to 1959–1960 and in 1961–1962, 1962–1963.[79] Lothal is located near the head of the Gulf of Cambay in Gujarat, in the southeastern part of the Indus Civilization that would have been a frontier with peninsular India. Lothal is the southernmost of the Sindhi Harappan settlements (figure 3.20).

Lothal A, the first occupation, dates the Mature Harappan. The second occupation, designated Lothal B, is Post-urban, circa 1900–1750 B.C. During the Mature Harappan, the settlement was about 4.2 hectares in size, not counting the area of the baked-brick-lined enclosure. The site was much smaller in Lothal B times.

Rao has claimed that Lothal was a port town of the Indus Civilization, a seat of maritime commerce linking ancient India with Mesopotamia. Some scholars propose that the large, brick-lined enclosure on the eastern side of the settlement was a dockyard or harbor for ships involved in commerce, but this has been disputed by others, including Thor Heyerdahl.[80] Most archaeologists feel that this enclosure was an ordinary tank for the storage of water.

The settlement was divided into three districts: an acropolis, a lower town, and the brick-lined enclosure. On the summit of the elevated mound is a building identified as a warehouse, as well as a long building with bathing fa-

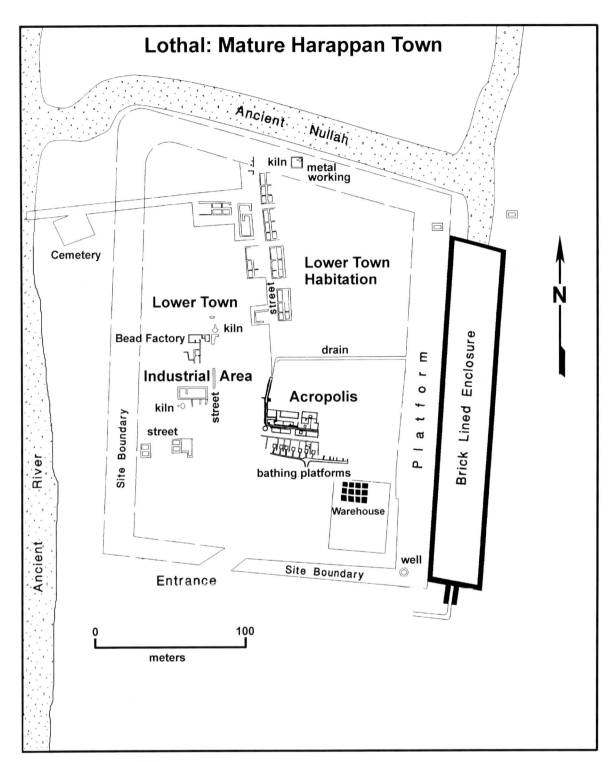

Figure 3.20 Plan of Lothal (after Rao 1973)

cilities and other structures of baked brick, a striking feature of Indus architecture. The elevated portion of the site was also provided with a baked–brick-lined well, a drain, and soak jars to take water from a building, the use of which has not been determined. These are all good Sindhi Harappan traits. To the north of this elevated platform were the domestic quarters of the town, with private houses. No formal market facilities have been documented. The western lower town was a manufacturing area, only a small part of which was excavated.

Lothal was a center of craftsmanship. The excavations uncovered finished products and waste materials from a wide range of natural resources: copper, bronze, gold, carnelian, jasper, rock crystal and other semiprecious stones, ivory, and shell. Many of these materials were associated with a bead-making shop similar to the installation at Chanhu-daro. The bead-making technology at Lothal, as documented by waste materials (beads broken in the process of manufacture and drills), is the same as that used at Mohenjo-daro, Mehrgarh, and Shahr-i Sokhta in Seistan.

Typical Indus seals and sealings were found at Lothal, most of which were the classic types. A number of more provincial glyptic objects were present as well. Perhaps the most important of these was a Dilmun-type seal, which was a surface find.[81]

The terra-cotta figurines of both humans and animals are simple, even crude, unlike those from Mohenjo-daro or Harappa. Fine examples were found of miniature animals (bull, hare, dog, and a bird-headed pin) probably cast by the lost wax process. The remainder of the material inventory includes typical Indus weights, triangular terra-cotta cakes, model terra-cotta carts, and baked bricks. Bun-shaped copper ingots have parallels in western Asia, but the metal implements are purely Indus in character.

A small cemetery to the northwest of the site contained a number of interments, twenty of which were opened.[82] This important feature of Lothal is discussed later in this book along with the other human remains of the Indus Civilization.

Rojdi

Rojdi is another of the well-known settlements of the Indus Civilization. It is strategically situated in the geographical center of Saurashtra, on a bank of the Bhadar River. It is a regional center of the Indus Civilization, one of the Sorath Harappan places. The location must have been significant in ancient times, since the site is approximately equidistant from all the borders of Saurashtra. This sense of centrality is also reflected in its size: approximately 7.5 hectares. While this hardly compares to Mohenjo-daro or Dholavira, it is large for an Harappan site in Saurashtra. Rojdi was a stable settlement in the sense that it was continuously occupied from about 2500 b.c. to 1700 b.c.[83]

The site is a low, oval mound about 500 meters long and 150 meters wide, sitting above the river (figure 3.21). Careful examination of the river edge of the site and a study of the outer wall, or circumvallation, has shown that the ancient settlement was essentially the same size as the modern archaeological site. There has been little erosion by the river, and the circumvallation is a feature

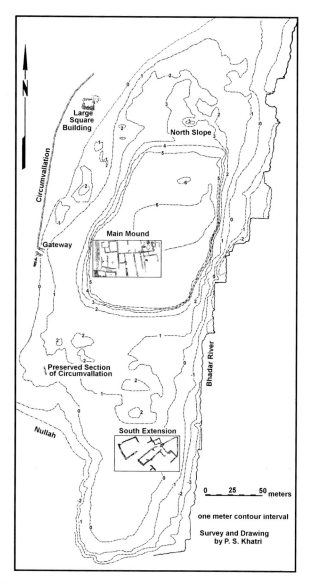

Figure 3.21   Plan of Rojdi (after Possehl and Raval 1989)

that accurately delimited the boundaries of the living settlement.

Builders in Stone

Two large excavation areas have been exposed at Rojdi: the South Extension and the Main Mound (figures 3.22 and 3.23). There was also a systematic excavation at an outer gateway (figure 3.24) and at an isolated structure on the northern slope of the site (figure 3.25). All of this very finely preserved architecture can be dated to Rojdi C, early in the second millennium b.c.

The people of Rojdi built their homes and associated buildings on stone foundations, probably with mud walls above them. No bricks were found, baked or otherwise, in

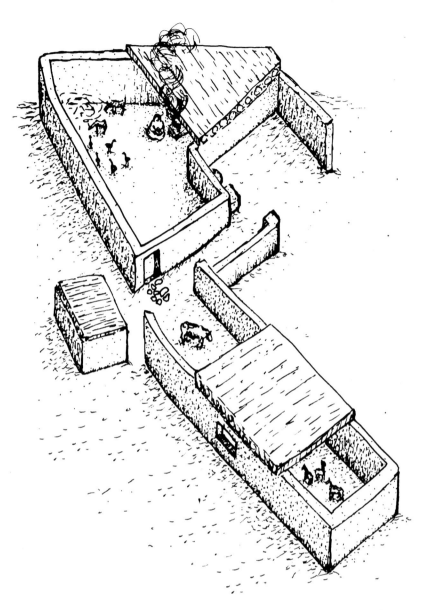

Figure 3.22 Reconstruction of a building complex on the South Extension at Rojdi (after Possehl and Raval 1989)

the excavations. No wells, bathing platforms, and the associated street drains, as found at such places as Lothal, Mohenjo-daro, and Harappa, were found either.

Rojdi Was Home to Farmers and Herders

The Rojdi excavation was geared to find out as much about the people of Rojdi as possible, so they took their subsistence system as another focus of investigation: the plants and animals that were used, the farming calendar, the place of pastoralism in the lives of these people. This part of the excavation strategy was generously rewarded with a huge collection of bones and paleobotanical remains.

The domesticated animals present were to be expected: cattle, water buffalo, sheep, goats, chickens. The ancient Rojdi folk were also hunters, and the wild ungulates of Saurashtra were part of their diet, including nilgai, sambar, chital, and black buck. There are also the remains of at least one elephant, a house cat, and the cuon, or dhole, a doglike animal. The animal that dominates the Rojdi faunal assemblage, and that of all other Sorath Harappan sites in this region, is the cow, the Indian zebu. Cattle were the most important animals to these people, and the people must have had large herds.

Paleobotanical research played an important role in the excavations at Rojdi. A systematic sampling and

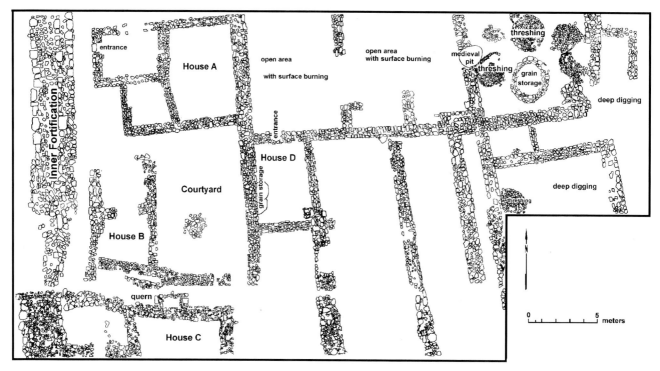

Figure 3.23 Architecture on the Main Mound at Rojdi

intensive recovery program was developed with the collection of soil from each stratum. This work yielded about 10,000 seeds from over seventy different plants. The ancient inhabitants of Rojdi did not rely on barley and wheat, as their cousins in Sindh and the Punjab did, but they had a diversified farming and collecting economy based on hearty species of plants that were drought resistant and needed little cultivation and care. For example, the ancient people of Rojdi used millets, such as *ragi* and *jowar*, still important in Saurashtra today. The millets were probably cultivated, but the use of wild plants was also significant. Because we know the life cycle of these plants, we were able to determine that Rojdi was occupied year-round.

The Material Culture
Much of the pottery from Rojdi is a hard, red to buff ware made from well-prepared clay. There are classic Indus forms, especially the dish, both as a plate and as the dish-on-stand. Many of the jar forms, especially the smaller ones, are alike, but the large storage jars are different, with various rims and none of the pointed bases found in Sindhi sites. Several of the diagnostic pottery types of Sindhi Harappans are not found in Saurashtra: The ubiquitous pointed-base goblet is missing, but so are the beaker, teacup, knobbed ware, feeding cup, and the elegantly tall, slender S-form jar with flanged rim. On the

other hand, the Harappans of Saurashtra had many pottery forms and types not found in other domains of the Mature Harappan world. For example, the most frequently found vessel form in Saurashtra at this time is the hemispherical red ware bowl, often with a stud handle, which accounts for over one-half of all the sherds recovered from Rojdi. Its function seems to have been as a drinking bowl.

The pottery often has graffiti with signs from the Indus script, such as the jar sign. There is also a short inscription in Harappan writing on the rim of a potsherd, as well as Indus weights, all seen in figure 3.26.

There is a reasonable amount of metal from Rojdi. Most of it is copper-based, but both gold and silver artifacts have also been found. Four complete flat axes of copper or bronze were found and another broken example, all in Rojdi C contexts. These are stylistically more like the axes of the Deccan Chalcolithic than the long, narrow axes of Sindh and the Punjab. There is also a very fine knife, or *parsu,* with an endless knot design, and an interesting ribbed object, possibly an ornament of some kind. Finally, there are fishhooks, and fish bones as well, but one of the hooks is flat, not fashioned from a round wire. Rather than having a loop on one end to fasten the line, there is a notch; not as good as a loop, but far better than nothing at all.

Conspicuous by their absence in any phase are signs of

Figure 3.24 Rojdi Gateway (after Possehl and Raval 1989)

nary Sorath Harappan village. We are not yet clear about this part of the Rojdi story, but the search should be pursued with further digging there.

The New Chronology for Bronze Age Sites in Saurashtra

The seven seasons of excavation at Rojdi between 1982 and 1995 produced a number of important results. Prior to 1982 it was assumed, actually for no particularly good reason, that the Harappan sites in Saurashtra dated to the Posturban, or Late, stage of the civilization. The renewed excavations at Rojdi were an opportunity to assess this. The new work confirmed three periods of occupation, called Rojdi A, B, and C. Twenty radiocarbon dates have allowed us to estimate the absolute chronology of Rojdi as follows:

Rojdi C	1900–1700 B.C.
Rojdi B	2200–1900 B.C.
Rojdi A	2500–2200 B.C.

These dates confirm that there are posturban Harappan sites in the region, but many of the sites are earlier, going back to the very beginnings of the Harappan Civilization circa 2500 B.C. Other research in Gujarat informs us that farmers and herders were present in the region even prior to 3000 B.C., but that is another story.

The Sorath Harappan

The ancient inhabitants of Rojdi were not "stamped-out" Harappans, clones of their cousins in Sindh and the Punjab. The Harappans of Saurashtra had their own way of life, their own farming economy, which was probably a unique blend of farming and pastoralism. Their architecture is also distinctive, with no drains and other water facilities so much a part of Harappan life in other Indus domains. The people of Rojdi built in stone and mud, not baked brick. Their material culture sets them apart from Harappans found elsewhere. The broad picture that emerges is that the Harappans of Saurashtra were part of the larger cultural mosaic we now call the Indus Civilization, but they had their own "flavor" and unique characteristics. Their ancestry goes back to Sindh and the old Neolithic homeland in Baluchistan through the Early Harappans, who are documented in North Gujarat.

Although their cultural heritage is the same as the Sindhi and Punjabi Harappans, they were also distinct, singular in their way of doing things, possibly with their own traditions and identity. In an effort to capture this sense that the inhabitants of Rojdi and their neighbors were both part of a larger Indus world, yet unique within it, I coined the term *Sorath Harappan*.[84]

industrial and manufacturing activity at Rojdi. There are no furnaces, kilns, wasters, or slag. In seven seasons of excavation we have found one bead broken while it was being drilled. Thus, if we look at Rojdi, with its houses, compounds, and food-processing and storage facilities, its overall character suggests a farmer's village. But the regional centrality of Rojdi, its comparatively large size, and the stability of a year-round settlement suggest that it was important in other ways and was not just another ordi-

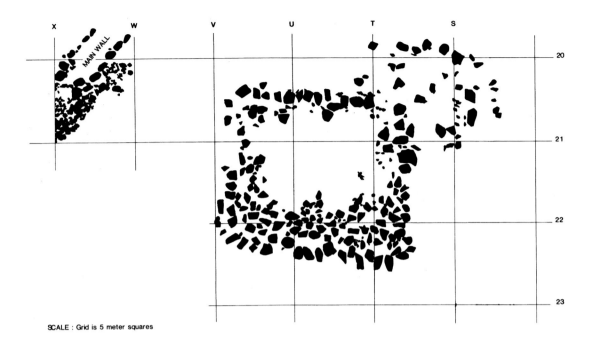

SCALE : Grid is 5 meter squares

Figure 3.25 Large Square Building (after Possehl and Raval 1989)

Rojdi and the Indus Civilization

What do the seven seasons of excavation at Rojdi contribute to our knowledge of the Indus Civilization? There are three main points.

First, the new chronology moved many of the villages, camps, and hamlets back in time by about 500 years. This correction brings the inhabitants of these places into a time when the Indus Civilization was flourishing. The Bronze Age peoples of Saurashtra can no longer be treated as "Late Harappan refugees" from Sindh or any other domain of the Indus Civilization.

Second, the investment the excavation team made in recovering bones and paleobotanical materials allowed them to define the Rojdi subsistence system. It was based on hardy, drought-resistant crops, adapted to the semi-arid monsoon climate of Saurashtra. The inhabitants of Rojdi were also cattle keepers par excellence. Rojdi is also one of the sites documenting the integration of the African millets into the Harappan subsistence system. This led to widespread double cropping in the Subcontinent, using both the *rabi* and *kharif* seasons. The work on the Rojdi subsistence system, taken as a whole, is a striking reminder that the Indus Civilization is best analyzed and discussed in terms of its various regional manifestations. This is the principal justification for speaking of the Harappans in Saurashtra as Sorath Harappans.

Perhaps the most important result of these excavations is an implication about the transformation of the Indus

Civilization. Rojdi C, which begins at about 1900 B.C., is defined by several important changes. Just as Mohenjo-daro was being abandoned, Rojdi was expanding in size. New houses and other structures were constructed on the fill of the South Extension; the Main Mound was rebuilt. The Large Square Building was constructed on the North Slope. The circumvallation, with a major gateway, was constructed around the landward side of the settlement, enclosing the South Extension and Large Square Building, as well as space between it and the Main Mound. This took the size of Rojdi from 2.5 to 7.5 hectares.

At about 1900 B.C., just as the major investments were made in the prospering community at Rojdi, Mohenjo-daro, Harappa, and many other Indus sites in Sindh and the Punjab were being abandoned or were shrinking in size. The excavations at Rojdi seem to inform us that the peoples of Saurashtra were solidly buffered against the dramatic changes taking place in many domains of the Indus world. This offers a caution that the so-called eclipse or end of the Indus Civilization might well be an overstatement and in need of radical reexamination.

NOTES

1. Possehl 1999b; J. Shaffer has also dealt with this theme, personal communication.
2. R. Ehrenreich, C. Crumley, and J. Levy 1995.
3. R. Blanton et al. 1996.
4. Jansen 1993a.

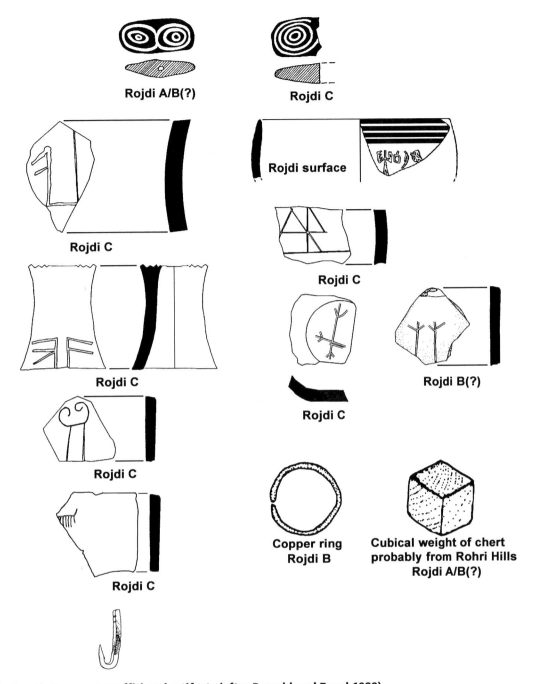

Figure 3.26 Sorath Harappan graffiti and artifacts (after Possehl and Raval 1989)

5. Wheeler 1968: 110.
6. Varma 1990.
7. Vidale and Miller 2000: 124–25.
8. Lamberg-Karlovsky 1975: 362–63.
9. Marshall 1931f: 91, 102–3. This is one of the themes that Wheeler and Piggott also took much to heart, but this observation speaks to order, discipline, a commitment to standards, the value of sociocultural homogeneity, and a single, overarching ideology.
10. Marshall 1931f: 95.
11. Mackay 1948: 25.
12. Shaffer and Lichtenstein 1989: 123.
13. Herodotus book III, 98; Godley 1926.
14. Shinde, Thomas, and Possehl 2001.
15. Marshall 1931e.
16. Hemphill, Lukacs, and Kennedy 1991: 172.
17. Kennedy 2000: 306.
18. Kennedy 2000: 302–7.
19. Dani 1970–71: 48.
20. Thomas and Allchin 1986; Allchin and Knox 1981: 106–8.
21. Possehl 1999b: 712.
22. Dani 1970–71: 47–48.

23. Khan, Knox, and Thomas 2000: 9–10.
24. Possehl 1999b: 727–845.
25. Mughal 1997; Possehl 1999b: 372–84.
26. Possehl 1979.
27. Possehl 1999b: 702 for map. These sites were first reported by Joshi 1986.
28. Possehl 1999b: 189–91.
29. Possehl 1999b: 191.
30. See Sharma 1974; Bokonyi 1997; Meadow and Patel 1997.
31. Belcher 1991: 114.
32. Possehl 1999b: 249–51.
33. Possehl 1999b: 250–51.
34. Jarrige et al. 1995: 248.
35. IAR 1986–87: 132.
36. Aitken 1907: 255.
37. Aitken 1907: 236.
38. Jarrige et al. 1995: 318–19.
39. Jarrige et al. 1995: 451, 461.
40. Flam 1981: 151–52.
41. Possehl 1975.
42. Weber 1991: 182–83.
43. This theme is developed in Possehl (1999b).
44. Possehl 1999b: 157–72.
45. Government of India 1884: 3.
46. Jansen, Mulloy, and Urban 1991.
47. See *Indian Archaeology, A Review* for yearly reports and Bisht 1991 and 1999.
48. Suraj Bhan 1975: 95–102.
49. Nath 1998, 1999.
50. See Nath 1999: 47, for a description of Period I.
51. Nath 1999: 48.
52. Nath 1998: pl. IV.
53. Khan 1965.
54. Mughal 1970.
55. Khan 1965: pls. XXVI, XXVIIb.
56. Mughal 1970.
57. Majumdar 1934: 35–44.
58. Mackay 1943.
59. Mackay 1943: 38.
60. Mackay 1943: 41–45.
61. Mackay 1943: pl. LVIII, nos. 1 and 2.
62. Possehl 1994.
63. Mackay 1943: 157, pl. LV, nos. 10, 11, 13, 14, 15.
64. Shar and Vidale 1985.
65. Lal 1979, 1981; Thapar 1975, 1989.
66. Lal 1970–71.
67. Thapar 1989: 196.
68. Sharma 1999.
69. Stein 1931: 118–27.
70. See Possehl 1986b: 51–55, for a description of Nindowari.
71. Possehl 1986b.
72. Stein 1931: 60–71.
73. Dales and Lipo 1992.
74. Stein 1931: 66–67.
75. Dales and Lipo 1992: 139.
76. Stein 1931: 63, 69.
77. Mackay 1937–38: pl. CXXI, nos. 1–5.
78. Dales and Lipo 1992: 148.
79. Rao 1979, 1985.
80. Leshnik 1968; Possehl 1976.
81. Rao 1963b.
82. Sarkar 1985.
83. Possehl and Raval 1989.
84. Possehl and Herman 1990; Shinde et al. 2001.

CHAPTER 4

The Technology of the Indus Age

The combination of elaborate social and economic organization over a huge empire with an isolation which rendered many of its technological processes astonishingly primitive makes one think not so much of contemporary Sumer or Egypt, but rather of the Central American, pre-Columbian Civilizations.

—S. Piggott, *Prehistoric India to 1000 B.C.*

INTRODUCTION

Stuart Piggott's statement on the technological sophistication of the Indus Civilization is very much outdated today. The high degree of Indus artistic and technological achievement can be seen in the cutting, polishing, etching, and drilling of the very long carnelian beads, the preparation of metal alloys, especially bronze, the use of lost wax casting and the very substantial quantity of metal, the quality of the carving of the square stamp seals, the manufacture of high-quality faience, and finally the preparation of very high quality ceramics, especially stoneware.[1] Equally apparent was the sophistication of the Harappan engineer. The building and maintenance of Mohenjo-daro is sufficient testimony to this skill, with the maintenance of the grid town plan, the elaborate drainage system that would have had to be regularly releveled as the contours of the city grew and changed, the digging of wells on a massive scale (estimated to be 700 at Mohenjo-daro alone), the engineering and architectural sophistication of the Great Bath. Contemporary thoughts on Indus technology are very much in line with the following:

> Although a large amount of field and laboratory research will be necessary to test many of the proposed interpretations, the available evidence is substantial enough to give a picture of the puzzling degree of sophistication of Harappan pyrotechnology . . . in artifacts such as the stoneware bangles we find not only the crystallization of impressive amounts of labor-force and specific know-how, but also the accumulated experience and skill needed to acquire and master a wide and diversified knowledge of chemistry.[2]

This high degree of technological sophistication, as well as accomplishment, was well enough developed that I think of it as a part of the Indus ideology. M. Vidale and H. Miller have used the phrase "Indus technological virtuosity" to describe the Harappan mastery of materials.[3] Theirs was not just a knowledge of pyrotechnology, it extended to techniques for crushing and refining, drilling, polishing, sophisticated engineering, city planning, and deep-water ocean sailing, including navigation, boatbuilding, and maintenance. There was also the work and skill needed to acquire the proper raw materials, some of which were fluxes and catalysts, that are not apparent parts of the finished product. Since the Indus virtuosity in such a wide a range of technological pursuits did not happen by accident, I have proposed that it was institutionalized within the ideology, which supported and promoted it.

Before moving to the substance of this discussion, I should make it clear that this is not an exhaustive coverage of Indus technology. There is much that could not be covered here, and some of it important.

PYROTECHNOLOGY AND THE INDUS AGE

Introduction

It can be shown that humans had an early interest in fire and heat. In the beginning this centered on practical, functional matters such as cooking, security, light, and warmth. These are matters of the hearth. But there seem to be other dimensions to humankind's interest in fire that go beyond the hearth and give the human species a prolonged interest in pyrotechnology.

Lime Plaster

Lime plaster and other products deriving from hydrated lime are useful materials for humankind. They have been manufactured for many millennia, going back to the seventh millennium in the Near East. Creating plaster begins with the heating of limestone. By placing the lime source in a kiln, the lime burner drives off carbon dioxide from the parent material and produces a substance called quicklime. This new product is a lively one, and the lime burner has to be careful since it can combine with water in a volatile way, expanding and producing heat.

Lime when combined with sand and water makes a fine mortar for binding bricks and stone together. Lime mortar was used at Mohenjo-daro, although simple earth was the mortar of choice in an overwhelming way.[4] Quicklime was also found in the bead factory at Lothal, near the updraft

89

kiln there.[5] There is some indication that it might have been used for the dehydration of steatite.

Ceramics

The early pottery from Mehrgarh is hand formed, pieced together, and lightly decorated.[6] There is also a basket-marked ware in early Mehrgarh that was made by packing a lining of clay inside a basket and then firing the entire unit. One would think that old, expended baskets were used for this purpose, but the basket itself would have provided some of the fuel for the burning.

It appears that some sort of slow potter's wheel was present in Period II at Mehrgarh, right at the beginning of pottery making. Other pots were made on a wheel and expanded by paddle and anvil. Wheel technology is vastly expanded in Period III, with beautiful, fine red wares. The precise kind of potter's wheel present so early is not certain, but a hand-turned table would be a good guess.

There is evidence during the Indus Age of the forming of pots using a slab technology, coiling, slow and fast wheels, as well as paddle and anvil. Some individual pots were made using more than one of these techniques.

During the Early and Mature Harappan, some pots have unmistakable signs that they were formed on a wheel. There is the corkscrew pattern on vessel walls that results from the potter's steady, slow, upward pull of clay, indicating a spinning pot and stationary hand. String marks on the bases of pots, made when the formed vessel was cut from the hump of clay on the wheel, are also good indicators. Mass-produced pottery, with striations exactly parallel to one another and the ground, with deep grooves also parallel to the ground can be taken as wheel made.

Some of the Mature Harappan pots are quite large: a meter or so tall and about that diameter. Mackay noted that these pots were made in sections he called "coiled strips of clay."[7] R. Wright tells us that they were made in three separate parts: the base, the body, and the rim.[8] The base was made in a chuck. This is an implement that serves two purposes: It holds and supports the base and the other parts as the pot is being assembled; the chuck also assists in forming the base.

The midsection of the pot was fashioned separately, possibly also using a chuck. After it had been formed the body of the pot was picked up and carried to the base, where it was placed. The potter then melded the two parts together. Doing this in an effective way, giving sufficient strength to the vessel so that it would not immediately (or ever!) break along this natural fault line is not easy. Since the midsection of these large pots was heavy and not strong, the Indus potters habitually tied string around the midsection to support the clay after it had been shaped.

The pressure of the soft clay against the string left an imprint on the outer surface, which remained with the pot when the string burned away during firing.

The rim portion of the pot was then made and wedded to the base and midsection; it too was melded into place. The assembled vessel was cleaned up and the external signs of the tripartite manufacturing process removed as best as could be done (generally very well). The pot was then slipped and decorated (figure 4.1).

Some Mature Harappan pots were formed in a preliminary way, then expanded by paddle and anvil. This is especially true of the *handi*-shaped cooking vessels.[9] Some pots were pared, shaved, scraped, and whatnot. These operations thinned and further shaped the pot and are documented to have occurred during the Indus Age almost from the beginning.

Clay Coverings, Slips, Glazes, Paints, and Decoration

The next stage in producing a pot is concerned with additions to the pot, generally on the outside, that play a role in determining the color, texture, and porosity of the vessel, as well as protection against thermal shock.

Early use of these clay coatings occurs with the Wet Wares of the Quetta area. These go back to Kechi Beg times, but flower in the Damb Sadaat and Quetta Stages. The Wet Wares were made by applying a viscous slurry of very fine clay over the body of a formed pot. The resulting pattern is both decorative and functional since the many ridges increase the surface area of the pot. Wet Ware vessels are globular, and the larger surface area enhanced evaporation; thus, they were probably conceived as water pots, although used for many purposes (figure 4.2).

It was common practice during the Indus Age, from Togau times on, to slip most if not all of the outside of pots with a thin clay coating that helped maintain surface color and texture as well as assisted in controlling the porosity of the vessel. Much of the slipped pottery of the Indus Age is red, but buff slips are also fairly common. There are also colors in between these extremes that seem

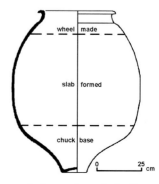

Figure 4.1   A large Indus pot made in three parts

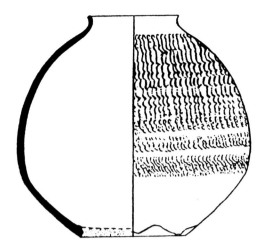

Figure 4.2   Wet Ware water pot (after Fairservis 1956)

to result from the imperfect control the ancient potter had over kiln temperature, oxygen, and the selection of raw materials.

The most common form of decoration for pots of the Indus Age was painting, and black was usually the color. Other colors that occur are red, orange, white, blue, and yellow. The paints were generally applied by brush or some brushlike implement. The paints of the Indus Age were generally minerals, iron and manganese oxides being very common, although lamp black was also used (figure 4.3).[10]

The chemistry of paints used on prehistoric pottery is a specialized field. The subject must have been quite intriguing to the prehistoric potter, since there is not necessarily a close relationship between the color before firing and the one the comes out afterward. For example, some iron minerals such as yellow ocher completely change in firing by losing their water, becoming a ferric oxide, and turning red. But raw clay, free of iron and organic impurities, probably looks white at the beginning and fires to that color.

There are no fully developed glazes of the Indus Age. One ceramic generally called Reserved Slipped Ware does have a kind of crypto-glaze. There is a short article on this ceramic, covering the basics of this ceramic and concluding quite rightly that it is not evidence for Indus-Mesopotamian contact.[11]

Glass, Faience, and Frit

There is no true glass from the Indus Age, but there is much faience.[12] Faience technology, which implies an ability to reach a controlled temperature of 1200 degrees Celsius, begins in the Early Harappan, as at Kalibangan.[13] By Mature Harappan times it is widely made and has been reported from Mohenjo-daro, Chanhu-daro, Lohumjo-daro, Harappa, Lothal, Desalpur, Rojdi, Chandi-

garh, Surkotada, Daulatpur, and Alamgirpur. There is also faience in the Posturban Phase at Sanghol, Ahar Period I, Navdatoli, and Nevasa.[14] Faience was found at Nal.[15] While there is probably faience in all of the domains of the Indus Civilization, it seems to have been most popular in the north, around Harappa and in the Eastern Domain, where it is especially well represented in the Posturban Phase.

A reasonably wide range of artifacts was made from faience and its allied materials. The sealings have already been mentioned. Other objects include boxes, bangles, beads, and inlay. Pots were also made, all small. Bangles are characteristic objects with long, flat projections on the other side. Vats called them "cog-wheels."[16] They are long and delicate, and complete specimens are rare; but they are the finest examples of faience craft from the Indus Civilization.

Kilns and Firing

There are many ways to fire pottery. Some methods use kilns, while others do not. It is possible to fire pots or clay figurines by simply piling these objects together with some fuel and setting the heap afire. Even the crudest of these arrangements gets the job done, maybe not in an even, fully satisfactory way, but the heat causes to occur some of the physical and chemical changes that transform clay to pottery. The most sophisticated and best-documented kiln in the Indus Age is the funnel-shaped, up-draft type (figure 4.4).[17] They have been found at Mohenjo-daro, Harappa, Lothal, Nageshwar, Balakot, Kot Diji, and Lal Shah. Kilns of this type are splendid little pieces of technology.[18]

The body of these kilns is a two-story affair: a lower chamber, where the fuel and fire are located, and an upper area, where the material to be baked or heated was placed. These are separated from one another by a floor with holes in it that allow for the circulation of heat and gas. Some provision for supporting the floor from below is made, which may be a pillar or a small wall of bricks, as in some of the Harappa examples.[19] This is all covered during firing with a dome that is usually taken apart at the end of firing to access the contents of the upper chamber, and it is therefore a temporary part of the facility. In front of the domed double chamber is a constricted neck, which gives the whole affair the look of a funnel when viewed on plan. This leads to the lower chamber, which is there for several purposes. It allows the kiln to be fueled and the fire stoked. It also controls the amount of air that gets to the fire and plays a role in determining the temperature and the oxidation/reduction reaction.

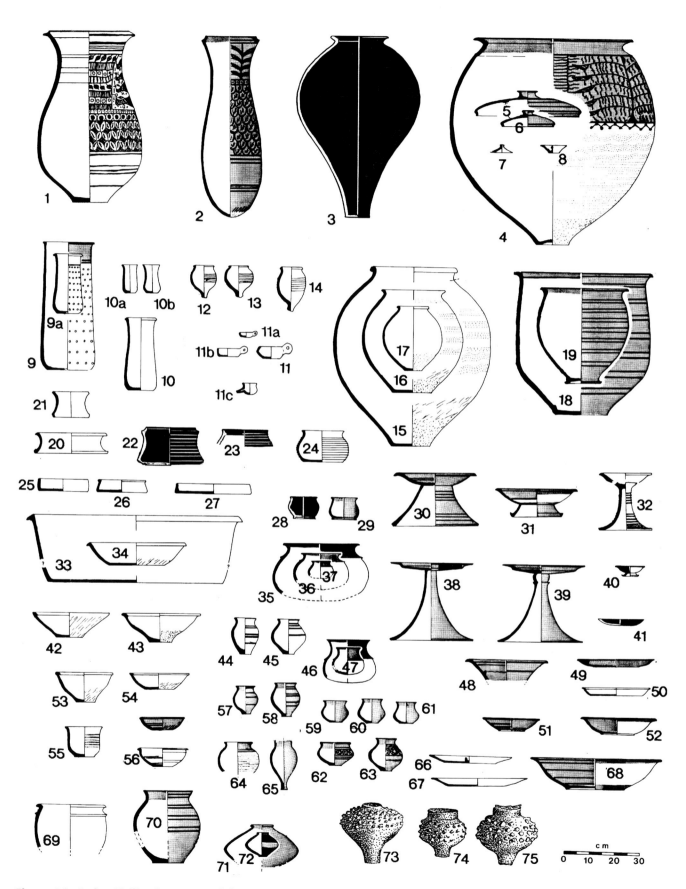

Figure 4.3   Indus Civilization pottery (after Dales and Kenoyer 1986)

Brick Manufacture

Burnt bricks are often said to be a characteristic of the Indus Civilization. There are millions of them at Mohenjo-daro.[20] The early literature on the Indus Civilization contains a small phrase, "bricks of the usual size," which captures the sense of the excavators and their observations on the standardization of this commodity.

> The bricks of Mohenjo-daro are exceptionally well made, yet have no straw or other binding material. They are always rectangular in shape with the exception of those that were used for special purposes, such as the wedge-shaped bricks almost invariably employed in the construction of wells. The bricks were made in an open mould and struck across the top with a piece of wood, as proved by their striated upper surfaces. The bases of bricks are invariably rough, showing that they were made and dried on dusty ground, which is borne out by the frequent presence of potsherds and bits of charcoal adhering to their bases. No bricks have been found that were made on matting.[21]

Baked bricks were obviously a valued commodity, and plundering them seems to be as old as their manufacture: "A stack of bricks against the eastern wall of the western wing of the palace (Block 1) provided eloquent proof of the collection of bricks from the lower levels to build the houses of later date. This stack included bricks of various sizes, to many of which the mud mortar still adhered."[22] While we do not have evidence for brick kilns, nor do we know where they were located, abundant use was made of brick kiln wasters.

Metallurgy

Introduction

There is an abundance of metal at sites of the Indus Age. These peoples regularly worked with copper, tin, arsenic, lead, silver, gold, and electrum.[23] The documentation of metal begins in a burial at Mehrgarh Period I with native copper in it. The story of Indus metallurgy is one of gradual change, in both technology and the scope of the metals commonly worked.

Copper Ores in the Greater Indus Region

Copper ores are widespread and are found in all of the major regions of the earth. In the Subcontinent copper ores are found principally in Baluchistan and the Khetri belt of Rajasthan, with other spotty occurrences.[24] There is also a good deal of copper in Oman. This was ancient Magan and was a partner in the maritime commerce of the second half of the third millennium, during the Mature

Harappan. Omani copper has a high nickel content and can probably be identified from this trace.

The Earliest Metallurgy in the Subcontinent

In Period III at Mehrgarh there are three compartmented seals that demonstrate the casting of copper at this time. There is also a pin with a double spiral head. There are also crucibles in Mehrgarh III.[25]

Shaffer has quite correctly noted that the copper–bronze metallurgy of the Indus Civilization is impressive due to the quality and variety of the artifacts as well as their widespread distribution.[26] The typology of Indus copper implements includes a wide variety of vessels (vases, jars, dishes, lids, even frying pans), ornaments (pendants, bangles, beads, necklace parts), tools and weapons (axes, knives, blades, projectile points, "razors"), stamp seals, and figurines.[27] While there is much smelted, cast, and forged Mature Harappan metal, especially copper–bronze, it is clear that not all of the "furnaces" ascribed to metalworking were used in this way, as shown by Kenoyer and Miller.[28] We should be particularly skeptical of older reports of this sort from Harappa and Lothal (figure 4.5).

Iron in the South Asian Bronze Age

Several pieces of iron have been recovered from Bronze Age sites in South Asia. To my knowledge none has been analyzed to determine their technical properties, and we do not know which of them is meteoric and which (if any) were smelted.[29] The sites with evidence of this early iron

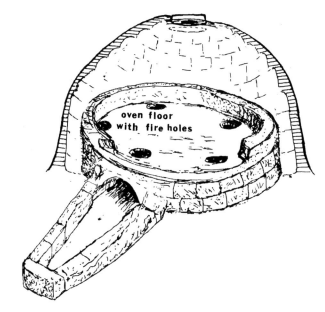

Figure 4.4 Indus Civilization funnel-shaped, up-draft kiln (by Jan Fairservis)

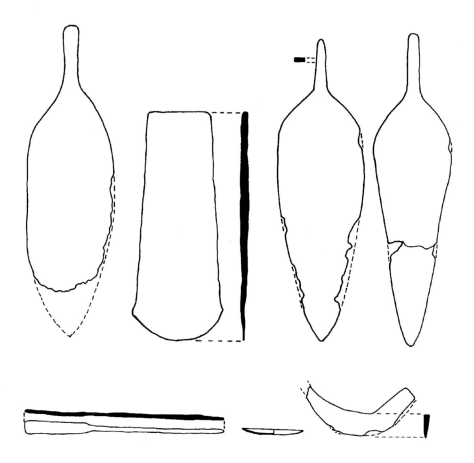

Figure 4.5   A selection of Indus Civilization copper–bronze artifacts (after Mackay 1942)

are as follows: Mundigak, Said Qala Tepe, Deh Morasi Ghundai, Ahar, Chanhu-daro, Lothal. "There is also very good evidence for smelted iron in Bronze Age contexts in the Near East and Egypt. Some of these materials have been tested and it can be demonstrated that they were smelted."[30]

Those who know the details of copper smelting have demonstrated that metallic iron can be produced as a part of this process.[31] This is a complex chemical matter and has to do with the uses of fluxes and their chemistry within the smelting process. The evidence just presented suggests that this actually happened there.

The Organization of Pyrotechnology during the Mature Harappan

It has been an assumption for many scholars working on the Indus Civilization that noxious pyrotechnological facilities such as pottery kilns and smelters were kept out of the Indus cities. Perhaps powerful families in good neighborhoods just did not want them around. Those pyrotechnological facilities found in Mohenjo-daro and Harappa were ascribed to the last occupations of these cities, when, presumably, there were no more "good neighborhoods."

Heather Miller has called this assumption into question, for Harappa, at least.[32] She has informed us of two important aspects of technology at Harappa. First, while there are many kilns there, as well as other sites, actual smelting/melting furnaces are rare. Second, the use of kilns in some areas of Harappa lasted for centuries, forming small areas of specialized activities over protracted periods of time. No one is sure why this took place. Perhaps these Mature Harappan facilities were not as noxious as we once thought.

Miller's observations at Harappa are somewhat different from those made at Mohenjo-daro: "The surface survey of Mohenjo-daro shows that most of the heavy, polluting industries (e.g., ceramic and brick firing and metallurgical activities) are not represented in the urban compound. It must be presumed that these activities were carried out in a series of peripheral settlements (now invisible due to alluviation) that supplied the center."[33] But in the Late Period the surface of Mohenjo-daro was littered with pottery wasters, sometimes in heavy concentrations.[34] A similar case can be made for metallurgy with not fewer than eleven occurrences of copper slag and crucibles there.

These observations are tentative, of course, since we know so little about Mohenjo-daro below the Late levels there. This is a contrast to Harappa, where the Early Harappan is much better documented. So, in the end, Miller could be right. We just need a good deal more work at Mohenjo-daro to confirm or deny this.

OTHER TECHNOLOGICAL FEATURES OF THE INDUS CIVILIZATION

There was much technology of the Indus Civilization that was not primarily dependent on heat, and it is to these important activities that attention is now turned.

Stamp Seal Cutting

The typical stamp seal was made of a soft gray stone in the family of minerals that can conveniently be called steatite. This is the softest of the minerals and is rated the lowest number 1 on the Mohs' scale of hardness, so soft that it can be scratched by a fingernail. The Indus craftspeople clearly selected this easily carved mineral to work with. The carving tools may have included shell, chert, or copper, all of which would have worked efficiently with steatite. Marshall notes that "it has been found by experiment that the sharp chert flakes cut steatite very well."[35]

If steatite is subjected to heat, it is slightly hardened to about 4 on the Mohs' scale. This was often done since it makes the seals wear better. The seals were also often glazed white, apparently to make their outer surfaces a uniform color, improving their luster and beauty. Mohammad Sana Ullah found that this covering was a fused powder of steatite.[36] Thus, furnaces are one of the pieces of physical evidence for a seal-cutting establishment.

The following description of the steps in making a square steatite Indus stamp seal is taken from my own observations as well as from observations in Mackay (see figure 7.1).[37]

The steatite was first sawn into blanks of the approximate size and shape of the seal, including the thickness needed to accommodate the boss. Mackay gives a table of seal sizes that range from 1.25 by 1.25 centimeters to 6.85 by 6.85 centimeters.[38] A rough boss was then cut. This was done with four saw cuts parallel to the face of the seal, thinning it. These "flats" were then removed by taking four additional saw cuts at right angles, at the edge of the reserved hump of the boss. We know from examples from Chanhu-daro that the boss was left in an unfinished state while the seal itself was smoothed of saw marks and prepared for cutting.

The animal or other device below the script was the first carving on a seal. We know from Chanhu-daro examples that the design was roughed out on the surface with a sharp point. Some unfinished seals were covered with a thick coating of red ocher, the use of which is not yet known. Various devices were completely carved and finished as a single operation, before even roughing out the inscription was undertaken.

The inscription was then carved. Mackay suggests that "the seal-cutters probably kept a stock of seals by them and added the inscriptions as required," something that has not yet been confirmed.[39]

The back of the seal and the boss were then finished. The boss was carved to a rounded shape and a deep V was carved along the length at right angles to the perforation, which was done next. This was most often a two-step drilling operation, which was usually angled slightly down into the body of the seal from opposite sides of the boss. We presume that this hole took a cord used to suspend, or hold, the seal. There are many broken bosses but few of the holes show wear along the edges, as would occur if the seal were moving back and fourth along a cord. This suggests that the seal was tied onto the cord so that it did not move. In fact, given the fragile nature of the steatite, the seal might well have been wrapped in cloth to protect it from being banged around and moving on the suspension cord.

As a final step, the seal was coated with a mixture of steatite dust mixed with water and then baked, fusing the coating and hardening the steatite body of the seal itself; pyrotechnology crosses our path once again. The resulting product was a seal with a beautiful, even white, lustrous surface.

Bead Making

Beads are by far the most popular form of ornamentation that survives in the archaeological record of the Indus Age. If one includes the masses of steatite microbeads, there are hundreds of thousands of beads, in a wide array of types and materials, each requiring its own manufacturing technology. This is a huge subfield, far larger than can be fully covered here.

Hard-Stone Beads

The most spectacular beads of the Indus Age are those made of hard stones, generally with a high silica content. The generic word I use for the most translucent of these is *agate*. Chalcedony, both banded and clear, is one among these rocks. The stones of this general class that the Harappans employed in bead making are given in table 4.1.

Table 4.1 Stones used for Mature Harappan bead making

Alabaster	Amazonite	Amethyst
Azurite	Bloodstone	Breccia
Caringorn	Chalcedony	Chert (brown and black)
Chrysoprase	Hematite	Hornblende
Jade	Jasper	Lapis lazuli
Limestone	Moonstone	Onyx
Opal	Plasma	Quartz (milky and rose)
Rock crystal	Serpentine	Turquoise

India and Pakistan have been famous for their native lapidary industries for millennia, since the Indus Age, in fact. Edward Balfour tells us that small stone cups from India were worth 70,000 sesterces in the days of Pompey.[40] Nero paid the round figure of a million sesterces for an Indian cup.

There is evidence for the manufacture of hard-stone beads at many sites of the Indus Age. The early sites are Mehrgarh III, Ghazi Shah I, Amri Ic and Id, as well as Shahr-i Sokhta II. During the Mature Harappan, we have a bead shop at both Chanhu-daro and Lothal. Mackay notes that "proof that some beads made from hard stones were actually manufactured at Mohenjo-daro is afforded by the unfinished specimens that we have found, though no actual bead factory has yet come to light."[41] More evidence in this regard comes from the intensive surface exploration of Mohenjo-daro. In the Moneer Area there was found the co-occurrence of several classes of artifacts indicating craft activity, but the "thousands of flakes of agate, chalcedony chert drills and other specialized tools form the largest assemblage of indicators of semi-precious stone working so far identified at Mohenjo-daro."[42]

The Sequence of Hard-Stone Bead Manufacturing
Based on hundreds of archaeological specimens, especially those from Chanhu-daro and Lothal, it has been possible to outline the sequence of hard-stone bead manufacturing.

Roughing the Bead This begins with chipping out a rough blank, then refining the shape with a second, more delicate round of knapping. There is also evidence for sawing during the early stages of shaping at Chanhu-daro.[43] Mackay felt that this implied the use of an abrasive, a sound idea without direct evidence. At this point the bead has its rough shape and size.

The chipping marks were then ground away on a hone. This was time-consuming handwork, at the end of which the bead had its final shape and size, but with an unpolished surface.

Drilling the Bead The bead was then drilled. Indus Age beads often show little cup marks, pecked into both ends,

which served the function of small starter holes.[44] A drill with a hard-stone bit was used. The stone we have from archaeological sites is chert or a hard green stone we believe to be phtanite. This was used with rotary motion, implying the use of a bow or possibly a pump drill. Drilling proceeded first from one end of the bead to about the center and was finished with a second hole penetrating from the opposite side, the two holes meeting in the middle. Even very small beads were drilled in this two-step manner. There is also evidence that not all beads were drilled. Sometimes the perforation was carefully pecked through using a delicate chipping technique.[45]

Polishing the Bead We have no direct evidence for the polishing process in prehistoric times, but the best guesses include moving the beads and a slurry of light abrasives inside a sealed bag of some kind (probably leather). The principle employed here is the same as that used by modern rock hounds and their tumblers; but the mechanics and materials would have been quite different during the Indus Age.

Making Carnelian
Carnelian, also known as sard, is a form of chalcedony that has been turned red by heating. It is rarely found in nature. Heating the stone causes the oxides of iron to become yellow, orange, and red. Some stones turn a uniform deep cherry red. These were prized objects for the Indus craftspeople.

Etching Carnelian Beads
One of the distinctive bead types of the Mature Harappan is that of etched carnelian. These are red with white designs (rarely black) that were traded far and wide as a part of the Middle Asian Interaction Sphere.[46] They were also prized by the Harappans themselves, who found them worthy enough to fake (figure 4.6).[47]

The art of etching stone is known in modern Sindh, and Mackay found one practicing craftsman in Sehwan near Lake Manchar who give him a demonstration.[48] The process began with the juice extracted from the tips of young shoots of a bush called *kirar* in Sindhi (*Capparis aphylla*). The informant then ground washing soda to a fine powder and mixed it with water in a cup. He poured a small quantity of this on the *kirar* and rubbed the whole carefully together to a semifluid mass. Then the craftsman strained this mixture through a piece of linen into a large empty mussel shell, and the "paint" was ready.[49]

This paint was applied to a carnelian stone using a reed pen. The painted stone was then allowed to dry, first in the hand, then by placing it on a metal plate over a charcoal

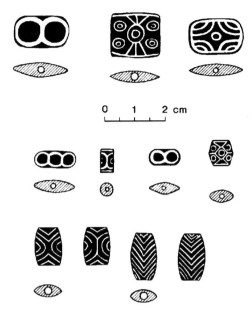

Figure 4.6 A selection of Indus Civilization etched carnelian beads from Chanhu-daro (after Mackay 1942)

fire. When fully dry, the carnelian was covered with live coals and the fire fanned for about five minutes. The piece was then removed from the heat and allowed to cool slowly for about 10 minutes under an inverted cup, at which point the craftsman "rubbed his piece of carnelian briskly with a rag and handed it over for inspection."[50] It was perfect!

Imitation Etched Carnelian

Etched carnelian was so prized during the Mature Harappan that it generated a market for a cheap imitation product. These have been found at Mohenjo-daro, and they are all of steatite or steatite paste.[51]

CONCLUDING STATEMENT ON TECHNOLOGY

The following sections discuss three statements of the broader patterns of Mature Harappan technology, mostly drawn from the research on craft organization at Harappa[52] and Mohenjo-daro.[53] These can be used to give us an overview of the Harappan way of organizing their technological activities.

Overall Site Structure

The supposed order of Indus sites is not seen in the distribution of craft activities. Pyrotechnological facilities were found in all of the major parts of both Harappa and Mohenjo-daro, at least during the Late Period at the latter site. There is also a suggestion that Mature Harappan technology took place at "a cloud of minor sites focused around the major urban center . . . many of the peripheral settlements appear to be specialized industrial sites."[54]

The Structure of Individual Mounds

There is an unexplained tendency at Harappa for manufacturing activities to be situated on the southern half of the settlement mounds. This is not due to prevailing wind patterns, since lapidary workshops are also located there and these involved the limited use of heat. No one is quite sure why this pattern is present.

The Distribution of Particular Crafts

There is a tendency at Harappa for copper smelting/melting debris and slags, as well as pottery firing debris, to be separate from debris from other crafts. On the other hand, lapidary activities (semiprecious stone, chert, steatite, and maybe ground stone) are usually found together, often in association with shell working. If this is a valid observation, one can see differences in the organization of pyrotechnological activities, as contrasted to the extractive-reductive crafts. According to Miller, this pattern might also be present at Mohenjo-daro.[55]

Blackman and Vidale note that the excavations and intensive surface survey at Mohenjo-daro inform us that nonpolluting industries were also located within the city.[56] These industries were involved in the manufacture of seals, beads and shell ornaments, and luxury and other prestige items probably consumed within the city. There is a "suburban" shell-working area, approximately 500 meters northeast of the Lower Town.

During the Late Period at Mohenjo-daro, there seems to have been two patterns of pottery production in the city. There was a kind of potter's district, as well as individual household potters.[57] We do not know enough about the earlier occupations at Mohenjo-daro, and whether this pattern was present then.

Sometimes the forming stages of such pyrotechnological crafts as pottery, faience, and copper were undertaken near their firing places. For example, pottery-forming tools were found during the excavation of a pottery kiln on the northwest corner of Mound E at Harappa. There is also evidence that the firing of steatite took place in the vicinity of its forming stages, as represented by the steatite-coated clay containers found together with talc/steatite and other lithic debris in the general debris levels of the southwest corner of Mound ET.[58]

Blackman and Vidale propose that some commodities may have been manufactured at only one Mature Harappan site and that others were the product of quite specific, if not exclusive, manufacture.[59] The first point is illustrated at Chanhu-daro: Blackman and Vidale propose that this may have been the only place where the very large "long-barrel" carnelian beads were made, since not one roughout or blank of this bead type has been found at either

Mohenjo-daro or Harappa. Their second point is made in the following way:[60] "The palaeo-technological analysis of the shell industries of Mohenjo-daro by Kenoyer[61] shows that the manufacture of ladles from murex . . . shells is definitely under-represented in that site, while this activity represents one of the most important industries at the coastal site of Nageshwar in Saurashtra[62] and in the workshops of Chanhu-daro."[63]

The study of these broad patterns in the structure of Indus technology is a growing field, one within which there is much more to be learned about the organization of Harappan life.

NOTES

1. Halim and Vidale 1984.
2. Halim and Vidale 1984: 96.
3. Vidale and Miller 2000.
4. Mackay 1937–38: 598.
5. Rao 1985: 582.
6. Vandiver 1995.
7. Mackay 1943: 86.
8. Wright 1991: 81–82.
9. Wright 1991: 80–81.
10. Wright 1986: 9.
11. Chakrabarti 1978.
12. Mackay 1931n.
13. Lal 1989: 321.
14. Lal 1989: 321.
15. Hargreaves 1929: 43.
16. Vats 1940: 448, pl. CXXXVIII, no. 2.
17. See Miller 1997 for a review of Indus kilns.
18. Wright 1991: 78.
19. Vats 1940: 471.
20. Fairservis 1967: 39 suggests 5 million.
21. Mackay 1931d: 266.
22. Mackay 1937–38: xiii.
23. Agrawal 2000.
24. Possehl 1999b: 232 for map.
25. Jarrige et al. 1995: 249.
26. Shaffer 1992: 448.
27. Agrawal 2000: 77–93; Heidi Miller 2000.
28. Kenoyer and Miller 1999.
29. Shaffer 1984; Possehl and Gullapalli 1999; Datta 1998.
30. Waldbaum 1980: 69–70.
31. Cooke and Aschenbrenner 1975.
32. Heather Miller 2000.
33. Blackman and Vidale 1992: 38.
34. Halim and Vidale 1984: 63.
35. Marshall 1925–26: 86.
36. Mackay 1931i: 379.
37. Mackay 1931i: 377–79, and 1943: 145–49.
38. Mackay 1931i: 372.
39. Mackay 1931i: 378.
40. Balfour 1885: vol. 1, 555.
41. Mackay 1937–38: 50.
42. Halim and Vidale 1984: 64.
43. Mackay 1943: 211.
44. Piperno 1973, 1983.
45. Kenoyer 1993: 513.
46. Reade 1979.
47. Mackay 1937–38: 517.
48. Mackay 1933: 143.
49. Mackay 1933: 144.
50. Mackay 1933: 144.
51. Mackay 1937–38: 517, pl. CLVII, nos. 8–12, and 506–7.
52. Heather Miller 2000.
53. Blackman and Vidale 1992.
54. Blackman and Vidale 1992: 38.
55. Heather Miller 2000.
56. Blackman and Vidale 1992: 38.
57. Tosi, Bondioli, and Vidale 1984.
58. Heather Miller 2000.
59. Blackman and Vidale 1992: 38.
60. Blackman and Vidale 1992: 38.
61. Kenoyer 1984.
62. Bhan and Kenoyer 1984.
63. Mackay 1943.

CHAPTER 5

The Architecture of the Indus Age

ONE OF THE MOST REMARKABLE FEATURES OF THE INDUS Civilization is the baked-brick architecture of Mohenjo-daro, with splendidly preserved buildings lining its streets and lanes. This is the largest Bronze Age city in the world where one can walk down streets well defined by the high walls of homes and other buildings, climb the stairways used in antiquity, peer down ancient wells, and stand in bathing rooms used over 4,000 years ago. One feels a sense of being in a living community; Mohenjo-daro is an extraordinary, unique place (figure 5.1).

The architecture and town planning of the Indus Civilization in some ways is another part of technology and it should be thought of as an aspect of that quite vigorous part of the Indus ideology. While this chapter addresses much of the architecture of the Indus Civilization, there is much more said on this topic in the tour of Mohenjo-daro (chapter 11).

THE EARLY MATERIAL
There is a great deal of mud-brick architecture in Stages Two and Three of the Indus Age. Many of the buildings were equipped with stone foundations and may have had some of the superstructure made in stone as well. This stone is useful for purposes of stability, but it also protects the superstructure from groundwater rising into the mud through capillary action.

An important feature of architecture in the first half of the third millennium was the growing use of large platforms, which served a number of purposes. First, they elevated settlements as protection against floods. At other times they served as solid, level foundations for buildings. These platforms, one side of which might be several tens of meters long, also served the purpose of protecting one edge of a settled area from general erosion and of forming a manmade boundary, segregating a particular settled area from those around it. Finally, some of the platforms were substructures that elevated large sections of a settlement, as in the case of the Mound of the Great Bath. Massive platforms emerge at Mohenjo-daro during the Mature Harappan as one of the fundamental architectural principles on which the city was built.

THE ARCHITECTURE OF THE INDUS CIVILIZATION
The architecture of the Indus Civilization is an immense subject, far more than can be summarized here. The expert on this topic is M. Jansen, whose writings have been liberally used here. Given the broad scope of the topic, along with the presence of a substantial number of sources which are both recent and of high quality, this discussion focuses on a restricted number of themes that have some base in technology: town planning, platform construction, well digging, streets, drainage, and both domestic and special buildings.

Three Misconceptions about Indus Architecture
There are three oft-repeated characteristics of the Indus Civilization that are in fact not true at all. These deal with the use of baked brick, the presence of a common pattern of civic organization, and the importance of grid town planning and design.

The Baked-Brick Cities of the Indus
It is often said that the ancient cities of the Indus were built of baked brick. Actually, Mohenjo-daro is the only Mature Harappan settlement where baked bricks were used for most of the buildings. At Harappa there is good evidence for baked brick, even in some houses.[1] But there is also a great deal of mud and mud-brick construction, and even evidence for baked and unbaked bricks used in the same building, as in the Granary.[2] Baked brick at Harappa, and such places as Chanhu-daro, Kot Diji, and Kalibangan, was used mostly where its durability and other physical properties suggested that it should be used: for drains, the lining of wells, bathing platforms, and the husking floors on Mound F.

There is no baked brick at Rojdi or the other Sorath Harappan sites, nor was the material used at the Kulli sites. The westernmost Indus site of Sutkagen-dor has no baked brick. There is little if any baked brick at Dholavira and Surkotada; the houses, walls, and drains were constructed of stone. The same is true for Allahdino near Karachi.

The Layout of Indus Settlements
It is also often held that the Indus Civilization brought forth planned settlements, with an acropolis to the west,

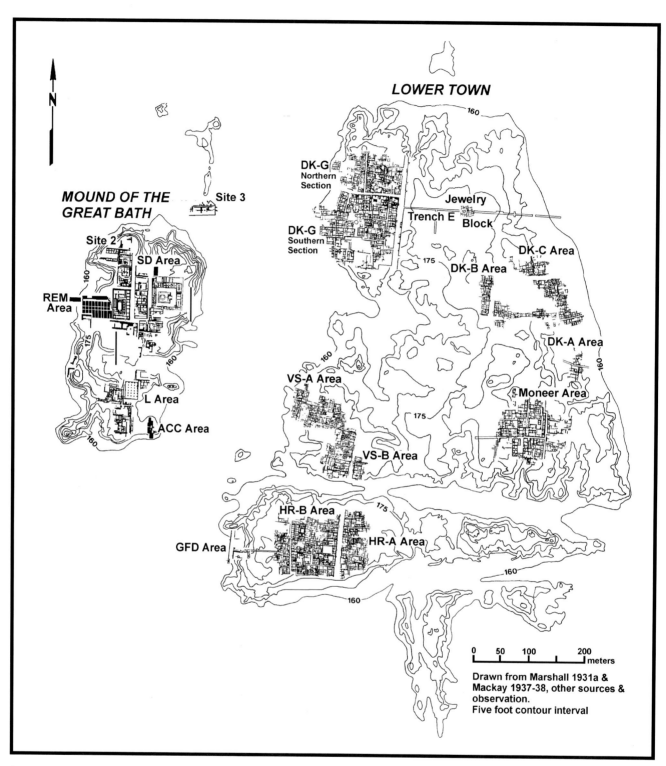

Figure 5.1 Plan of Mohenjo-daro (by Gregory L. Possehl)

separated from the lower living spaces of the community.[3] Mohenjo-daro is used as evidence for this pattern. But most Mature Harappan settlements are not planned like Mohenjo-daro: for example, Allahdino, Amri, Lothal, Rojdi, Surkotada, Ropar, Hulas. We know that

Harappa was an old place by the time the Indus Civilization began, and this would have probably constrained the would-be civic planners there. Thus, a close examination of the plan of Harappa will reveal, I think, that it is only vaguely like Mohenjo-daro. There is an acropolis to the west, but there is also an important part of the city to the north of the acropolis, called Mound F, with the Granary and husking floors. The other mounded parts of the city (Mounds E and ET) were built out from the southern end of the A-B Mound, like the lower extension of the letter L. The pattern is not evident at Chanhu-daro, which is simply a set of three mounds separated from each other. Dholavira has the acropolis near the middle of the enclosed settlement.

The Indus settlement most like Mohenjo-daro in layout is Kalibangan, but that is the only one with such close similarities. Thus, out of some 1,050 Mature Harappan sites, there are two that are proved to conform to the pattern said to be typical of the civilization as a whole.

The Grid Town Plan and Streets

The best example of Mature Harappan grid town planning is found at Mohenjo-daro, although Kalibangan and Nausharo also provide good evidence for this practice. While there is an overall sense of planning at Mohenjo-daro, the settlement does not seem to be perfectly organized. Two avenues, First Street (7.6 meters wide) and Second Street (9.1 meters wide) run north-south through the Lower Town. They have both been "proven" through excavation, although Second Street is only documented in DK-B Area. The east-west streets are a bit more problematic. Central Street (5.5 meters wide) is the northern east-west thoroughfare in DK-G Area. It is certainly a wide, straight street, but it terminates at First, where it runs into a building wall. Eleven meters to the south of Central, another wide street joins First. This is Dikshit's Trench E. It is 3.8 meters wide, on par with Central. The size of these two streets and their propinquity suggests that, if the civic planners of Mohenjo-daro were serious about their grid town plan, they would have aligned these streets, rather than incorporating a dogleg. Mackay thinks "the town planning regulations of Mohenjo-daro were evidently stretched beyond this occasion."[4] Clearly, this dogleg complicates the grid town theory more than a bit (figure 5.2).

Piggott and Wheeler in their reconstruction of the grid town plan ignore Mackay's Central Street and place the principal east-west axis in the northern part of the site at the bottom of DK-G.[5] This is excavated only on the northern side, so we are not even certain that it is a street. There is a rough alignment between this feature and a street (9.1 meters wide) in DK-C Area, 245 meters to the east. But the street in DK-C is only exposed for 55 meters and seems to dip to the south, not head straight across the mound toward DK-G. In fact, the DK-C street might be a byway internal to the local neighborhood—no one knows.

The southern east-west street was called East, despite the fact that it cries out to be "South Street." This has not been exposed let alone proved by excavation. It is placed on the maps only because there is a gully that suggests the presence of a deep, narrow architectural depression.

In the end, there is very good evidence for First Street, a main north-south thoroughfare in the Lower Town at Mohenjo-daro. The evidence for Second Street is thin, a possibility but not quite proved. The southern east-west street is unexcavated, but a possibility. The northern east-west street, Central and Trench E, or the street at the southern edge of DK-G South, can be debated but not proved.

Inside the major blocks the streets are not well aligned. There are many doglegs and some deadends. The walls along streets and lanes may pinch in on the avenues that grow narrower and narrower, but curves are rare in the Mohenjo-daro system of roads.

While there is regularity in the layout of Mohenjo-daro, it is far from perfect. The regularity itself suggests that the founders of this city started with a clean plate, virgin soil, on which they began the construction of their metropolis. This has been very carefully addressed by Jansen, who believes that the foundations of Mohenjo-daro lie in massive platforms that were used to raise the city above the surrounding floodplain.

Platforms

Mohenjo-daro was designed in part as a city on the floodplain of a tremendously powerful, violent river. Serious flooding of the Indus River in historical times has been recorded every five to seven years. The solution to this problem at Mohenjo-daro was to build platforms to raise the buildings and streets above the floods. Jansen has developed a general model for this scheme.[6] He sees four principal functions for platforms in the Harappan context.

1. Foundations, or substructures, for building areas, as in the case of the Mound of the Great Bath.
2. Foundations, or substructures, for single buildings.
3. Substructures for elevating single buildings, in whole or part, as in House 1 in HR-A Area.
4. The often complete infilling of older, abandoned structures to form a new occupational level and surface. This was found in virtually all of the older houses at Mohenjo-daro.

The story of Mohenjo-daro begins with the original, as yet unlocated settlement. I think that the beginnings of Mohenjo-daro may be another phenomenon of the Transitional stage, admitting the possibility that there could have been a small Early Harappan site there, the plan of which was totally abandoned and submerged by the founders' settlement. As Jansen says:

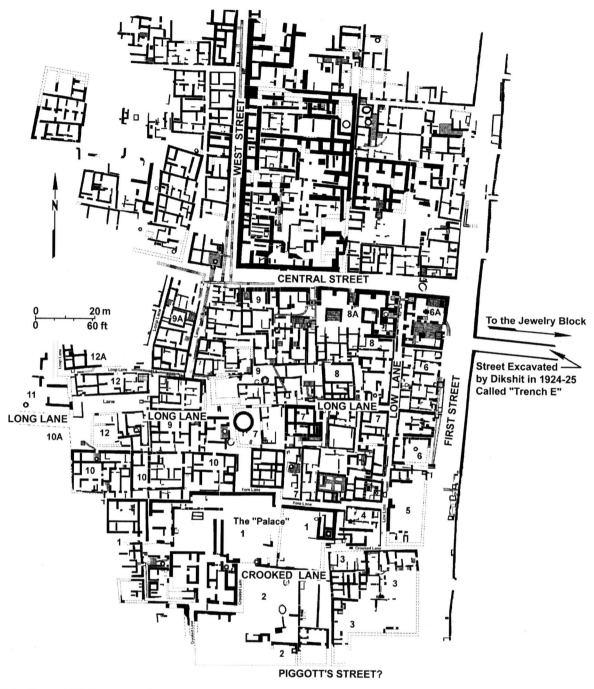

Figure 5.2 Plan of DK-G showing intersection of main streets (after Mackay 1937–38).

We are dealing with a rather small time gap of not more than 80 years around 2400 B.C. where all these elements must have been developed, most probably not in Mohenjo-daro, but in a place close enough to the alluvial plain to study the river carefully. It seems that the first urban settlement of Mohenjo-daro was constructed as a whole in a very short period of only a few years, equipped from the beginning with vertical water-supply systems such as wells, which could hardly have been constructed later when the city was already flourishing.[7]

Platforms of the Lower Town
Evidence for platforms around the Lower Town is available. In 1964 Dales found "a massive structure of mud brick with a solid, burnt brick wall. It provided a facing and

support to the mud brick structure for a length exceeding 183 meters along the western face of HR mound."[8] There is evidence for a clay or mud-brick platform at the very southern end of Mohenjo-daro, below HR Area, which was gained from a geophysical survey carried out in 1981–1982 by M. Cucarzi, who found a linear anomaly some 400 meters long which "could represent part of a clay or mud brick platform marking part of the southern limit of a constructional phase of Mohenjo-daro."[9] Finally, the deep digging at Mohenjo-daro has consistently encountered masses of mud brick, often recognized as platforms, at the lowest levels of the site.[10]

The early platforms were foundation structures that substantially raised the city above the Indus plain, out of the way of the floods. It was a massive amount of work, and a huge investment. One can assume that a laborer can move about a cubic meter of earth a day, so it must have taken approximately 4 million days of labor. This means 10,000 laborers working 400 days, or just over a year. That is a very large labor force. If it were 2,500 laborers, it would have taken 1,600 days, or about 4 years and 4 months, and that was just to put the "foundations" in place.

Interesting implications flow from the theory of platforms at Mohenjo-daro. They make it a clear that someone, or some group of people, had a plan for the entire city before they built it. This is seen most clearly in the layout of the Lower Town, with the alignment of the main avenues, First and Second Streets running north-south, with East and Central running east-west, if they can be fully confirmed. Planning on this scale, especially planning that was accompanied by the will and means to bring it into reality, is something special for the third millennium B.C. because the Harappan Civilization is nowhere better defined than at this city; we may be justified in thinking that, in some ways, it represents what it meant to be Harappan. This takes us further in the direction of contemporary thought, that ideology was the defining quality of the Harappan Civilization and that it was a definition that developed in the third millennium as a new way for people to organize themselves in terms of their social configuration and their system of beliefs and practices.

A second implication derived from Jansen's position is that the platforms would have limited the settled area of the city, which was defined by the elevated ground. This means that ancient Mohenjo-daro would have been about the size of the modern mounds and that the other traces of human habitation around them are either trash deposits or suburban communities vulnerable to flood and therefore not permanent and somehow not part of the urban core.

Several smaller points need to be made about the plat-forms. Mohenjo-daro changed over time. As the city rose higher and higher on its own debris, there was a great deal more filling and platform building that went on.[11] Rooms were filled in with alluvium and crude brick, even trash deposits, as in rooms 77–80 of House XIII in VS Area[12] or the rooms below 15 and 16 in House XIII of HR-A.[13] Providing a one-story-high podium for at least one section of a house seems to have been a well-documented part of house construction at Mohenjo-daro. The city grew vertically over time, and there is a remarkable continuity of brick walls, with the tops of old walls forming the foundations for new ones.

Mound of the Great Bath: Platforms and Retaining Walls

Marshall excavated a deep trench north of the Buddhist stupa on the Mound of the Great Bath. He found seven strata in this trench. The lowest had a low wall, adjacent pavement, and Mature Harappan pottery.[14]

This trench and the exposure of retaining walls around the Mound of the Great Bath allowed Marshall to reconstruct the rough history of the place. It is an artificial hill, probably begun in the Early Harappan–Mature Harappan Transition or the early Mature Harappan. The Mound of the Great Bath functioned as a massive platform to elevate the buildings on its top above the surrounding floodplain and the Lower Town. The Great Bath and Warehouse there were built together as a part of the first set of buildings (figure 11.8).

These were important civic facilities, and on the Mound of the Great Bath they were segregated from the Lower Town, even hidden from view. Elevating them, especially the Great Bath, above the Lower Town can be presumed to have been an important symbolic act.

Reasons to Reject Wheeler's Proposals on Indus Citadels

A central theme in the Wheeler–Piggott paradigm for the Indus Civilization is that the cities incorporated citadels, from which a ruling elite ruled a vast empire. The Mound of the Great Bath at Mohenjo-daro is thought to have been one of these citadels. It is reasonable to presume that if the Mound of the Great Bath had been effectively fortified, it would have to have been fortified all the way around. This does not appear to have been the case. For example, the Warehouse, a large storage facility of some importance, was placed on the western side of the mound. It is open to the Indus plains, vulnerable, and not a place that could be observed from the Lower Town. Thus, the notion that the "Great Granary" was on a "Citadel" makes no sense from a defensive, protectionist, point of view.

Since the Warehouse was built just after the Mound of the Great Bath had been raised, the placement of the facility would have been part of the planning and could have been set anywhere on the Mound. But it was put at the center of the western side, in perhaps the most vulnerable position from a military point of view.

The Mound of the Great Bath is manmade and built of Indus alluvium. To contain the earthen fill and inhibit erosion, the builders of the Mound of the Great Bath put a retaining wall around their "hill." This helped to keep everything in place; it also defined the Mound of the Great Bath architecturally and provided defense against floods. The retaining wall would have been a useful feature for the defense of the Mound of the Great Bath, as well. Solidly built walls like this retaining wall generally emerge as multipurpose features. But this one is an imperfect fortification, and the placement of the Warehouse suggests that this acropolis was not a citadel at all, but the place that the peoples of Mohenjo-daro built as a platform to symbolically elevate important public edifices.

Jansen sees Mohenjo-daro as defined by two Indus innovations: platforms and brick-lined wells. He believes that the location of the wells throughout the city was also planned from the beginning, a contention that can be supported. In any event, they are interesting facilities.

The Architecture of Water Management: Indus Ideology Expressed in Architecture

Water and the management of water has been proposed to have been central to the ideology of the Indus peoples. This is most fully expressed at Mohenjo-daro, but is also found at many other Indus sites, most notably Dholavira.

Well Digging

A distinguishing feature of Mature Harappan settlements is the brick-lined wells. Jansen has estimated that there were about 700 at Mohenjo-daro.[15] Brick-lined wells are also found at Harappa, Chanhu-daro, and Lothal.

Wells are lined with bricks for two reasons. First, the bricks support the earth and guard against cave-ins and erosion, especially of the well opening. Brick-lined wells also deliver clean, sweet water with a minimum of silt and other large-particle contaminants. Properly dug and maintained, brick-lined wells can deliver perfectly clear water, even on a river floodplain.

Archaeological observations trace the continuity of well location over the stratigraphic buildup of Mohenjo-daro. Courses of bricks were added to wells as the city mound grew. Also, there is no direct evidence for the construction of wells. Excavations at none of the sites with brick-lined wells have backdirt from digging or wells that cut through older, buried structures. Remarkable as it may seem, the well locations at Mohenjo-daro seem to have been laid out when the original platforms were built and were maintained over the history of the city with almost no changes. Some were abandoned, but we know of no wells newly sited and constructed after the initial platform building.

Some wells at Mohenjo-daro are as small as 60 centimeters in diameter; one was as large as 2.1 meters. The average is about 1 meter.[16] Ardeleanu-Jansen has provided the information for table 5.1 concerning the 75 wells exposed at Mohenjo-daro.[17] Some recomputation was done due to the availability of updated excavation data.[18] The GFD (or UPM) Area is not included in the study of wells.

The area served by each well and the mean distance between wells is remarkably consistent in the Lower Town; another reflection of the planning that went into Mohenjo-daro from the very beginning. A few wells were abandoned during the life of the city. Mackay suggests that this took place because someone jumped into them.[19] Dig and discover!

Table 5.1   Wells at Mohenjo-daro

Excavation Area	Excavation area (m²)	Number of wells	Area per well (m²)	Mean distance between wells (m)
Mound of the Great Bath				
SD, DM, REM	16,500	4	4,125	56.3
L and ACC	6,400	2	3,200	36.5
Total or average	22,900	6	3,662	46.4
Lower Town				
DK-G	28,000	21	1,333	36.5
DK-A-C	12,200	10	1,525	39.0
VS	13,000	10	1,300	36.0
HR	20,600	23	1,030	32.0
Moneer	7,200	5	1,440	38.2
GFD	2,000			
Total or average	83,000	69	1,326	36.3

Mackay observes that the social context of wells at Mohenjo-daro seems to have changed over time:

> In the early days of the city it is probable that the wells were private, as there seem to be no means of reaching them from the street, but later on, as the population grew, they were thrown open to public use. The rooms in which the wells were situated were, as a rule, carefully paved, and the floor in many cases was worn into deep depressions where countless water-jars had been set down.[20]

Many of these wells, especially those thought to be public, have deep grooves in the inside coping, witness to the thousands of times the well was used, ropes raising pottery vessels hand over hand as the inhabitants of the city drew their water.[21] Occasionally, low brick platforms provided seats around the well. It is not difficult to imagine knots of people, some sitting, others standing, passing the time, sharing gossip and news while waiting their turn to draw water.

The rationale for lining wells with bricks and the well-digging technology that the Indus peoples may have employed is discussed in Ardeleanu-Jansen.[22] The wells were just one element in the water management system of Mohenjo-daro. The drainage system was another element.

The Drainage System and Domestic Water Facilities

One of the most remarkable features of Mohenjo-daro and several other Mature Harappan settlements (e.g., Harappa, Kalibangan, Nausharo, Chanhu-daro, Allahdino, Dholavira, Lothal) is the drainage system. At Mohenjo-daro the streets and lanes in all of the neighborhoods were provided with drainage.[23] There was also provision for the management of wastewater inside the houses, with intramural drains, vertical drain pipes in the walls, chutes through walls to the streets, and drains from bathing floors into street drains. Mohenjo-daro receives less than 13 centimeters of rain per year, probably about what it received in the third millennium. This would not seem to be enough rain to justify such an elaborate system.

At Mohenjo-daro drains were found at all levels of the site. They seem, therefore, to have been made at the very beginning of the Indus Civilization and may be another technology of these peoples that was developed in the important Transitional Stage. The street drains at all sites were generally made of baked brick, although the one at Allahdino is of stone.

In SD Area of Mohenjo-daro there are some drains where the bottom was made of gypsum and lime plaster with sides of baked brick. In most instances ordinary baked brick was used, but specially dressed brick was noted in some drains of SD and DK Areas. Specially shaped bricks were used to form the gently rounded corners of drains. The integrity of the drains was achieved by closely fitting the bricks with a bit of mud mortar. Dressed bricks made the fit even better.

Drains were often reused from building period to building period at Mohenjo-daro. This was done by simply raising the walls with more bricks. At the southern end of First Street in DK-G the walls of a drain were repaired and raised at least twice. In its last construction phase this drain was 42 centimeters wide, but 2 meters deep in places.[24] Most of the drains had brick or stone covers because they were under the street or ground surface. Open drains have been found along the sides of streets, a common feature of contemporary villages in Pakistan and northwestern India. The most frequent cover was simply an ordinary baked brick laid flat across the sidewalls, although bricks laid on edge across the channel are also well documented. The wider drains were covered with large limestone blocks quarried from the nearby Rohri Hills. These blocks are especially common on the Mound of the Great Bath.

The drains were mostly hidden underground, out of the way of the traffic. Mackay estimates that the average depth was in the range of 46 to 60 centimeters, but some drains were very close to or at the surface. Limestone drain covers in SD Area sometimes had a distinct polish on their upper side—"polish that must have been caused by the feet of passers-by."[25] We should imagine the tops of these covering blocks right at ground level, some slightly buried, and that as the earth of the street surface changed and moved, some were periodically exposed and the slight polish of wear was applied to them.

Small settling pools and traps were built into the system of drainage. This allowed coarse sediment and other materials to drop out of the flow in places were it could be periodically collected.

> That the drains of Mohenjo-daro were cleaned out periodically is attested by the little heaps of greenish-gray sand that we frequently found alongside them. The more finely levigated clays would be readily carried off by the rush of water whereas the heavier particles of sand were deposited.[26]

The wider drains, or culverts, could not be covered in an ordinary way. Sometimes special bricks of extra length were baked.[27] The corbelled arch was used for the culverts. The Great Bath was provided with the largest of all the Mature Harappan culverts (figure 5.3).

Water from inside houses was sometimes led directly

Figure 5.3 Elevation of a culvert with a corbelled arch (after Marshall 1931i)

into a street drain, but there are other facilities that were used as well: brick-lined cesspits and pottery jars along the streets. But it was clearly important for the water from bathing floors to be moved out of the home and for it not to be allowed to sink directly into the ground. This suggests that the water from bathing (and other domestic activities) was polluted and dirty beyond the simple scientific sense, leading to the close connection with ideology.

Bathing Facilities

One of the most common features of a house at Mohenjo-daro was a special platform for bathing (figure 5.4). These are usually on the order of 1.5 meters on a side, sometimes not square, but always rectilinear. The bricks of the floor were very carefully prepared, sawn and ground to shape, with right angles where faces met and smoothed upper surfaces. This was specialized, careful work, expensive in terms of time, but then the jobs were relatively small in scale. The bricks varied in size, even within a single platform. A raised rim around the platform was achieved by ringing the platforms with a course of bricks on edge. The surfaces of these bathing platforms were slightly tilted so that water would run to a corner and out of the bathing area through a drain in the wall.

Not only were the floors of these platforms sloped, they were very smooth, probably ground down after all of the bricks had been fitted to give a seamless surface. Then they were coated with a plaster of lime and brick dust that was polished by the plasterer and the feet of the users.[28]

Bathing facilities are also found in abundance at Harappa, where they conform to the patterns outlined here. Somewhat different is the line of thirteen bathing platforms on the High Mound at Lothal. This seems to have been a civic facility, open to many, but not likely all, of the relatively few people at this small site.

These bathing platforms seem to be the chief source of water that went into the drainage system of Mohenjo-daro, except, of course, for those few days when there was a really good rain.

Privies

The issue of latrines, or privies, in the Indus Civilization begins with Marshall's discussion of the vertical terra-cotta pipe in the wall of a house:

> From its small size it is clear that this vertical pipe was meant to convey fluid only, not solids; and this seems to be true of the house drains of Mohenjo-daro. . . . [However,] in House XLIX of HR Area, Section B, Block 7 privies with seats (as to the character of which there can be no question) are directly connected with brick drains of the usual type, which must therefore have been designed for sewage of any kind, solid or fluid.[29]

There is one more privy as well, but that is all, and the drains of Mohenjo-daro seem not to emerge as conduits for solid waste. There are just too many good points against it, as noted by Mackay (figure 5.5).[30]

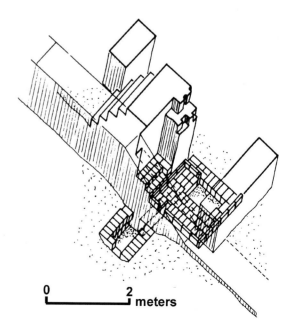

0   2 meters

Figure 5.4 Bathing platform at Mohenjo-daro (after Jansen 1993)

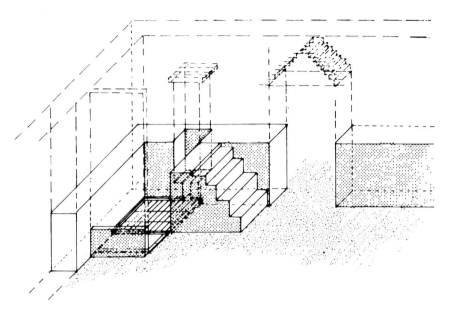

Figure 5.5   Privy in DK-G at Mohenjo-daro (after Jansen 1993)

In a discussion of triangular terra-cotta cakes, Wheeler once said: "Their great abundance, especially in drains, would be consistent with a use in the toilet, either as flesh rubbers or as an equivalent to toilet paper."[31] Hummm!

The Indus Civilization and Water: Summary
Water was important in the Indus Civilization in two ways. From a practical point of view, it sustained the life of humans, plants, and animals. But it also played an important symbolic role as an essential part of the Indus ideology. Clean, fresh water was provided to urban peoples from deep, brick-lined wells. Dirty, polluted water was moved out of the houses of urban peoples by an expensive system of drains. The Great Bath at Mohenjo-daro was a special place for the ablutions of elites.

Residential Architecture: Mohenjo-daro
Most of the buildings of the Lower Town of Mohenjo-daro seem to have been used as residences. Some of them, perhaps even most, may have served other purposes as well, but the Lower Town is the part of Mohenjo-daro where the people lived and worked. The buildings there were the prime setting for these activities. Marshall offers a vivid, well-illustrated picture of two buildings that might have been houses.[32]

There are several recurring features of the residences at many Mature Harappan sites. The best preserved are found at Mohenjo-daro, and extensive use is made of these data. But there are also residences at other sites, and they will serve to broaden these observations.

Extensive Use of Baked Brick
The standard baked brick at Mohenjo-daro was 28 by 14 by 7 centimeters. The 1:2:4 ratio is one of the most efficient proportions for laying bricks and was an improvement over the Early Harappan 1:2:3 standard. The largest brick found at Mohenjo-daro is 50.65 by 26.25 by 8.75 centimeters. It was incorporated into a wall of the Late Period on the Mound of the Great Bath and may originally have been used to cover a drain.[33] The smallest brick is 23.75 by 10.875 by 5 centimeters.

Baked brick was used at Harappa, but there were many structures of unbaked brick as well.

> Side by side with burnt brick middle class houses of the Intermediate Period dwellings of the poor were made of mud and mud brick, e.g., Houses 1–4 in Trench I, Mound D. Sometimes in the better class houses mud bricks were used in alternate courses along with burnt brick masonry. Mud brick was also used for raising solid terraces to guard against the danger of floods. Where used in masonry it was always well molded, and once the walls were plastered over with mud and straw, no distinction would be possible between the two.[34]

The use of sun-dried brick at Mohenjo-daro was different. There are no complete structures made of this material. Sun-dried brick was also extensively used as fill there.

Substantial Buildings at Mohenjo-daro
The buildings of the Lower Town are also generally substantial and solidly built. Walls with a thickness of a meter

or two are common. The very latest levels of the site have shabby squatters' quarters. Mackay informs us that this was generally true at Mohenjo-daro.

> The sizes of the bricks tell us nothing, and it is practically impossible to distinguish between the brickwork of the early and intermediate periods, the brickwork of the Late Period is as a rule quite unmistakable . . . the majority of the rooms and buildings at Mohenjo-daro are out of truth in the Late Period, and this feature is noticeable in even the largest buildings.[35]

Vats says something similar about the late architecture at Harappa:

> During the Late Period, however, most of the foundations of numerous fragmentary walls seem to have been laid on any kind of slipshod debris, possibly as a majority of them had nothing more than a thatched roof to support. Indeed, this is exemplified by the Late III dwellings in the extension of Pits I and II in Mound AB where a considerable quantity of charcoal of pinewood rafters, bamboos and reeds was brought to light.[36]

More Than One Floor

The thickness of the walls of the houses at Mohenjo-daro and the presence of stairways leading up (to open sky today) seem to imply that many, perhaps most, of these buildings had an upper story. The stairs could have led to the roof, but the thickness of the walls argues against this, at least as the general pattern. The number of floors cannot be determined in an accurate way, but one story above the ground floor can be hypothesized securely. It is entirely possible that the general pattern was a ground floor, another with living space, and then a roof. But some of the larger buildings could have had two, even three, additional floors below the roof.

Hearths, Kitchens, and House Fires

The frequency of fires at Mohenjo-daro is a minor, but intriguing, topic. There is much evidence for burning at Mohenjo-daro and fires consumed many of the buildings.[37] Additional information on fire at Mohenjo-daro comes from Dikshit's report on his excavation near the "Jewelry Block": "The destruction of the latest city in this quarter seems to have been caused by fire. This was evident from the existence of stratified layers of ashes, alternating with debris of fallen structures."[38] These statements can be contrasted to Mackay: "Evidence for houses having been burnt out is extremely rare and accidental fires were carefully guarded against."[39]

It is difficult to know exactly what the frequency of fires was at Mohenjo-daro, and an examination of the standing remains is not really helpful, given postexcavation cleanup and conservation. Fresh digging is needed to resolve the issue, but it is two diggers against one right now. If there were a significant number of fires this could be contrasted to the small number of hearths.

Marshall notes only three doubtful hearths at Mohenjo-daro.[40] Mackay informs us that these fireplaces were simple platforms of brick, slightly raised, usually placed along one side of a room. "In one house in HR Area there was an arrangement for boiling water; the vessels were set on a high brick stand with an ample space beneath for fuel."[41]

Here is an interesting situation. Very few hearths on the ground floor, but abundant evidence for house fires. If the hearths and kitchens were not on the ground floor, then they must have been on the parts of the buildings with wooden floors. We can be certain that the hearths would not have been laid on the bare wooden floors. A base of bricks, possibly several courses thick over a good area and covered with mud plaster, that baked to terra-cotta through use would have been there. But, over time, these open fire hearths so near the wooden floors were a bad combination. They would not pass code today. No matter what the precautions, over the long run they were very dangerous and frequent house fires resulted.

In this case, if house fires were a result of this pattern of living, why did the people of Mohenjo-daro persist in their "suicidal" ways? A difficult question, but the situation is reasonably clear: frequent house fires and almost no hearths. The hearths and therefore the cooking seem to have been done upstairs.

Windows, Doors, Roofs, and Other Features

There are some windows in Mature Harappan buildings. Terra-cotta fragments that look like grilles could be "window" filling. Mackay observes that the trick at Mohenjo-daro was to keep the heat out, just as we do with cold, and windows work counter to this.[42]

There are a few door sockets, but not as many as one would expect if every door had one. Lack of door sockets may indicate wooden doors and frames with sockets in the frame.[43] Dales found a portion of a door frame in his 1964 excavations at Mohenjo-daro but made no mention of a socket (figure 5.6).[44]

The only coherent discussion of roofs on Mature Harappan buildings deals with those from Mohenjo-daro. Marshall opts for flat roofs set on timbers for all of his buildings at Mohenjo-daro, as does Mackay.[45]

There is no direct evidence for furniture although a number of individuals depicted on the stamp seals sit on a

Figure 5.6 Wooden door jam from Mohenjo-daro (after Dales 1982: 103)

kind of dais. There appears what may be a chair on a seal, and one or two figurines depict furniture. The high dish-on-stand suggests to me that it is a raised plate and that the people who used them sat on the ground, probably cross-legged with this utensil in front of them.

Architecture of the Lower Town: A. Sarcina's Study
There is a special study of the residential architecture at Mohenjo-daro that was undertaken by A. Sarcina.[46] Her study of the ground-floor architecture found that there were five recurring house plans in the city, which she identifies with color names (figure 5.7). Table 5.2 lists the number of occurrences as well as the sizes of each building type.

Table 5.2 Sarcina's counts for houses of different types at Mohenjo-daro

Model	Number of buildings	Size (m²)
Yellow model	58	104.27
Red model	42	97.35
Green model	6	183.60
Brown model	4	106.70
Blue model	2	130.42
Total	112	

Note: After Sarcina (1979: 435).

SUMMARY: THE ARCHITECTURE OF THE INDUS CIVILIZATION

In some ways the substance of the Indus Civilization is its architecture, and the artifacts found within these contexts. This chapter has attempted to give an overview of architecture, not as an architect would necessarily

view it, but from the perspective of an archaeologist. Such topics as town planning, civic and domestic drainage, platforms, and well digging have provided a glimpse into the subject as have discussion of bricks, roofs, fires, and doorways. More is found in the individual site surveys on buildings, town planning, and architecture generally. Mohenjo-daro is the defining settlement for the Mature Harappan and Indus urbanization, so a special tour of the ancient city highlights and deepens the discussion of architecture and other qualities of the Mature Harappan.

NOTES

1. Vats 1940: 12.
2. Vats 1940: 15.
3. Wheeler 1968: 26; Piggott 1950: 151; Rao 1973: 11–23.
4. Mackay 1937–38: 29.
5. Piggott 1950: 152; Wheeler 1968: 36.
6. Jansen 1987, 1993a, 1994: 269.
7. Jansen 1987: 15.
8. Dales 1968b: 60.
9. Cucarzi 1984: 195.
10. Mackay 1937–38: 42–44.
11. Jansen 1985: 12.
12. Marshall 1931b: 21.
13. Marshall 1031b: 19
14. Marshall 1931i: 124–27. As an aside: Wheeler criticized Marshall for his lack of attention to stratigraphy, but here Marshall tells a coherent story of the buildup of the mound, and the subsequent order of building during the Indus and Buddhist periods. He even places his Arabic strata numbers in small circles; very Wheelerian.
15. Jansen 1989b: 252.
16. Mackay 1948: 38.
17. Ardeleanu-Jansen 1993: 1.
18. Jansen 1993a: 266.
19. Mackay 1948: 39.
20. Mackay 1948: 38.
21. Mackay 1931d: 270.
22. Ardeleanu-Jansen 1993.
23. For general discussion, see Mackay (1931d: 277–82).
24. Mackay 1937–38: 27, 29, 31, 34, and so forth.
25. Mackay 1931d: 278.
26. Mackay 1937–38: 27.
27. Mackay 1937–38: 91, 428.
28. Mackay 1931d: 273.
29. Marshall 1931b: 21.
30. Mackay 1931d: 281.
31. Wheeler 1968: 93.
32. Marshall 1931c: 18–22, pls. IV–VI.
33. Mackay 1931d: 267.
34. Vats 1940: 12.
35. Mackay 1931d: 262.
36. Vats 1940: 12.

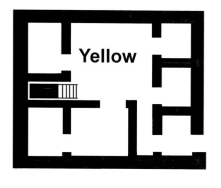

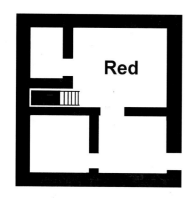

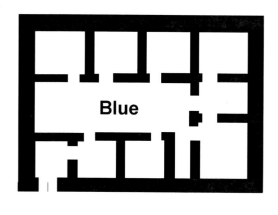

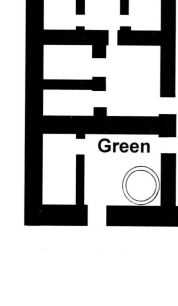

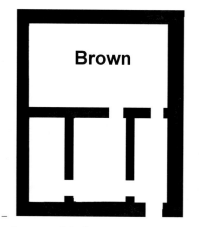

Figure 5.7   Sarcina's models for Mohenjo-daro houses (after Sarcina 1978–79)

37. Marshall 1931c: 15.
38. Dikshit 1924–25: 69.
39. Mackay 1937–38: 163.
40. Marshall 1931b: 16.
41. Mackay 1931d: 276.

42. Mackay 1948: 27.
43. Mackay 1948: 28.
44. Dales 1982: 103.
45. Mackay 1931d: 277.
46. Sarcina 1978–79, 1979.

CHAPTER 6

The Art of the Indus Civilization

INTRODUCTION

The study of the art of the Indus Civilization has not been fully developed, making it one of the most important areas of scholarship on this civilization open for growth. I am an archaeologist, not an art historian, and will not pretend to be one. What follows is therefore a statement on Indus art from an archaeological and anthropological perspective.

HUMAN SCULPTURE IN THE INDUS CIVILIZATION

There is a modest amount of human sculpture from Indus sites, mainly Harappa and Mohenjo-daro. There are no examples of life-size works of art from the Indus Civilization as we know it today. The following is a description of the principal pieces of human sculpture.

Human Sculpture from Harappa

The Red Jasper Male Torso from Harappa

One of the best-known art objects—and the most controversial—from an Indus site is a red jasper torso found by Vats at Harappa during the 1928–1929 field season (figure 6.1). The find was made in the vicinity of the circular brick threshing floors to the south of the great Granary and was ascribed by Vats to stratum III, the modern Period 3C (c. 2200–1900 B.C.).[1]

The piece is 9.5 centimeters high, broken at the legs, with the head and both arms missing. It is a striking frontal nude. The genitalia seem to have been carefully modeled, although they have been defaced. This torso was carved in a natural, well-rounded way with "the refined and wonderfully truthful modeling of the fleshy parts."[2]

There are holes for the attachment of the head and arms, but none are apparent for the legs. Prominent circular indentations, probably made by a tube drill, are located on the front of each shoulder. Their function is unknown, but it has been suggested that they were somehow related to the way a garment might have been affixed to the original sculpture or for the inlay of ornaments. Holes for the breast nipples are apparently intended for inlay.

Vats insisted from the beginning that the piece should be attributed to the Mature Harappan in spite of other opinion that it was best attributed to an historical era. As evidence for a prehistoric date, Vats cited the use of the tube drill, that it was made in pieces (not a practice in historical India for small sculpture), and that there is no piece of historic sculpture made of the same material. The pronounced abdomen, in relation to the chest, is characteristically Indian. There is a Gupta occupation of Mound AB at Harappa, but it is well removed from the find spot on Mound F. Vats says: "And let me state at the outset that, although a large area—larger than anywhere else at Harappa—has been explored on this Mound [F], not a single object which is not referable to the prehistoric period has ever been found on it."[3]

In a long footnote to the Vats preliminary report, Marshall counters the excavator's arguments for an early date. He attributed it to an historic age, possibly the Gupta Period, and concludes with a reference to this object in relationship to other Harappan sculpture: "They are, without exception, crude, archaic and lacking in anatomical correctness, whereas the figure in question is anatomically correct and the work of a sculptor in possession of an advanced technique."[4]

Figure 6.1   Red torso from Harappa (after Vats 1940)

Figure 6.2 Zebu seal number 337 (after Marshall 1931i)

Over time Marshall's position softened somewhat. Noting the exquisite portrayal of the zebu on Mohenjo-daro seal number 337, he said: "Experienced sculptors whom I have consulted on the subject take the view that an artist who could engrave the seal in question (no. 337) would have had little difficulty in carving the statuette; archaeologists will probably take another view and prefer to wait for further discoveries before committing themselves" (figure 6.2).[5] Wheeler considered the date of this torso to be "disputed."[6]

The torso is a small masterpiece, not comparable to any other Harappan art (seal number 337 not withstanding). The find spot is impeccably documented and no one has challenged Vats's assertion that Mound F was not reoccupied after Mature Harappan. It seems reasonable, then, to accede to his judgment on this magnificent piece and use it as an example of the heights to which the Indus artist could rise.

Gray Stone Torso of a Dancer from Harappa
Sahni found the broken torso of a male dancing figure, made of dark gray stone, during his excavations at Harappa (figure 6.3). Curiously, this statuette does not figure in his preliminary reports on the work there, but it is a significant piece of Indus sculpture. Vats informs us that the piece was found on Mound F in an Intermediate I stratum, which is the Great Granary area associated with Building IV on the central-aisle side.[7] It is about 150 meters north of the spot where the red jasper torso was found. Everything in this part of the site can be safely assigned to the Mature Harappan.

This torso is 9.9 centimeters high, with the head, arms, and legs all missing. The legs have been broken off, but there are holes for the arms and head, just as with the red jasper torso. Posed as a dancer, his right leg is firmly fixed, the left lifted in movement. The torso is nicely twisted, which gives it a sense of movement. Holes on the back of the neck were probably intended to hold hair in place, suggesting that the face was looking almost directly at the ground. Nothing remains of the arms to suggest their position, but Marshall's reconstruction of the pose may not be far off the mark (figure 6.4). Wheeler considered this piece also to be "disputed" as to the period in which it was made, but he agreed with Marshall that there is an attractive historical link between it and historical "Dancing Siva."[8]

On examination, the gray stone torso of the dancer has a naturalism that does not compare to the red jasper torso, but it is still a credible interpretation of a dancing figure. It does have life and movement and should be placed in the top rank of Harappan art. Except for the bronze dancing girl, it is filled with more life than anything from Mohenjo-daro.

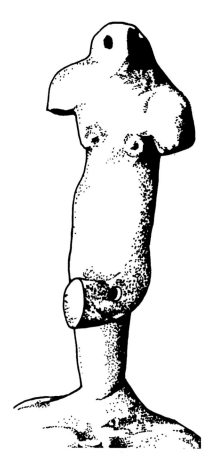

Figure 6.3 Gray stone dancing figure from Harappa (after Vats 1940)

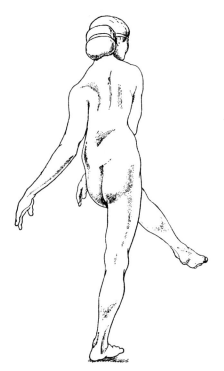

Figure 6.4 Reconstruction of the gray dancing figure from Harappa (after Marshall 1931i)

Human Sculpture from Mohenjo-daro

Much of the sculpture from Mohenjo-daro was described just as it came from the earth in the preliminary reports that were published annually through the field season of 1936–1937. Ardeleanu-Jansen has reviewed the sculpture.[9] The seven principal pieces are discussed here (figure 6.5).

Bronze Dancing Girl from Mohenjo-daro (HR-5721)

The most captivating piece of art from an Indus site is probably the bronze dancing girl from HR Area at Mohenjo-daro (figure 6.5). She was found in a Late-level house of Block 7 by Sahni during the 1926–1927 field season.[10] The house is a small structure, deep within the urban maze of the southwestern quarter of the city. She is 10.8 centimeters high and was cast in bronze using the lost wax process.

The figure is a very thin young woman, standing upright, with her head tilted slightly back, her left leg bent at the knee. There is little sense of flesh on the body or anatomy to the joints, which is a stylistic feature shared with some later Indian sculpture. Her right arm is bent, with her hand placed provocatively on the back of the hip, the thumb outside a clenched fist. The left arm rests slightly bent on the thigh of her left leg. The thumb and forefinger of this hand form a circle, and it is apparent that she once held a small object, possibly a baton of some kind.

She is naked, except for some adornments. Around her neck is a small necklace with three large pendant beads. On her left arm she wears twenty-four or twenty-five bangles, which would have severely restricted the mobility of the elbow in a living person. The right arm has four bangles, two at the wrist and two above the elbow. Her hair is

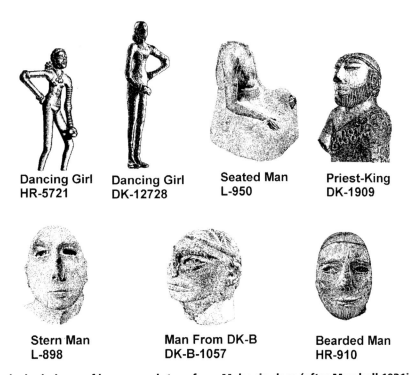

| Dancing Girl HR-5721 | Dancing Girl DK-12728 | Seated Man L-950 | Priest-King DK-1909 |

| Stern Man L-898 | Man From DK-B DK-B-1057 | Bearded Man HR-910 |

Figure 6.5 The seven principal pieces of human sculpture from Mohenjo-daro (after Marshall 1931i and Mackay 1937–38)

0   5
cm

Figure 6.6   The Priest-King of Mohenjo-daro, DK-1909

coifed into a kind of loose bun, held in place along the back of her head much the same as some Indian women wear their hair today. The artist has rendered this feature in detail.

Whether this small statuette actually portrays a dancer is open to question. Only the pose seems to convey this. If she was a dancer, it would foreshadow later Indian sculpture, which is much influenced by this theme.

Some think that the broad nose and large lips of the dancing girl can be used to indicate a racial affiliation: Dravidian;[11] Nubian;[12] Baluchi Proto-Australoid.[13] Piggott even ventured: "When we are describing the Harappa culture we shall, I think, recognize a Kulli girl in a foreign city."[14] Phenotypic features on such a stylized piece of art are difficult to interpret, and there is every chance that she is representative of women of one of the Indus peoples.

Marshall referred to this bronze statuette as "a small figurine of rather rough workmanship."[15] But he did catch something special in the figure as well: "It gives a vivid impression of the young aboriginal nautch girl, her hand on hip in a half-impudent posture, and legs slightly forward, as she beats time to the music with her legs and feet. . . . The modeling of the back, hips and buttocks is quite effective."[16]

On detailed examination of the bronze dancing girl from HR Area one sees a subtlety to the expression and pose that defies description and cannot be captured by the

camera. In spite of the stylized, even abstract, nature of the figure, there is a sense of "impudence" as Marshall noted, certainly youthful superiority, self-confidence, even arrogance. In the 1973 autobiographical television film *Sir Mortimer Wheeler, the Archaeologist,* the principal described his favorite statuette.

> There is her little Baluchi-style face with pouting lips and insolent look in the eye. She's about fifteen years old I should think, not more, but she stands there with bangles all the way up her arm and nothing else on. A girl perfectly, for the moment, perfectly confident of herself and the world. There's nothing like her, I think, in ancient art.[17]

We may not be certain that she was a dancer, but she was good at what she did and she knew it.

A Second Bronze Dancing Girl from Mohenjo-daro (DK-12728)

There is a second bronze dancing girl from Mohenjo-daro, found by Mackay in his final full season of 1930–1931. It was associated with Late level II of DK-G Area, Block 9, House X, Room 81, an undistinguished building just off Central Street. The preservation is not as fine as the first dancing girl, but, as Mackay observes, "Despite the damage by corrosion it is clear that the workmanship and finish of this later figure is inferior to that found earlier."[18]

The Priest-King of Mohenjo-daro (DK-1909)

Excepting possibly the Mahayogi seal (also known as "Proto-Siva"), nothing has come to symbolize the Indus Civilization better than the so-called priest-king from Mohenjo-daro (figure 6.6). This "steatite" bust was found by Dikshit during the 1925–1926 season in DK-B Area, Chamber 1, Block 2, 1.37 meters below surface.[19] This chamber was a small enclosure with some curious parallel walls that Mackay suggested might have enclosed the hypocaust for an ancient *hammam* (sauna). The priest-king was in one of the small passages between the parallel walls, and, as Mackay says: "This could hardly have been the place for such an object: it probably rolled here when the walls fell in."[20]

This piece can be attributed to the Late Period at Mohenjo-daro. It is broken at the bottom and survives to only 18 centimeters in height. A toga-like garment is draped over the left shoulder and under the right arm. The garment is covered in the trefoil design, found on a number of other objects of the Indus Civilization. It also occurs in Mesopotamia and Central Asia. The trefoil is interspersed with occasional circles. The trefoils and circles were left roughened on the interior, to allow a red paste filling to adhere. One hole is present below each ear, apparently intended to hold a necklace. The back of the head has been smoothed; Mackay suggests "broken."[21] This is possible but it might also be that the sculpture was intended to be placed in a niche with a sloping back, and this unseen portion of the work was created to allow it to sit farther back than it could have with a full head of hair.

The nose is straight and broken, but does not seem to have dominated the face. The unusual eyes appear to be partially closed, or hooded, but are not of an "eastern physical type," according to Mackay.[22] One shell eye inlay survived. "Rai Bahadur Ramaprasad Chanda has ascertained that the half-closed eyes concentrated on the tip of the nose proclaim this figure to be a yogi."[23] The ears are fashioned rather crudely as simple C shapes, characteristic of Harappan sculpture. In fact, they are out of place with the other physical features of the priest-king, which are far more sophisticated in their representation.

The hair is parted in the middle and kept in place by a simple band, which hangs down the back of the head to below the shoulders. There is no bun of hair at the back of the head. The figure's beard is close cropped. Some suggest that there is a mustache,[24] but Wheeler declares the upper lip to have been shaved, which is probably wrong.[25]

Priest-King Not Finished   The priest-king may not be a finished work of art. As seen in figure 6.6, the stone of the upper lip has been left slightly thicker than the cheek. The lip is thus on the same plane as the beard, but no attempt was made to portray the mustache hair. The raised mustache area is smooth, and it seems that the artist stopped working prior to carving the mustache hair lines. This sense of being unfinished is also seen at the point where the beard meets the skin of the face. The instrument used to create the beard hair lines strayed across the raised boundary for the beard and disfigured the cheek. These stray work lines were not smoothed away, as they would have been in a fully finished work. This feature is visible in figure 6.6, and runs counter to Mackay's claim that "the general finish of this head is exceptionally good."[26]

Neither a Priest nor a King, Let Alone Both   The suggestion that this work of art portrays a priest was first made by Mackay. Marshall mentions this piece as a possible "king-priest," but Wheeler seems to have coined "priest-king," a notion perfectly in line with his vision of the Harappan Civilization.[27] That the person portrayed here was either a priest or a king, let alone someone who held both positions in Harappan life, is without foundation. Nor can it be demonstrated that it is a portrait or even a representation of a real person.

Ardeleanu-Jansen's Reconstruction   Ardeleanu-Jansen has created an interesting reconstruction of the priest-king as a statue of a seated man, with his left leg raised and bent at the knee (figure 6.7).[28] This is a posture assumed by other statuary found at Mohenjo-daro; one of which I have named the "Seated Man," another, the "Sad Man," as well as figures from Bactria (figure 6.8).

Parpola's Thoughts   A. Parpola attempts to demonstrate that the robe of the priest-king is something called the *tarpya*, found in Vedic ritual and said to be the garment of the divine king Varuna.[29] Parpola postulates that this statue is a representation of a seated deity, which had an elaborate, changeable headdress of the type he proposes is found on the Mahayogi seal.[30]

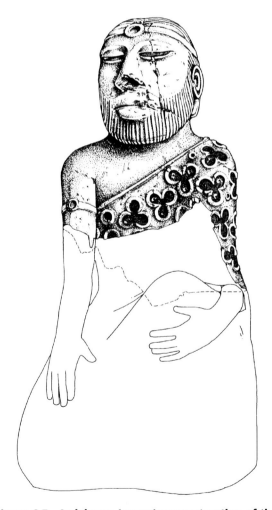

Figure 6.7 Ardeleanu-Jansen's reconstruction of the Priest-King (after Ardeleanu-Jansen 1991)

Figure 6.8   Vase from Bactria with men dressed as the Seated Man (L.950) and possibly the Priest-King (after Ardeleanu-Jansen 1991)

The Man from DK-B (DK-B-1057)

One of the finds from DK-B Area at Mohenjo-daro is a brown limestone bust of a male (figure 6.5). It comes from Block 5, Room 20 of DK-B and was found 0.96 meters below ground surface in a Late level of the site.[31] The bust was cleanly broken at the neck and is not severely weathered, although the nose is defaced. It is 14.5 centimeters high. The expression is not animated, but if viewed from the left, he appears to be scowling. The chin is short, comparing well with the Bearded Man from HR Area and the Stern Man of L Area, but not with the priest-king. The face has no beard, but the hair is depicted with the herringbone pattern that suggests a wavy quality, like that of the Bearded Man from HR Area. The hair was placed in a bun at the back of the head and held in place by a fillet. This was either tied in a bow or used in conjunction with a barrette, or possibly two pins. There are no bands extending down from the fillet on the back of the head. The ears are prominent and simple C shapes, much like the other sculpture from Mohenjo-daro, comparing well with the priest-king. The eyes are ovate, somewhat narrower than those of the Bearded Man from HR Area, but much wider than the priest-king's.

The Bearded Man from HR Area (HR-910)

In 1925–1926 a well-preserved limestone head was found by Hargreaves in House I of HR-A Area, a large building just off Deadman Lane (figure 6.5). The head was 2 meters below ground surface in a Late Period context. The building is an interesting structure, unconventional in plan; it had been suggested that was a temple.[32] HR-910 was one of two human sculptures found in this building, the second was found in pieces (HR 163/193/226) and was called the Sad Man of HR-A.

HR-910 is a well-preserved piece that has been fully described by Mackay.[33] It survives to 17.5 centimeters high and has no trace of color or other finish. Some of its fea-

tures contrast with those of the priest-king. The mass of this head is almost as big as the entire priest-king, as it survives today. An attempt had been made to represent wavy hair, and it is quite striking. Clearly seen on the left side of the sculpture, the hair was long and had been arranged in a bun at the back of the head and held in place with a string fillet and a small hairpin with a round top. The priest-king had short-cropped straight hair, not held in a bun.

The head has a short beard, and the upper lip seems definitely to have been shaved. The mouth is held in a slight smile; the lips, which are not full, are slightly pursed. The nose is of medium size, but broken. This man's ears are also portrayed in a very simple way, being almost closed ovals, rather than the more usual C. The almond-shaped eyes, originally provided with inlay, are in distinct contrast to the heavily lidded eyes of the priest-king. HR-910 is more lifelike than the priest-king, less formal; and the overall sense of this head is one of attempted portraiture.

The Seated Man (L-950)

A headless seated male statue made of gray alabaster was found by Mackay in L Area on the southern half of the Mound of the Great Bath.[34] It has been attributed to the Late Period (figure 6.5).

This seated figure survives to 29.2 centimeters in height. Based on the thickness of the clothing around the waist, Mackay hypothesized that he was wearing a thick, kilt-like garment, which was covered by a thinner garment or shawl that went over the left shoulder and under the right arm, just as with the priest-king. The left arm is at the outer side of the left leg, which is raised and bent at the knee. The right hand rests on the right knee. The hands are crudely and ineptly rendered. A "rope" of hair hangs down the back, asymmetrically to the right. "A squarish projection at the back of the head is evidently intended to represent a knot of hair. It is, however, unfinished and shows the chisel marks of the preliminary stone dressing."[35]

This is the one statue from Mohenjo-daro that clearly is seated and costumed in the same manner as those seen in Bactrian art (figure 6.8), and the pose has been proposed by Ardeleanu-Jansen for the priest-king. This admits the possibility that the Mohenjo-daro representations are of Bactrians. The men on the Bactrian vase are "floating" in the sky above other men behind plows being pulled by *Bos taurus*, not the Indian zebu. Everyone looks perfectly at home. Of course, the dress could be Harappan and the Bactrian vase could represent "Harappans" floating in the sky above the plowmen. But nowhere else in the art of the Mature Harappan do we find this form of dress, so the balance tips a bit toward the notion that the Seated Man from L Area, and the priest-king, if Ardeleanu-Jansen is correct, represent Bactrians at Mohenjo-daro in the Late Period there. This might be late enough to somehow figure in the contacts between the Indus Civilization and the Bactria-Margiana Archaeological Complex, and the Middle Asian Interaction sphere (see chapter 12).

The Stern Man (L-898)
Mackay found a second piece of statuary during his first season of excavation at Mohenjo-daro (1926–1927), here called the Stern Man from L Area (figure 6.5).[36] This is a yellow limestone piece found 60 centimeters below the ground surface in Chamber 77. It, too, comes from the Late Period.

The head survives to 19.7 centimeters high and is beardless. The figure is thought to be a male based on the way in which the hair has been portrayed: It is arranged in a bun at the back, held in place by a fillet extending around from the front, just as in the Bearded Man of HR Area. Though there is not as much detail present in the Stern Man, the handling of the hair bun is very similar on both pieces; close enough to guess the probable gender. The mouth is full and straight, without expression. The nose is broken, but appears to have been carved in a fashion not unlike the other sculpture from Mohenjo-daro. The eyes are hollow, although they were drilled to take an inlay of some kind. The bust is expressionless; a real poker face. The ear is again, a simple crescent, matching that of the Bearded Man of HR Area. If they were properly studied, it might be determined that these two heads, the Bearded Man and Stern Man, were created by the same hand.

Human Figurines of the Indus Civilization
The human terra-cotta figurines of the Mature Harappan are varied in style, size, and theme. There are both males and females, as well as some examples whose gender can-

not be determined. C. Jarrige is the expert on terra-cotta figurines of the Indus Age. One of the most distinctive terra-cotta figurines of the Mature Harappan is female, with a fan at the back of the head, sometimes with a basket, pannier-like container at one or both sides of the head (figure 6.9). This type is found at both Mohenjo-daro and Harappa, but is rarely encountered outside these urban centers. These females may be equipped with a girdle around the waist, or even a kind of miniskirt. (Perhaps an early precursor to the style of the 1960s?) Many of these figurines are bedecked with jewels and necklaces.

Most of the figurines are loaded with jewelry, which is sometimes cleverly portrayed with little effort. In the

Figure 6.9   A classic terra-cotta figurine of a female from Mohenjo-daro (after Marshall 1931i)

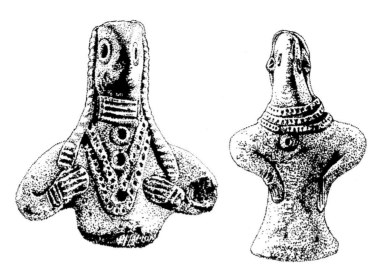

Figure 6.10   Kulli-style human terra-cotta figurines (after Possehl 1986)

longest of the strings worn by the figure shown in Pl. XCIV, 14, each bead is represented separately by a pellet of clay. The highly ornamental collar worn by this figure looks a most uncomfortable affair. A similar collar, if anything a little higher, is seen on no. 1 on the same Plate.[37]

There are figurines with exaggerated collars. Others from Mohenjo-daro have tightly fitting neck rings, or chokers.[38] It might be that some community within the Mohenjo-daro population found long necks a mark of beauty and distinction and achieved them through artificial means. Physical anthropology might be used to confirm or deny this.

Kulli Human Figurines   The figurines from the Kulli Domain have a distinctive look, adding to our sense of cultural diversity during the Mature Harappan (figure 6.10).[39] The Kulli folk were fond of figurines of several kinds, but animals, especially painted bulls, consistently outnumber the humans.[40] At Nindowari the 173 animal figurines and 28 humans came mostly from one stone paved cell at the site—a rather spectacular and unusual concentration.

Masks and Busts of Humans and Animals   Masks and busts of humans and animals are part of the material inventory from Mature Harappan sites (figure 6.11). The hu-

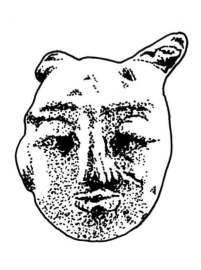

Figure 6.11   "Masks" from Mohenjo-daro (after Marshall 1931i)

Figure 6.12 Double-sided seal from Mohenjo-daro with the "devil" on two edges (after Marshall 1931i)

mans appear to be males, but this has not been demonstrated conclusively in all cases. They are invariably horned and one has a goatee, so his sex is reasonably certain.[41] His horns are also of the corkscrew variety; many of the others are straight, rather "devil-like."[42] There is also the representation of two devil-like individuals, complete with horns, cloven feet, and a pointed tail, in a posture of hailing someone (figure 6.12).[43] These representations are on opposite edges of a stamp seal that has unicorns and script on the two large faces. It therefore has no boss. While each of the faces has a unicorn, the inscriptions are different.

These devil-like representations come through with just enough strength and clarity to make us suppose they were part of the Indus system of beliefs. How they fit with the overall pantheon of the male animal deity and a female plant goddess is not known, but the "devil" is there and he was part of Indus life.

The Ithyphallic Males from Mature Harappan Sites and Mesopotamia

Some years ago Dales published a discussion of the links between the Indus Civilization and Mesopotamia, including dice and male figurines.[44] The figurines interested Dales because two nearly identical examples have been found, one from Chanhu-daro, the other from Nippur (figure 6.13).

The objects in question are small handmade terracotta figurines of potbellied, naked males, about 12 centimeters tall. The legs are an integral part of the body, but the arms were attached separately, as with puppets, which seem to have been to the liking of the Harappans. The sexual organs of both pieces are broken, but the gender of the representations is not in doubt. In fact, they both seem to be in an ithyphallic state. Both figurines also have the remnants of small tails.

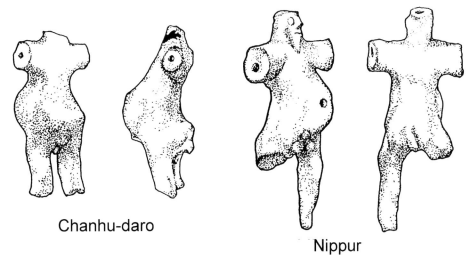

Chanhu-daro

Nippur

Figure 6.13 Ithyphallic terra-cotta figurines from Chanhu-daro and Nippur

The Art of the Indus Civilization 119

There are five human figurines of this general type from Mohenjo-daro.[45] Other examples come from Lohumjo-daro and Lothal. Figurines of this type have not been found at Harappa.

The figurines from Chanhu-daro and Nippur were tested to see if they were made of clay from the same source.[46] They were not. The Chanhu-daro figurine was made of Sindhi clay, and the Nippur figurine was made in Mesopotamia, further strengthening the notion that there were Harappans there.

Ethnicity and Figurine Style

One of the assumptions in this study of the Indus Civilization is that there were many kinds of people in the region from the beginnings of food production through the Mature Harappan and posturban times. The principal evidence for this is diversity in the artifactual record. While "pots are not people," the diverse archaeological assemblages, especially after Togau Phase times, are highly likely to indicate some degree of ethnic diversity. Although this is a kind of principle, it should be remembered that it is inappropriate to think of the "Kot Diji people" or the "Amri-Nal folk" simply because there is an archaeological assemblage by that name. Moreover, there is every possibility that within as large and diverse an archaeological assemblage as the Amri-Nal, there was cultural and ethnic diversity as well. And the same ethnic group might have spread between areas like the Kot Dijian and Amri-Nal Early Harappan assemblages.

Support for this proposition of ethnic diversity also can be obtained from the human skeletal record, which indicates some degree of biological diversity. One can also look to the representations of people in the figurines of the Mature Harappan. There is a good deal of diversity in dress, headgear, and hairstyles—all of which can be used as indicators of ethnicity. This topic has not been explored well, but within the context there is a cautionary word from F. Barth:[47] He warns that while ethnicity is often displayed in material culture, only a limited number of articles from the wide spectrum of available objects will carry this marker or be used in this way. There is no simple one-to-one correlation, so what is said here should not be seen as a conclusion but an indication that serious work on this corpus of material, from this perspective, might be rewarding.

In some ways the figurines offer the most intimate insight into the peoples of the Indus Age, since many of the representations seem to have been taken from daily life. Jan Fairservis has created a drawing based on Indus figurines that shows some of the diversity of dress and hairstyles (figure 6.14). The Indus people come in great variety, with many poses: sitting in chairs, lying on beds, holding babies and animals, kneading bread, and other things that people do to round out their existence. They form a loose style, compared to a distinctive Kulli style of the same period. A vast quantity of human figurines, both male and female, come from the long sequence at Mehrgarh, giving us a strong sense of the depth of the figurine-making traditions of the Indus Age.

Animals in Art: Menagerie of the Indus Age

Many plants and animals are represented in the archaeological record of the Indus Age. Some were exotic, such as peacocks and pangolins; others were very much a part of the day-to-day life of these peoples and played a critical role in their survival: cattle, sheep, and goats, for example. Animal life has been discussed in detail elsewhere in the literature.[48] Some animals, such as the lion and Indus porpoise, are missing from the archaeological record even though they were certainly present in the Greater Indus region.

While plant life is very much a part of Indus imagery, only a few species can be positively identified; for example, the pipal and the water lily. It has not been possible to produce a great deal of information on plants, but perhaps someone with a botanical background might be more successful.

There are several interesting, relatively large reclining caprids in the Indus Civilization. They are all from Mohenjo-daro and have been nicely summarized by Ardeleanu-Jansen.[49]

The Fantastic People and Animals of the Indus Age

There are many animals in the art of the Indus Age that are clearly a part of the natural world. Scholars agree that there are good representations of zebus, water buffaloes, elephants, tigers, gavials, and rhinoceroses on the seals. But there are others that are the product of the imagination of the Indus peoples: unicorns with elephant trunks, for example (figure 6.15). This is an exceptional motif in Mature Harappan art since the animal presented here is a true patchwork of animals. Moving from head to rear, one notices a rather human face and an elephant's trunk hanging from the chin. There is a slight suggestion of tusks, which is better shown on FEMD seal number 411. The head is crowned with double horns, rather like the one on zebu seals. The neck has the ornamentation of the unicorn, and the forelegs and sometimes the body are a part of the same animal in Mature Harappan art. Depending on the seal, the rear of the body may have tiger stripes, sometimes only the rear legs are treated this way. The rear legs are not bovid but felid, with claws not cloven hoofs. On one of the seals the tail is raised and looks

Figure 6.14 Indications of possible ethnicity from terra-cotta figurines from Mohenjo-daro and Harappa (in a drawing by Jan Fairservis)

something like a scorpion tail with the stinger at the end. There is also the representation of two unicorns emerging from the top of a standard adorned with pipal leaves (figure 6.16).

There are many representations of "humans" with horns, some or all of which could be simply headdresses; others may be representations of an Harappan notion of humans with this biological feature. The Mahayogi seal

might fit in here as would the very nice terra-cotta masks. Horned females are also known, as depicted on the seal with a woman in combat with a horned tiger; there is no doubt that is the figure possesses a rather pendulous breast, so the gender identification seems reasonably secure (figure 6.17).

There is also the well-known incised triangular terra-cotta cake from Kalibangan (figure 6.18). One side has a

Figure 6.15 A composite animal on an Indus seal (after Mackay 1937–38)

Figure 6.16 Seal with "unicorns" emerging out of a pipal tree (after Marshall 1931i)

human with a tethered animal, of which the species is still undetermined. The face of the cake has a horned human with what is generally thought of as a plant growing out of the top of his or her head. But this could be hair, as demonstrated by an ethnographic analogy from Greenwich Village, New York, in 1989, shown in figure 6.19.

There is another composite creation of the Harappans. This is the centaur-like creature, with the torso of a human on the body of an animal with claws and a long straight tail, perhaps of a tiger. The human has a long braid, char-

Figure 6.17 Horned female in combat with a horned tiger (after Marshall 1931i)

acteristic of many Indus representations of humans, as well as a set of horns generally parallel to the ground. This creature also appears on the cylinder seal from Kalibangan approaching (probably not departing from) the central group of three humans, two of whom hold spears over the head of a smaller individual (figure 6.20).

There is a window here into the world of the Harappans. These representations of fantasy do not, however, seem to dominate their art. On the whole, the Indus peoples in their art, as in other aspects of their lives, come across as people with a practical bent, a tendency to deal with and represent the real world as they (and we) see it. There is just enough of the fabulous world there for a bit of spice to be sensed, and the same is true for their painted pottery.

INDUS PAINTED POTTERY

There is a variety of painted wares and motifs at Mature Harappan sites. Some of these seem to be intrusive, clearly having been made elsewhere and transported to a new "home." The Ahar white painted black and red ware common on many Sindhi Harappan sites in Kutch (e.g., Surkotada and Dholavira) is a good example of this. The occasional Kulli-style sherd has been found in the Indus Valley, even at Mohenjo-daro. There was also a great deal of line painting on pots during the Mature Harappan, the simplest kind of painted decoration, just enough to break the monotony of a plain surface. Slips on the pottery were also common, almost always red. Slips are a kind of paint used to cover all or virtually all of the visible surface of the pot. They are generally applied before firing and serve to give the vessel a pleasant consistent color, difficult to

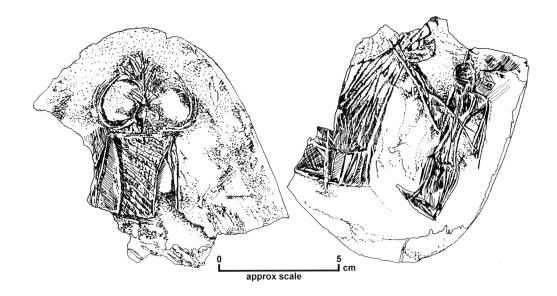

Figure 6.18   Incised triangular terra-cotta cake from Kalibangan (after Thapar 1975)

achieve if the plain clay surface was unaltered. Some of these red-slipped pots were painted in a way that I have come to think of as the "classic" Indus black paint on red slip decorative style (figure 6.21). There is nothing like it anywhere else in the world, making it easy to identify.

The pottery painting style of the Indus Civilization is never found as a high proportion of the total pottery assemblage. The only site in Sindh where statistics are available is Allahdino, where it is 3 or 4 percent of the total inventory. Red-slipped pottery is about a quarter of the inventory there. This painting style is entirely absent in the Sorath Harappan, and it has a provincial sense in the Eastern Domain, something that needs more rigorous definition. The Kulli Domain has its own painting style, related to but different from the Mature Harappan painted ware discussed here. The classic painting style is found in the Sindhi, Cholistan, and Harappa Domains.

At first glance this style might look rather slapdash. The lines tend to be thick and variable in width and density, often continuing past the point at which they should have stopped. The painting is not carefully controlled and there is an effort to cover the entire design area with work, a pronounced tendency toward *horror vacuui*. But, on closer examination, one can find order here, a plan for the layout and execution of each painted vessel.

CONCLUSION

Several points emerge from this discussion of Mature Harappan art. The best of the sculpture of the Indus Civilization are the red jasper torso from Harappa and the

bronze dancing girl from HR Area of Mohenjo-daro. In terms of its artistic merit, the jasper torso is comparable to the achievements made on the seals, which allows me to not doubt its authenticity.

The differences between Harappa and Mohenjo-daro

Figure 6.19   A scene from New York titled "Sunrise, Greenwich Village" (1989) (from *The New Yorker*, April 10, 1989, page 99; drawing by Cline; copyright © 1989; The New Yorker Magazine, Inc.)

Figure 6.20 Centaur-like creature (after Marshall 1931i)

in terms of the sculpture in the round is worthy of note. The red jasper torso and gray stone torso are the only pieces of note from Harappa, and there is nothing that is very much like them from Mohenjo-daro. The two bronze dancing girls and the eleven other major pieces that have been found at Mohenjo-daro are vastly larger in terms of number and once again do not have parallels at Harappa. The two cities that we know best are simply very different in terms of the corpus of sculpture in the round. It is as though they were not even of the same culture. It is also interesting to note that these are the only two Mature Harappan sites to have produced high-quality stone sculpture in the round. There is none at Chanhu-daro, Kalibangan, Banawali, or Lothal. One poorly preserved seated male has been found at Dholavira.

There are many pieces in this repertoire of Harappan terra-cotta art that are alive with a sense of humor. The animal puppets come across in this way. It does not require much imagination to visualize an Harappan parent or grandparent delighting in play with a child, showing it how the bull can shake his head, or using it to pull a model cart. Some of the simpler terra-cotta figurines convey the same sense of delight and play; simple toys to amuse people, young and old, each in their own way, often sharing the pleasure. These objects offer the most human face of the Indus Civilization, a sociocultural system that can often appear to be quite severe. At Mohenjo-daro one thinks of most of the citizens closeted in their brick homes, hidden behind the immense, unbroken outer walls, living a rather private even austere life. But the art, especially the figurines, tell us that there was another side to these people equally important to understanding them and their lives.

The Indus black-on-red painting style is not just a slap-

dash, hurried way of the painting. The artists who created these vessels did have a plan, a model for painting. A relatively small percentage of Indus ceramics were decorated in this fashion, and one wonders how the artists that practiced this art were organized. With so little painting being done at any one site, who were the painters trained in this canon? How was the style maintained if there were many painters spread over the million or so square kilometers of the Indus world? This may suggest that there were small numbers of highly skilled, well-trained ceramic painters who did this work, and most of the other potters did not. These black and red ware painters could have been located at permanent workshops or could have traveled to various settlements and done their work on site. Or both these modes of production may have occurred, and even this could have changed over the 600 years of the Indus Civilization.

Finally, there seems to be a great disparity between the very best of the art of the Mature Harappan and the rest. While the seals are numerous and demonstrate without doubt that there was widespread appreciation of art and high-quality craftsmanship, the rest of the material by and large is of distinctly lesser merit. There are relatively few pieces that bridge the differences—it seems to be either very, very good, as with the red torso and the dancing girl, or artistically somewhat lacking, and it seems to me

Figure 6.21 An Indus painted jar (after Mackay 1942)

that this is a statement of some sort on the civilization as a whole.

NOTES

1. Vats 1940: 74–75.
2. Marshall 1931d: 46.
3. Vats 1940: 75.
4. Marshall, in Vats 1928–29: 79.
5. Marshall 1931d: 47; the seal is published in Marshall 1931a, seal number 337.
6. Wheeler 1968: 86, 89.
7. Vats 1940: 22.
8. Wheeler 1968: 86, 89–90.
9. Ardeleanu-Jansen 1984; see also Mackay 1931g.
10. Sahni 1926–27: 81.
11. Huntington 1985: 16.
12. During-Caspers 1987.
13. Piggott 1950: 150.
14. Piggott 1950: 111.
15. Marshall 1931d: 44.
16. Marshall 1931d: 45.
17. Hawkes 1982: 367, quoting Wheeler.
18. Mackay 1930–34: 60.
19. Mackay 1925–26: 90–91, pl. XLIIIa; see Possehl 1999b: pl. 2.25 for a staged photograph of the recovery of the priest-king.
20. Mackay 1931c: 237.
21. Mackay 1931g: 357.
22. Mackay 1931g: 357.
23. Mackay 1931g: 357, n. 2.
24. Mackay 1931g: 357.
25. Wheeler 1968: 86.
26. Mackay 1931g: 357.
27. Mackay's first statement is in Marshall 1925–26: 91, but see Mackay 1931g: 357, where he changes his mind suggesting it represents a deity; see also Marshall 1931e: 54 and Wheeler 1953: 65, and 1968: 87.
28. Ardeleanu-Jansen 1991: 167–69.
29. Parpola 1985a, 1985b.
30. Parpola 1985a: 387; Hiltebeitl 1978.
31. Ardeleanu-Jansen 1984: 140.
32. Wheeler 1968: 52–53; see also Jansen 1985.
33. Mackay 1931g: 359.
34. Mackay 1931g: 358–59, pl. C, 1–3; Ardeleanu-Jansen 1991: 166.
35. Mackay 1931g: 359.
36. Mackay 1931g: 358, pl. XCIX, 7–9.
37. Mackay 1931f: 339.
38. Mackay 1937–38: pl. LXXV, nos. 3, 9, 10.
39. Stein 1931; C. Jarrige 1984; Possehl 1986b.
40. C. Jarrige 1984: 130.
41. Mackay 1937–38: pl. LXXIV, no. 26.
42. Marshall 1931i: pl. XCV, nos. 1, 2, 3; Mackay 1937–38: pl. LXXIV, nos. 21, 22, 26, pl. LXXXVI, nos. 1–4.
43. Marshall 1931i: pl. CIX, nos. 227, 230; see also Shah and Parpola 1991: 151, M-1224.
44. Dales 1968a.
45. Marshall 1931i: 549, pl. CLIII, 38; Mackay 1937–38: pl. LXXVII, nos. 3, 12, and pl. LXXXI, nos. 8, 14.
46. Possehl 1994.
47. Barth 1969: 9–38.
48. Possehl 1999b: 173–231; Meadow 1993.
49. Ardeleanu-Jansen 1984, 1987; see also Pittman 1984: 88; Allchin 1992.

CHAPTER 7

The Indus Script

INTRODUCTION

Writing is one of the hallmarks of civilization. I think of it as symptomatic of the size and complexity of ancient urban systems, be it the archaic state or a more corporate organization such as the Indus Civilization.[1] They all have large volumes of information to record, process, retain, and transmit. These include accounts and economic records, dynastic histories, genealogies, religious and ideological documents, literature, and personal identifiers. People who lived in most archaic complex sociocultural systems found it expedient to "write it down" as a fix for these practical information problems. There is a more active, aggressive aspect to writing, too, with the manipulation of information, like accounts, history, especially dynastic history, and genealogy. Writing could be easily used to gain political and personal advantage.[2]

We do not know much about the sociocultural locus of writing in the Indus Civilization. There are no accounts, at least among the documents we have, so it does not look like a writing system that was deeply embedded in economics. The best-known written documents are the small stamp seals, and these seem to have been personal identifiers, with messages that seem to be names, titles, places of affiliation, and the like. There is no Indus written literature, but literacy, or control over some of the Indus writing, was widespread. For instance, there are thousands of examples of Indus messages scratched onto the surfaces of ordinary fired pottery. This indicates that ordinary people probably controlled some small part of the writing system and used it in their daily lives. Potters put stamped messages on wet pots that were probably used by ordinary people in their daily lives. These messages must have had meaning to the people who used the pots. There are many things yet to

be learned about the Indus script, not the least of which is how to read it.

In spite of many claims to the contrary, the writing system of the Indus Civilization remains undeciphered. It is one of the unsolved puzzles regarding the peoples of the ancient cities of the Indus. Perhaps some qualification is needed for this claim, in the sense that none of the would-be decipherers can demonstrate that their reading of the script is the correct one. This being the case, there is the logical possibility that one of them is correct, in whole or part; we just cannot prove it! A review of the most important decipherment efforts is available.[3]

SOME GENERAL OBSERVATIONS ON INDUS SEALS AND THE WRITING SYSTEM

The Indus script is found principally on stamp seals, pottery, and copper–bronze tablets, tools, and weapons (figure 7.1). No writing has been found on organic materials like paper, papyrus, leaves, or bark. Important sources on the Indus script include two concordances.[4]

No one has an exact count of the number of inscriptions, but in 1977 I. Mahadevan included 2,906 texts. The number has not changed substantially since then, although several new seals and other glyptic materials have been reported from new excavations at Harappa, Dholavira, and Rakhigarhi.[5] The total number might have grown to something approaching 3,100. This does not count most of the graffiti (stray single signs and symbols on pottery) that occurs with great frequency. Using the Mahadevan concordance, about 87 percent of all Indus inscribed materials come from Mohenjo-daro and Harappa (table 7.1). The large number of "other" objects from Harappa reflects the presence of 272 "miniatures," very small objects inscribed with simple messages (figure 7.2).

Table 7.1 Inscribed material from various Mature Harappan sites

Site	Seals	Sealings	Copper tablets	Bronze implements	Other objects	Total
Mohenjo-daro	1,232	119	135	5	49	1,540
Harappa	350	288	—	3	344	985
Chanhu-daro	58	3	—	1	4	66
Lothal	89	75	—	—	1	165
Kalibangan	56	21	—	2	20	99
Other sites	13	4	—	—	17	34
West Asia	16	1	—	—	—	17
Total	1,814	511	135	11	435	2,906

Note: From Mahadevan (1977: 7).

Figure 7.1   A selection of Indus seals (various sources)

The animal devices on the stamp seals have been enumerated by Mahadevan, as presented in table 7.2.

The Seals Themselves

The typical stamp seal is square to rectangular, 2 to 3 centimeters on a side, but larger and smaller examples exist. Fairservis has the best description of seal cutting.[6] It seems that a grid was used to lay out the placement of the devise and the line of script above it. However, there are instances where the logographs are cramped at the end of the inscription, so the planning process was not perfect (figure 7.3).[7] The seal was cut with sharp tools, probably of flint and/or copper–bronze. The analysis of

the "micromorphology" of seal cutting and design has led to some interesting suggestions about the unicorn-type seal, which is the most frequent device.

P. Rissman undertook the first analysis.[8] Using the decorative elements on the head and neck of the unicorn, and the stand or "brazier" in front of it, he constructed a contingency table that reveals two groups of unicorn seals: (1) the hatched-faced type found in the north around Harappa as well as Cholistan, and (2) those with collared necks and straight cages on the brazier, found in the south, around Mohenjo-daro.

U. Franke-Vogt undertook the second analysis.[9] She deals with the unicorn seals from Mohenjo-daro. Franke-

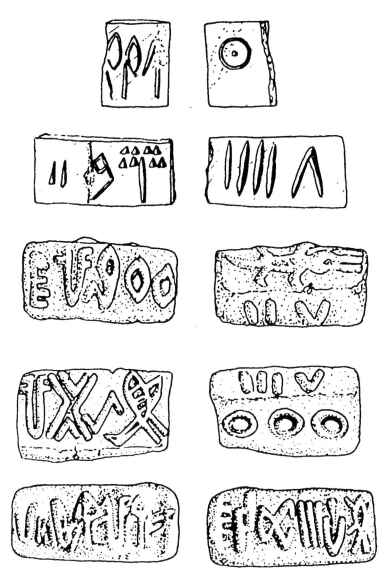

Figure 7.2 Inscribed miniatures from Harappa (after Meadow 1991)

Vogt made a determined effort to replace these objects in their horizontal and stratigraphic contexts. Her examination of the resulting distribution tables demonstrates that the seals are not randomly distributed at the site.[10] For example, they are relatively rare on the Mound of the Great Bath, where only 25 percent of the expected number of seals was found. HR and VS Areas also yielded relatively few inscribed objects, but in DK-G and DK-I the number of inscribed objects was high. From the middle to late levels of Mohenjo-daro there appears to be a trend for fewer seals to have been found in the excavations; but there is a corresponding increase in the occurrence of copper tablets (figure 7.4).

Franke-Vogt also deals briefly with the emerging thought that there are provincial carving styles. The seals from Mohenjo-daro, Chanhu-daro, Harappa, and the

Table 7.2 Frequency of animal devices on Indus seals

Unicorn with standard	1,159
Short-horned bull	95
Elephant	55
Zebu (humped bull)	54
Rhinoceros	39
Goat-antelope	36
Bull-antelope	26
Tiger	16
Buffalo	14
Hare facing a bush	10
Bull-like unicorn but with two horns	5
Horned tiger	5
Hare	5
Two short-horned bulls, face to face	2
Horned elephant	1
Two rhinoceroses	1
Two goats flanking a tree	1

Note: From Mahadevan (1977: 793).

Figure 7.3   Seal with signs cramped at the end of the inscription (after Marshall 1931i)

other sites in the Sindhi, Harappa, and Cholistan Domains have a consistency in their carving style that can be identified. In her opinion, for example, 40 percent of the seals from Lothal are of a "lower quality" than those from the cities. At Banawali the unicorn is less frequent (20 percent) than the goat and antelope (53.3 percent), reinforcing Rissman's basic conclusion that there were regional workshops for seal production.[11]

Were They Really Stamp Seals at All?

The Indus seals may not have been made as a part of seal-based administration known from Mesopotamia. This important aspect of the Indus Civilization is just emerging from a renewed interest in the writing system and the corpus of glyptic materials. It is a topic that deserves a separate in-depth study, but an outline can be made here. The first, and perhaps the most important, observation is that the number of seal impressions is very small. There are only four seal impressions from Mohenjo-daro, four from Harappa, and another from Banawali. Kalibangan has five impressions, and Lothal the largest number, thirty-seven, most from the warehouse there. Three other examples come from Bagasra in northern Saurashtra. These are all impressions of stamp seals on lumps of clay that preserve the imprint of a package, jar, or other material indicating that the intent was to seal something. They do not include the hundreds of sealings, made mostly from molds that served as amulets or identification of some kind. Nor are the seal impressions made directly into the fabric of pots included here.

Mackay has noted that in the excavations of Mohenjo-

daro through 1926–1927 no seal impressions were found at all. In speaking of the corpus of impressed glyptic material from the site, he says:

> It is not quite certain whether these objects should rightly be classed as seals only or as amulets, for the reason that up to the present there has not been found at Mohenjo-daro a single true sealing; that is, an impression on a piece of clay or other substance that had been attached to a jar or other article of merchandise, of the kind so well known at other ancient sites, where they were fastened to the object to be sealed by means of a cord, or else they bear traces on their backs of some fabric to which they were once attached.[12]

This lack of data is not due to poor digging, since Mackay excavated several sites in the Near East, and he found many true seal impressions there, at Kish, for example. If seal impressions had been made at Mohenjo-daro he would have found them there, too.

Another important observation regarding the function of the square stamp seals has to do with wear. Most of the Indus seals (not all) still retain the crisp edge of the original carving. They are unworn and clearly were not used to make many impressions, especially since the steatite from which they are carved is the softest on the Mohs' scale of hardness, soft enough to be marked by a

Figure 7.4   A copper tablet from Mohenjo-daro (after Mackay 1937–38)

fingernail. Even when baked and hardened, this family of minerals registers as only about four on the Mohs' scale. In contrast, the cylinder seals in Mesopotamia were intensively used and were consequently carved from hard stones: agate, crystal, lapis lazuli. There are many examples of Mesopotamian seals that were heavily worn from the taking of many impressions, even some that have been recut in antiquity to rejuvenate the scene and the written message. This fits well with the large number of seal impressions that have been recovered in archaeological excavations there.

There is a terra-cotta "seal" from Allahdino, complete with a boss on the back. The elephant and the script have been incised on the face in the manner of graffiti on pottery. The incisions are so shallow that they would leave little or no imprint on clay.

Some Indus seals have rather heavily abraded outside edges, especially those directly adjacent to the face. Joshi and Parpola have some excellent color photographs that nicely illustrate this.[13] These are worn only on the edges; the interior carving retains a fresh, crisp line. This pattern suggests that the seal was wrapped in cloth (or another material).

Thus, the Indus seals were not used to make huge numbers of impressions, which in turn suggests that they may have been used primarily for visual identification. The seal itself, not the impression, was shown. It identified, or gave some form of legitimacy, to the bearer.

It is emerging that the Indus peoples and Mesopotamians used their seals in significantly different ways. The kind of text and seal administration found in the Mesopotamia archaic state was not a part of the economic fabric of the Indus. With the growing consensus that the Indus Civilization was not organized as an archaic state,[14] the notion that a seal-based administration was used in the Indus political economy also comes into doubt.

The usual typology includes many objects in the "seal" category because of their form, not their function. At the moment, it makes sense to allow them into the domain of the seal and let the category of function expand to accommodate them.

The Indus Unicorn: A Real or "Fantastic" Animal?

There has been some discussion of the one-horned "bull" on the seals, usually called a "unicorn." The question centers on whether this is a real animal, with the single horn shown for purposes of artistic perspective, or is it fantastic, a creation of the Indus mind? Mahadevan's concordance lists 1,159 seals with this device, so it must have been important.[15] C. Grigson is a recent proponent of the fantastic

animal hypothesis, which is not without merit.[16] But most others, including Marshall and Mackay, agree that "the artist intended to represent one horn behind the other."[17] This point of view is supported by the fact that there are a few seals with unicorn-type bulls with two horns.

On the other hand, the original reference to the Indian unicorn was made by Ctesias the Cnidian, a Greek physician resident for seventeen years (c. 415–398 B.C.) in the Achaemenid court under Darius II and Artaxerxes Memnon.[18] There are also terra-cotta figurines that look like bulls with one horn coming out of the middle of the forehead from Harappa, Chanhu-daro, and Lothal.[19] In the end, I believe that the single horn on the unicorn seals was an artistic convention. This implies that the animal is probably a real bull and that the unicorn of India as reported by Ctesias is a separate matter.

A Typology of What Is Inscribed

Indus inscriptions are found on a variety of objects, none of them lengthy texts. Since the context of Indus writing is an important element in decipherment, a typology of inscribed objects is needed, as in table 7.3.

Indus Pictographs

The Indus script is usually thought of as pictographic. There is a "fish" sign ⚲, a "rake" ⊤, a "house plot" ⊞, a "diamond" ◇, and others. The Mesopotamian writing system also passed through this stage. Since these pictographs are so simple, there is, not surprisingly, some correspondence between their pictographs and those of the Indus system (figure 7.5).

The Proto-Elamite, or Linear Elamite, script of the Iranian Plateau is also pictographic and roughly contemporaneous with the Indus script. It has been found in eastern Iran, as near as Tepe Yahya and probably Shahr-i Sokhta. There is even better correspondence between this script and that of the Indus Civilization than there is between Sumerian and Indus. Unfortunately, Proto-Elamite is also undeciphered, although the counting system on the tablets is understood. The correspondence between the pictographs of Proto-Elamite and Indus script is close enough that G. R. Hunter noted: "That the languages (Proto-Elamite and Indus) are unconnected is probable, and the phonetic value of the signs may well be different. But that they are unrelated in origin seems to be contradicted by the number of resemblances that seem to be too close to be explained by coincidence."[20] Fairservis once did a transliteration of a Linear Elamite tablet into the Indus writing system, further documenting the close correspondence between the two.[21]

Table 7.3 Typology of inscribed material

I. Seals		
	I.A. Stamp seals with an Harappan-type boss	
		I.A.1. Standard stamp seal with an Harappan boss
		I.A.2. Stamp seals with an Harappan boss and geometric designs
		I.A 3. Narrative stamp seals with an Harappan boss
	I.B. Harappan bar seal	
	I.C. Cylinder seals	
	I.D. Round seals of Persian Gulf type	
II. Seal impressions		
	II.A. Standard seal impressions on clay	
	II.B. Seal impressions on pottery	
III. Sealings and moldings		
	III.A. Sealings and moldings with only writing	
	III.B. Narrative sealings and moldings	
IV. Inscriptions that are not seals, sealings or moldings		
	IV.A. Miniature inscriptions	
	IV.B. Copper tablets	
	IV.C. Inscribed copper artifacts	
	IV.D. Inscribed ivory and bone objects	
	IV.E. Graffiti	
V. Miscellaneous inscribed material		

The Total Number of Signs

While there is substantial disagreement on the total number of Indus signs, all experts agree that it is in the range of a few hundred. This number indicates that the writing system was not like our twenty-six-letter alphabet or as expansive as Chinese and Japanese writing, with thousands of logographic characters. This strongly suggests that the writing system was based on syllables, or something akin to them, and was neither alphabetic nor logographic. Virtually all scholars who have studied the Indus script agree on this point and have used the term *logosyllabic* to describe it.

The exact number of Indus signs, however, is an unresolved question. This is principally due to the fact that what could be considered one sign is open to interpretation. No one is quite sure which are variants and which are signs unto themselves.

The number of pictographic signs is important for several reasons. It sets the limit on the number of signs to be deciphered as well as determines which signs might be related and therefore have similar meanings or functions in the writing system. It also plays a role of fundamental importance in an examination of sign frequency, which can be a source of many clues and productive lines for research for the would-be decipherer. The thinking of some scholars is reflected in the number of signs they assign to the total size of the script, as given in table 7.4.

The Length of the Inscriptions

Indus inscriptions are usually short; they vary from isolated signs to as many as twenty-six characters in length. The longest inscription comes from two molded terra-cotta "bars" from Mohenjo-daro, both from the DK Area (figure 7.6). Inscriptions on one line are the most common, but they range up to seven lines.[22]

Sign Frequency

Since the number of signs and their frequency is important to most decipherment efforts, an example of where experts disagree on this matter is in order. The "diamond" and the "rounded diamond" θ were treated as separate signs by Langdon and Fairservis[23] but as variants of one sign by Mahadevan and Koskenniemi, Parpola, and Parpola.[24]

Of the 417 signs given by Mahadevan, 113 occur once, 47 occur twice, and 59 occur fewer than five times.[25] The

Table 7.4 Number of signs in the Indus script as estimated by various scholars

Langdon (1931b)	288
Hunter (1932)	149
Von Meriggi (1934)	270
Dani (1963: 16)	537
Koskenniemi and Parpola (1982)	396
Mahadevan (1977)	417
Fairservis (1992: 6)	419

Indus Sign	Sumerian Sign	Phonetic Value	Picture Value
		BAR	Shrine
		GI.	Reed
		GAN MAL	Land Measure
		GA	Dwelling
		—	—
		GIL	Double Reed
		GIR AD	Scorpion
		KHA	Fish
		SAR.	360
		GAL.	Great
		SAG	Heart in
		BAD	Dead
		KU ŠU	to
		ŠU	Hand
		VŠ	Unknown
		E	House Plot of Land

Figure 7.5 Comparison of Mesopotamian and Indus pictographs (after Smith and Gadd 1924)

Table 7.5 Sign frequency according to the Finnish team

Total frequency of a sign	Total number of signs with this frequency or higher
Over 800	1
Over 200	6
Over 100	24
Over 50	46
Over 20	86
Over 10	100

Note: After Parpola et al. (1969: 9).

frequently used. But this could be a sort of diacritical mark, and not a full sign in and of itself—another sign definition/counting problem. Sixty-seven signs account for over 80 percent of the use. Of Mahadevan's 417 signs, about 200 could be said to have been in general use.[26]

The Origins of the Indus Script

There is little conclusive evidence for the development of the writing system in the Greater Indus region; although there is new evidence emerging from the ongoing excavations at Harappa. It is reasonable to assume that it arose from the same set of general culture processes that brought urbanization to the plains of the Greater Indus Valley.[27] The Early Harappan–Mature Harappan Transition would be the time period within which the writing system developed from isolated signs to a system of symbolism that involved multiple characters. B. B. Lal has attempted to

Figure 7.6 Longest inscription

"jar" sign 𝕌 is the most frequently used sign, occurring 1,395 times. Frequencies, as given by the Finnish team, for suffix signs appear in table 7.5.

The "jar" sign is the only one that occurs more than a thousand times. It also has a very broad distribution, occurring at Rojdi as a graffito in the Posturban Harappan Rojdi C (c. 2000–1700 B.C.) and possibly as a design on the painted pottery of Cemetery H (see figure 9.9a). The "marker" ‖ sign occurs 649 times and is the second most develop a sense of correspondence between the signs used in the writing system and the potters' marks and painted designs on pottery from the Early Harappan Phase.[28] It could be expected that the inventors, or codifiers, of the writing system drew on parts of their own culture when they turned their attention to writing. Lal's position is interesting, but falls short of being compelling. In spite of observations from Harappa, there is not yet a convincing bridge that allows us to see a progression from the use of single signs to sign combinations, sign standardization, and the development of a system of representation that has an institutional rather than an individual quality.

Prototypes for the square Indus stamp seal have been found at the site of Kunal as well as Harappa, as published on the Internet.[29] These "proto-seals" seem to date to the Early Harappan–Mature Harappan Transition, which is just where they should be in terms of cultural history.

The apparent short period of development for the Indus script is a contrast to the history of writing in Mesopotamia, where cuneiform writing begins in the sixth millennium with three-dimensional counters or tokens. These slowly developed into the primitive texts of the late fourth millennium B.C.[30]

Lack of Change in the Indus Writing System

At the moment, it appears that the Indus script "arrives" full-blown, with the dawning of the Indus Civilization. As we learn more about the Early Harappan–Mature Harappan Transition this will change, and we will be able to trace the development of Indus writing within the 100 to 200 years of this transitional phase. With one or two possible exceptions, no one has detected any change or development in the writing system over the 600 years of the Mature Harappan. This is almost certainly due to the general lack of control over the detailed history of the Indus Civilization. It makes little sense to suppose that such a system was invented and then used for hundreds of years throughout the entire Indus region without any modification.

Two hints of change, not in the writing system itself, but in the inscribed objects, already exist. The first comes from Harappa, where Vats observes:

"Stamp seals . . . diminish in both size and numbers from the IVth stratum downwards in Mound F; and so also do the terracotta and faience sealings. Their place is taken by a class of very small seals and sealings which are not represented at all at Mohenjo-daro presumably because the strata exposed on that site are posterior to the age to which these early seals belong.[31]

The second piece of evidence comes from Mohenjo-daro, where the copper tablets "were especially characteristic of the 'Late Period,'"[32] something confirmed by Franke-Vogt.[33]

B. M. Pande has also studied the evolution of signs and has produced some interesting suggestions, especially concerning the development of a sign ⋈ that he derives from a quadruped.[34] Pande's list significantly expands the corpus of copper tablets over that presented by Mackay.[35]

If the matter is given sensitive attention, evidence of change and variation n the Indus script will almost surely emerge. This is but one of many tasks that can be done with this writing system that does not necessarily involve the decipherment directly.

The Direction of Indus Writing

It is generally conceded that Indus script should be read from right to left in the impression.[36] C. J. Gadd was the first to set forth this argument in detail.[37] He noted that the Indus signs seem to face both to the right and the left, so the rule followed in Egyptian hieroglyphics that one reads into the face of the symbol is of no help. Of more significance, Gadd pointed out that on some seals signs (e.g., H 5629) seem to be cramped, as the engraver ran out of room (see figure 7.3). There are a number of other seals with this characteristic.[38]

Evidence for *boustrophedon* (the way an ox turns in plowing) writing has been noted by several scholars.[39] One of the seals published by Marshall is of this general type with the "jar" sign at the end: ⊍⋉〰⥾⥿⊍⋔⟐.[40] Seal number M 247 is also written in this form ⟐⥾⊍⊍⫴⊍.[41]

Other important observations on the direction of writing have been drawn from split-sign sequences and one seal with writing on three edges on the face. The manner in which the strokes forming a character overlap, especially on unbaked pottery, is also a useful guide. The arguments for the direction of writing are covered in Possehl.[42] In the end, we know that there is an occasional inscription written from left to right (in the impression). The *boustrophedon* form is present, but most Indus writing was to be read from the right to left, in the impression, and this feature of the Indus writing system is one of its the most securely known.

What You See Is What You Get?

A curious feature of the Indus script is that the writing system does not seem to have been expressed in texts or economic documents. The small "formulae" of the seals and sealings are all perfectly fine examples of ancient writing, but there are no lists, ledgers, letters, or law codes. It may have been that the Indus scribes used a perishable material, such as cloth or bark, to compose longer documents; both materials served as paper in historical times.

There is always a chance that a large corpus of long inscriptions in the Indus script will emerge, perhaps on imperishable materials. Bilingual texts might also appear. But after a lot of digging there is no evidence for them today, and this may suggest that we know the principal cultural contexts of Indus writing, which is quite unlike Mesopotamia and Dynastic Egypt. The context for early writing in these civilizations, or archaic states, was administration. In the Indus it seems to be personal identity.

Professor J. Baines, an Egyptologist at Oxford University, made an intriguing observation pertinent to Indus texts written on perishable materials.[43] There are many unique and low-frequency signs in the corpus of inscriptions on nonperishable materials, and Baines noted that this may well be evidence that the inscribed materials that have been recovered are sufficiently specialized that the balanced expression of the Indus corpus of signs is not present. If this is true, then it implies that at least some of the unique and low-frequency signs that are recorded are simply a reflection of the deep bias on the corpus of texts and that if we had the whole range of texts (e.g., those on perishable materials), this statistical point would vanish. A real writing system with 113 unique signs, or one where over half of the pictograms occur less frequently than five times, is odd. The point that Baines makes is not a complete answer, but I think it is important and should be kept in mind by students of this ancient script.

The Language Family of the Indus Writing System

Many researchers in their attempts to read the Indus script have had to make an assumption on the language affinity of the writing system. Other researchers (e.g., the Soviet team) claim to have discovered this affiliation as a part of their conclusions; they believe it to have been a form of early Dravidian. From the beginning of the work on the Indus Civilization, it has been assumed by the most credible researchers that there were people speaking more than one language in the vast area covered by Indus remains. Marshall stated: "Of the language of these texts little more can be said at the present than that there is no reason for connecting it in any way with Sanskrit. . . . Possibly, one or other of them (if, as seems likely, there was more than one) was Dravidic."[44]

Was the Indus script a rendering of one, or more than one, language into written form? Cuneiform was certainly used to write more than one language, and languages in different language families, just as the Roman alphabet is used today. There is no certain answer to this question for the Indus materials. Some internal consistencies of sign placement and combination suggest that it may be one language, but there are exceptions to these patterns that could be interpreted as a second language.

Since an assumption of two languages, possibly from entirely different language families, would vastly complicate the research methodologies of some scholars who are attempting to bring order to this body of data, they have proceeded on the assumption that the Indus script renders one language into written form. This is not a proven fact and is a potential source of error in readings attempted so far.

Another structural feature of the Indus script that is agreed upon is that it admits suffixes but not prefixes or infixes. This feature of the writing powerfully suggests that the parent language was not one of the Indo-European tongues, Sanskrit, in particular. Dravidian languages are possible, but so too are those of the Altaic family.

No one can draw a linguistic map of the northwestern portion of the Subcontinent in the third and fourth millennia B.C., but there are studies of the larger linguistic scene that help archaeologists to deal with these complexities. For example, D. McAlpin has proposed the existence of a "Proto-Elamo-Dravidian" language family.[45] It would have been a set of living languages in the second and third millennia B.C., covering a vast stretch of land possibly extending from southeastern Iran across the southern portion of the plateau into Pakistan and northern ancient India. McAlpin hypothesized that it was languages of this affiliation, not Dravidian itself, that were in the Indus region at the time the Indus script was developed and used. The working hypothesis that many researchers have adopted, which is partly backstopped by the Soviet findings and the structure of "fixes," is that the script renders one of the Dravidian, or Proto-Elamo-Dravidian, languages into written form.

THE STATE OF RESEARCH ON THE INDUS SCRIPT

Introduction

Decipherment is an art; unfortunately, in the case of the Indus Civilization, an art not yet perfected. It takes commitment and courage to engage in the decipherment game. The decipherment of Hittite is a case in point. The Norwegian, Knutson, saw as early as 1902 that Hittite was an Indo-European language. But he was a temperamental man, unable to accept criticism challenging his insight, and this defeated him. But B. Hrozny had the same thought and pushed his ideas, countered his critics, and stayed with his beliefs. His reward was fame and recognition as a brilliant decipherer.

The lesson learned from this is that it seems to take a particular kind of scholar to succeed in this decipherment business: someone with the courage to stick with his or her convictions, the will to withstand severe criticism, possibly even public ridicule from colleagues. It even seems to require an unwillingness to recant but to "go down with the ship," a particular kind of strength.

While these qualities may be ingredients for success, they do not guarantee it. Hrozny was correct with Hittite and took on a decipherment of the Indus script without apparent success. But he stuck to his hypothesis on Indus writing to the end of his life.[46] Strong men such as W. Fairservis, S. R. Rao, A. Parpola and his team, and Knorozov and his Soviet colleagues must be credited with this kind of self-confidence. They have the courage to venture into difficult and "dangerous" intellectual worlds and stay with their beliefs. Through the efforts of these scholars, and others like them, there is agreement on some issues dealing with this writing system, but they fall short of decipherment.

Some Common Ground

K. Zvelebil offers some thoughts on points about the Indus script that are (or ought to be) agreed upon.[47] These ideas, combined with my own distillation, are as follows:

1. The script is to be read from right to left (seals, left to right, but their impressions right to left).
2. The system admits occasional uses of left-to-right readings as well as the *boustrophedon* form.
3. The script makes extensive use of suffixes, but lacks prefixes, infixes, and inflectional endings.
4. The script is best seen as a form of logosyllabic writing.

Zvelebil reiterated these points of convergence and added the following:[48]

1. The total number of signs tells us that the Indus script is not alphabetic or quasi-alphabetic.
2. The Indus script is not closely related to other writing systems of the second and third millennia B.C.; although some convergence might be found with Proto-Elamite.
3. The Indus script is not related to any later Indian script. This includes Brahmi and Kharosthi.
4. None of the grids have proved powerful enough to lead to decipherment.
5. The Indus script is not likely to have been a written form of an Indo-European language since it apparently lacks prefixes, infixes, and inflectional endings.

6. The Indus script is not likely to be a written form of a West Asiatic language since the attribute is placed after the substantive head of the attributive phrase in them. However, there may be a distant, as yet poorly understood, relationship to Elamite.
7. The common supposition that the common ending signs of the Indus inscriptions (e.g., the "jar" sign and the "arrow" sign) represent grammatical suffixes like case endings has not been confirmed.
8. None of the proposed decipherments of the Indus script can be proved to be true.

This is the common ground. When one looks at the decipherment efforts, one finds a great deal of diversity in the readings.

Lack of Agreement in Reading the Script

While we have the agreed-upon points, there is much disagreement as well. The language affiliation has been proposed to be Dravidian, Indo-European, Sumerian, Egyptian, even Malayo-Polynesian. The method of the decipherer, when method can be determined, ranges from the use of the rebus principle, to the world of tantric symbols. Comparative analysis has been made with scripts far removed for the Indus Civilization, like that of Easter Island. This work was so far-fetched that it is almost comical. The Easter Island script dates to the eighteenth or nineteenth century A.D. The Indus script dates to circa 2500–1900 B.C. Easter Island is 21,000 kilometers from Mohenjo-daro, across vast oceans.[49]

The various attempts at decipherment have yielded significantly different readings of the individual signs:[50]

1. The "jar" sign ᚑ has been taken to be a genitive case marker or the third-person-singular honorific.
2. The "arrow" sign ⌃ has been taken to mark the nominative case, or the genitive case, or the dative case. Some consider it to be a suffix of the oblique case. For Fairservis, it is the term "be powerful," which is homophonic with the third-person singular in proto-Dravidian.
3. The human stick figure ⚠ is thought to mean simply "man." Another interpretation is that it is a determinative for "man," or a word forming the suffix for masculine gender. The Finns consider it a marker for masculine gender. For Fairservis, it is "rule" or "ruler."
4. The "comb" sign ☰ has been called "from," as well as a marker for feminine gender, or still another use as marker of the dative case. For Fairservis, it is, among other things, "his mark" or "belongs to," if it is a terminal sign.
5. The "porter" sign ⚇ has been called a plural marker and even a separate word interpreted as "god-saver" or "defense." For Fairservis, it is "watchman."

This diversity of thought on the meaning of these and other signs would be vastly expanded if every reading were included. But this is enough to demonstrate that there is no agreement among the various researchers as to the meaning of individual signs, so there should be no surprise that longer messages on the seals have been read in different ways. For example, the message on the "Proto-Siva" or Mahayogi seal ⅄ ⅄ ⅄ ⅃ ⅃ ⅄ has been read by different scholars as follows:[51]

Bedrich Hrozny: "Here is the tribute offered to the god Kueya."

Swami Sankarananda: "The (aquatic) birds have covered all the waterways."

B. M. Barua: Barua believes the message is in Sanskrit and translates into English as "the mountain-worshipped one."

Finnish team: "Man of the Star (Siva), the lord of . . ."

B. Chakravorty: "*Satta Kosika* with *kosika* being found in *Dictionary of Pali Proper Names*."

B. Priyanka:

The seal transliteration is: *ha-sa-hi-ma-ma-tra,* read from right to left. This suggests that the Indus words sounded something like: *trama mahis_a-ha* (left to right) which has a Sanskrit equivalent in *tri Maha_ mahis_a.* Mahis_a has appeared in connection with Krishna Rao's decipherment. The word means "buffalo" in Sanskrit and would fit with the headdress of the central figure on the Mahayogi seal. *Tra* for "three" would then refer to the postulated three faces of the Proto-Siva and *Maha_* would mean "great."

W. A. Fairservis: "An-il the Ruler, He (who) Gathers the Assembled Clans."

FUTURE WORK AND THE NEED FOR A TEST OF DECIPHERMENT

It is possible to identify some areas of research that need the immediate attention of those interested and qualified to undertake original research on the Indus writing system.

Some Problems That Need Attention:
The Working Hypotheses

In addition to the points of broad agreement already noted about this writing system, several working hypotheses have been formulated that could be useful to those attempting to further our understanding of the Indus script.

1. Proto-Dravidian remains the best working assumption for the language affiliation of the script. Broadly conceived, this could include McAlpin's Proto-Elamo-Dravidian.[52]

2. Other language families, perhaps even Munda, can be seen as vying for the current position of Proto-Dravidian as the language for the best working hypothesis. Work on this matter is encouraged since the "Dravidian hypothesis" is not proved, and such research will tend to stimulate thought.

3. The apparent lack of prefixes, infixes, and inflectional endings in the Indus script rules out Sanskrit as the language of the Indus writing system.

4. The rebus principle is a potentially "powerful tool" for deciphering the Indus script.[53]

5. The "additions" thought by some to constitute meaningless allographs are in fact functional elements, perhaps phonetic indicators.

6. Determinatives were employed.

7. Ligatures occur systematically.

8. The structural analytical approach of I. Mahadevan has considerable methodological merit and is largely independent of decipherments employing the rebus principle. Both of these approaches should therefore be employed in parallel, seeking places where the results from each method converge to form a single conclusion.[54]

This series of working hypotheses needs to be confirmed by independent work. The confirmation process should form part of the normal science of day-to-day research on the script.[55]

The Need for an Agreement on a Sign List

There is no general agreement on the number of signs in the Indus script. Virtually all of the people who have studied this writing system agree that the sign counts and characteristics place it within the range of a logosyllabic system. There are too many signs for an alphabet and too few for a logographic system like Chinese. But there is disagreement concerning a number of important variables. What are the primary or core signs? What are the variants of these core signs? And which signs are ligatures (combinations) of signs? What constitutes scribal and stylistic variation within the signs? Is there change in these variables over time and between places like Mohenjo-daro and Harappa?

Dealing systematically with these questions is important for a number of reasons. If answers can be found and independently confirmed (tested), decipherers will have authoritative data to begin making sign identifications based on the shape of the signs, that is, their pictographic qualities. It stands to reason that once the primary signs are identified, then combinations of them in the form of ligatures could be more easily determined and deciphered. It also would be easier to see additions to signs for what they are, either as elements with meaning or as scribal variations or stylistic variants. As the situation now stands, everyone is guessing about the set of primary signs and making claims about sign variation that may or may not be true. From an epistemological point of view, these claims are nothing but assertions and therefore baseless speculation.

There is one possible exception to this critical observation. When Mahadevan was working on the problem of "sign variation" in connection with his concordance, he attempted to distinguish "sign" from "variant" based on the statistical and positional behavior of signs. Those that looked alike and had similar "behavioral" characteristics within inscriptions were deemed to be variants. Signs that looked alike but had different "behavioral" characteristics were determined to be different signs. This is a beginning, but the undertaking is far from over. More work has to be done to reach a satisfactory conclusion, as seen from the fact that he disagrees with Fairservis on a number of cases.[56]

While the Indus writing system has pictographs, this observation does not necessarily help in relating signs to known objects. For example, the "fish" sign ⚲ was said by Fairservis to be a "knot." Maybe Fairservis is right; maybe he's not. Who is to say? Where is the test?

What about the identifications of the other signs? Is the "arrow" sign ⚲ an "arrow" or a "spear" or a staff with a triangle on top? What is the relationship between the various "arrow" signs ⚲ ⚲ ⚲? These questions, and many others, arise when we try to identify the Indus signs as an initial step to decipherment. What is needed is a detailed study of individual signs that is published, critiqued, and open to revision. With this kind of iteration, conclusions might be reached that would provide confirmation and broad acceptance among the scholars with the special knowledge and skills to address decipherment in a professional way.

The Need to Study the Writing System in Its Various Contexts

Fairservis has been the most convincing voice for studying the Indus script within the context of the Indus Civilization. This is intuitively obvious to me, and I tend to neglect its importance when addressing nonarchaeologists, but it is of paramount importance. We must understand the script within the larger context of what we know of the Indus Civilization. This is a matter of theory and of practice. For example, "Fairservis pleads for a reconstruction by the Dravidianists of the obvious artifactual vocabulary familiar to the archaeologist which would include words for characteristically Indus objects (he offers such a word list)—another idea worth attention."[57] In fact, this contextualization of the script is the strongest element in Fairservis's work with the writing system.[58] These skills are not matched by many other workers, Lal and Pande being notable exceptions.

The Indus script was used in diverse cultural contexts from square stamp seals to signs scribbled on potsherds. It is found in the Greater Indus region at great city sites and in small villages on the frontiers of the Indus Civilization, as well as in the Arabian Gulf and Mesopotamia. There are two primary dimensions to this diversity: (1) the kinds of objects that were inscribed, and (2) the geographical contexts of these finds. It seems highly likely that the message on the typical Indus stamp seal with the unicorn and other devices is different from that on the copper tablets, Indus miniatures, and copper tools. If this is the case, then the statistical study of sign position and count should take cognizance of it. The decipherment efforts should not be directed at the script as a general, undifferentiated writing system, but as one delivering messages within the context of different media. The occurrence of Indus writing in the Gulf and Mesopotamia, in contexts whose writing systems are understood, presents special opportunities in terms of deciphering messages.

The kind of work I have suggested has already been tried, but in a very limited set of examples. Pande's research on the copper tablets addressed a well-defined body of glyptic material. His more speculative paper on the evolution of an individual sign within the script is another example of the sort of intensive, small-scale research that needs to be done.[59] Another example is Franke-Vogt's excellent study of stoneware bangles from Mohenjo-daro.[60] These hard-fired objects are often inscribed and might carry one or more of a variety of messages (owner's identification, maker's identification, place of manufacture, etc.). The restricted contexts for writing here, and the number of inscribed stoneware bangles, gives promise to research on these objects.

The Need for an Independent Test of Proposed Decipherments

The question of how to test the legitimacy of a claim for decipherment remains a significant one. The appearance of an exemplar with a substantial bilingual inscription, one in Indus script, the other in a writing system that could be read (at the moment, not Proto-Elamite), would settle this. Failing that, the tests have to fall back on how well the proposed decipherment and statistical data available on the script fit together. In the absence of a good bilingual text, the test of decipherment might have to rely on meaningful and consistent patterns; unfortunately, these are concepts that elude precise definition.

CONCLUSION

There seems to be a certain amount of impatience on the part of some researchers working on the Indus script. So many scholars who have ventured into this area of Indus scholarship have been captured by their own work and have moved quickly from an initial hypothesis to a series of conclusions and readings. This has meant that the patient, somewhat dreary work that would increase our understanding of the internal workings of the script and its cultural environment has been neglected. A more methodical, deliberate approach to the decipherment program, with a kind of team spirit (as with the Finns and Soviets), would almost certainly increase the chance for progress on this important subject. As it is now, researchers barrel ahead in their own directions, showing little evidence that they can, or even care to, draw on the work of their colleagues. There is some congenial give and take, and occasional critical asides noting disagreement with the conclusions of others, but entire books can appear with the author paying almost no attention to anyone else's research. It is sad, but true, with the exception of the concordances of the Indus script, that we are no nearer a decipherment than G. R. Hunter was with his groundbreaking work in 1929.

NOTES

1. This chapter draws liberally on Possehl 1996b.
2. Goody 1978.
3. Possehl 1999b.
4. Mahadevan 1977; Koskenniemi and Parpola 1982; Joshi and Parpola 1987; Shah and Parpola 1991; Franke-Vogt 1991; Parpola 1994a.
5. Mahadevan 1977: 9.
6. Fairservis 1976: 24–30.
7. Possehl 1996a: 59–60.
8. Rissman 1989.
9. Franke-Vogt 1992.
10. Summarized in Franke-Vogt 1992: 104–5.
11. Franke-Vogt 1992: 104.
12. Mackay 1931i: 380.
13. Joshi and Parpola 1987: 379, no. M-66; 380, no. 238; 386, no. M-375.
14. Possehl 1998.
15. Mahadevan 1977: 793.
16. Grigson 1984.
17. Marshall 1931e: 68; Mackay 1931i: 382.
18. McCrindle 1882: 2.
19. Mackay 1943: 157, pl. LV, nos. 10, 11, 13–15 and pl. LVI, no. 2; Rao 1985: 482, 494, pl. CCVI, c.
20. Hunter 1932: 483.
21. Fairservis 1976: figs. 15a and 15b.
22. Mackay 1937–38: pl. XCIV, 405.
23. Langdon 1931a; Fairservis 1992: 82.
24. Mahadevan 1977: 789; Koskenniemi, Parpola, and Parpola 1973: sign no. 380.
25. Mahadevan 1977: 32–35.
26. Mahadevan 1977: 17.
27. Possehl 1990, 1998.
28. Lal 1992.
29. Khatri and Acharya 1995.
30. Schmandt-Besserat 1979.
31. Vats 1940: 324.
32. Wheeler 1968: 107.
33. Franke-Vogt 1992.
34. Pande 1973, 1974, 1985.
35. Mackay 1931i: 398–401; 1937–38: 363–69.
36. Possehl 1996b: 59–62 for illustrations.
37. Gadd 1931.
38. Marshall 1931i: nos. 100, 233; Mackay 1937–38: no. 68.
39. Parpola et al. 1969: 18.
40. Marshall 1931i: pl. CIX, no. 247 and pl. CXV, no. 555.
41. Marshall 1931i: pl. CIX, no. 247.
42. Possehl 1996b: 59–62.
43. J. Baines, 1994, personal communication.
44. Marshall 1931d: 42.
45. McAlpin 1981.
46. K. Zvelebil, personal communication.
47. Zvelebil 1970: 195–96.
48. Zvelebil 1990: 96–97.
49. Possehl 1996b: 90–101 reviews the story of the workers who proposed a relationship between the Indus and Easter Island scripts.
50. Possehl 1996b: 163–64 for documentation.
51. Possehl 1996b: 163 for documentation.
52. Zvelebil 1990: 97.
53. Zvelebil 1970: 195.
54. Zvelebil 1990: 97 for comments on Mahadevan's method.
55. Zvelebil 1990: 97.8 for discussion.
56. For example, Fairservis 1992: 82.
57. Zvelebil 1990: 93.
58. Zvelebil 1990: 93, 97.
59. Pande 1973, 1974.
60. Franke-Vogt 1989.

CHAPTER 8

Indus Religion

INTRODUCTION

Considerable attention has been given to the religion of the Indus Civilization, and not only from trained archaeologists.[1] The best early study of the religion of the Indus peoples was that done by Marshall.[2] The term *religion* in the context of the Indus Civilization must be broadly defined as "an institution devoted to the world of deities, the premise(s) of which are believed to be true by the adherents, but cannot be either proved or disproved." It includes the system of belief in the otherworld as well as in gods and goddesses. Indus mythology and astronomy/astrology are also included, in part because the nature of the evidence makes it so difficult to disarticulate them.

Ideologies have a similarity to religion. Both are based on institutions founded on principles, or beliefs, that can be neither affirmed nor falsified. They are just "believed." The differences between them lie in the fact that by definition religions are concerned with "gods" and a "spiritual world" and ideologies are part the world of politics and economics. But they both rest to no small degree on notions of belief and faith.

INDUS RELIGION: SOME POSSIBLE CONFIGURATIONS

Marshall's comments on Indus religion were perhaps the most sophisticated of his thoughts on these ancient peoples. His commentary has been called "brilliant."[3] While there are parts of Marshall's syntheses that are no longer tenable, many of the fundamentals are sound. This is especially true for the great divisions of this institution into the domains of a Great Mother Goddess and a Great Male God.[4]

The Great Female Goddess

The Great Mother Goddess was made manifest in female figurines and other iconography. Some of the female figurines manufactured by Harappans were toys, but others were possibly votive offerings or perhaps cult images for household shrines (see figures 6.9, 10.9, and 10.10).[5]

Marshall hypothesized that the terra-cotta female figurines are of three general types: toys, objects of sympathetic magic, and mother goddesses. He saw broad parallels in the mother goddess cult in Baluchistan, the Northwest Frontier, extending as far as the Aegean.

The evidence for mother goddesses in Indus religion is not terribly robust. Just which functions the terra-cotta female (and male) figurines played in Indus life is open to question. It might well be that some of them were multifunctional. Based on the material record in general, female sexuality is deeply engrained in Indus religion and ideology, and attention is paid to this point as this exploration of ancient beliefs progresses. The evidence for a Great Male God is a bit less ambiguous.

The Great Male God: Marshall's Proto-Siva

Perhaps the best-known part of Marshall's comments on Indus religion is the identification of a seal found by Mackay as a "Proto-Siva," thought to have been a forerunner of the consummate Hindu deity (see figure 3.2).[6] The seal was discovered during the 1928–1929 field season in DK-G Area, Southern Portion, Block 1, at minus 3.9 meters below datum.[7] Mackay ascribes it to the Intermediate I Period. It is steatite and 3.56 by 3.53 by 0.76 centimeters. This is seal number 420 in Mackay's report, and it is sometimes referred to as simply "seal 420."[8]

Marshall properly describes this figure as being in the attitude of a practitioner of yoga. McEvilley agrees with this determination.[9] The male sits on a dais with legs bent double beneath him. The heels are together, the toes down. His arms, covered with bangles, are outstretched with hands resting lightly on his knees, thumbs out.[10]

There is a claim that this figure on seal 420 is three-faced and that "the lower limbs are bare and the phallus . . . seemingly exposed, but it is possible that what appears to be the phallus is in reality the end of the waistband."[11] The head is surmounted by a pair of large horns, meeting in a high central headdress. These horns are those of a water buffalo, with the ribbing clearly depicted. Four wild animals surround the figure: an elephant, rhinoceros, water buffalo, and tiger. Beneath the dais are two quadrupeds: antelopes or ibexes, animals presented in a style that is paralleled on other Indus seals. Seven Indus pictographs are included on the seal, but one of them, a simple human stick figure, is out of place, and it may have been put there "for lack of room at the right-hand top corner."[12] On the other hand, this character could have been placed there for some special purpose, and until we have a decipherment of the Indus writing system, we probably will not be able to resolve this issue.

Marshall finds some connection with the historical Siva, although the name *Siva*, for a god does not appear prominently before 200 B.C.[13] The Vedic god with Siva's powers was Rudra, who possessed vigor and the ability to punish. He is something of an ascetic and a controller of destinies. In time Rudra and the new god Siva became one.

Marshall saw three faces on this seal, and this was one of the reasons he saw it as a Proto-Siva. But it is not entirely clear that the three faces are there.[14] Marshall is on safer ground when he addresses the more obvious yogi features of this seal. He draws on the connection with Siva as "pre-eminently the prince of Yogis—the typical ascetic and self-mortifier, whence his names *Mahatapah, Mahayogi* . . . in the course of time the yogi came to be regarded as a magician, miracle-monger and charlatan."[15]

Siva is not only the *Mahayogi* but also *Pasupati*, the lord of the beasts. In historical times this was thought of as the lord of cattle, but in the Vedas *pasu* signified a beast of the forest, thus the presence of wild animals on the seal appropriately follows the more ancient usage. "Rudra, the Vedic God, whose cult was amalgamated and identified with that of Siva, also bore the title of *Pasupati*, and this might conceivably have been one of the reasons for identifying him with Siva."[16] Marshall draws attention to the "master and mistress of animals" of Minoan Crete, but this is surely irrelevant in today's view of ancient religion.

Rai Bahadur Ramaprasad Chanda has noted that the famous priest-king image from Mohenjo-daro seems to have his eyes concentrated at the tip of his nose in the attitude of a yogi.[17]

Marshall next deals with the animals beneath the dais on which his Proto-Siva sits. "Two deer in a like position are portrayed on many medieval images of Siva . . . and a deer . . . held in one of his hands is a frequent attribute of the god in other manifestations."[18] Deer are a frequently used image in Indian religious art, employed by both Hindus and Buddhists. (The Buddha's first sermon was at the Deer Park at Sarnath.) But the animals on this seal are more probably antelopes or ibexes.

Marshall's position on his identification of this seal can be summarized as follows:

My reasons for this identification are four. In the first place the figure has three faces and that Siva was portrayed with three as well as with the more usual five faces, there are abundant examples to prove. Secondly, the head is crowned with the horns of a bull in the form of a *trisula*, and both the bull and the *trisula* are characteristic emblems of Siva. Thirdly, the figure is in a typical *yoga* attitude, and Siva was and still is, regarded as the *Mahayogi*—the prince of *Yogis*. Fourthly, he is surrounded by animals, and Siva is par excellence the "Lord of Animals" (*Pasupati*)—of the

wild animals of the jungle, according to the Vedic meaning of the word *pasu*, no less than that of domesticated cattle.[19]

Many authors have expressed a favorable view of Marshall's identification of the figure on this seal as a Proto-Siva.[20] I. Puskas has proposed that the central figure is a Proto-Brahma, a great Creator, rather than Proto-Siva.[21] Marshall's position has also been the object of a number of critiques.

A Critique of Marshall's Proto-Siva

Three scholars dispute Marshall's position on his Proto-Siva seal. One of the first is Sullivan.[22] He disagrees with Marshall on almost every point, including the possible presence of a phallus and the three faces. Sullivan submits that the figure is, in fact, female: There is no phallus and so on.

Srinivasan has two important papers reviewing seal 420.[23] The first is a fine review of the history of the problem. She holds that there are many "non-proto-Siva" images with the horned headdress; the figure is not "three-faced," moreover, there are no other tricephalic images in Harappan art; the posture of the yogi is indeterminate; her survey of Rudra in the Vedas indicates that this aspect of *Pasupati* does not protect wild animals, and Rudra's predominant trait with respect to all animals is wrath, rather than protection, compromising the notion that the Lord of the Beasts is a protector.

An interesting and provocative paper has been published by A. Hiltebeitel, who drew heavily on the work of B. Volchok, one of the Russian scholars who worked on their attempted decipherment of the Indus script.[24] Hiltebeitel's critique is much like Srinivasan's, but he makes much of the fact that the horns on the central figure are those of a buffalo. Indian tradition is rich in mythology and symbolism concerning *Mahisha*, the Buffalo God. Water buffalo also seem to occur in various contexts in the Indus Civilization (figure 8.1). For example, there is seal 279 showing a man hurling a spear at a buffalo.[25] "This has been regarded as depicting a mythic scene: a prototype of *Skanda* killing *Mahisasura*, the 'Buffalo Demon,' with a spear (*sakti*; *Mahabharata* 3: 221, 66, Poona Critical Edition) or *Valin* killing the buffalo *Dundubhi* (*Ramayana* 4, 11, 7–39; Baroda Critical Edition), or as the prototype of a Dravidian style buffalo sacrifice."[26]

Turning to other iconography on seal 420, Hiltebeitel begins to deal with the surrounding animals: the elephant, rhinoceros, tiger, and buffalo. In a long presentation he tries to associate these animals with the "vehicles" (*vahanas*) of later Indian tradition, particularly those of the deities of the four quarters, the *dik-* or *lokapalas*, or "World

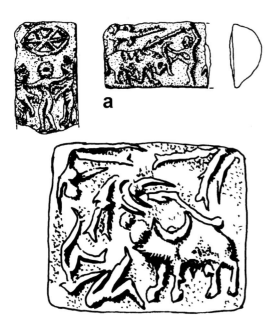

Figure 8.1 Seals with humans combating water buffalos (from *Indian Archaeology, A Review* 1962–63)

Regents." This was first suggested by Marshall, but relegated to a footnote and never pursued in his commentary.[27] This proposition between the animal iconography on the seal and *vahanas* remains interesting but not proved.

A Revision to the Proto-Siva Hypothesis

There is considerable merit in the contemporary critiques of Marshall's hypothesis on the Proto-Siva seal. He seems to have taken his thought on the significance of this figure one or two steps too far. The same is true, to some degree, with notions that the animals surrounding the central figure can be seen as "proto-*vahanas*" and that there was a sacrificial cult in the Indus Civilization. But there is something significant about this seal and other objects with similar figures, and it would be wrong to abandon the idea that in the Proto-Siva seal we have an insight into the Harappan system of belief, even later Indian tradition. There are three points, discussed in the following sections, on which I believe there is reasonably safe ground.

The Central Figure on Seal 420 Is a Deity

The pose, demeanor, and dress of the figure all combine to suggest that the central figure on seal 420 is a god of some sort. The buffalo horn headdress is especially important, given the other cultural contexts for this imagery. Also, the figure is not intelligibly human; there is even a slight chance that it is three-faced. There is ultimately no proof for the contention that this figure is a god, but the look of the figure elicits an irresistible conclusion for me—it is a god because it looks like a god!

The Headdress on the Deity of Seal 420 Is Derived from the Water Buffalo

There is a clear association between the god and the buffalo based on the headdress. These are clearly buffalo horns in both the sweeping curve and the fact that the artist who carved this seal attempted to indicate the distinctive ribbing of buffalo horns.

The importance of the buffalo to the Indus peoples is revealed in two contexts. The number and frequency of remains of this animal demonstrate its importance to the subsistence economy. Combat between humans and the buffalo is also a part of Indus iconography (see figure 8.1).

The buffalo horn motif first appears in the Early Harappan–Mature Harappan Transition. The famous pot from Kot Diji is undoubtedly the best and clearest representation of this motif (see figure 3.12). From the Mature Harappan at Kalibangan there is the famous horned figure incised on the broken triangular terra-cotta cake (see figure 6.18). A more recent discovery comes from the site of Padri in Saurashtra, where there is a large, complete storage jar with a human figure in a horned headdress.[28] The horns in this case seem to be those of a buffalo, based on the ribbing that the artist has portrayed. The Padri figure is flanked by a motif that is more plantlike, but retains the ribbing of the buffalo horns (figure 8.2). This is important documentation of the fact that these two sweeping motifs, one animal the other plant, might travel together and be combined on a single object.

There is evidence for a "buffalo cult" in ancient India, at least as old as the Puranas of the first millennium B.C.,

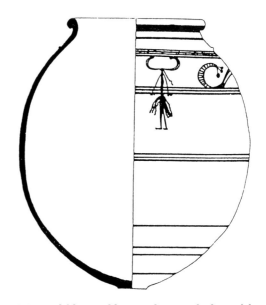

Figure 8.2 Padri horned human in association with a "horned" plant motif (after Shinde 1991)

and it was especially prominent in south India, where the Dravidian languages are spoken.[29]

The Posture of the Deity on Seal 420 Is a Form of Ritual Discipline, Suggesting a Precursor of Yoga

The posture of the central figure on Seal 420 is clearly not "naturalistic" as claimed by Sullivan.[30] Who sits "naturally" with their heels together?—only someone who has practiced the art sufficiently for it to have become cultural, a nonbiological adaptation. The structural biology of humans is not such that we take to such a position naturally.

There is an excellent article by T. McEvilley, a scholar who knows the Indian tradition of yoga, that evaluates the pose of the god on seal 420.[31] He concludes that the pose is the same as one used in yoga and can be taken as early documentation of a tradition of physical and mental discipline that emerges as yoga in the first millennium B.C.

According to B. Walker, yoga in later Indian tradition is said to have been founded by the sage Yajnavalkya and was later codified by Patanjali in his *Yoga Sutra*.[32] It is a form of mental and physical discipline, a code for ascetics. There are several forms: *karma-yoga*, salvation through works; *bhakti-yoga*, salvation through faith. *Hatha yoga*, the one most familiar to Westerners, is salvation through physical culture. Thus, while the origins of yoga are sometimes said to be pre-Aryan, it should be emphasized that the Hindu tradition has its own origin myth, as well as a story for the codification of the system of belief. If yoga as yoga goes back to the Indus Civilization, these latter points must be dealt with and not simply brushed aside as irrelevant.

There are several other yogi images in the corpus of Mature Harappan materials. A catalogue of those that have come to my attention is given in table 8.1. These diverse images suggest that the Indus pose of ritual discipline was used in more than one way and that their buffalo god did not have exclusive access to it. Taken as a whole, it appears that the pose may have been used by deities and humans alike, possibly best seen in the Ashmolean prism. This presents an interesting possibility: Some of the Harappans were devoted to ritual discipline and concentration, and this was one of the preoccupations of at least some of their gods.

Parpola has observed that this pose of ritual discipline may also occur in the West.[33] There is, for example, a potsherd with a sitting personage in this attitude from Tepe Yahya IVa in southeastern Iran (c. 2400–1800 B.C.).[34]

Horns and Plants in the Indus Age

The Indus Age is filled with imagery relating to bulls and buffalos. Seal 420 is one that is clearly a buffalo. But there are others that seem to be zebus, and these are not restricted to the stamp seals. Many examples of the latter come from the Early Harappan occupations at sites in the Gomal Valley. There is also a very fine example of a Kot Dijian vessel found at Burzahom in Kashmir, with the motif, which may date to the Late Kot Dijian, contemporary with the Mature Harappan (figure 2.10).

There are some "human" terra-cottas with horns.[35] The example in Mackay's plate LXXII has no sign of breasts, which are usually placed on female figurines, and so it might tentatively be identified as a male, as the central figure on seal 420 must be.

The Early Harappan period at Kalibangan is rich in imagery, and here we have the evidence for the broadening of this theme into motifs that are definitely plantlike and may represent a synthesis or merging of a plant/animal theme during the Indus Age (figure 8.3). There is a formal similarity in these various motifs. It is evident that the sweep of the lines, whether of a water buffalo's horns or those of a bull, is paralleled by the portrayal of stems and leaves of plants. The kind of plant motifs from Kalibangan

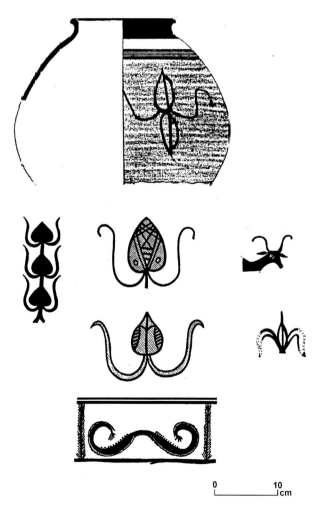

Figure 8.3　Plant and animal motifs from Kalibangan

Table 8.1 Yogi glyptics from the Indus Civilization

Designation	Reference	Site	Location
DK-5175 "Mahyogi"	Mackay 1937–38: 382, pl. XCIV, no. 420, pl. C, F	Mohenjo-daro	DK 1 II 7
DK-7991	Mackay 1937–38: 362, pl. CII, no. 9	Mohenjo-daro	DK 7 V 66
DK-12050	Mackay 1937–38: 376, pl. LXXXVII, no. 222	Mohenjo-daro	DK 15 I 5
VS 210	Marshall 1931i: 395, pls. CXVI, no. 29, CXVIII, no. 11	Mohenjo-daro	VS, Lane 5, House XXVII
Ashmolean Prism	Parpola 1994a: fig. 10.11	Mohenjo-daro	Surface
H97-3343/8029-28	Meadow and Kenoyer 2000: fig. 3, no. 1	Harappa	
H97-3346/8029-31	Meadow and Kenoyer 2000: fig. 3, no. 2	Harappa	
H97-3352/8029-32	Meadow and Kenoyer 2000: fig. 3, no. 3	Harappa	
H97-3301/8035-01	Meadow and Kenoyer 2000: fig. 3, no. 4	Harappa	
H97-3349/8102-41	Meadow and Kenoyer 2000: fig. 3, no. 5	Harappa	
H97-3345/8029-30	Meadow and Kenoyer 2000: fig. 3, no. 6	Harappa	
H97-3429/8010-76	Meadow and Kenoyer 2000: fig. 3, no. 8	Harappa	
H95-2486/4651-01	Meadow and Kenoyer 2000: fig. 3, no. 12	Harappa	
	Meadow, Kenoyer, and Wright 1996: fig. 21.1	Harappa	
	Meadow, Kenoyer, and Wright 1996: fig. 21.2	Harappa	
11466	Vats 1940: 344, pl. XCIII, no. 303, pl. XCII, no. 2	Harappa	Mound F

I type are also found at Kulli and Mundigak IV.3, contemporary with the Mature Harappan.[36]

This duality of motifs, with broad sweeping lines either as horns or plants or even indeterminate in these terms, is incorporated into the iconography of the Indus Civilization. There are numbers of sites in Saurashtra with a plant motif that document this ideographic element there during Sorath Harappan times. A fine example of the combination of motifs is found on a Period II pot from Lewan.[37] It has both the horns of a bullock, probably the zebu, and those of what appears to be a water buffalo. In the space between the horns of each of these beasts are stylized pipal leaves, seemingly growing out of the head of the animal.

The motif from Kulli, and others like it from Kalibangan, appears to be a representation—*stylization* is a probably a better description—of a water plant resembling the lotus, with its central bulblike flower and streamers. The shape of the bulb can also be seen as a play on female genitalia, giving us some reason to think of the plant motif as "female" and the animal, male, as in the Mahayogi seal, extending Marshall's male-female dichotomy.

Shaktism

Fundamental to the Marshall synthesis of Harappan religion is that it marks the beginning of a later Indian sect called Shaktism: "The underlying principle of shaktism is a sexual dualism, which has been aptly described as 'duality in unity.'"[38]

According to Walker, "*Sakti*, or 'energy,' is the term applied to the role of a god, and signifies the power of a deity manifested in and through his consort. The deity and his wife represent the dual aspect of the divine unity, and together symbolize the power of the godhead."[39]

In Marshall's view this primitive mother worship led to the transformation of the goddess into a personification of female energy (*shakti*) and the eternal productive principle, which was in turn united with the eternal male principle to become the creator and Mother of the Universe.[40] Support for the presence of this duality has been proposed here in the form of the plant/animal motifs. It came to Marshall in the form of cult objects representing human sexuality: phallic, baetylic stones, as well as the female, *yoni* ring stones.

Seven Attending Figures on the Seal of Divine Adoration (Seal 430)

One of the most famous of the Indus seals is seal 430, with what seems to be a narrative scene, possibly a mnemonic of some sort. It shows a goat and a kneeling human in front of a tree with a human inside it. Below that is a row of seven attending figures (see figure 3.4). This is not the only representation with seven attending humans, as seen in figure 8.4.

Seven is an important number in Indian culture, and in the Rgveda in one of the "Sarasvati Hymns," the river is venerated as one of seven sisters:

> She hath spread us beyond all foes, beyond her Sisters,
>   Holy One. As Surya spendeth out the days.
> Yea, she most dear amid dear streams, Seven-sistered,
>   graciously inclined. Sarasvati hath earned our praise.
> Guard us from hate Sarasvati, she who hath filled the
>   realms of earth. And that wide tract, the firmament!
> Seven-sistered, sprung from threefold source, Five
>   Tribes prosper, she must be invoked in every deed of
>   might.[41]

The geography of the Rgveda is centered on the Punjab, and we know that the reference to seven sisters is to

Figure 8.4 Indus glyptics with seven standing figures (after Vats 1941)

the *Sapta Sindhava,* the "seven rivers" of the region which include the Indus on the west and moves to the Ghaggar-Hakra to the east. Given the continuities in belief marking ancient India, that this notion of the "seven river sisters" came to the Vedic pundits from an Harappan source is at least as possible as the idea that they made it up for themselves.

Allchin and Allchin note that the seven figures have been "identified with the seven Rishis (seers) and with the seven Mothers of recent times."[42] Parpola has proposed that they represent the children of Brahma and Sarasvati, the seven sages of the constellation Ursa Major. Or, he notes, it could represent the Pleiades.[43]

Zoolatry

There is widespread evidence for the place of animals in Indus ideology. Two Indus sealings, in fact, show small figures carried above the crowd in a procession (figure 8.5). One of them is a bull, or cow, just another small observation that

supports the idea that cattle were a source of wealth for these people and entered their ideological world as well.

There are many portrayals of composite animals, some with three heads on one body; or tigers entwined; human torsos on four-legged bodies (see figure 6.20), "minotaur-like"; tigers with horns (see figure 6.17); unicorns with elephant trunks (see figure 6.15); and unicorns growing out of trees (see figure 6.16). At least one authority has suggested, with some reason, that the unicorn of the stamp seals is a mythical creature and not a bull at all.[44]

Mesopotamian Themes in Indus Iconography

Two iconographic themes appearing on Indus seals have parallels in Mesopotamian mythology; both are related to the Gilgamesh epic. The first is shown on a seal from Mohenjo-daro (see figure 6.17).[45] It shows a half-human female, half-bull monster attacking a horned tiger. This Indus seal may be construed as portraying the story of the Mesopotamian goddess Aruru, who created Ebani or Enkida as a bull-man monster to do combat with Gilgamesh, but who ultimately became his ally and fought with Gilgamesh against the wild animals.[46] The second motif is the well-documented Mesopotamian combat scene, with Gilgamesh fighting off rampant animals on either side (figure 8.6). The presence of this theme in objects associated with the Indus Civilization is perfectly in keeping with the notion that the Indus region and Mesopotamia were in contact with one another. That some aspects of Mesopotamian religion and ideology would have been accepted by the Indus peoples is a reasonable notion at face value, given the many historical examples of this sort of cultural exchange around the world. This theme has been further developed by A. Parpola.[47]

The Important Place of Water in Harappan Ideology

Marshall deals briefly with the importance of water to the Harappans.[48] Of the sanctity of water in the abstract, no tangible evidence has yet been found. But that water was held in great reverence and played a highly important part in the daily lives and practice of religion of the citizens of

Figure 8.5   Sealings with processions, possibly in Mohenjo-daro (after Marshall 1931i)

Figure 8.6 The "Gilgamesh" seal from Mohenjo-daro (after Mackay 1937–38)

Mohenjo-daro is demonstrated by the Great Bath as by the universal arrangements made throughout the city for drainage, wells, and bathing facilities, a theme very nicely developed by M. Jansen.[49] Indeed, it is safe, I think, to affirm that in no city of antiquity was so much attention paid to this matter of bathing as in Mohenjo-daro; and we can hardly believe that the practice would have been so ubiquitous and firmly rooted there had it not been regarded in the light of a religious duty. That such emphasis should have been placed on bathing—even in this remote age—is not a surprise given the importance the Indian has attached to ceremonial ablutions in sacred tanks, pools, and rivers since time immemorial.

F. R. Allchin's Interpretation of a Seal from Chanhu-daro

Mackay found an extraordinary seal in his excavations at Chanhu-daro.[50] It shows a short-horned bull, *Bos gaurus,* above a prostrate human figure (figure 8.7). He thought that the scene depicted an attack by the bull, and the human on the ground was attempting a defense against the trampling animal. In an essay on this seal, F. R. Allchin explains that the gaur is standing on his hind legs, slightly elevated above a human figure; its front legs are shown in excited motion. The bull's erect penis is shown in correct anatomical position. The figure below the gaur is less clearly shown and consequently more difficult to interpret. Allchin and Mackay see a headdress to the far right bottom of the seal impression.[51]

Seen from Allchin's perspective, the scene is very dy-

namic and excited; the bull is about to take a female goddess in an act that might be seen as sexual violence, and yet the clear appearance of her open, exposed genitals tells us that she is a willing partner in this deed.

Allchin rightly rejects the notion that this scene has any serious connection to the ancient Indian horse sacrifice (*Asvamedha*). Instead, he turns to the Vedas and forms an interesting hypothesis. This argument must be read in the original to gain a full sense of the detail, but it concludes:

> In the Chanhu-daro seal we have a representation of Heaven, the Bull, who is at once the consort and father of Earth; and of Earth who is at the same time the consort of the Bull, Heaven, and the mother of the Bull, her calf; and that these themes can be understood by reference to the Creation myths found in the Rgveda and Atharvaveda. It would be fascinating, but beyond the scope of this paper, to trace these themes through into the mythology of later periods of Indian thought. There is unquestionably prolific and rich material to use, both from textual and from modern ethnographic sources.

But for our understanding of the Indus civilization and its religion the discussion appears to be pregnant with suggestive meaning. We are led to wonder whether the omnipresent "bull," whether unicorn, bison or zebu, may not be the symbolic representation of the Heaven Father, just as the deity with the plant sprout emerging from head or genitals may not be the Earth Mother. How well the Vedic epithets Earth Mother (*Mata bharni*), mother of plants (*Mate osadhñam*) Aditi uttanapad (Aditi with the extended legs) and Aditi of the people (*Aditi jananam*) seem to fit the Indus representations! How suggestive that Sayana commenting on the word *uttanapad* should have linked it with vegetation and the whole creation of upward germinating plants![52]

Figure 8.7 Gaur ravaging a female on Chanhu-daro seal number 13 (after Mackay 1943)

Allchin takes this a step further, using the work of M. Eliade concerning the widespread theme of "Heavenly Father and Earth Mother." He seems to have given us good reason to see one possible contribution of the Indus Civilization to the concepts of heaven and earth as propounded in the Vedas.

Summary Thoughts

With the ethnic and cultural diversity that seems so clearly implied by the Early and Mature Harappan remains, there is still a chance that there never was a single Indus religion, but simply the sum of the belief systems of the peoples we see united within the archaeological context, as suggested in Wheeler's use of the term *Harappan religions*.[53] However, in the Indus Civilization, there was a high level of intense communication throughout the Greater Indus region that would have promoted a corresponding amount of change, adjustment, synthesis, and sharing of the older, diverse beliefs of the Early Harappan Stage. The emergence of an Indus religion would not be out of place, assuming the validity of these observations. It can be seen in the iconography that the religious aspect of ancient life in the Greater Indus region was exceptionally complex and that the surface has been barely scratched here.

Some insights into the nature of Indus religion, or perhaps religions, can be gained through an examination of the various architectural remains considered in this context. They were a poorly developed part of life during the Mature Harappan.

INDUS RELIGIOUS ARCHITECTURE

One of the more interesting observations about the Indus Civilization is that no temples have been found. Nor is there much to be said of monumental architecture with a religious function or monumental architecture of any kind. The temples and pyramids of Dynastic Egypt and the ziggurats of Mesopotamia have no parallel in the Indus Valley. Even if a crisp definition of the Indus religious institution or institutions eludes us, it is clear that religion was there; but they expressed this institution in a totally different way from that of their neighbors to the west. Constructing these kinds of huge, physical monuments to their gods and goddesses was apparently inappropriate to their belief systems. There can be little doubt, given the large Mature Harappan urban centers, that the capability—in both engineering skills and the ability to mobilize a workforce—was there to build such edifices. That this was not done is an important element in understanding the nature of this civilization.

Another contrast between Egypt and Mesopotamia and the Indus Civilization is the absence of palaces, the large abodes of the heads of government and their powerful associates charged with managing the fortunes of the political apparatus. It is possible that there was no single personage on whom the Indus political system focused.

The tension and competition between the religious and political institutions of Egypt and Mesopotamia were a source of creativity. The construction of ever larger temples and ziggurats, funerary monuments, palaces, and city walls was fueled by this rivalry. Without suggesting that this competition was the only source of inspiration for the construction of such monuments, it is an important focus. The absence of such monuments in the Indus Civilization suggests that the fundamental organizing and operational principles there were different from those of Egypt and Mesopotamia. It does not necessarily mean that the Indus Civilization was any less complex or less developed in a sociocultural sense. The absence of temples and palaces and other forms of monumental architecture should not be seen as an indication that the Harappan Civilization was a lesser development, a chiefdom, for example.[54] It is simply a good example of an alternative way in which a civilization, or a form of highly complex sociocultural system, has expressed itself.

There are several structures at Mohenjo-daro proposed to have been buildings used by the Indus religious establishment. Marshall lists several candidates, which fail the test, on detailed examination.[55] The best candidates include four buildings on the Mound of the Great Bath (see figures 11.3, 11.4, and 11.9): the Bath itself, the so-called College of Priests, a temple said to be below the stupa, and the Assembly Hall in L Area. House XXX in HR-B, House I in HR-A, and two buildings in DK-G Area (Blocks 11 and 8A) have also been discussed in this context. The structures that have been called fire altars at both Lothal and Kalibangan, along with the "ritual structure" at the latter site and the bathing platforms at Lothal, should also be mentioned. Harappa is conspicuous for the absence of architectural remains associated with religious activities.

Structures on the Mound of the Great Bath

The Great Bath

The Great Bath is the only convincing example of a ritual structure in the Mature Harappan. It does not look like a temple, but it does very strongly suggest a place of ritual (see figure 11.3). There is a discussion of the function of this important structure in the tour of Mohenjo-daro of-fered in this book, but the following points serve to justify the judgment just made. First, the building in which the bath is housed is elevated and secured away from the Lower Town, both highly symbolic. The bath was, in fact, filled with water and was a place of bathing or taking one's ablutions, in part evidenced by the bathing rooms on the eastern side of the building. The symbolic nature of water (especially at Mohenjo-daro) and cleanliness, both physical and ritual, seems to apply here, especially given the Great Bath's elevation and location. Thus, the notion that the bath was a place for ritual bathing makes a great deal of sense.

The College of Priests

The College of Priests, across Main Street from the Great Bath, is a very large building and might have functioned as a complement to the Great Bath (see figure 11.9). But there is no compelling evidence for this, save for its size and location. The thought that this building was a temple has no corroborating evidence.

A Temple under the Buddhist Stupa

Wheeler has referred to "the pious hope, often repeated but entirely unbased, that a temple may underlie the stupa on the (Mound of the Great Bath)" (see figure 11.3)[56] Mackay was the most outspoken proponent of this idea, and in his popular book, he said: "When further excavations are made on this site, the axiom will probably once more prove true that once a site becomes sacred it remains so, even to the followers of other religions who may occupy it later."[57] This is a good idea and one that is often true, but we have reason to believe that it may not be true at Mohenjo-daro.

So far as can be judged from the plans and sections of the buildings exposed around the stupa, there is nothing that sets the area apart from the rest of the city. There are "well-paved rooms and courtyards, bathrooms, drains, water-chutes, and the like—all well made though not better made than in some other buildings, and all seemingly in conformity with the standard patterns, but with no features out of the common. This is no proof, of course, that the few remnants exposed did not form part of some temple or other sacred edifice, or perhaps I should say, series of such edifices, since they belong to several strata and to various ages."[58] The prevailing view is that a detailed examination of excavation records shows that there has been sufficient digging around the stupa to ensure that there is no large building under it, an observation corroborated by M. Jansen.[59]

Other Buildings at Mohenjo-daro Proposed to Have Been Religious Architecture

House I in HR-A Area

House I in HR-A Area is an unusual, even exceptional structure, almost certainly not a domestic building (figure 8.8). A large number of seals and other finds came from it, along with two major pieces of sculpture: the Bearded Man and the Sad Man. The original description of the building leaves much to be desired, and it is not clear that Marshall knew exactly what to do with the finds.[60] Wheeler has said of the building:

> Amongst the other buildings attention may be drawn again to the HR Area, and more especially to the so-called House A1, bounded on the north by "South Lane" and on the west by "Deadman Lane." The significance of the plan is not brought out by the published record, which amalgamates walls of very different periods and is in several respects incomplete.[61]

Some portion of this inadequacy has been corrected in an excellent article by M. Jansen.[62] Access to original field records has enabled him to plot the find spots for twelve seals found in House I, all of which are unicorns or bar seals.

This structure is actually three buildings, interlinked into a single, integrated whole by staircases flanking the entrance. The elevated northern portion of the building has parallels in other structures, notably the Great Bath and House VIII in HR-A, the significance of which is not fully understood.[63] It cannot be demonstrated that this house was a temple or even associated with the religious institution. But it does not fit the pattern for an ordinary house: "From every point of view, House 1 is an extraordinary structure."[64]

House XXX in HR-B

There is a massive building, designated House XXX, in HR-B Area (figure 8.9). The exterior dimensions are approximately 24 by 11 meters. Most of the building, as we see it, is of the Intermediate Period; but Late Period walls also seem to be present, and the plan as published should not be relied on to settle detailed issues of interpretation. The outer walls are approximately 1.37 meters thick and preserved to a height of over 2 meters in places. Many of the interior rooms have no apparent entrances but are solid podia of mud-brick packing. Except for the southern rooms, associated with a well, the whole seems to have been a very solid understructure for another building, either vanished or never built, which would have been very substantial indeed.

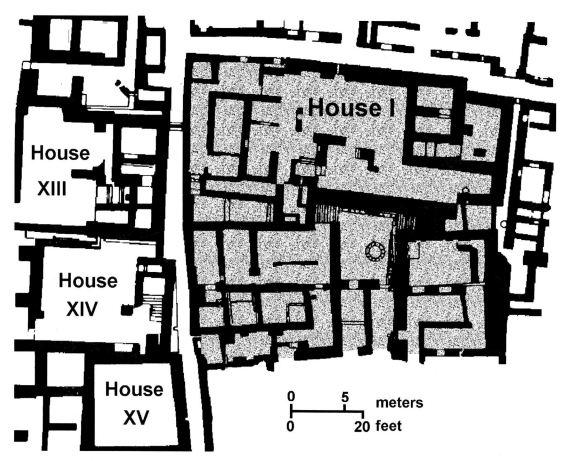

Figure 8.8   Plan of House 1 in HR-A (after Marshall 1931i)

House XXX's massive character and its unusual configuration have led to its consideration as a religious structure, and the proposal that it was a temple has no more merit than these two factors.

House L in HR-B Area
House L in HR-B is another massive structure, near House XXX. There is no more reason to believe that it was a temple than there is for House XXX.

Block 11, DK-G Area
This is a building of the Intermediate II Phase (figure 8.10). It is irregular in shape and associated with Loop and Long Lanes in DK-G Area.[65] The structure has not been completely excavated, but it contains a courtyard and three wells, a culvert, and water chute. There were many modifications in the Late Period. Mackay stated in the Marshall report:

> This building seems to approximate more closely to our idea of a temple than any building yet excavated at Mohenjo-daro. The three wells, which are almost in a straight line, probably provided water for ablutions in the

temple precincts. Not many antiquities were found within this complex beyond a few baked pottery figurines in the chambers on the south of the courtyard.[66]

It was later cleared more completely by Mackay, who gave four reasons for identifying this building as a "great khan," or hostel, rather than a temple. His reasons include such things as the block's propinquity to a gateway he thought was present, but never found, as well as an undocumented open-air market.[67]

Block 8A, DK-G Area
Located at the southwestern corner of the intersection of Central Street and Low Lane in DK-G Area is an L-shaped structure with very solidly built walls and interior buttresses (figure 8.11). The buttresses are unusual features at Mohenjo-daro and may have carried a second story or a continuous gallery around the building. The entrance off Low Lane is in the southeastern corner of the building, with a well room adjacent to the north. A later modification of the building led to the creation of a new entrance in about the center of the northern wall on Central Street,

Figure 8.9 Plan with Houses XXX and L, in HR-B Area, with privies (after Marshall 1931i)

and the blocking of the one off Low Lane. This remodeling seems to have also involved the creation of a double drain and the emplacement of a soak jar, connected with a terra-cotta pipe from the upper levels of the building. A separate latrine with its own entrance from Central Street and a drain into a cesspit on Low Lane also appears at about this time. The general level of this neighborhood was rising and this necessitated the construction of a set of stairs down into the well room off Low Lane.[68] While Block 8A is an unusual structure, not like a private home or domestic structure at Mohenjo-daro, there is really no evidence that it was a temple.

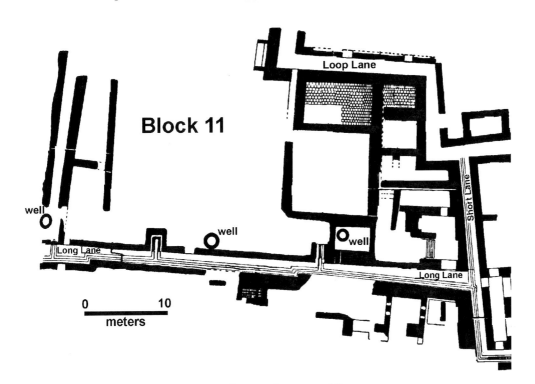

Figure 8.10 Plan of Block 11 in DK-G Area (after Mackay 1937–38)

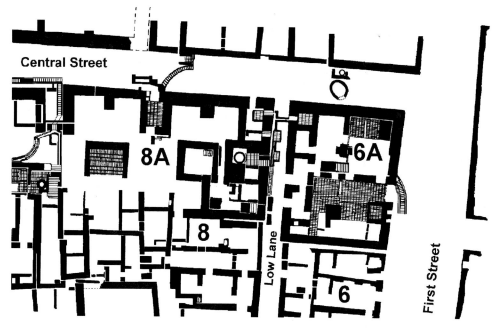

Figure 8.11   Block 8A in DK-G Area (after Mackay 1937–38)

Fire Altars

Small pits filled with ash and other debris have been identified as fire altars at the following Mature Harappan sites:
Rakhigarhi, Kalibangan, Lothal, Vagad, and Nageswar, the
latter three are in Gujarat. Similar structures were identified at Navdatoli on the Narmada River and Dangwada, a
site near Ujjain in western Madhya Pradesh.[69]

There is little merit to the proposal that there are fire
altars associated with the Indus Civilization. The case for
fire altars at Kalibangan is by far the strongest, and it includes the so-called ritual structure to the east of the
Lower Town. The rest of the evidence is weak, including
that from Nageswar, where the "fire altar" is in all likelihood a regular Indus funnel-shaped updraft kiln.

Religious Architecture: Summary

The only building, or building complex, that can be associated with the Indus Civilization that is religious or ritual
in nature is the Great Bath. Its location and size suggest
that it was used by a small number of people in an exclusive way. The importance of water, cleanliness, and elevation all contribute to the notion that this was an
important element in the Harappan religious establishment, perhaps even preeminent. The remainder of the
buildings falls short of the mark, especially those in DK
Area. House I in HR-A Area is an intriguing structure, but
it could be seen as the seat of a political potentate as easily
as a temple or seat of religious authority. Buildings XXX
and L in HR-B are simply massive structures.

HARAPPAN FUNERARY PRACTICES AND RELIGION

We have a strong sense that there was a diversity of Indus
funerary practices, suggesting the kind of ethnic diversity
that other observations tend to support. There is evidence for extended supine burial in pits and coffins, in
line with modern practices of Muslims and Christians.
The best evidence for this comes from Cemetery R-37 at
Harappa, the Kalibangan cemetery. Fractional burials,
for which the human remains were exposed to the elements and reduced to skeletons before being gathered for
final inhumation, also exist. Good evidence for this practice comes from Mohenjo-daro and Harappa in the Mature Phase and from Nal during the Early Harappan. The
evidence for cremation is not particularly robust, but
then, ash is ash, and if the practice is properly done, the
resulting material does not survive well, especially if the
teeth and residual bone are crushed. Mohenjo-daro and
Harappa both produced evidence for "postcremation
urns" that contain Mature Harappan artifacts—mostly
pottery and some ash and bone, but almost none of it human. There is a Mature Harappan crematory located in
western Rajasthan at Tarkhanwala Dera.[70]

There is also a sense that, for some Indus persons, the
care they received at death was somewhat casual. Stray human bones and teeth are a part of the excavation records at
a number of sites, for example, Rojdi. Moreover, many of
the fractional burials have remains from more than one
person in them, sometimes mixtures of adults and children.

The Indus dead are discussed more in the next chapter.

SYNTHESIS

There are two themes that come through to me in this review of Indus religion. The first is diversity of practice; the second is the absence of a robust representation of the religious institution in monumentality.

The diversity theme is seen at Mohenjo-daro in a number of ways. First, Marshall's Great Mother Goddess and Great Male God, synthesized in a body of iconography that plays on the plant/animal dichotomy—with the importance of water worked in—in a way that is not well understood. I include the water theme because of the magnitude of its presence (the Great Bath, drains, wells, bathing platforms) at so many Indus sites. But there are other themes as well: Shaktism, zoolatry, lingas and yonis, ritual discipline, even Mesopotamian ideas that complement the first theme.

As seen at Mohenjo-daro and to some extent other sites, the "big" theme, perhaps as close as the Harappans got to a Great Tradition, is the one that deals with the dichotomy of female/male and plant/animal and the importance of water. This is complemented by the "little tradition" of Shaktism, zoolatry, lingas and yonis, and the like.

There is geographical diversity as well. Harappa has no Great Bath, and the water theme there may be more muted than it is at Mohenjo-daro. The same is true for Kalibangan. If the fire altars there are in fact ritual facilities, perhaps we have a fire theme that contrasts to the water theme at a place like Mohenjo-daro. Such a north-south opposition would fit well with the provinces that have been suggested for stamp seals and the human population. There is nothing at a place like Rojdi to suggest much of anything about religion.

The absence of ostentatious buildings and facades says nothing of a priesthood, which may or may not have been present. We could even consider the possibility of an individual anointed as the supreme religious leader, a kind of Harappan Pope. But it is just as possible that this, too, was a weakly developed part of the institution and that priests, if present at all, were not organized into their own hierarchy, but functioned more individually, as in Islam or Buddhism. As a further alternative—and this is not an exhaustive treatment of possibilities—some category of "respected elder" might have been the source of religious leadership, training, and inspiration. We just do not know how the Indus peoples organized themselves in this area, and there does not seem to be a class of evidence in the remains of the Harappan Civilization that will answer the question, as intriguing as it may be.

It appears that the practice of religion may have been a rather individualized obligation, possibly done in the home by family members without significant amounts of paraphernalia. This is perhaps the most appealing suggestion to emerge from this study of the Indus system of beliefs because it is so harmonious with the artifactual and architectural evidence. The terra-cotta figurines, lingas, *baetyls,* and yonis could all be very nicely accounted for in this view of Indus beliefs. The same is true for the fire altars at Kalibangan and perhaps Lothal; although at Kalibangan there is a suggestion of some civic level of use as well. If fire was used as a part of Indus ritual, and there is no reason to say that it was or was not, many of the hearths that have been found in Indus settlements might have been used for such daily worship. The Indus practice might even have involved using the household cooking hearth as the ritual hearth in some very sensitive expression of household renewal linked to the preparation of food, sustenance, and continued well-being. This speculation has gone well beyond the ability of the evidence to support it, but the key point is that the ordinary domestic hearth should not be ruled out as a possible center for daily worship.

There is some direct evidence for public performances of a somewhat religious nature. This comes from the two sealings from Mohenjo-daro that show a procession with participants carrying banners, statues of cattle, and what may be models of the "standard" that is generally found in front of the unicorn on the stamp seals (figure 8.5).

If the primary expression of worship in the Indus Civilization was an individual or family matter, there is still some sense that devotion was carried out at some higher institutional or civic level as well. The best evidence for this comes from the Great Bath and possibly the bathing floors at Lothal as an extension of the practice.

The raison d'être for the Indus Civilization was an ideology, an Indus Great Tradition, fashioned in part from the heritage of the Early Harappan Stage, in part from the genius of the Harappans themselves. This would have been a distinctively Indus way of looking at the world, an all-encompassing philosophy of life. The inhabitants of the settlements clearly within the Indus fold, such as Mohenjo-daro and Kalibangan, would have shared significantly in at least these core beliefs. If this hypothesis is anywhere near correct, the Indus ideology would have been both universalistic and powerful, capable of molding the lives of hundreds of thousands, if not millions, of people.

LATER INDIAN TRADITION BEGINS IN THE INDUS CIVILIZATION

The proposed historical links between the Indus Civilization and later Indian civilization is a difficult, complex, sometimes contentious, even politicized topic. There is evidence from Mature Harappan times for a female/male duality, something like Shaktism, the importance of water and possibly fire in worship, the presence of yoga-like ritual discipline, and Allchin's proposed representation of heaven as a male and earth as mother. These are all reasons for us to suspect that the Indus Civilization provides a logical, if somewhat arbitrary, starting point for some aspects of the later Hindu tradition. Wheeler touches on this when he notes:

> And finally the importance—not necessarily the deification—of water in the life of the Harappans is stressed by the Great Bath on the citadel of Mohenjo-daro and by the almost extravagant provision for bathing and drainage throughout the city, and may provide yet another link with the later Hinduism. The universal use of "tanks" in modern Indian ritual, and the practice of bathing at the beginning of the day and before principal meals, may well derive ultimately from . . . the Indus civilization.[71]

A complete discussion of the cultural historical connections, suggesting the process whereby the Indus cultural tradition met and was accepted by the Aryans, who composed the Vedic texts, is more properly part of a discussion of the transformation of the ancient cities of the Indus. There are, after all, continuities other than religious ones to be considered. At the conclusion of the paper on seal 13 from Chanhu-daro, Allchin makes the following comment:

> This should warn us against any premature attempt to see in the Chanhu-daro seal evidence of the presence of the Indo-Aryan speaking people; and equally against any over simple attempt to derive the ideas in the *Rgveda* from an Indus source. But having said so much, it must still be admitted that the correspondences in the present case appear to be so profound, and so harmonious, that they must have involved some kind of fairly direct culture contact. Several times in recent years we have expressed our view that Indo-Aryan speaking people must have arrived in the Indus Valley during the lifetime of the mature Indus civilization, and that there must have been a period of cultural synthesis between the two very different elements. It is still not possible to say when the first Indo-Aryans arrived, nor over how long a period they continued to move into the Indus region from their earlier homelands in Central Asia, but the model of this period of cultural interaction provides in our view the most plausible indication of the medium within which the sort of cultural synthesis suggested by the Chanhu-daro seal and the Rigvedic myths could have taken place.[72]

Allchin's notion that there were Indo-Europeans in the Greater Indus Valley during Indus times is perfectly reasonable, in theory. These were not the people who com-

posed the hymns of the Rgveda, nor even necessarily the direct ancestors of the composers, since the codification of the Rgveda, the earliest Vedic text, is thought to be circa 1000 B.C. The history and ritual in the Rgveda is older than this, some of it possibly as much as several hundred years older, but surely not much more. Thus, placing the beginnings of the composition of the Rgveda at 1500 B.C. is reasonable, but certainly not proved. The composition process could have begun as late as 1100 B.C., or even decades later. In any event, it is hundreds of years removed from the date that Allchin has proposed for the earliest appearance of Indo-Europeans in the Greater Indus region. To satisfy Allchin's suggestion and make a connection to the Vedas, we must imagine that there were early Indo-Europeans who became one of the peoples of the Indus Civilization. They must have maintained their own language and traditions, but participated in Indus cultural life as well. Their sense of self-identity preserved their own heritage in a way that allowed them to interact in a positive way with other Indo-Europeans. Allchin suggests that there may have been a more or less regular southerly migration of these peoples. While this is possible, and may well have been one part of a complex pattern of movement, we should also admit that the seasonal migration of cattle-keeping peoples, like the Aryans of the Rgveda, may have taken these peoples back north into Central Asia on a periodic basis. Moreover, various Indo-European peoples may have moved south on a seasonal or some other relatively short-term basis, thus coming into contact with both the Harappans themselves as well as their Indo-European-speaking brethren who had moved on a permanent basis into the Punjab, possibly Sindh, and other areas.

The position just stated is congruent with the linguistic findings of F. Southworth, who sees a variety of language influences in the Vedic texts.[73] Moreover, with the excavations at Dadheri and Baghwanpura,[74] as well as Posturban Phase Harappan sites such as Hulas,[75] Mitathal,[76] and Banawali,[77] we now have a complete, unbroken cultural historical sequence linking the Mature Harappan settlements to the north Indian Early Iron Age, which is associated with Painted Gray Ware.

Bringing the Harappans and Indo-Europeans together in time and place for a period of cultural synthesis is not an insurmountable problem in the cultural history of the Subcontinent. Getting archaeologists to stop thinking in terms of a single Indo-European migration is far more of a challenge.

NOTES

1. A bibliography on this subject is Atre 1987; F. R. Allchin 1985; Hiltebeitel 1978; Marshall 1931f; McEvilley 1981;

Parpola 1985a, 1985b, 1992, 1994a; Srinivisan 1975–76, 1984; Sullivan 1964.
2. Marshall 1931e.
3. Allchin and Allchin 1982: 213.
4. Marshall 1931e: 49–58.
5. Marshall 1931e: 50.
6. Marshall 1931e: 52–56.
7. Mackay 1928–29: 74–75, pl. XXVIIIf.
8. Mackay 1937–38: pl. XCIV, no. 420.
9. McEvilley 1981.
10. Marshall 1931e: 52.
11. Marshall 1931e: 52.
12. Marshall 1931e: 52.
13. Walker 1968: 406.
14. Marshall 1931e: 53.
15. Marshall 1931e: 53–54.
16. Marshall 1931e: 54.
17. Marshall 1931e: 54.
18. Marshall 1931e: 55.
19. Quoted in Mackay 1928–29: 74–75.
20. Mackay 1948; 56–57; Wheeler 1968: 105; Allchin and Allchin 1982: 214; Walker 1968: II, 406; Fairservis 1975: 275, 277; O'Flaherty 1973: 9.
21. Puskas 1984: 164.
22. Sullivan 1964.
23. Srinivasan 1975–76, 1984.
24. Hiltebeitel 1978.
25. Mackay 1937–38.
26. Hiltebeitel 1978: 773–74.
27. Marshall 1931e: 53 n. 1.
28. Shinde 1991.
29. Hiltebeitel 1978: 773–75.
30. Sullivan 1964: 120.
31. McEvilley 1981.
32. Walker 1968: II, 616–17.
33. Parpola 1984: 181–83.
34. Lamberg-Karlovsky and Tosi 1973: pl. 137.
35. Mackay 1937–38: pl. LXXII, no. 37, pl. LXXIV, nos. 21, 22, 25.
36. Stein 1931: Kulli V.ix.3; Casal 1961: fig. 102.
37. Allchin et al. 1986: 112.
38. Marshall 1931e: 57; see Walker 1968: 336–38 for more.
39. Walker 1968: II, 336.
40. Marshall 1931e: 57–58.
41. Rgveda VI.61.10–12, after Griffith 1896.
42. Allchin and Allchin 1982: 215.
43. Parpola 1990: 265.
44. Grigson 1984.
45. Marshall 1931i: no. 357.
46. Marshall 1931e: 67.
47. Parpola 1984.
48. Marshall 1931e: 75.
49. Jansen 1993a.
50. Mackay 1943: pl. LI, no. 13.
51. Allchin 1985.
52. Allchin 1985: 381.
53. Wheeler 1968: 108.
54. Fairservis 1986.
55. Marshall 1931c: 22–23.
56. Wheeler 1968: 53.
57. Mackay 1948: 15.
58. Marshall 1931h: 124.
59. Jansen 1998, personal communication.
60. Hargreaves 1931: 176–79.
61. Wheeler 1968: 52.
62. Jansen 1985.
63. Jansen 1985: 166 n. 1.
64. Jansen 1985: 184.
65. Mackay 1931c: 251–52, pl. LXIV, and 1937–38: 118–20, pl. XIX.
66. Mackay 1931c: 252.
67. Mackay 1937–38: 119.
68. Mackay 1937–38: 92–93; Wheeler 1968: 51.
69. Sankalia, Deo, and Ansari 1971: 49, pl. IVB; Chakravarty, Wakankar, and Khare 1989: 43–45.
70. Ghosh 1962.
71. Wheeler 1968: 110.
72. Allchin 1985: 382.
73. Southworth 1990, 1992.
74. Joshi 1993.
75. Dikshit 1984.
76. Bhan 1975.
77. Bisht 1982.

CHAPTER 9

Burial Customs and Biological Diversity of the Peoples of the Indus Civilization

INTRODUCTION

The discovery of the Indus Age took place at a time when the concept of biological races was much in vogue, and the older literature on the Indus Civilization speaks of its peoples in these terms.[1] In their report on the excavations at Mohenjo-daro, Colonel R. B. Seymour Sewell and B. S. Guha used anthropometric measurements and descriptive features of twenty-six skeletons and found four racial groups: Proto-Australoid, Mediterranean, Alpine, and Mongolian branch of the Alpine stock.[2] This racial typology of Indus peoples has been widely referenced despite the fact that the use of such data has been discredited for many years.[3]

A list of the principal sites where there is evidence for the disposal of the dead during the Indus Age is given in table 9.1. This list does not cover all the sites at which human remains have been found, those with stray human bones and teeth, for example.

The human remains associated with the Indus Civilization have been collected from diverse archaeological contexts: from cemeteries to cremation platforms; some even came from cesspits. While we know of no cemetery there, the human remains from Mohenjo-daro deserve first treatment.

Mohenjo-daro

The apparent absence of a cemetery at Mohenjo-daro is one of the important facts in the funerary record of the Indus Civilization. The interments at this city all seem to be of a rather hasty character. There is a total of forty-two individuals represented in the Mohenjo-daro skeletal series. These are human skeletal materials that can be examined and measured. There are more fractional interments and postcremation urns from seventeen other distinct archaeological contexts.

Wheeler implies that some of the humans whose remains were found at Mohenjo-daro may have died as part of a massacre associated with the abandonment of the city and the decline of the Indus Civilization.[4] This has been thoroughly debunked by Dales and Kennedy.[5] Whatever their cause of death, its association with war and then abandonment of Mohenjo-daro or the eclipse of the Indus Civilization cannot be proved. Neither Indra nor his Aryan believers stand accused of these deaths. Table 9.2 is a list of the places at Mohenjo-daro where human remains or possible funerary materials have been found.

The skeleton in House I of HR-A is a later interment since its jewelry includes glass beads and a zinc ornament.[6] The funerary record at Mohenjo-daro is indicated in figure 9.1.

A Note on Fractional Burials and Postcremation Urns

Marshall notes possible fractional burials in several places at Mohenjo-daro (e.g., VS Area, House XXVII), but they are not associated with human bone.[7] Most of the occurrences are from late in the occupation of the city. These are doubtful cases in relation to funerary activity, but serve to illustrate how elusive the Indus treatment of the dead is to us. These occurrences are discussed here since Marshall has described them as "funerary," and we note, of course, the absence of human bones.

There are also postcremation urns, said to be funerary relics, but most often they, too, contain no human bone. These urns occur at both Mohenjo-daro and Harappa. It may seem strange to seriously entertain the notion that the Indus peoples had a funerary custom that involved interring cremated human remains in urns with other objects if there is hardly a shred of human bone to back up the proposition.

Special mention should be made of the two urns buried at the entrance of the Great Bath. Whether or not these urns actually resulted from some funerary rite, these deposits are of special significance because of their location at the entrance of this important building. They should at least be considered a "foundation deposit" or a "commemorative offering" marking something of consequence to those who used the Great Bath.

Marshall, a deeply committed champion of this proposition, put the best face he could on the matter.[8] Wheeler leaves no doubt as to his opinion: "I also omit the so-called 'postcremation burials' from both sites, since there is no evidence whatsoever that these have anything to do with human burial."[9] The following sections discuss the human remains from Mohenjo-daro in excavation-area order.

Table 9.1 Sites with evidence for the disposal of the dead during the Indus Age

Site	District	Phase
Allahdino	Karachi	Indus Civilization
Bagor	Bhilwara	Bagor
Bajaniya-no Thumdo	Banaskantha	Amri-Nal Burial Pottery
Bhamaria Thumdo	Banaskantha	Amri-Nal Burial Pottery
Binjor Three	Ganganagar	Indus Civilization or Sothi-Siswal
Burzahom	Srinagar	Northern Neolithic
Chandigarh	Chandigarh	Indus Civilization
Chanhu-daro	Nawabshah	Indus Civilization
Dabar Kot	Loralai	Indus Civilization
Daimabad	Ahmednagar	Posturban Harappan
Damb Buthi	Dadu	Amri-Nal
Damb Sadaat	Quetta-Pishin	Quetta
Damboli	Kachi	BMAC
Dauda Damb	Kachi	BMAC
Derawar Ther	Bahawalpur	Indus Civilization
Dher Majra	Ropar	Indus Civilization and/or Posturban Harappan
Gemuwala Dehar	Bahawalpur	Indus Civilization
Gumla	Dera Ismail Khan	Gandhara Graves?
		Late Kot Diji
Harappa	Sahiwal	Indus Civilization and Cemetery H
Harthar-no Timbo	Mehsana	Amri-Nal Burial Pottery
Isplinji Two	Kalat	Quetta?
Kalibangan	Ganganagar	Indus Civilization
Kashi Qalat Cemetery	Makran	Shahi Tump?
Kulli	Makran	Kulli?
Langhnaj	Mehsana	Bagor
Lothal	Ahmedabad	Indus Civilization
Madhvya-no Timbo	Banaskantha	Amri-Nal Burial Pottery
Mahra Sharif	Dera Ismail Khan	Gandhara Graves
Mehi	Kalat	Kulli?
Mehrgarh	Kachi	BMAC
		Early Harappan–Mature Harappan Transition
		Kot Diji
		Kechi Beg
		Togau
		Burj Basket-marked
		Kili Ghul Mohammad
Moghul Ghundai	Zhob	Kot Diji
Mohenjo-daro	Larkana	Indus Civilization
Moti Pipli	Banaskantha	Amri-Nal Burial Pottery
Nagwada One	Surendranagar	Amri-Nal Burial Pottery
Nal	Kalat	Amri-Nal
Periano Ghundai	Zhob	Kot Diji
Quetta Treasury	Quetta-Pishin	BMAC
Rakhigarhi	Hisar	Indus Civilization
Rampara Two	Bhavnagar	Sorath Harappan?
Randal Dadwa	Rajkot	Sorath Harappan?
Rojdi	Rajkot	Sorath Harappan or Late Sorath Harappan
Ropar	Ropar	Indus Civilization
Santhli Two	Banaskantha	Amri-Nal Burial Pottery
Santhli Four	Banaskantha	Amri-Nal Burial Pottery
Sarai Khola	Rawalpindi	Iron Age Cemetery
Shahi Tump	Makran	Shahi Tump
Sibri Cemetery	Kachi	BMAC
Sur Jangal	Loralai	Kechi Beg?
Surkotada	Kutch	Transitional
Sutkagen-dor	Makran	Indus Civilization
Tarkhanwala Dera	Ganganagar	Indus Civilization
Uchali	Rawalpindi	Northern Neolithic?
Waddanwala	Bahawalpur	Indus Civilization

Table 9.2 Human remains at Mohenjo-daro

Excavation area	Human remains	Site report documentation
HR-B Area, Block 2, House V, Room 74	14 skeletons: 13 adult males and females and 1 child; the HR Area tragedy. These remains are skeletons numbered 2 and 4–16 in the reports.	Marshall 1931f: 79–80; Hargreaves 1931: 184–86, pls. XLIIIa and XLVIa and b; Sewell and Guha 1931: 602–5
HR-B Area, Block 2, House X, Room 126	Fractional burial.	Marshall 1931f: 83; Hargreaves 1931: 184
HR-B Area, Block 2, House V, Room 49	1 cranium of a female found 1.8 m below the surface. This is designated skeleton 19 in the reports.	Sahni 1931a: 191; Sewell and Guha 1931: 630–31
HR-A Area, Deadman's Lane	1 skeleton and parts of a small cranium. This is designated skeleton 17 in the reports, and the cranium seems to be number 26.	Marshall 1931f: 79; Sahni 1931a: 179, pls. XLIIc and d; Sewell and Guha 1931: 605
HR-A Area, House III, Courtyard 13	Fractional burial. This is designated skeleton 3 in the reports and consists only of a cranium.	Marshall 1931f: 82; Hargreaves 1931: 180–81, pl. XLIIId; Sewell and Guha 1931: 602
VS Area, Block 3, Lane 4 between Houses XVIII and XXXIII	6 skeletons, including 1, possibly 2 children; the VS Area tragedy. These are designated skeletons 20–25 in the reports.	Marshall 1931f: 79; Sahni 1931b: 222–23, pl. LIXc; Sewell and Guha 1931: 605–6
VS Area, Block 4, House XXVII, Room 72 at the south end of Lane 5	Fractional burial.	Marshall 1931f: 83; Sahni 1931b: 228
VS Area, Block 4, House XXVII, Room 66	Fractional burial.	Marshall 1931f: 83; Sahni 1931b: 228, pl. LXXX, nos. 41, 44, 52
VS Area, Block 4, House XXVII, Courtyard fronting Rooms 69 to 71	Fractional burial.	Marshall 1931f: 83; Sahni 1931b: 228, pl. LXXIX, no. 18, pl. LXXXI, no. 23, and pl. LXXXII, no. 35
VS Area, Lane 3 south of House XIX	Postcremation urn.	Marshall 1931f: 86; Sahni 1931b: 223, pl. LXXXIV, no. 19, pl. LIXb
VS Area, Block 1, House V, Room 15	Postcremation urn.	Marshall 1931f: 87; Sahni 1931b: 217, pl. CXIII, no. 444
VS Area, Block 4, corridor in House XXVI	Postcremation urn.	Marshall 1931f: 87; Sahni 1931b: 228–29, pl. CXVI, no. 29, pl. CXVIII, no. 11
VS Area, Block 4, Lane 5	2 postcremation urns.	Marshall 1931f: 87; Sahni 1931b: 227
VS Area, Block 4, Building XXI, Chamber 3	Collection of charred human bones.	Marshall 1931f: 87; Sahni 1931b: 224
SD Area, Great Bath	2 postcremation urns.	Marshall 1931f: 86, 137 n. 5, pl. XXVa
DK-G Area, Block 10A	9 skeletons in the Long Lane Group.	Mackay 1937–38: 116–18, 648, pls. XXXIIa and b, pl. CX, no. 43, pl. C, no. 15, pl. CXI, 11, 72, pl. CXXXIX, nos. 25, 45, 69, pl. CXLII, no. 14; Guha and Basu 1938: 613–23, fig. 1
DK-G Area, Block 8A, Well Room 42	2 skeletons lying on a stairway; the Well Room Tragedy.	Mackay 1937–38: 94; 648, pls. XX and XLIIIa, b, and c; Guha and Basu 1938: 624
DK-G Area, Low Lane, opposite Block 8, Well Room 42	1 cranium lying in Low Lane.	Mackay 1937–38: 95; 648, pls. XX and XLIIIa; Guha and Basu 1938: 624
DK-G Area, Block 8A, Low Lane	1 cranium in a cesspit on Low Lane.	Mackay 1937–38: 95; 648, pls. XX and XLIIIa; Guha and Basu 1938: 624
DK-G Area, Block 7, House I, Room 19	1 skeleton.	Guha and Basu 1938: 623
DKG Area, Western Court of Block 1	1 skeleton.	Mackay 1937–38: 49; Guha and Basu 1938: 623
GFD Area	5 skeletons.	Dales 1968b: 61

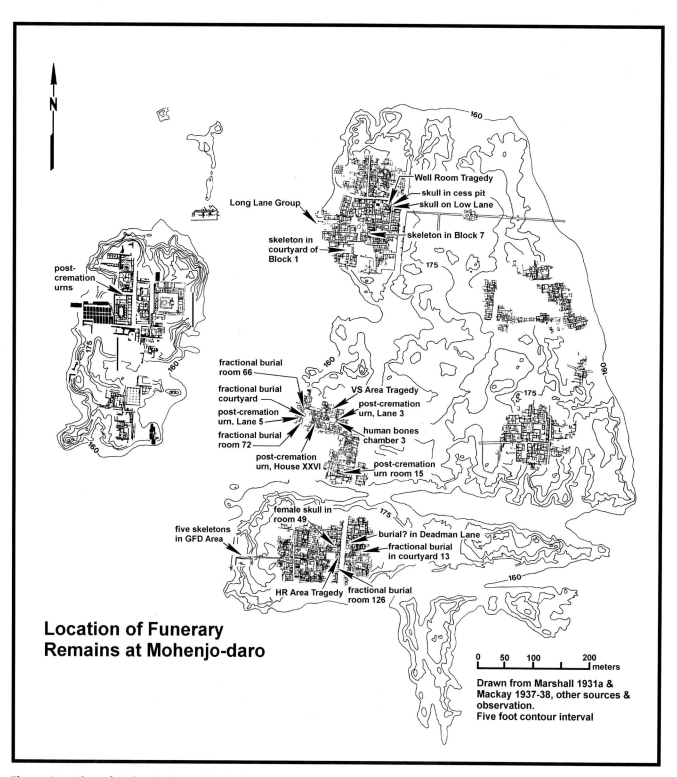

Figure 9.1   Plan of Mohenjo-daro with the locations of human remains

Human Remains in HR Area

HR-B Area, Block 2, House V, Room 74; the "HR Area Tragedy"   Perhaps the most prominent of the "massacre" scenes at Mohenjo-daro was found in HR Area

(figure 9.2). It consists of 14 skeletons: 13 adult males and females and 1 child.[10] Many have thought this group of skeletons were the victims of the invading Aryans in their conquest of the Harappan empire. Wheeler's thoughts on this scene are as follows:

Figure 9.2   The "HR Area Tragedy"

Figure 9.3 Unicorn seal found with one of the victims of the "HR Area Tragedy" (after Marshall 1931i)

That final blow has often enough been described. It is represented by groups of skeletons—men, women and children, some bearing axes or sword-cuts—which have been found lying on the topmost level in the sprawled or contorted positions in which they fell. They had been left there by raiders who had no further use for the city which they had stormed. In that moment Mohenjo-daro was dead.[11]

The HR Area tragedy was found very close to the surface, with the first sign of a skeleton being only 30 centimeters below ground level. These skeletons are sometimes thought to be in room 74 of House V; however, they were found above the wall levels of this room as with skeleton number 2.[12] All of the skeletons were on approximately the same level, but skeleton number 2 was 15 centimeters higher than the legs of skeleton number 8. Variation of this kind can be an indication that we are not dealing with a single event here. There were no signs of actual graves.

Hargreaves believes that these people were dispatched on the spot:

The remains of the fourteen bodies found in Room 74 appear to indicate some tragedy, for the manner in which the skeletons are intermingled points rather to simultaneous death than synchronous burial, for the positions of the individual bodies are rather those likely to be assumed in the agony of death than those of a number of corpses thrown into a room.[13]

Marshall has a slightly different view:

In regard to Group A, though prolonged denudation had obliterated the surface remains, there can be little or no doubt that later structures once rose above the ruins of House V in which this group occurs, and presumably it was beneath a room or court of one of these vanished structures that a pit was dug and the bodies thrown into it, or it may be that the living were put to death in it; for it is possible, though I do not think likely, that these groups of skeletons represent sacrifices to the dead.[14]

A general sense of the chronology for this scene comes from the stratigraphic position, high in the deposits, and the artifacts associated with them. These included a variety of personal ornaments, some of which still encircled the bones and a unicorn seal (figure 9.3).

One of the individuals was found with 75 faience beads, which seem to have been part of a girdle, two copper rings, and two copper beads along with a fragment of another copper ornament—all artifacts of the Indus Civilization.[15]

Sewell and Guha note what they believe to be traumatic injuries to some of the individuals in the HR Area tragedy.[16] Kennedy, who had an opportunity to examine these same materials firsthand, believes that Sewell and Guha have overstated the case. Kennedy agrees that there are signs of trauma on skeleton 10; however, "the 'cut' is not fresh and its margins are characterized by considerable bone resorption."[17] His assessment of this wound is that it may have contributed to the death of this individual, but the degree of resorption indicates that it was received thirty to seventy days prior to death. Kennedy also noted an old, healed lesion on skeleton 1: "However, it is likely to be a skeleton of more recent date than others in the series and its relevance to the massacre is nil."[18] This is a subject in which I believe we should respect Kennedy's more recent professional assessment.

We, therefore, have skeletons without mortal wounds found in a context in which they all may not be associated or even in the same "room." We lack definitive evidence for the context of this macabre scene, and it could have taken place any time after the abandonment of House V at the close of the Intermediate I period. In the end, no one knows how or why these people died, but the disposition of the bodies suggests a very hasty interment.

HR-A Area, Deadman Lane   The report on the skeleton(s) in Deadman Lane is very short:

At the point where the lane turns westward, part of a skull and the bones of the thorax and upper arm of an adult were discovered, all in friable condition, at a depth of 4 ft. 2 in. The body lay on its back diagonally across the lane. Fifteen inches to the west were fragments of a tiny skull. It is to these remains that the lane owes its name.[19]

The skeleton was found rather deep, at 1.25 meters, and Marshall makes the following point about the date of this find: "Deadman's Lane, where one of the skeletons lay, was completely built over in the Late Period, and it was apparently during that period (either Late I or Late II) that the body was interred there under the floor of the then existing houses."[20]

This case seems to document intraurban burials at Mohenjo-daro in the early part of the Late Period. It has not been demonstrated conclusively, however, that this took place in a lane, since the architectural context for the early Late Period in this part of the site has not yet been established.

Human Remains in VS Area

VS Area, Lane 4, between Houses XVIII and XXXIII; the "VS Area Tragedy" This tragedy consists of six skeletons, including one, possibly two, children.[21] It is another of the massacre scenes, and the positions of the remains are quite graphic (figure 9.4).[22] Four of the bodies lay on their backs, two of them facing one another. But the other two (numbers 23 and 20) were found lying face down, seemingly preserved where they fell at death. Number 20 fell fully stretched, legs slightly bent, with arms thrown forward and bent at the elbows. No artifacts were found on or near the skeletons, and they had been covered with loose earth, free of bricks. A shell ball and some inlay were discovered in the vicinity, but they might not be associated with the skeletons; and the same is true of the reported faunal remains. Marshall says that they must have been buried during the Late I or Late II Period, but that there is no certainty that the area was a street at the time.[23]

These corpses, and the others at Mohenjo-daro, must have been covered soon after death, or animals and the elements would have led to the dispersal of the body parts. This "burial" could have been done as an act of respect by relatives or friends, or simply to control the stench and pests of putrefaction. These skeletons are unremarkable, except for number 23, which was an individual who was slightly over 1.8 meters—rather tall for the Indus population.

Human Remains in DK Area

DK-G Area, Block 10A; the "Long Lane Group" The Long Lane Group is the third of the so-called massacre scenes. It consists of nine skeletons.[24] They were found, along with two complete elephant tusks, in DK-G, Block 10A, associated with Long Lane (figure 9.5). The presence of an Indus-style comb and beads of faience associates this group with the living city of Mohenjo-daro, and Mackay's suggestion of a Late Period date, possibly Late IA, is reasonable.

The contorted disposition of the skeletons suggests violence; but the elephant tusks and the other artifacts seem to preclude theft as the motive in these deaths. Mackay prefers to blame raiders for this act, an hypothesis that is examined in the summary. Some sign of violence is present here since one of the skulls has evidence of a severe wound:

> This is the *single* case where trauma is evident and in all probability was the cause of immediate death. The large depressed area extending from the left frontal-parietal region to the left mastoid process is of a completely different form from a fracture formed by erosional processes.[25]

DK-G Area, Block 8A, Well Room 42; the "Well Room Tragedy" This is the fourth and final of the massacre scenes at Mohenjo-daro. The deaths seem to have taken place during the last occupation of Mohenjo-daro, in a well room close to the intersection of Central and First Streets (figure 9.6). The skeletons of two people were found on the stairs leading down to the well. They seem to lay where they died in an unsuccessful attempt to claw their way out of the well room up to Low Lane. "Of one of them, the badly crushed cranium lay on the partly missing top step facing north, the pelvis was on the step below and the vertebrae in position between the two. The left leg which had been flexed and drawn up rested on the same step as the pelvis, and the right leg was still extended."[26] The second skeleton was so badly preserved that the position of the body could not be determined, but it appears that he or she fell over backward just prior to death. There is no mention of any artifacts associated with either of these individuals, the better preserved of which was thought to be a male by Guha and Basu.[27]

DK-G Area, Low Lane, Opposite Block 8, Well Room 42 We know little of this find of a skull. Mackay says: "The remains of a . . . skull lay in the lane . . . but no trace was to be seen of the other bones of the body."[28] No artifacts are mentioned, and this seems to simply be the find of a

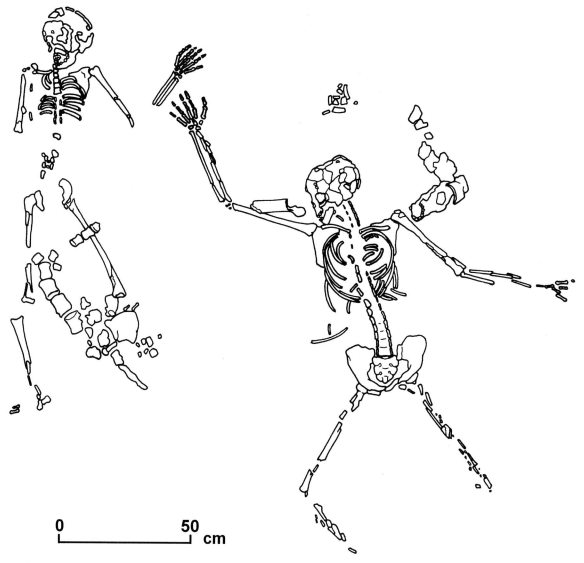

Figure 9.4 Sketch of the "VS Area Tragedy"

stray skull in a Late Period lane. However, there is a small sediment pit on Low Lane close to this skull and just to the north of the entrance to the well room containing the two skeletons just mentioned. A lone cranium was found in this brick structure: It "must have been thrown or fallen in when the pit was still in use, for it rested on the floor."[29] One might well believe that this represents a grave insult against the deceased, throwing his or her de-capitated head into a cesspit!

Of course, there are many scenarios that could ex-plain how this cranium got to where it was found. But the lane just off the intersection of Central and First Streets seems to have been a dangerous place during the last days of Mohenjo-daro, perhaps frequented by peo-ple with murder on their minds who had little or no re-gard for their victims.

General Observations on the Mohenjo-daro Funerary Record

The lone skeleton on Deadman's Lane in HR-A Area is the only place where there may have been something like a thoughtful burial at Mohenjo-daro. The context for this find is not conclusive, however. The significance and sometimes the date of the remaining material are quite ambiguous for the most part.

The Four Tragedies The four tragedies and the Long Lane Group are all associated with the upper levels of the site and can be dated to the Late Period, possibly even Late I, as in the Well Room Tragedy. Some experts on an-cient Indian history have faith in the proposition that these deaths were cause by invading Aryans.[30] There are, however, many problems with this theory, not the least of

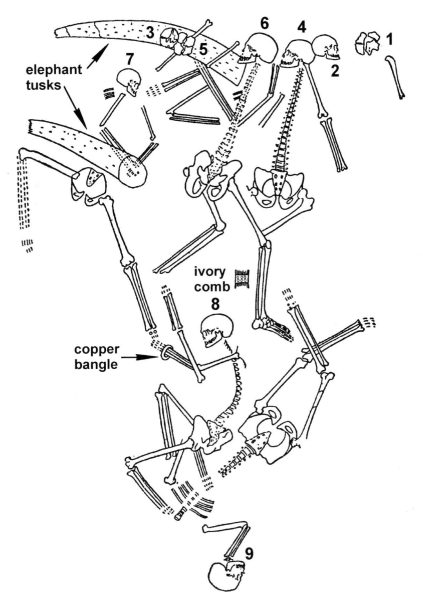

Figure 9.5 Sketch of the "Long Lane Group" (after Mackay 1937–38)

which is chronological: While there may have been speakers of one or more Indo-European languages in the Greater Indus region earlier, there is a gap of centuries between the abandonment of Mohenjo-daro at about 1900 B.C. and the documentation found in the Rgveda, which probably dates to circa 1000 B.C. Also note that the Rgveda is not a text documenting the invasion and conquest of the Subcontinent, but speaks of the feuding among the Aryans as well as with the indigenous peoples. Sindh is a peripheral area in the Vedic literature: The center of this world was the Punjab. It is therefore noteworthy that there is no evidence for a massacre at Harappa or any of the other Indus settlements in the geographical area described most prominently in the Vedas.[31]

If not Aryans, then who might have been responsible for these four tragedies? Mackay thinks that the culprits were hill peoples and those of the Indus frontier.[32] This is one possibility, but the cause of death of many of these people is not at all apparent. If violence was involved, we can imagine that as the civic order of Mohenjo-daro failed, the place would have become an increasingly unpleasant environment, perhaps eventually becoming a huge slum. The law-abiding citizenry would have largely (wholly) departed to be replaced by those not having much respect for the property and lives of others. Thus, the victims we see in these tragedies, if they did indeed die violent deaths, may have been victims of decaying city life, not invading Aryans.

Figure 9.6   Sketch of the "Well Room Tragedy"

Fractional Burials at Mohenjo-daro   There are only two reasonable occurrences of fractional burials at Mohenjo-daro: a "basket of human bone" from House XXVII in VS Area, and the cranium from House III in HR-A Area. The rest have to be considered doubtful because of the absence of human remains associated with the artifacts inside urns and the like.

Cremation at Mohenjo-daro   The evidence for cremation at Mohenjo-daro requires some comment. There are only two instances, both in VS Area, where reasonable

evidence for this practice may be present (Block 4, corridor in House XXVI and Block 4, Building XXI, Chamber 3; see table 9.2). Mackay believes that cremation was the predominant method of disposing of the dead at Mohenjo-daro and, by implication, the other settlements of the Indus Civilization. This is supported by the lack of burial and other forms of interment. He proposes that someone or some group hastily cremated these people to comply with one of the norms of Harappan society, and then just covered over the partially (very partially) burned remains.

Table 9.3 Human skeletal remains from Lothal

Grave	Phase	Skeleton number	Comments
1	Posturban Harappan	1	Cranium and other bones missing
2	Indus Civilization	2 and 3	2 is adult male, 3 is young adult without definite sexual determination
3	Indus Civilization	4	Very disturbed interment
4	Posturban Harappan	5	Interment very disturbed by cultivation
5	Posturban Harappan	6	Interment very disturbed by cultivation
6	Indus Civilization	7	Red ware jars and 2 teeth of *Bos indicus*, male skeleton 6'2" in height
7	Indus Civilization	8 and 9	Brick-lined pit, both adult males. Copper earring with skeleton 9
8	Indus Civilization	10	Disturbed, feet missing
9	Indus Civilization	11	Dish on stand and 2 jars, male skeleton 6'0" in height
10	Posturban Harappan	12	Dish on stand, lota, and pot
11	Indus Civilization	13 and 14	Both adult males, but 14 is published with a '?' for sexual determination. Skeleton 13 badly damaged. Grave as a whole greatly disturbed
12	Indus Civilization	15	Child (9–10) with possible trepanation; lota pot
13	Indus Civilization	16	Disturbed, skull missing, goat bones present. Additional human bones reported
15	Posturban Harappan	18	East-west orientation, head to the west. No grave goods
14	Indus Civilization	17	Partially disturbed, 5 pots as grave goods; the richest Lothal grave
16	Indus Civilization	19	A few carpal and metacarpal bones found in the southern half (Rao 1979: 169)

Lothal

Lothal is the southeastern most Sindhi Harappan site. It is located near the head of the Gulf of Cambay in the delta of the Sabarmati River. A small cemetery was located within the bounds of the site.[33] Kennedy examined the Lothal skeletal series, and we have the benefit of his observations.[34]

Table 9.3 was prepared from material given in the reports on the Lothal cemetery. In addition to these interments, two other "stray" skeletons were found in the cemetery area.[35]

The Joint Burials at Lothal

The occurrence of three joint burials at Lothal brought some attention to this cemetery. In addition, Rao notes: "In grave 13, bones of another individual besides skeleton no. 16 were found."[36] This would be a fourth possible double inhumation. Two bodies in one grave brings the ancient Indian custom of *sati* to mind. This is the practice associated with some Hindu communities in the past in which a wife joins her late husband on his funeral pyre. The case is weak at Lothal since we are dealing with burial, not cremation, and some of the Lothal double interments are of the same sex. Sankalia raises a host of objections to this proposition as well.[37]

K. A. R. Kennedy's Observations on Phenotypic Diversity at Lothal

Kennedy examined the entire Lothal skeletal collection and makes the following observations:[38]

1. There is a high degree of phenotypic heterogeneity in the skeletal biology of the Lothal population when it is compared with the mortuary series from Mohenjo-daro and Harappa.
2. The ancient people of Lothal are similar enough in phenotypic pattern to their contemporaries in the Indus Valley centers as to support a theory that the inhabitants of the settlement were not reproductively isolated from the macro-populations of the region.
3. There is evidence of a biological continuum of ancient and present-day populations in this part of the Subcontinent.
4. A number of physical variables present in the Lothal skeletal series suggest that their closest biological affinities are with some of the hunting-gathering communities whose descendants survive as tribal enclaves in modern India.

A principal components analysis of the Lothal specimens, along with those from 14 other South Asian sites demonstrates the close affinity of this population with that from the hunter-gatherer site of Langhnaj, on the north Gujarat plain to the north of Lothal (Kennedy, Chiment, Disotell, and Meyers 1984: figure 2). This serves to reinforce our notion that there was a regular gene flow between Harappan and hunting-gathering populations in prehistoric Gujarat.[39]

The interaction between the Indus Civilization and the aboriginal peoples on its eastern frontiers is an interesting

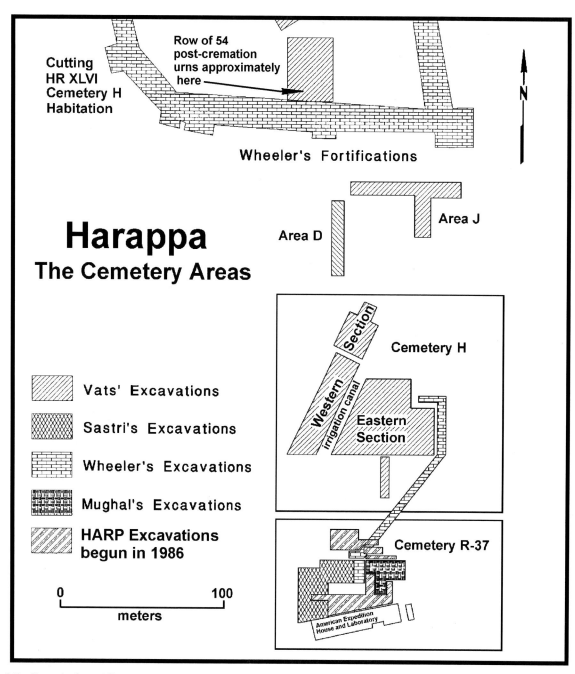

Figure 9.7 Cemeteries at Harappa

and important topic. Both Langhnaj and Bagor have evidence of trade or exchange between the Indus peoples and hunter-gatherers, who seem to have been important agents for the acquisition of raw materials, especially semiprecious stones.[40]

Human Remains from Harappa

The largest corpus of data on the funerary customs of the Indus Civilization and the longest skeletal series come from Harappa. This includes remains from the two fa-

mous cemeteries, Cemetery H (named for its mound) and Cemetery R-37 (named for its excavation square; see figure 9.7).

Stray human bones and two clusters of what may be fractional interments have also been found at Harappa. A significant number of postcremation urns have been found in the city. As noted at Mohenjo-daro, these are controversial and must be considered in a critical way.

The human skeletal series from Harappa is summarized in table 9.4.

Table 9.4 The human skeletal series from Harappa:
Number of individuals represented by skeletal remains

Excavation area	Vats (Gupta, Dutta, and Basu 1962)	Sastri (Gupta, Dutta, and Basu 1962)	Wheeler (Gupta, Dutta, and Basu 1962)	Mughal (Mughal 1968)	HARP* (Kennedy et al. in press)
Cemetery H Stratum I	78	0	0	0	0
Cemetery H Stratum II	23	0	3	0	0
Habitation area	25	0	0	0	0
Area G 289	23	0	0	0	0
Cemetery R-37	0	47	61**	11	90
Total	149	47	64	11	90

Note: Grand total = 361 individuals.
Most of the skeletons are incomplete, some of them only fragmentary.
*HARP = Harappa Archaeological Research Project.
**Wheeler found 10 graves, but Gupta, Dutta, and Basu (1962: 13) list 108 individuals, of which the 47 found by Sastri should be subtracted.

Human Remains from Cemetery R-37

The discovery of this cemetery was an accident, and the credit for reporting it goes to K. N. Sastri, who is also the principal source for the first four seasons of excavation there.[41] We know from the pottery and other artifacts found in association with the skeletal materials that this cemetery dates to the Mature Harappan.

The Cemetery and Interments The full extent of Cemetery R-37 is not known; however, the excavations in 1987 and 1988 did help to expand knowledge of the area through the extensive use of small test pits spread over a broad grid. It seems unlikely that the overall cemetery area is larger than 50 by 50 meters.[42] The internal chronology of Cemetery R-37 covers the time from Period 3B to early 3C, or from about 2450 B.C. to 2150 B.C.

The norm for interment in Cemetery R-37 was to place the deceased in a grave pit with a north-south orientation. Some pits were lined with bricks, others contained wooden coffins (figure 9.8). Most burials were extended, the bodies were supine, and some grave offerings, often large numbers of pots, were included. The dead were also interred with some of the ornaments they apparently possessed in life: beads, bangles, copper artifacts, and the like. Only women wore shell bangles in the Cemetery R-37 interments.

Physical Anthropology at Cemetery R-37 A team of physical anthropologists studied a population of thirty-three well-preserved individuals from the 1987 and 1988 excavations in R-37C as well as thirty-four similar specimens from previous work (R-37A; see tables 9.5 and 9.6).[43] The general health and robustness of the population of Harappans identified in Cemetery R-37 was quite good. The following points are made in Dales et al.[44] No cases of nutritional inadequacy, such as rickets, scurvy, or anemia, were identified; however, there are three cases of arrested

growth lines. There was a low incidence of traumatic injury, chronic infectious disease, and no malignant neoplastic disease. Arthritis mostly associated with the spinal column was the most common health problem. There were several cases of severe arthritis in the neck, including fusion

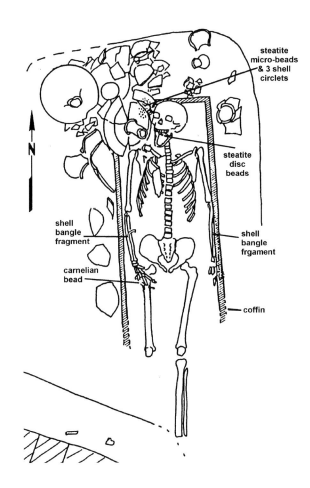

Figure 9.8 Indus coffin burial from Harappa (after Meadow 1991)

of adjacent elements. This could be associated with unusual stress on the neck vertebrae, such as would result from carrying heavy loads on the head. (This is one of the most common customs in South Asia today, especially among women, and this observation might indicate considerable time depth for this practice.) Examination of the teeth reveals that the incidence of dental caries is high, in 46.3 percent of the individuals.

Table 9.5 Sex distribution of Cemetery R-37

Sample	Males	Females	Unknown	Total
R-37A	38	55	13	106
R-37C	19	29	42	90
Total	57	84	55	196

Note: After Hemphill, Lukacs, and Kennedy (1991: table 11.1).

Table 9.6 Age distribution of the sample from Cemetery R-37C

Category	Age range	Number
Subadult	<16 years	15
Young adult	17–34 years	35
Middle-aged adult	35–55 years	27
Older adult	>55 years	13
Total		90

Note: After Hemphill, Lukacs, and Kennedy (1991: table 11.2).

Cluster analysis of cranial data suggests that the R-37C series is most closely related to other individuals interred in this cemetery as well as to those of the two phases of Cemetery H and Timargarha, an Iron Age site in northern Pakistan.[45]

Postcremation Urns at Harappa

The postcremation urns from Harappa are pottery jars of several descriptions, filled with a wide assortment of materials, including smaller pots, seals, chert, terra-cotta toys, animal bones, cereal grains, ash, and charcoal.[46] Almost never is any human bone included. At Harappa, where 230 postcremation urns were found by Vats, only one contained human bone.[47] There is a remarkable row of fifty-four postcremation urns.[48]

Most of the postcremation urns at Harappa come from AB and F Mounds, but that is also where most of the digging took place. These urns are concentrated in the Late and Intermediate Periods, but then very little is yet known of the earlier levels of the city, so this is to be expected.

Cemetery H

Cemetery H is located adjacent to R-37 at the foot of the southern end of the AB Mound at Harappa (figure 9.9). The interments in Cemetery H and the remains associated with this type of pottery in the habitation area at Harappa date to Posturban times (c. 1900–1500 B.C.).

There are two strata at Cemetery H, each quite different from the other.

Cemetery H, Stratum II: The Earth Burials As Vats describes them, the burials of Stratum II were different in the Eastern and Western Sections.[49] Those to the east were generally complete burials, while those to the west were invariably fractional. Neither area produced evidence of pot burials, but there was ample evidence for grave goods, including artifacts and animal bone; food for the departed. The animal bone included the remains of a goat.

The complete interments in the Eastern Section are generally supine, although there is some flexing. Most are oriented in an east-west direction, although northeast-southwest is also noted, and one (H698) is west-east. There were two fractional burials and two others that Vats describes as "dismembered burials."[50] The bones of these latter two burials were basically all there, but seem to have been disrupted in a purposeful way.

No earth burials were found in the Western Section; however, several fractional burials of Stratum II occurred in the Extension of the Western Section. These consist of fragmentary skeletons and Cemetery H–type pottery not clearly associated with grave pits. These are generally fragmentary skeletons, often badly broken, that had been exposed elsewhere. The bones, or most of them, were then gathered and interred in Cemetery H, along with some pottery. Below the interments in the Western Section, the remains of three rooms were found, including a wall 12 meters long.[51]

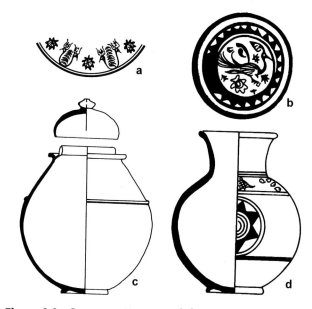

Figure 9.9 Cemetery H pottery (after Vats 1941)

Cemetery H, Stratum I: The Pot Burials The latest of the prehistoric burials at Harappa belong to Cemetery H, Stratum I. They were found in both the Eastern and Western Sections and consist of a pottery vessel into which human bone had been stuffed. These also contained animal bone, birds, and rodents, being specifically mentioned along with "antler."[52] The remains of more than one individual were sometimes placed in the same pot, and mixing of adult and child remains was common. Some pots, however, contain only the remains of very young children. The burial vessels were sometimes covered with proper lids. No artifacts were found inside the Stratum I pot burials. Vats found twenty-three examples of this type of interment, and Wheeler, another three.[53]

The pots in which these remains were placed are relatively small, ranging from 25 to 60 centimeters in height. They are quite different from postcremation urns in that they actually contain human bone! It is also clear that whoever gathered the bones together to deposit them in the pots probably did so from a place rich in human remains, possibly with many individuals all decaying together. They seem to have paid more attention to simply gathering bones than they did to finding precisely those person(s) they came to fetch. It is possible that the rodent bones are from animals who burrowed into the pots after they had been sunk and then died there.

Summary of Human Remains from Harappa

The data from Harappa on postcremation urns and fractional interments are not so different from the materials encountered at Mohenjo-daro, and postcremation urns would seem to be another of the shared cultural features of the Mature Harappan, at least within the domain of the cities. However, the uncertainty about their true function still remains—they might not be postcremation urns at all—and is another of the archaeological problems associated with the Indus Civilization needing additional attention.

The two cemeteries at Harappa are, of course, not paralleled at Mohenjo-daro; however, R-37 shares many features with the cemetery at Kalibangan, Lothal, and other examples of Mature Harappan burial grounds. The lack of significant differentiation of grave goods and the general excellent health of the population found in Cemetery R-37 are important observations. They suggest that only one segment of the overall Harappan population was interred in this way. Therefore, this form of interment may not reflect a cultural norm for Indus society, but rather that of some segment, possibly small and at the upper end of the socioeconomic hierarchy.

Evidence for biological continuity as seen from the Harappa skeletal series is interesting and important. Three questions about it are summarized here.[54]

1. What is the biological relationship between the population from cemeteries R-37 and H at Harappa? Hemphill, Lukacs, and Kennedy note that there is a close affinity between the skeletons in Cemetery R-37 and those in the lower interments of Cemetery H; but both of these samples are different from the interments in the upper stratum of Cemetery H. The difference of burial practice between these samples (earth burial versus fractional pot burial) is in agreement with this observation.

2. How do the interments from the Harappa cemeteries compare with populations from other sites?
   a. There is evidence for some biological differentiation of the Indus population, with a reasonable argument for a northern population centered around Harappa and a southern one centered on Mohenjo-daro. This north-south distinction was also suggested in the style of the stamp seals. The individuals from Mohenjo-daro did not have close biological affinities with any other South Asian group, but the sample is small and the dating of some of the remains is uncertain.
   b. Cluster analysis and principal components analysis suggest that the individuals from Cemetery R-37 and the lower stratum of Cemetery H have a close biological affinity with the burials from the Early Iron Age (c. 800 B.C.) site of Timarghara in Dir District. This is strong evidence for biological continuity from the Bronze Age into the Iron Age.

3. When South Asian samples are compared to samples from outside this region, especially to the west, is there evidence for prolonged continuity within the Subcontinent? There is some evidence suggesting that a biological discontinuity exists in the Indus Age at some point following the transformation of the Indus Civilization but prior to the Iron Age at Sarai Khola (c. 200 B.C.).[55]

These general observations and others made by these authors concerning the pattern of biological continuity and discontinuity within the early history of the northwestern regions of the Subcontinent are discussed later.

Human Remains from Kalibangan

There is a cemetery at Kalibangan approximately 300 meters west-southwest of the western High Mound. It was found after a rainfall produced an efflorescence of salt in a pattern that suggested there were graves beneath the surface (figure 9.10).[56] A. K. Sharma observed that the Kalibangan cemetery is located downwind from the habitation mound and that it is also "situated on the

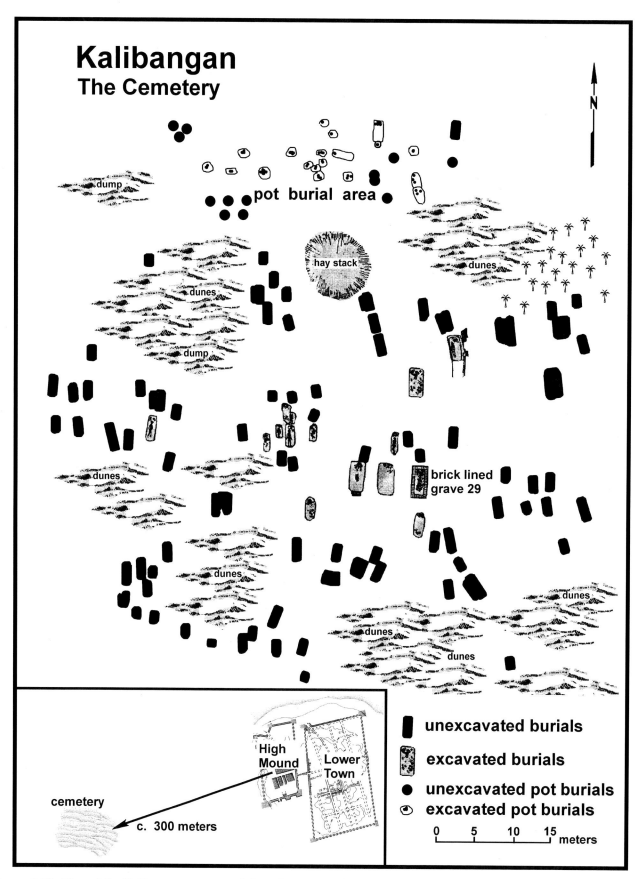

Figure 9.10 Plan of the Kalibangan cemetery (after Sharma 1999)

Text within the figure:

Kalibangan
The Cemetery

N

dump

pot burial area

hay stack

dunes

dump

dunes

dump

dunes

dunes

dunes

dunes

dunes

dunes

brick lined
grave 29

High
Mound

Lower
Town

cemetery

c. 300 meters

■ unexcavated burials

▨ excavated burials

● unexcavated pot burials

◉ excavated pot burials

0   5   10   15
meters

downstream floodplain. Water first passes by the side of the habitation mound and then touches the fringes of the cemetery. The chance that flood waters from the cemetery could ever reach the habitation were thus remote."[57] While Kalibangan has two periods of occupation (Sothi-Siswal and Mature Harappan), all of the interments are of the latter period. The survey and excavation of the cemetery area show that this area contains 102 inhumations, too small to represent the entire population of the site.

Burial Types at Kalibangan

Sharma notes that there are three types of burials at Kalibangan, only the first of which contains human skeletal remains.[58] This is a typical Harappan extended inhumation in a rectangular or oval pit, generally containing pottery as grave goods. There are eighty-eight type 1 interments reported in the Kalibangan cemetery (figure 9.11).

The second two types of interment are technically cenotaphs, in that neither of them contains human remains. Sharma's type 2 consists of pots buried in circular pits; and his type 3 consists of pottery deposits in rectangular or oval pits, much like the extended burials, but without the skeletal remains.

Burial types 1 and 2 are the most common grave forms. The pot burials in circular pits (type 2) were found in an area to the north, separate from the area with the type 1 and type 3 inhumations. It is further apparent that the type 1 interments were found in groups, suggesting to Sharma family burial areas.

Possible Social Implications of the Kalibangan Cemetery

The extended inhumations in rectangular pits are associated with a ritual interment. These seem to cluster spatially in the cemetery, suggesting that there is a sociological unit behind the arrangement; the family is the most obvious unit. The type 2 interments (cenotaphs in pots) are quite different and are spatially separated from the other burials. This suggests a second pattern of burial, possibly associated with another social group, or stratum, within the Indus population at Kalibangan. It is also possible that the Kalibangan type 2 interments represent individuals who died or were lost while away from their homes at Kalibangan and that their relatives chose to remember them in this particular way. There are certainly other possibilities, but the preceding are the most obvious, if not certain. Also, there may be a relationship between the pot burial cenotaphs at Kalibangan and the postcremation urns at Mohenjo-daro and Harappa.

If it is assumed that the entire population of Kalibangan lived in the Lower Town, an area of about 8.6 hectares, and

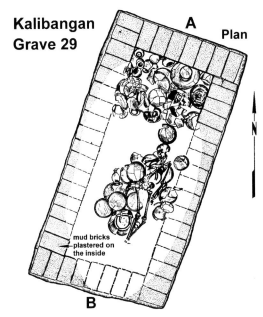

Kalibangan Grave 29

Plan

mud bricks plastered on the inside

Section A-B

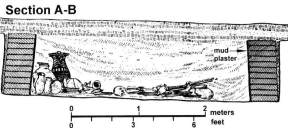

mud plaster

Figure 9.11 A brick-lined grave at Kalibangan (after *Indian Archaeology, A Review* 1964–65)

that this entire area was generally inhabited, the population of the town would have been between approximately 860 and 1,160 individuals. The chronology for the Mature Harappan at the site indicates that it had a duration of about 600 years, but there is no age profile for those interred in this cemetery. If we estimate that only five individuals died each year, from the thousand or so people living there, that amounts to 2,500 graves over the life of the settlement. There are, however, only eighty-eight interments with skeletons in them—far short of the estimated number. Since the survey and excavation of the Kalibangan cemetery were done in such a thorough and competent way, we can reasonably depend on its findings. Perhaps some graves were missed in the excavation, but even if we double the number of graves found, it still falls far short of the estimated number of deaths. This suggests that the cemetery at Kalibangan may contain only the remains of some small portion of the population for whom burial was seen as the appropriate method of disposal after death. The most obvious of the two major axes for such differentiation are, of course, ethnicity and class, perhaps working together in some complex way.

Pathologies of the Kalibangan Population

The Kalibangan cemetery has evidence for (1) trepanation of a child, (2) a serious, unhealed axe wound to the knee, (3) the remains of an individual with serious bodily deformation, (4) some differentiation in the grave goods with skeletons, mostly expressed in the amount of pottery included.[59]

Summary of the Kalibangan Cemetery

There is not much anthropometric information on the Kalibangan population. But the available reports suggest evidence of ethnic differentiation based on burial type. While the evidence for cremation is equivocal at Kalibangan, it is not at Tarkhanwala, just downstream on the Sarasvati River.

Human Remains from Tarkhanwala Dera

Some 90 kilometers to the west of Kalibangan, but very much on the ancient Sarasvati, is the small site of Tarkhanwala Dera. An exploratory trench was laid at this Early Harappan–Mature Harappan site by A. Ghosh as a part of his exploration of the Sarasvati.[60] On the top of an artificial platform he found evidence for at least five cremations that can be associated with the Indus occupation of the site. This is the only unequivocal evidence for cremation at an Indus site.

BIOLOGICAL ANTHROPOLOGY OF THE HARAPPANS

The study of the skeletal biology of the Indus peoples has produced several important inferences concerning the nature of their society. There is also some information on their predecessors.

Prior to entertaining this fascinating topic, a word of caution, or perspective, is necessary. When we contrast the human remains of hunter-gatherers with farmers and herders, it appears that food producers tend to be smaller, more gracile people, with fewer, or diminished, differences between males and females. Food producers are not necessarily healthier than hunter-gathers; they do suffer from bad teeth, more sickness, and a higher incidence of broken bones and wounds. Thus, when we notice that the people buried in Mature Harappan graves were healthy, this must be understood not as a contradiction of these conclusions, but true in relative terms.

Inferences from Observations on Human Teeth

J. Lukacs, a biological anthropologist specializing in the study of human dentition, focused on the results of his study of ninety-eight specimens from Mohenjo-daro and Harappa.[61] He found that four dental diseases occurred with some frequency: an abundance of dental caries and abscesses, tooth loss prior to death, and gum disease. The relative incidence of these dental diseases was consistently higher at Harappa than at Mohenjo-daro, except for ante-mortem tooth loss, which was equal. He observes that in an overall way, his study of these materials is consistent with what could be expected from an urban, agricultural population, eating soft, starchy foods. The human remains from Mehrgarh were found to have high levels of fluorine, which may have protected them and the Mature Harappans from the worst incidence of these conditions.[62]

Disease and Sickness among the Harappans

Some diseases leave a clear record in the skeletal biology. There are signs of some nutritional stress in some bones, but on the whole the Indus population was healthy. There is one paleopathological anomaly that occurs: thinning of the bones of the cranium, or porotic hyperostosis. It was observed by Kennedy on skeletons 6, 7, 8, 11, 14, 19, and M in the Marshall series from Mohenjo-daro. Kennedy considers it to be one of the pathologies that he "consistently" observes, occurring on about 25 percent of the specimens. This condition is related to anemia, and there is an intriguing story of why it is important:

> When these data are applied to questions of the health profile of the ancient peoples of the Indus, we feel confident in associating the frequencies of porotic hyperostosis encountered in examination of Harappan skeletal materials with the types of hereditary abnormal haemoglobins described [earlier]. Furthermore, probability is high that these diagnostic markers of thalassaemia and sicklaemia are associated with endemic malaria as a balanced polymorphism in ancient times in Harappan settlements just as the situation exists today in the Indian subcontinent. A very strong argument that we may be able to document the antiquity of malaria in the South Asian land mass is afforded by our examination of the skeletons of pre-Harappan, i.e., Mesolithic, temporal or cultural context in this part of the world. With one exception known to the author, Mesolithic human skeletal remains in India and Sri Lanka do not exhibit porotic hyperostosis, thromboses of postcranial bones or marrow hyperplasia and osteomyelitis. Whatever the date of mutation of the genes for haemolytic disorders may be for the Mediterranean basin and Nilotic Africa, its manifestation in the Indian subcontinent would appear, on the basis of present biological evidence, to be somewhat later.[63]

The large-scale research recently undertaken at Harappa has brought more data to bear. While malaria is still seen as a health problem for the Indus peoples, Kennedy notes: "Only one case of porotic hyperostosis was encountered at

Harappa in 1987, a situation that suggests that the disease stressers peculiar to the environment of Sind may have been quite different from those at Harappa in the Punjab during the same period of time."[64]

THOUGHTS AND CONCLUSIONS CONCERNING HARAPPAN PEOPLE AND SOCIETY

The physical attributes of the Harappan peoples allow us some thoughts on Indus society.

Features Characteristic of Food Producers

The first, and perhaps most important, conclusion would be that the Indus peoples, as well as their immediate predecessors in the long preurban period of gestation, have features that physical anthropologists associate with food-producing peoples. This includes a general reduction in tooth size, a high incidence of dental caries, as well as the loss of significant prognathism.

Population Stability

A second conclusion that rises from the data sets at hand is that the Harappans and their predecessors represent a population, or populations, that are quite stable.

> The important message for archaeologists . . . is that whatever the racial origins of the Harappans may have been, they were a relatively stable population inhabiting the northern and northwestern sectors of the Subcontinent for several millennia prior to their climactic moment of urbanization.[65]

Kennedy notes that this stability has continued to the present day: "One is on surer ground when one speaks of the Harappans themselves, for which there is in evidence a relatively large skeletal sample. One recognizes a biological continuum of many of their morphometric variables in the modern populations of Punjab and Sind."[66]

Looking at the significant human remains from all Indus sites, other interesting observations on the biological affinities of the Mature Harappans and their predecessors include the following:

1. All Indus sites, except Mohenjo-daro and Lothal, were inhabited by people with relatively strong affinities to one another.
2. Individuals from Mohenjo-daro are somewhat different in their biology than individuals from other Indus sites.
3. There is an affinity between the individuals in Mature Harappan Cemetery R-37 and those in the lower interments of Posturban-Stage Cemetery H; however, both of these samples are different from those in the upper stratum of Cemetery H.

4. The individuals from Cemetery R-37 have their closest affinities with the individuals from Periods III through VII at Mehrgarh.
5. There may be some kind of biological discontinuity between the individuals from Periods I and II of Mehrgarh as compared to Periods III through VII.
6. The population of Periods I and II at Mehrgarh has rather close affinities with the Deccan Chalcolithic, as seen from data on skeletons from Inamgaon.
7. The skeletal series from Early Harappan Sarai Khola is closely affiliated to that from Iron Age Timargarha.

Nutritional and Health Indices of the Indus Peoples Are Similar

It is widely thought that in societies like the Indus Civilization, with social differentiation and class, there would be physical differences between individuals from different segments of this hierarchy.

> But . . . observations from Harappan skeletal series from five major sites, which comprise about 350 individuals, have not revealed significant differences in patterns of growth and development as would be recognized by lines of arrested growth in long bones and hyperplasia or dental enamel. Osseous malformations suggestive of nutritional stress are absent as well. Nor are there any striking differences in incidents of dental attrition and common dental pathologies such as caries, abscess, malocclusion and ante-mortem tooth loss in Harappan skeletons.[67]

We should remember that this tells us that the people of the Indus Civilization who were "buried" have these characteristics. This may not be representative of the whole Indus population in terms of either its ethnic diversity or social hierarchy. Kennedy's sample of 350 individuals seems to represent a relatively well-fed, well-cared-for segment of the Indus population, probably one of the upper classes. Individuals from other classes, including the possibility of other upper classes, may not be a part of this sample, and it should not be concluded that all Harappans were so well fed and "prosperous." To be fair, an alternative to this should also remain open as a working hypothesis: "Social control may have been exercised by the Harappan elite in a way that did not invoke the usual dietary stresses so often imposed elsewhere upon an urban proletariat. The absence of royal tombs in Harappan centers may be significant in this connection."[68] These data do not allow us to rule out the notions that the entire Indus population was generally well off, possibly relatively egalitarian.

NOTES

1. Kennedy 2000 is the up-to-date source on the ancient human populations of the Subcontinent.
2. Sewell and Guha 1931.
3. Kennedy 1977.
4. Wheeler 1968: 129–32.
5. Dales 1964; Kennedy 1984, 1995, 2000: 308–26.
6. Hargreaves 1931: 178.
7. Marshall 1931f: 82–84.
8. Marshall 1931f: 88.
9. Wheeler 1947: 83.
10. Marshall 1931f: 79–80; Hargreaves 1931: 184–86, pls. XLI-IIa and XLVIa and b; Sewell and Guha 1931.
11. Wheeler 1959: 113–14.
12. Hargreaves 1931: 184.
13. Hargreaves 1931: 186.
14. Marshall 1931f: 81.
15. Hargreaves 1931: 186.
16. Sewell and Guha 1931: 617, 624.
17. Kennedy 1984: 429.
18. Kennedy 1984: 428.
19. Hargreaves 1931: 179; see also Marshall 1931f: 79; Hargreaves 1931: 179, pls. XLIIc and d; Sewell and Guha 1931: 605.
20. Marshall 1931f: 81.
21. Marshall 1931f: 79; Sahni 1931b: 222–23, pl. LIXc; Sewell and Guha 1931: 605–6.
22. Marshall 1931i: pl. LIXc.
23. Marshall 1931f: 81.
24. Mackay 1937–38: 116–18, 648, pls. XXXIIa and b, CX, no. 43, C, no. 15, CXI, 11, 72, CXXXIX, nos. 25, 45, 69, CXLII, no. 14; Guha and Basu 1938: 613–23, fig. 1.
25. Kennedy 1984: 429.
26. Mackay 1937–38: 94.
27. Guha and Basu 1938: 624.
28. Mackay 1937–38: 95.
29. Mackay 1937–38: 95.
30. For example, A. L. Basham 1967: 26–28.
31. Dales 1964; Kennedy 1984.
32. Mackay 1937–38: 647–48.
33. Rao 1979: 137–69; Sarkar 1985.
34. Kennedy and Caldwell 1984: table I; Kennedy et al. 1984.
35. Rao 1979: 139, 169.
36. Rao 1979: 137.
37. Sankalia 1974: 375.
38. Possehl and Kennedy 1979: 593; Kennedy 2000: 301.
39. Possehl and Kennedy 1979: 593.
40. Possehl 1980: 67–80.
41. Sastri 1965: 1.
42. Dales, Kenoyer, and staff 1991: 191–99, 206–13.
43. Hemphill, Lukacs, and Kennedy 1991: 139; Dutta 1983.
44. Dales et al. 1991.
45. Hemphill et al. 1991: 150–60, table 11.7.
46. Vats 1940: 251–74.
47. Vats 1940: 252, 254.
48. Vats 1940: 272–74.
49. Vats 1940: 221–35.
50. Vats 1940: 222, 224.
51. Vats 1940: 231.
52. Vats 1940: 242–45.
53. Vats 1940: 205–20; Wheeler 1947: 89–90.
54. Hemphill et al. 1991: 172–74.
55. Hemphill et al. 1991: 173.
56. Sharma 1999.
57. Sharma 1982: 297.
58. Sharma 1999: 17–90.
59. Sharma 1999: 91–98.
60. Ghosh 1952, 1962.
61. Lukacs 1982.
62. Lukacs 1985.
63. Kennedy 1984: 432.
64. Kennedy 1990: 71.
65. Kennedy 1982: 290; see Kennedy 2000: 302–7 on this topic and others.
66. Kennedy 1982: 291.
67. Kennedy 1982: 290.
68. Kennedy 1982: 291.

Gender and the Indus Age

INTRODUCTION

The men and women of the Indus Age were part of an internally differentiated, structurally specialized social system. They participated in their sociocultural system in different ways; gender made a difference. Not a great deal is known about this aspect of the Indus Age, but some observations can be made. The most important data come from figurines and Cemetery R-37 at Harappa. The splendid corpus of figurines from Mehrgarh adds time depth to this investigation and allows us to move from the Indus Civilization to the Indus Age. Since the gender of the figurines there is often obvious, Mehrgarh is a good place to start.

MEHRGARH–NAUSHARO FIGURINES

Figurines appear at Mehrgarh from almost the very beginning of the settlement. Catherine Jarrige specializes in the study of these objects.[1] Most of her data comes in the various preliminary reports on the site.[2] The figurines from Periods I and II are very simple, without clear gen-

der marking. Broad hips and large buttocks have been used to suggest a voluptuous woman. They are generally seated, have no arms, and the legs are joined. Adornment, in the form of necklaces and belts, is shown by strips of clay and small clay pellets applied to the body. Some of the figurines have been coated in red ocher, a pigment also used in some interments in the Mehrgarh cemeteries (figure 10.1).

Period III at Mehrgarh (Togau Phase) is an important time for craft innovation and some indication of new genes in the human population. There are no human figurines from this period, but there are a large number of bull figurines.

Composite figurines appear in Period IV, just after 4000 B.C. (figure 10.2). They are generally female, have heads that are rodlike in shape and often quite elongated. There may be a small, pointy nose and hollowed eyes. The torso is rounded, with prominent hips, and the legs, manufactured separately, were attached to it. Typically, large breasts, some conical in shape, were appended to the torso. These women were equipped with somewhat elaborate necklaces represented by clay strips. The legs point

Figure 10.1 Figurines from Mehrgarh I (after Jarrige, Jarrige, Meadow, and Quivron 1995)

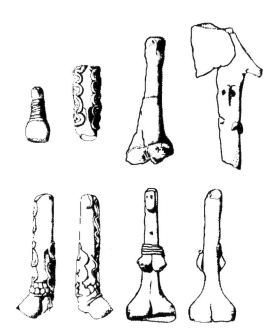

Figure 10.2 Figurines from Mehrgarh IV (after Jarrige, Jarrige, Meadow, and Quivron 1995)

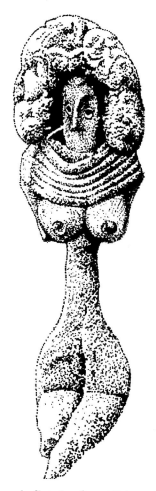

Figure 10.3 Female figurine from Mehrgarh V (after Jarrige, Jarrige, Meadow, and Quivron 1995)

to the front and are joined, a feature from Periods I and II that continues through time. Although joining the legs is a stylistic attribute, it may be that the individuals who made the figurines had bad luck with thin, independent legs breaking, so they joined them together for strength. The other feature that might be thought of as both stylistic and functional is the lack of arms.

The figurines of Mehrgarh Period V are refinements of the figurines seen in Period IV. The manufacturers used very fine, well-prepared clay and fired the figurines at high temperatures in an oxidizing atmosphere, which produced a buff-colored finished product. The head and torso are a kind of rod, broadened at the shoulders in order to take large appended breasts and shoulders supporting necklaces. The hips continue to be a prominent feature in the representation of female anatomy (figure 10.3).

The Period V figurines also begin to have elaborate coiffures, large and fluffy. The way the face was completed also changes. A nose was appended and is often large in proportion to the face. The eyes are represented by a small

pellet of applied clay, which was then pierced. Jarrige calls them "mask faces."[3] The holes for the eyes become larger and larger over time. The women are still seated, with joined legs to the front.

Figurines become more popular in Period VI, with some very interesting, elaborate, individual coiffures. They also have prominent breasts with nipples and an abundance of jewelry. The necklaces now have some individuality, with small incisions marking individual elements. Arms are shown, sometimes tucked neatly under the breasts, which completes the anatomy. By Period VIB, these female representations are widespread at the site (figure 10.4).

Some simplification of hairstyles is found in Period VII (c. 2900–2600 B.C.). Locks are tied at the back of the neck, flowing in ringlets down the sides of their heads. There is even a sense that some of the figurines represent women with wigs. Some of the figurines are standing, with modeled knees and feet, and have arms in more or less natural postures. Some females hold small infants modeled in clay. The prominent pinched nose and eye with the pellet pierced by a sharp tool is also seen (figure 10.5).

The jewelry is also shown in a more sophisticated way, with greater individuality. There is an increase in the variety of adornment, with more necklace types, bangles, diadems, and pendants.

Some of the Period VII figurines were painted. Black was used for the hair and eyes. Some ornaments were picked out in yellow. The figures are sometimes completely slipped in a brown ocher pigment. There are also male figurines in Period VII. One is a standing representation, with a turban-like headdress (figure 10.6).

Figure 10.4 Mehrgarh figurine Period VI (after Jarrige, Jarrige, Meadow, and Quivron 1995)

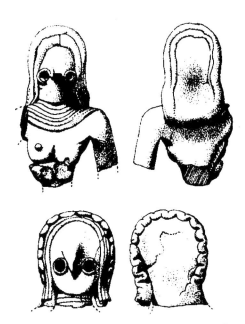

Figure 10.5 Mehrgarh female figurines Period VII (after Jarrige, Jarrige, Meadow, and Quivron 1995)

tion in this deposit is shown with features hitherto reserved for males. Only her breasts are fuller than those of the male figurines, not the voluptuous spheres of the familiar Mehrgarh tradition.[5]

There is an interesting reversal of the proportion of female to male figurines. From Period IV to the beginning of Period VII the emphasis is on female features, large, prominent breasts, and broad hips. Male figurines begin to be found early in Period VII: Their chests are flat, the genitals are represented, arms and legs are stiffly held. But, by VIID, the proportion of female to male figurines is reversed, the latter then accounting for up to 85 percent of the human representations.[6]

In a neolithic context, the idea of a fertility goddess is . . . (not) improbable in a society where reproduction plays an all important role. . . . As in many other developing cultures, this preoccupation with fertility is expressed in the

At the beginning of the period the male hairstyles were braids or knots. They were replaced in VIIB by a pair of strands flowing over the shoulders to the front, covering parts of their necklaces. The males can be identified by the presence of male genitalia, breasts barely marked, and their own style of jewelry, some of which might be seen as phallic in nature.[4] Some of the males wear loincloths made of broad strips of clay, a feature of later Indus figurines, especially those from Mohenjo-daro. Jarrige feels that the male representations are stiffer in carriage than the relaxed women.

Extreme simplification predominates in Period VIIC. . . . The traditional figurine types are now being mass-produced: whole series of ornamented female figurines, of mothers with babies and of turbaned male figurines are turned out, monotonously uniform, totally lacking in artistic inspiration and roughly modeled. . . .

This simplified uniformity is soon enlivened by a new development . . . the rise of a composite type of figurine of high quality towards the end of Mehrgarh Period VII. . . . This new composite type is finely modeled, with a small hole in the centre of each of the applied oval eyes. The male type, with two strands of hair hanging down and turban head-dress, predominates to the extent that, by the end of the period, it is practically the only human type represented. The loin-cloth, still the exception at the start of Period VII, now becomes more common in the form of a band of clay wrapped round the hips. Curiously, the male type becomes so dominant that the only figurine found holding a baby in a late Period VIID deposit is actually that of a male, whereas the only female representa-

Figure 10.6 Male figurine holding a baby from Mehrgarh VII (after Jarrige, Jarrige, Meadow, and Quivron 1995)

exaggerated pelvis of the figurines, which results in their typical biconic shape. From Period IV onwards . . . certain features are emphasized to draw attention to the idea of fertility, e.g. broad hips, voluptuous bosoms, and motherhood. . . . [But, by the end of Period VII] male figures are shown with babies in their arms, while females lack any feature which could be related to the idea of fertility.[7]

This may well reflect important changes in gender-based roles in the Early Harappan and the Early Harappan–Mature Harappan Transition. Just what is heralded here, and what it has to do with the rise of the Indus Civilization, is not quite clear. But Jarrige's data set seems to tell us that there are interesting things to be known.

THE SOCIOCULTURAL FUNCTIONING OF THE FIGURINES

It is not known what these figurines were used for. Jarrige notes that they are most frequently found broken, even smashed, sometimes burnt, in secondary trash deposits. Once they were used, for whatever purpose, their disposition does not seem to have been a concern to the people of Mehrgarh. Archaeologists have a long history of thinking of figurines such as this in rather simplistic ways—mother goddesses, Venus figurines, and other thoughts along those lines. In our own culture this would be akin to thinking of every Barbie doll as a representation of a goddess, an object of ritual and religious adoration. Figurines without gender markings, some of which look quite male, are often classed as "female" based on the theory that there was a universal "Neolithic mother goddess cult" in Europe and Asia. This model has serious limitations.

The ethnographic record, and our own life experience, suggests that some figurines in some cultures were toys or playthings, made for the kids and entertainment. On the other hand, many cultures use facsimiles of humans, animals, and plants in their ritual lives, as religious, magical, and mythical representations. They provide a focus for consciousness during worship and can be objects for sympathetic magic. Some people believe that such physical objects become the gods, not just representations of them. They might represent humans and animals as cultural "ideals," models for young and old to try to emulate.

There is then a range of activities or representations for figurines—from gods to toys. In some cultures they could be both simultaneously. Or they might be gods at some point, and once used, could be recycled into the toy arena, perhaps to be resuscitated to divinity by the uttering of a culturally loaded incantation. In some cultures they might be neither, as in objects used for storytelling or as mnemonic devices. There are many other mixings and matchings within this cultural arena also possible. The archaeologist should therefore be conscious of the fact that human figurines of the type found at sites of the Indus Age should not be thought of simply as either "religious" or "toys." Some of the figurines might serve one purpose, and others, another.

There is little to go on to determine what the inhabitants of Mehrgarh used their "little women" for, especially before Period VII; but two or three points tip the scales slightly in one direction. Prior to Period VII, when gender is indicated, it is wholly in terms of females. It is not possible to say that no male figurines were made, but of those found, none was demonstrably male. When gender was shown, it represents the feminine, but in a special way. The pubic region does not receive attention in these figurines; it is the breasts and hips that mark the women.

When the Mehrgarh figurines carry something, it is a small human. It is not a rabbit, or a dog, or a sheaf of grain; it is a human infant. This establishes a connection to the gender markers and fertility. It should be emphasized that it is a tentative connection, but a connection, nonetheless. This seems to indicate that the figurines were meant to represent human fertility and reproduction, possibly "motherhood," in some abstract sense.

If this hypothesis is correct, why did some of the inhabitants of Mehrgarh choose to represent motherhood? For a start, human fertility is an important part of survival. Representing a culturally "ideal" physical type for reproduction offers a model to everyone. In this sense, the Mehrgarh figurines do share something with the Barbie dolls of American culture. They are, after all, not just toys, since they also represent a kind of ideal cultural type. The Barbie doll is slim, blond, blue-eyed—an attractive young woman to be admired, even imitated. At Mehrgarh the ideal type seems to have been quite different. These women had hips built for childbearing and breasts to feed the young, to make them strong, healthy members of society. Rather than Barbie (the American ideal), the female figurines of early Mehrgarh are reproducers (the Indus Age ideal). The figurines may have also represented a kind of sympathetic magic or wish fulfillment. By creating a figurine of a mother and a baby, the people of the Indus Age might have believed this could bring motherhood to someone.

Thus, the balance of evaluation of the Mehrgarh human figurines tips slightly toward the concept of motherhood, fertility, reproduction. It does not seem to favor religion, ritual, and goddesses quite as much; although there can be elements of magic and wish fulfillment.

There is an important change at Mehrgarh VIII also apparent at neighboring Nausharo I. The emergence of males and males holding human infants suggests a shift in society. This change is doubly interesting since it seems to come within the Transitional Stage, when South Asian urbanization was in the making. The only coherent thought about what might have been going on at Mehrgarh–Nausharo is something that parallels our own society in recent years. That is, increased sharing of the birthing experience and a greater involvement of males in the parenting process. Today, this has been stimulated in part by the increased involvement of women in careers outside the household. It is certain that the ancient Indian experience and that of modern America were very different, but it could be that during the Transitional Stage there were forces at work in the society of Mehrgarh–Nausharo that brought males closer to the process of creating and raising children.

Jarrige has emphasized the cultural continuity between the figurines of the Transitional Stage at Mehrgarh–Nausharo and those of the Indus Civilization: "These figurines, recovered principally from the pre-Indus period levels at Nausharo, already incorporate in embryonic form all the elements of the Indus Civilization figurines with their elaborate hairstyles, loin cloths and applied ornaments."[8]

FIGURINES OF THE INDUS CIVILIZATION

Indus figurines are significantly more varied than those of Mehrgarh. A quick scan of the site reports from Mohenjo-daro and Harappa substantiates this observation. But this diversity is rooted in the Transitional Stage and even earlier.

The gender of the human figurines from Indus sites is not always obvious. The presence of a prominent beard helps to distinguish males from females. Beards are also often indicated on the steatite and limestone sculpture from Mohenjo-daro (figure 6.6). Male genitalia are also commonly built into the figurines. Some of these men appear to be nude, but wear hats and jewelry (figure 10.7). Beardless figurines with very prominent breasts seem to represent females. But males can have indications of breasts, too (figure 10.8). It seems that the figurine makers of Mohenjo-daro sometimes chose to show breasts in ways that lead the modern observer to wonder which sex they were attempting to portray. For example, the breasts on the bronze dancing girl from HR Area at Mohenjo-daro are not particularly prominent, but the figurine is definitely that of a female (see figure 6.5).

The ambiguity of gender markers in the figurines brings up the distinct possibility that some Indus figurines may represent beings that were both male and female, or androgynous. Or the figures may represent possibly a male or female who portrayed themselves as the opposite sex (as

in figure 10.8). The figurines portraying individuals combining two sexual markers may not represent the realities of Indus life, although cross-dressing is a common enough feature of cultures around the world. Sexual ambiguity is very much a part of Hinduism, as in one of the aspects of Siva *Ardhanarisvara*, half-male, half-female.

While female breasts are a prominent feature in the corpus of Indus figurines, portrayal of the female pubic region is not. The only figurine with clear representation

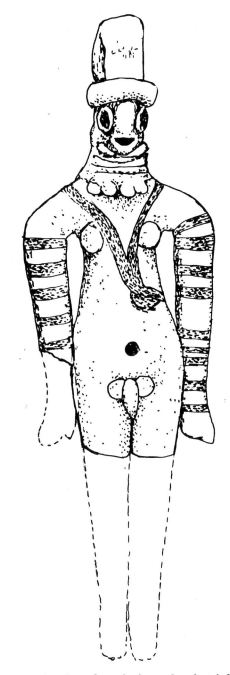

Figure 10.7 Figurine of a naked man in a hat (after Marshall 1931i)

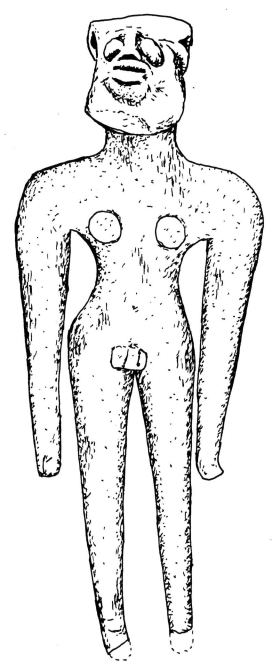

Figure 10.8 Representation of a possible androgen from Mohenjo-daro (after Mackay 1937–38)

may well show the suckling child at a woman's breast. None of the sources mentions males holding children at either site.

A real treasure of a figurine, with clear female gender markings, is the woman either kneading bread or grinding grain (figure 10.10). She comes from Mound F at Harappa, where the Granary is located. By inspecting the original, Vats believed that she is kneading bread.[10] This is good evidence for the involvement of women in food preparation. We do not know if males also kneaded bread, but this shows that women did it. It is also interesting to see that the figurine is all dressed up, with the hair fan, panniers, and head cone. Could this portrayal of Indus daily life show that at least some of the Indus women actually dressed this way?

EVIDENCE OF GENDER FROM INDUS CEMETERIES

The cemeteries at Lothal and Harappa have information on gender. Recall the series of double burials at Lothal discussed earlier. There is some disagreement about the sex of the skeletons in the three joint burials. Sarkar says that one of them has two males and that two of them have a male and another individual of indeterminate sex, or possibly a male.[11] Kennedy has also examined this skeletal series and reports that, in two cases, these double inter-

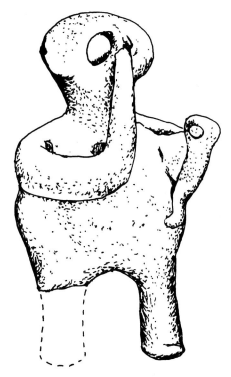

Figure 10.9 Woman holding a child (after Mackay 1937–38)

of this gender marker is the superb copper–bronze dancing girl. On the other hand, male genitalia are commonly shown. It seems possible that the display of male genitalia for the Indus peoples was mature, even dignified—simply a nude male, as in the red jasper torso from Harappa (figure 6.1).

Women carrying children are a feature of the figurines at Mohenjo-daro and Harappa.[9] Mackay lists four examples from his excavations (figure 10.9). This illustration

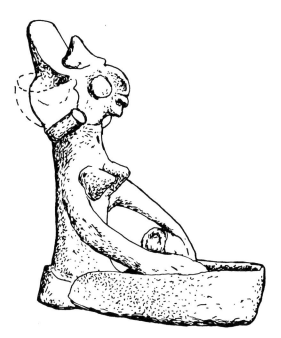

Figure 10.10   Figurine from Harappa of a woman kneading bread or grinding grain (after Vats 1941)

ments each contained one male and one female skeleton, while the third consisted of two males.[12] Although there is a difference of opinion here, it does seem that at least one of these joint burials has two males, and it is wise to rely on the careful work of Kennedy.

CONCLUSION

While this small foray into gender in the Indus Age has a severely limited scope, it does demonstrate that there are data on this aspect of life in ancient South Asia. Much more productive research could be done on the figurines in terms of gender issues as well as the ethnic diversity that dress and hair treatment seems to indicate. The data that the physical anthropologists bring forward from analysis of the interments, especially at Harappa, are extraordinarily promising, and archaeologists working on the Indus Civilization must devote attention to the discovery of more cemeteries, using subsurface prospecting and other techniques.

NOTES

1. Jarrige 1991.
2. Jarrige et al. 1995.
3. Jarrige 1991: 89.
4. Jarrige 1991: 90.
5. Jarrige 1991: 91–92.
6. Jarrige 1991: 92.
7. Jarrige 1991: 91–92.
8. Jarrige 1991: 92.
9. Marshall 1931i: pl. XCV, no. 20; Vats 1940: pl. LXXVII, no. 31.
10. Vats 1940: 296.
11. Sarkar 1985.
12. Kennedy and Caldwell 1984: table I.

Mohenjo-daro

INTRODUCTION

Mohenjo-daro is arguably the most impressive, best-preserved Bronze Age city in the world (see figure 5.1). The city was constructed of baked brick, and when it was abandoned, no widespread destruction took place there. It was simply left to deteriorate.

I have come to think of Mohenjo-daro as a kind of ideological center of the Indus Civilization. This is because the Indus ideology seems to be best, and most expansively, expressed within its urban landscape. This city was probably founded on virgin soil, as a "new city," a kind of ancient "Alexandria," thus expressing both Indus nihilism and the urban nature of the Indus ideology. *Wasserluxus* is wonderfully displayed there, and in a diversity of ways. It was also, at least in its later years, a place of technological vigor and innovation.

The name of the city is derived from the Sindhi language and is commonly written "Mohenjo-daro." Some claim that this implies a connection to Mohan, the Hindu divinity, one of the avatars of Krishna.[1] Sorley believes that it should be written "Muyan-jo-Daro" or "Moenjo-Daro," *moen* or *muyan* being the inflected, objective plurals of the past participles of the verb *maran*, "to die." *Muo*, the singular form, means "the dead man." *Daro* is the Sindhi word for "mound" or "heap." The Sindhis clearly intend to convey "Mound of the Dead Men" when they refer to the ancient city, and this is "Moenjo-daro" in their language.

The revised spelling of *Mohenjo-daro* as "Moenjo-daro" is widespread and perfectly appropriate. I happen to like the older spelling, one that has been recognized as a standard since at least 1931, when Marshall's *Mohenjo-daro and the Indus Civilization* appeared, especially since there is no evidence that anyone, other than Sorley, has made a connection to Mohan.

GENERAL DESCRIPTION OF THE SITE

The layout of Mohenjo-daro is quite distinctive. There is a high mound to the west that is roughly 400 meters by 200 meters (8 hectares) in size. This mound has had several names. Marshall refers to it as the "Stupa Mound." It was Wheeler's "Citadel." In *The Indus Civilization* it is the "Mound of the Great Bath." This artificial *daro* is separated from the Lower Town to the east by open space, which excavation and boring have shown to have been unoccupied. The Lower Town at Mohenjo-daro measured from the ground plans using the contour line 160 feet above mean sea level as the limit of the mounds is approximately 1,100 by 650 meters, or 71.50 hectares.[2]

Some archaeologists believe that Mohenjo-daro was larger than the settlement that can be seen above ground today. Subsurface prospecting has detected remains in at least two, possibly three, places (figure 11.1). One of them is a large area, two or three times the size of the city itself, located a little over a kilometer south of the ancient city where the remains of brick buildings and pottery can be detected to a depth of 18.3 meters. Two other areas were discovered in 1987 and 1988 just below ground surface, to the east of the Lower Town, on the river side of the city. These are in the vicinity of "Spur Number 3," a bund intended to protect the site from floods (figure 11.2).[3] Well-preserved building foundations of baked brick associated with Indus pottery and square stamp seals were found there. Finally, Dikshit noticed Indus pottery and baked bricks 1.5 kilometers southwest of the Mound of the Great Bath, as well as about a kilometer from Mohenjo-daro on the road to the village of Hasanwahan.[4] Thus, there are Mature Harappan remains around Mohenjo-daro, but these seem to be separate from the mounded area we see today. The size of Mohenjo-daro is therefore given here as 100 hectares, with the thought (as elsewhere in this book) that it will be revised, if new facts warrant a change.

THE MOUND OF THE GREAT BATH

The Mound of the Great Bath is an artificial *daro*. Marshall put in a deep trench to the north of the stupa. From this work, we learn that there were signs of Indus people at or near the original plain level.[5] These would seem to date from the very earliest years of the Indus Civilization or the Early Harappan–Mature Harappan Transition. Above this was fill of earth and broken bricks to the level of the stupa, providing the people of Mohenjo-daro with a high platform on which to place their special buildings, among them the Great Bath and Warehouse. The platform was held in place, and erosion checked, by stout retaining walls of baked brick built all around it. This gave the Mound of the Great Bath the appearance of a "citadel," but that was not its function. The walls around the Mound of the Great Bath were to hold the earthen filling in place, not protect priest-kings.

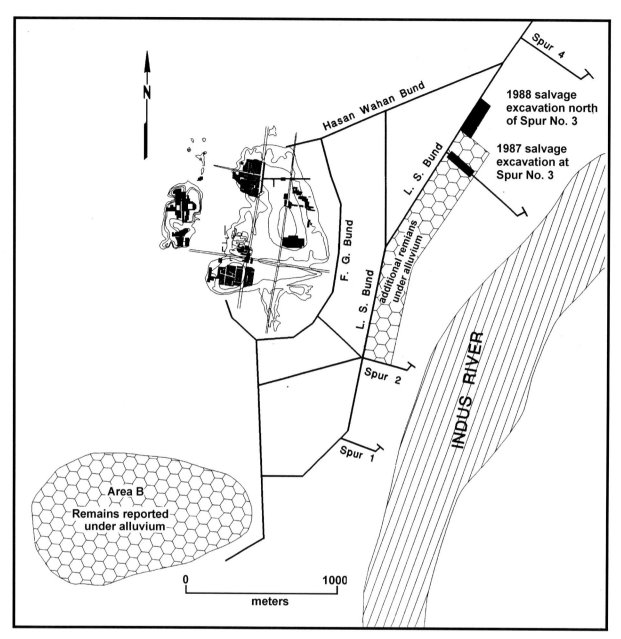

Figure 11.1   Mohenjo-daro and sites around it (after van Lohuizen-de Leeuw 1974)

The original entrance to the Mound of the Great Bath is obscure. There is a grand staircase almost 7 meters wide from the plain to the top of the Mound of the Great Bath (figure 11.3).[6] This is one of the entrances, but it is on the back, or western side, of the mound, possibly used in connection with the Warehouse (Wheeler's "Granary"). It is not likely to have been the entrance for those coming from the city side. There is also a small postern gate at the southeastern corner of the Mound of the Great Bath.

Today one ascends the Mound of the Great Bath by a series of comfortable footpaths. The best way to reach the Great Bath, avoiding the steep northern slope, is through the saddle separating SD from L Area. Climbing a gentle rise moving west, one passes a set of rather unsorted walls of baked brick. Then there is an opening on a wide unnamed street that draws the visitor north toward the center of the area, to the Great Bath.

The Great Bath

It is a few steps on a dogleg course to Main Street, which separates the Great Bath on the west from the College of Priests, as Mackay called the building to the east. Main Street itself is wide (4 to 5 meters) and straight, excavated for a length of just over 100 meters. There is a

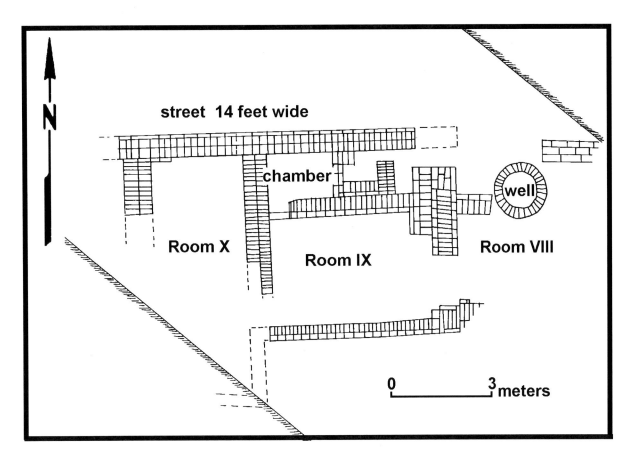

Figure 11.2   Structures at Spur Number 3, east of Mohenjo-daro (after Hussein 1989)

series of drains here, one of them large and covered with rough-hewn white limestone blocks brought in antiquity from the Rohri Hills. This was an area of heavy-duty drainage given the presence of the Bath to one side and a large building, the College of Priests that can be reconstructed plausibly as a residence, at least in part, on the other. There was a concentration of people here, and they appear to have been deeply involved in ablutions (figure 11.4).

The ancient visitor to the southern end of Main Street would have looked up an unpaved, shadowed road, with imposing buildings on both sides. There was probably little relief on these walls: a door into the College, but probably no windows; and a slit to enter the well room of the Bath was all that relieved that facade. Unless we are missing something major (festive, multicolored murals, brightly dressed young men and women)—always a possibility in Indus archaeology—it was all pretty dark and plain.

The Bath itself is set just off center of the Mound of the Great Bath, slightly to the north and west. The Warehouse abuts the southwestern corner of the Bath structure, and this suggests that they may have functioned in tandem, at

least in some contexts. Marshall's description of the Bath seems to capture it very well:

> The Great Bath . . . was part of what appears to have been a vast hydropathic establishment and the most imposing of all the remains unearthed at Mohenjo-daro. Its plan is simple: an open quadrangle with verandahs on its four sides, and at the back of three of the verandahs various galleries and rooms; on the south a long gallery with a small chamber in each corner, on the east a single range of small chambers, including one with a well; on the north a group of several halls and fair-sized rooms. In the centre of the open quadrangle is a large swimming-bath some 39 feet long by 23 feet broad and sunk 8 feet below the paving of the court, with a flight of steps at either end, and a the foot of each a low platform for the convenience of bathers who might otherwise have found the water too deep. . . . That the Great Bath had at least one upper storey is evident from the stairway ascending to the latter . . . as well as from drains descending from it. . . . We know too from quantities of charcoal and ashes found in the course of my excavations that a great deal of timber must have gone to the building of the upper storey.[7]

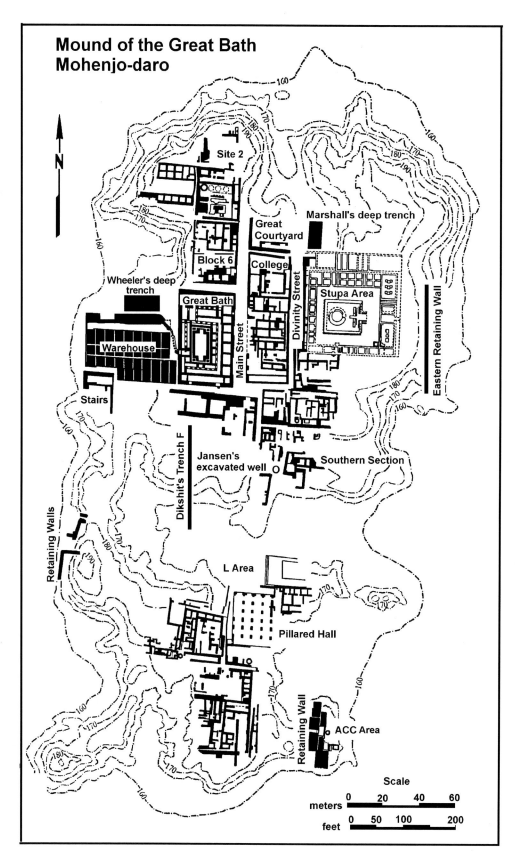

Figure 11.3   Mound of the Great Bath (after Wheeler 1968)

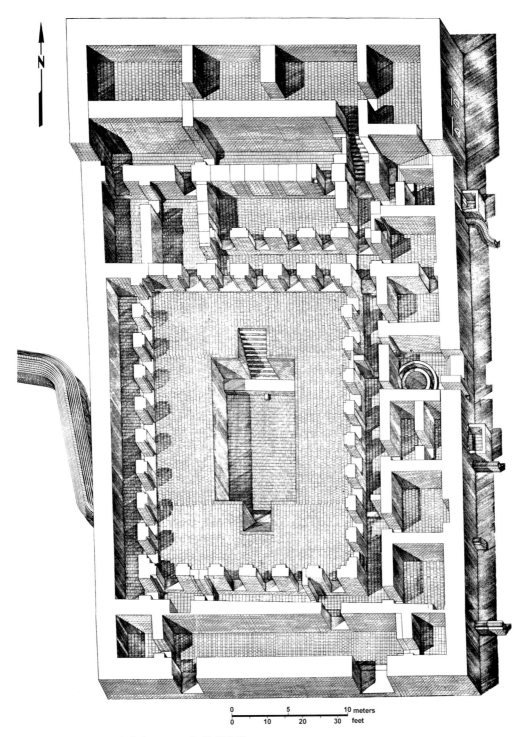

0   5   10 meters
0   10   20   30 feet

Figure 11.4   Plan of the Great Bath (after Marshall 1931i)

The bathing pool was fashioned of very precisely fitted baked bricks. The finish was said by Mackay to be "so good that the writer has not seen its equal in any ancient work."[8] The four walls of the bathing pool were uniformly 1.36 meters thick. This had been covered and made waterproof by a regular lining of bitumen (tar) 2.4 centimeters thick that was kept in place by a course of brick. The

bottom of the pool was not probed in sufficient depth to know if the bitumen sealed the bottom as well, but this is a more than a fair presumption (figure 11.5).

There is a well on the eastern side of the bath, within the enclosing structure itself. Marshall proposed that it was used to fill the bath and provide water for its operations; Mackay doubts this.[9]

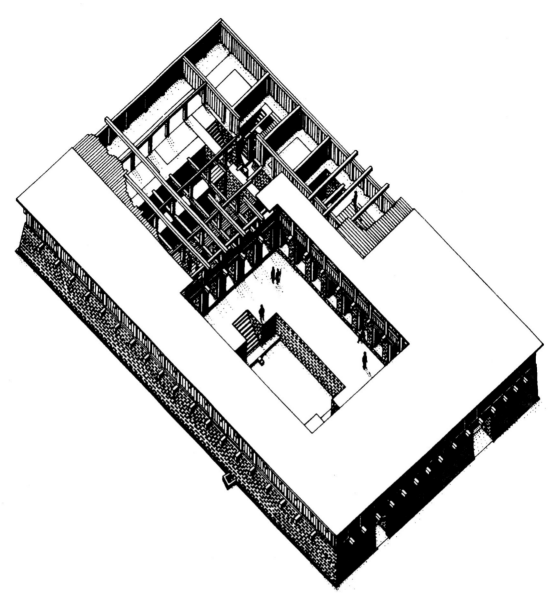

Figure 11.5   Reconstruction of the Great Bath (after Wheeler 1966)

A drain was found in the southwestern corner inside the bath. This was a hole in the brick facing 38 by 20 centimeters that goes through two baked-brick walls and an intervening packing of clay, all 3.12 meters thick. The water exiting the pool would have flowed into a burnt-brick channel, which enters a culvert with a beautiful corbelled arch, 0.71 meters wide by 2.3 meters high, large enough for a fair-sized man to walk in. There is a manhole at the bath end of the culvert, which would have allowed for the inspection and cleaning of the drain, a feature also found with the sumps in the drainage system of Mohenjo-daro. The end of the drain has been removed by erosion of the western edge of the mound and cannot be traced. Thus, we do not know how the effluent was handled, but it presumably was routed, ceremoniously or not, down onto the plain.

Marshall proposes that the impressive corbelled arch of the bath drain was provided for cleaning and "may have served as a secret exit in times of need."[10] If it was only a drain, there was certainly no need for it to be 2 meters high. It simply enlarges an area of flow to no particularly good end. But Mackay has the answer, I think, by proposing that the culvert was where the bathwater was blocked and the water to fill it put down the manhole, causing the drain in the bottom of the pool to flow backward.[11]

The sunken bath could be entered at either end by two flights of steps, which were baked brick covered with wood held in place by bitumen. The stairs at either end terminate on a platform 1 meter wide and 40.6 centimeters high. If filled to the brim, the bath would have been about 2 meters deep; given the stature of most Harappans at about 1.5 meters, even this extra 40.6 centimeters of depth would not have allowed them to stand on the platform without treading water. Thus, assuming that the platform was for comfortable standing, with the water at about shoulder level for the bathers, the level of the water in the bath would have been kept at least 40 or 50 centimeters below the top, making Mackay's use of hydrostatic pressure for filling it even more plausible.

The Bath was surrounded by a colonnade, seven across the width, and ten along each side. These would have supported a roof, but given the span, most reconstructions leave the bath open to the sky as an interior courtyard. On the eastern side of the Great Bath is a series of seven, possibly eight, bathing chambers of typical Mohenjo-daro design, with doors offset to one side to ensure privacy and a drain to carry away the dirty water to the large drain in Main Street.

A Chronology for the Great Bath

The Great Bath was built just following the raising of the mound on which it is sited. The modified building that one sees has been assigned to the Intermediate Period at Mohenjo-daro but it was probably built much earlier.[12] It is apparent that the Great Bath was no longer in use during the last phases of the Late Period at the site, when most of the architecture that we see today at Mohenjo-daro was inhabited.

In a formal analysis of the Great Bath, the German research team that worked at Mohenjo-daro notes that the original architectural concept for the building should be considered a representative piece of Harappan architecture: It is rectangular, proportions of about two by three, with robust enclosing walls, concentric layout, strong central axis, and the like. This team has noted the following additional points concerning this building:

> Functional alteration . . . indicated by the blocking up of all entrances but one in the south, raising of floor level in many compartments, bricking up of parts of inner fenestrated wall intersecting inner circumambulatory, blocking up of northern staircase necessitating the sealing of room 20, building activity in the north and west resulting in the obliteration of these portions of the outer surrounding streets (outer circumambulatory).
>
> Complete abandonment of primary function probably coincidental with the destruction of the complex. Filling of the central tank with debris, removal (destruction?) of eastern and western rows of pillars, partial reuse as production area.
>
> Construction of a drain close to the surface traversing the southeast entrance and ignoring the structure underneath which was already completely buried.

The change in function is further documented by the fact that "prestige and ideology" artifacts, seals, luxury goods and the like diminish in frequency as one moves from lower levels to upper strata; but "production" artifacts show the reverse trend, with more of them in the upper levels.[13]

The Great Bath was abandoned and filled in. The area was then used as a craft production site. Wheeler, who excavated the adjacent Warehouse, noted that "to a height of 30 feet or more, the tall podium of the Great Warehouse on the western side of the citadel, was engulfed by rising structures of poorer and poorer quality."[14] We do not know how deep the fill covering the Great Bath was; however, a photograph suggests that about 3 meters separated the local ground surface from the floor level of the bathing rooms around the pool.[15]

The sequence that can be pieced together then is something like this. At an early time in the history of Mohenjo-daro, but within the Mature Harappan, or the Early Harappan–Mature Harappan Transition, there were settlers near plain level under the Mound of the Great Bath. The inhabitants raised a platform and equipped it with proper buttresses and reinforcing. Two of the buildings they constructed at this time were the Great Bath and the Warehouse. Both of these structures were abandoned at about the beginning of the Late Period of Mohenjo-daro. During the Late Period, there is much evidence for craft activity in this area. This relative sequence of events is reasonably well documented and there is some archaeological evidence for all of it.

Departing through the southern doors of the Great Bath, a turn to the right takes one down a well-trodden street leading to a small stairway up into the Warehouse.

The Warehouse

The Warehouse would have been an imposing building, mostly of wood, with a heavy, thick, flat roof (figures 11.6 and 11.7). This was probably repaired many times, with added layers of Indus rushes and mud crisscrossed and piled on. Not terribly sophisticated, and weighing many tons, it took a substantial set of supports to keep it up. The Warehouse is one story, lower than the Bath, and the light on this side of the mound is not nearly as dark and shadowy as Main Street. The building walls and supports are wooden planks and timbers. The pattern of the outside wooden planks is up and down. These may have been taken from huge deodar trees of the mountains and were floated down to Mohenjo-daro from Kashmir.

We do not know precisely what function the goods stored in the Warehouse played in the life of the inhabitants

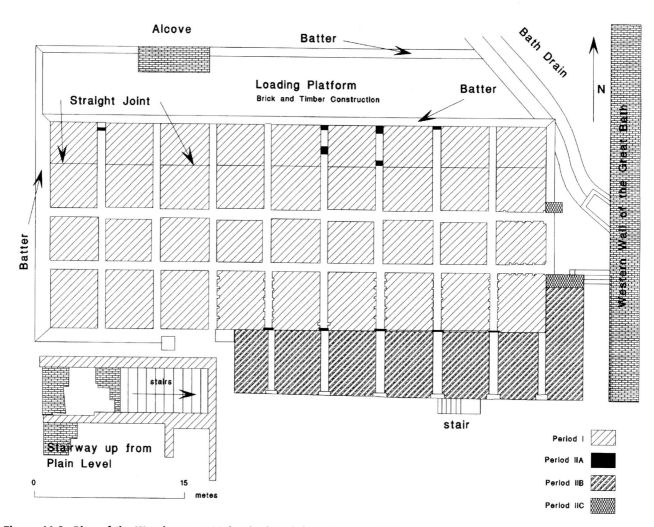

Figure 11.6 Plan of the Warehouse at Mohenjo-daro (after Wheeler 1968)

of Mohenjo-daro or the Mound of the Great Bath (figure 11.8). But propinquity and the similarity of history suggest that the people in charge of the Great Bath had these goods at their disposal. They probably stored things for their own use (food, cloth, leather, wood, fuel, etc. in raw and finished form) as well as for patronage, or "giveaways." That all of this fits into an institutionalized state economy based on redistribution cannot be demonstrated. The fact that the Great Bath and Warehouse seem unique to Mohenjo-daro, with a possible parallel at Lothal, suggests that whatever the function of these two interrelated buildings, it was confined to this city (and possibly Lothal) and may not apply to the civilization as a whole.

A broad staircase of baked bricks took visitors from the Warehouse down to the floodplain of the Indus. Once there, one can turn around for a broad, unobstructed view of the land. The mountains of Baluchistan are visible in the winter, but the haze of the monsoon heat obscures them other times of year. There is no wall

around Mohenjo-daro, not even on this side of the city with the major storage depot on the very edge of inhabited space.

The College of Priests
The College of Priests is now a stabilized set of walls that are difficult to understand without the help of a technical drawing and a trowel. The possible institutional function of the College "was probably the residence of a very high official, possibly the high priest himself, or perhaps a college of priests" (figure 11.9).[16] The overall size of the building is approximately 70.3 meters long and 23.9 meters wide. There were many internal changes to this structure over its lifetime. It was probably conceived with large rooms to the north and south, and smaller ones in the middle. One of the more interesting spaces seems to have been patterned after the northern end of the Great Bath, with interior fenestrations. The western wall of the College appears to have had the principal entrance.

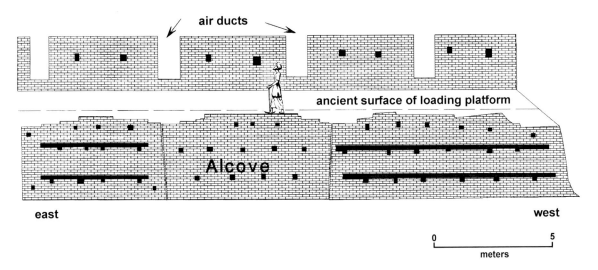

air ducts

ancient surface of loading platform

Alcove

east

west

0 _____ 5

meters

Figure 11.7   Elevation of the Warehouse at Mohenjo-daro (after Wheeler 1968)

Who Came to the Bath, Warehouse, and College of Priests?

Who among the citizens of Mohenjo-daro would have found themselves at the southern end of Main Street? We do not know for sure, but some of them would have been the men and women who were allowed by their society to use the Great Bath. I think of them as a group of individuals who were dedicated to acting out the rituals for which the Great Bath had been constructed. They may well have been "career specialists," possibly by birth, but it may have been something that individuals advanced to over the course of their lives. They may have lived in or around the College of Priests. There were probably other visitors at this intersection: high officials from the city, responsible citizens, respected elders, senior families, and all sorts of special people defined by Indus society as privileged. They, too, may have come here to partake of bathing, ritual, study, and socializing with the "permanent" residents. I do not take this area to be the playground of the Indus hoi polloi, folks at the lower end of the social pyramid.

The foregoing could be read as very "Wheelerian," with the Mound of the Great Bath as the headquarters of a priestly administration wielding autocratic, absolute power from their citadels.[17] This is not what I want to convey. First, we do not know what role the religious specialists, who are proposed to have been primary users of the Great Bath, played in the government of Mohenjo-daro or some larger part of the Indus Civilization. There is no compelling reason to think of them as priest-kings. That they had some form of political influence, perhaps even power, is a reasonable proposition, but we do not know how this worked itself out within the contexts of

the Indus political institution. Moreover, there is nothing quite like the Mound of the Great Bath at any other site of the Indus Civilization. Kalibangan might come the closest, with the separate High Mound to the west, but there is no Great Bath there. Such a facility is not a part of Harappa itself, where there is a high mound, but, again, no Great Bath. Lothal's "tank" comes to mind, but the scale of this feature is so much larger than the Great Bath at Mohenjo-daro.

The Area North of the Great Bath: Blocks 6 and 10

Remounting the Mound of the Great Bath via the western stairway, one can return to Main Street and walk north between the Great Bath and College. Today this is another jumble of walls, mostly of the Late Period, and not at all well understood. The Buddhists were also in this area and seem to have used it as living space. More bathing rooms were found by Mackay in 1927–1928 in Block 6, to the north of the Great Bath.[18] He dates these to the Late Period and makes the quite reasonable suggestion that they may have taken over the function of the Great Bath at this time. Wheeler has an excellent description of the new bathing rooms.[19]

Just across Main Street from Block 6 is what seems to have been a large open courtyard, Mackay's Block 10. This feature probably originated at or about the same time as the Warehouse and was one of the original features of the Mound of the Great Bath. The surrounding wall is thick (approximately 2 meters) and is preserved in only the southwestern corner and extensions there from. There are later structures inside, but I feel that it was probably conceived as an open space, possibly also connected to the ritual/religious establishment.

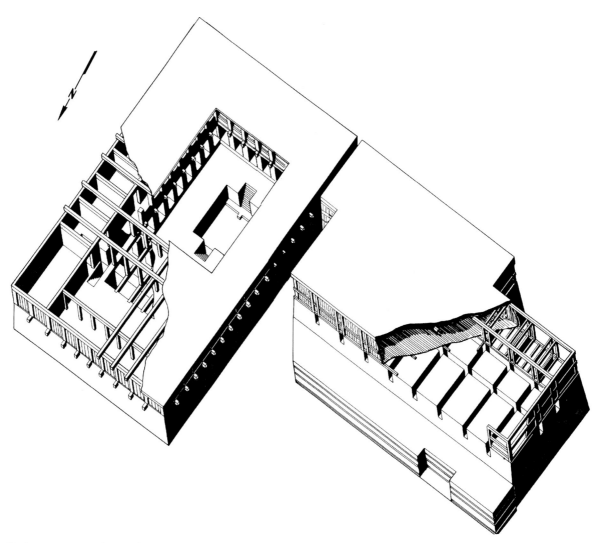

Figure 11.8   Reconstructions of the Warehouse and Great Bath at Mohenjo-daro (after Wheeler 1966)

L Area: The Southern End of the Mound of the Great Bath

It is less than a 200-meter walk from the neighborhood of Block 6 to the complex of buildings on the southern end of the Mound of the Great Bath. Getting there takes a matter of minutes, walking across the saddle of open, eroded turf. Today the ground is sufficiently salty so that a crust forms on the surface. After rain and a period of time for drying, one "crunches" across the skin of lightly consolidated earth and salt.

The southern end of the Mound of the Great Bath was designated "L Area." It was excavated by Mackay in 1926–1927, his first year at Mohenjo-daro (figure 11.20).[20]

L Area is clearly an important place, but what went on here during the heyday of the city is still obscure. The principal feature of L Area has been construed by Marshall as a place of assembly for monks or priests and has

been compared to Buddhist caves,[21] although Mackay thought of it as a marketplace.[22] Siding with Marshall for once, Wheeler believes it to have been an assembly hall: "The general scheme of the building is a little reminiscent of an Achaemenian *apadana* or audience chamber."[23] We call it the "Pillared Hall" here.

The structure is an open, columned hall approximately 23 by 27 meters. The building seems to have had its principal entrance in the center of the northern wall. The roof was supported by four north-south rows of five columns each. The bases of the columns are made of baked brick. Mackay dates the original building to the Intermediate Period and notes that later additions have obscured some parts of the original plan. At the same time, strips of pavement, arranged in a peculiar way not found elsewhere at Mohenjo-daro, were laid down between the columns (figure 11.21). This curious arrangement of paving is a mys-

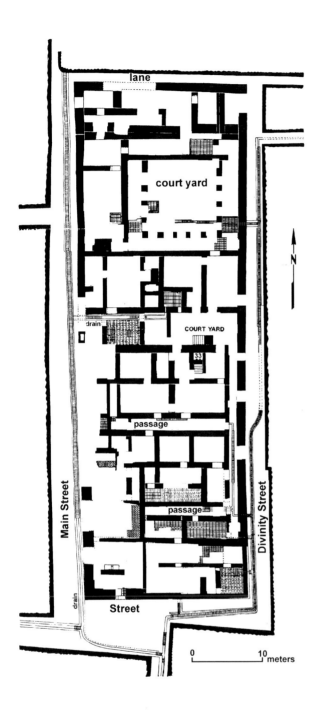

lane

court yard

drain

COURT YARD

33

passage

Main Street

passage

Divinity Street

drain

Street

0   10 meters

Figure 11.9   The "College of Priests" (after Mackay 1937–38)

tery, and I have no good idea as to its function. Wheeler says that the entire matter "cries aloud for intelligent re-excavation,"[24] which is probably the best thing.

There is a great deal of Late Period material above the curious paving, and most of the artifacts that have been found in L Area seem to be best placed in this latter time frame. The most interesting of the artifacts is a large (61

by 54 by 37 centimeters) worn stone that is dark brown or black in color. The top is flat and polished and "it was possibly used by a leather-cutter or sandal-maker."[25]

The Latest Occupations on the Mound of the Great Bath

The presence of the "leather cutter's stone" is in agreement with the general observation that the Late Period on the Mound of the Great Bath, when the Bath and Warehouse were abandoned, was a time when it was used for craft activities and daily life. This seems to be a significant change from the function(s) envisioned by the builders of the place. This leather cutter's stone brings the Mound of the Great Bath down to earth, with the real, daily needs of people. Whoever lived on the southern part of the Mound of the Great Bath needed sandals and other leather items, and the local *chamar* set up shop in the neighborhood to take care of them. It also may inform us of the fact that the people who lived here did not exclusively use the bazaars of Mohenjo-daro to fill their needs, but that day-to-day living activities were a part of life on the Mound of the Great Bath. In fact, the late levels in L Area are filled with objects of daily life: pottery, storage jars, bangles, seals, beads, and the like. And there is evidence for craft activities there, including lapidary work and shell work, along with the leather cutter's stone.[26]

Mound of the Great Bath: Overview

The Mound of the Great Bath is an impressive place, even forty centuries after its abandonment. Set aside and elevated over the Lower Town gives it a special quality. Its separateness suggests exclusivity, a position where the upper rank or ranks of Indus society would have been comfortable, possibly even at home. The elevation suggests dominance and complements the sense of being exclusive. There would have been a wide view of Mohenjo-daro and the surrounding plain from the Mound of the Great Bath, where the elites could look down upon the workings of the city and the lower and middle classes that were the warp and weft of their society. Thus, whoever conceived of Mohenjo-daro as a totality was intelligent enough to use two dimensions, separateness and height, to symbolically set apart the functions and functionaries of whatever went on within the precincts of the Mound of the Great Bath. This was symbolism, since we can be quite certain that it was simply another representation of a social reality that all of the members of Mohenjo-daro society would have recognized from their day-to-day lives. So, the construction of the Mound of the Great Bath incorporated aspects of those clever tricks that are at the heart

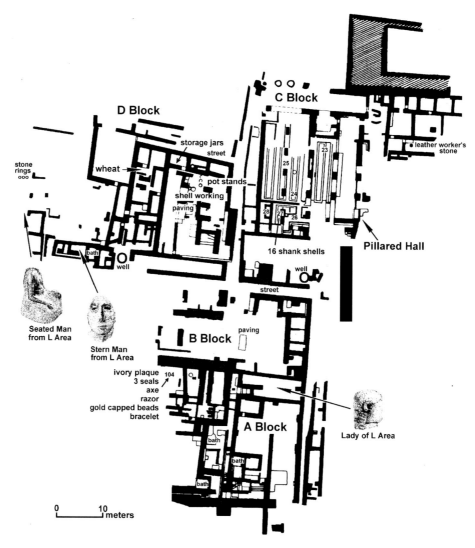

Figure 11.10 L Area on the Mound of the Great Bath (after Marshall 1931i)

of every society by using symbols in a rich and effective way to manage, govern, and perpetuate a social order. How different all of this is from the sprawling, urban functionalism of the Lower Town.

THE LOWER TOWN AT MOHENJO-DARO

The best way to enter the Lower Town of Mohenjo-daro today is to walk into HR Area in the southwestern quarter of the archaeological mound, just where it meets the remains in the GFD Area.[27] GFD Area informed us of a number of things at Mohenjo-daro, such as a late "squatters' level" there and evidence for a conflagration very late in the history of the site.[28] The other documentation we find is for "a massive structure of mud brick with a solid, burnt brick wall. It provided a facing and support to the mud brick structure for a length exceeding 600 feet (183 meters) along the western face of HR mound."[29] Here we

have sound evidence for platform building and that the Mature Harappan pattern at Mohenjo-daro was to face walls with baked brick.

HR Area

The best view of HR Area is straight north, up First Street, which was a linear depression of some magnitude on the surface of unexcavated Mohenjo-daro (figure 11.12). Excavators went to this depression hoping to uncover a major street, and they did. First Street is just over 10 meters wide in this part of Mohenjo-daro. It is wide enough for wheeled vehicles to use, although there is no good documentation for carts in the city, and there are some reasons for us to believe that their use inside the municipality was restricted.

The starkness of First Street is readily apparent. There are blank walls of baked brick, broken by the lanes that

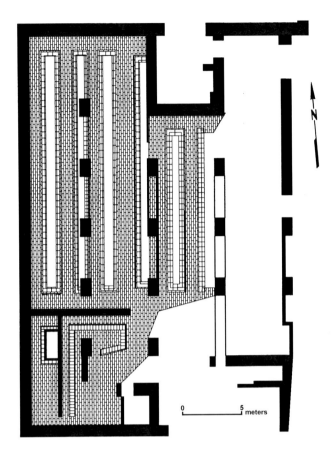

Figure 11.11 Detail of paving in the Pillared Hall (after Marshall 1931i)

join into it. There are few doors and windows, little sense of an eagerness to welcome visitors to share the hearth and company—all very Harappan.

There are two modern parts to HR Area: Section A to the east and Section B to the west. Coming north, up First Street, one sees to the right House 1 of HR-A, a building proposed to have been a temple.

The southern end of Deadman's Lane, is also open to traffic, and it is a nice stroll north, past South Lane on the right, where the second part of the Sad Man was found. One passes doorways of houses in this little neighborhood of the third millennium B.C. It is 70 meters to the end of Deadman's Lane, where it turns left and joins First Street. Just at the turning, Hargreaves found a skeleton lying on its back, giving the street its name.[30]

Most of the buildings in this part of Mohenjo-daro are thought to have been the houses of the Mohenjo-daro elite, or at least those who could afford large houses and the expensive baked-brick architecture. I would like to describe one of them here.

The Building in HR-A, Block 3, House VIII

The building with the Mohenjo-daro address of HR-A, Block 3, House VIII, hereafter simply called "House VIII," is in the northern part of this excavation area. Marshall described it in detail and took the time to have an isometric drawing prepared of the place (figure 11.13).[31] The original core of the building was said to have been built in Intermediate II times, modified in Intermediate I, and then burned down.[32] This chronology is not necessarily correct.[33]

The main entrance to House VIII is on High Lane, just 15 meters east of First Street. There is also a back door on the northernmost wall. This can be considered typical for a residence in the city, since it places the entrance off of a major thoroughfare. House VIII is surrounded by buildings that one could reasonably think of as residences, and this would have been an upper-class neighborhood of the ancient metropolis. The front of the house, or its southern wall, is approximately 26 meters long. Including the little extension of the core building to the north, House VIII is 29.5 meters deep (north-south). The walls that surround it are of baked bricks and 1.2 to 1.5 meters thick. There are two exterior doors, but no windows or other large apertures in the exterior walls.

The main entrance was originally 3 meters wide, but was narrowed to 2.3 meters in a remodeling. There is an entrance foyer (space 5) fronting a small room (5a) that Marshall and I feel was a place for the *chowkidar*, or watchman, to sit. The walls of space 5 were plastered with about 2 centimeters of mud and chopped grass finished by a wash of fine clay; they were preserved because of the house fire.

Having entered House VIII, and passed through security, one took a dogleg turn to the right, passing the entrance to space 17 on the left and entering the central courtyard (spaces 18 and 18a), which has eight small spaces (6–13) on its southern and eastern sides. The courtyard was a focus of the house and was probably open to the sky. If it was not open, the ground floor of House VIII would have been very dark, as dark as a cave, in fact, given the absence of windows and the door placed so as to shield the entry of light.

The whole of the courtyard and other rooms on the ground floor of House VIII were paved in baked brick, and there is a small raised area (18a) with a protective coping on the outside. There is an intramural floor drain fronting spaces 12, 12a, and 11. This is connected to a vertical earthenware pipe in space 12a and another in space 9, not shown on the oblique projection.

But a strange thing about this drain is that it discharged, not, as was usually the case, into one of the street drains,

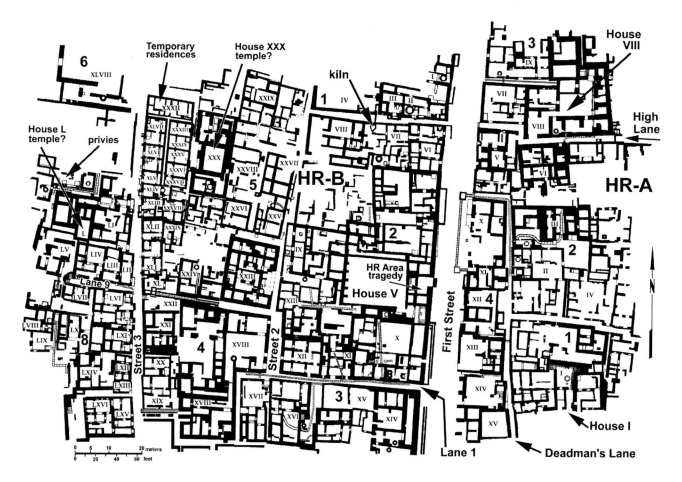

Figure 11.12 Plan of HR Area (after Marshall 1931i)

but into a moderate sized earthenware vessel sunk beneath the courtyard pavement in front of Room 11. That this receptacle was intended to take the whole discharge from the vertical pipes which served the upper story, is perfectly clear from the slope of the courtyard drain itself, which falls from both directions towards the vessel. The point of interest, because it is evident that in this house at any rate the main drain was not intended to carry off either the bath water from the upper or lower floor, or rainwater from the roof. Indeed, it seems as if it was meant to serve the upstairs privies only, the vessel into which it discharged being cleaned as often as was necessary and the contents conveyed by hand to one or other of the street drains or soak-pits.[34]

I rarely have an opportunity to absolutely disagree with Marshall on matters of this sort, but his interpretation of this drain makes no sense at all. First, without huge amounts of running water, the drains would be completely plugged in no time if this facility was used for the servicing of privies. Moreover, drains and pipes used to convey raw sewage can be identified by the residual material, usually a

slightly greasy, green glaze or patina, and there is no mention of this. Also, the earthenware vessel that would have been regularly emptied is buried as a permanent facility below a neatly paved floor. There is no evidence that it was ever opened, let alone opened daily (or more) once it had been paved over. Finally, one can imagine the implications of this entirely malodorous facility in the middle of the prime space of an upper-class Mohenjo-daro house. This family may have well put an open privy in the dining room. How can this interpretation be matched against the fastidiousness of the people who are said to have inhabited the city? The drains in question were intended for rainwater, possibly bathwater, and other light-duty domestic waste, not the "upstairs privies."

Space 6, which could be entered by rising three steps, has a brick-lined well (number 3) in it, so its function is reasonably clear (figure 11.14). There is an opening between the well room and spaces 7 and 8 large enough for vessels of water to be passed from the well to the aforementioned spaces, which were a bathing-washing facility. Space 7 was a typical Mohenjo-daro bathing floor, with a

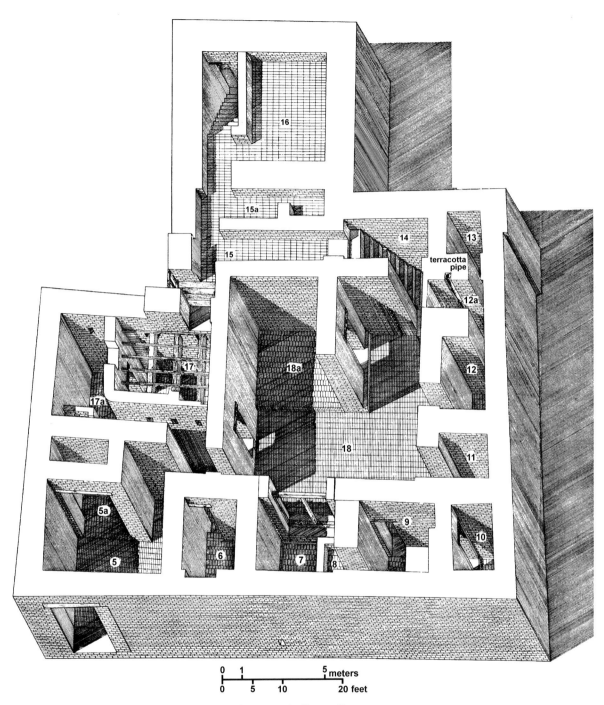

Figure 11.13 Oblique projection of House VIII (after Marshall 1931i)

small drain through the outer wall, emptying into the street drain on High Lane.

Space 8 is an extension of the bathing room, and both it and 7 were provided with a window onto the courtyard. This was lined in wood, and Marshall suggests it may have been covered with a latticework. He further suggests that the opening was convenient, so that clothes could be passed out of the bathing space into the courtyard, imply-

ing the possibility that the *dhobi* washed clothes there. There were several modifications made to this part of House VIII over its lifetime, and the original arrangement of spaces 7, 8, and 9 is not clear. Marshall's oblique projection shows stairs descending from above in space 9. This would have allowed the family members to come down to this bathing space from the private rooms on the southeastern side of the upstairs without having the

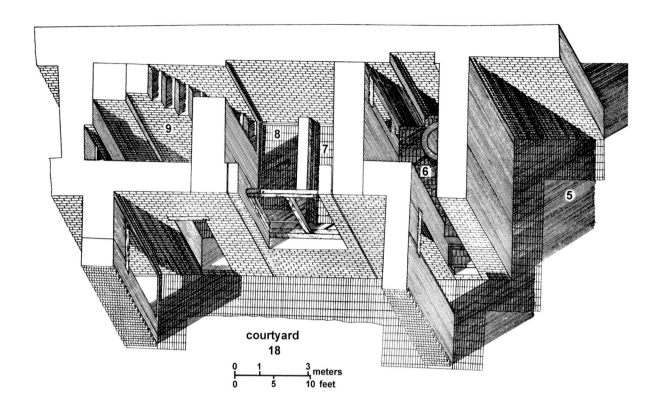

Figure 11.14 Oblique projection of the southern chambers of House VIII, from the north (after Marshall 1931i)

inconvenience of moving through the more open parts of the house. One could also enter space 7 from the court-yard, via a door in space 9.

Spaces 10 through 13 are very small. Number 10 is 2.1 by 3.6 meters, and 13 is 1.5 by 2.4 meters. Marshall be-lieves these to be used by "menials," but they could have been storerooms as well and may have served both these purposes, and others, in antiquity. The jambs of the open-ings into 10 through 12 were rebuilt over the life of the house. This might be taken to indicate hard use, harder than that a "menial" might inflict on his or her room, but the kind of use that storage facilities get, tilting the bal-ance slightly in this direction. But household staff have been known to live in what we might think of as store-rooms, and we have to imagine that the notion of clear-cut, single-purpose functions for these spaces, especially over the lifetime of House VIII, is not likely. They proba-bly served a number of functions, and this shifted over time, depending on the needs of the inhabitants and the taste of those in charge of space allocation. Whatever the case, space 13 was a pretty mean, dark little room, what-ever it was used for.

Before proceeding upstairs, something more should be said of space 17, near the High Lane entrance. This is ac-tually a room inside a room (17a). The largest of these is approximately 8 by 5.5 meters. The inner space is approx-imately 5 by 4 meters. The larger space could be entered either off the dogleg from the High Lane entrance or di-rectly from the courtyard. There is a small space in the southwestern corner that might have been a bathing area, but this is not mentioned by Marshall. The inner room has a hidden entrance, in the sense that no one but those who had entered the space and moved to the western hall could see into it. The ceiling had been lowered, and there were rafters of deodar and sissoo placed in beam holes.[35] The craftsmanship employed in creating the inner room is also seen in the brickwork of the southwestern corner of the space. The outer corner has been very carefully rounded, doubtless for the comfort of the inhabitant(s). The inner corner, however, was kept square. Marshall thought of space 17 as a guest chamber, and this fits well with the evidence. But it also has the look of a "grand-mother's apartment." It is on the ground floor, so no stairs to climb. There is privacy and quiet in a place obvi-ously carefully crafted near water and bathing facilities. This could have been a place for the senior generation of a family to live in relative peace and comfort, slightly away from the normal hustle and bustle of children and day-to-

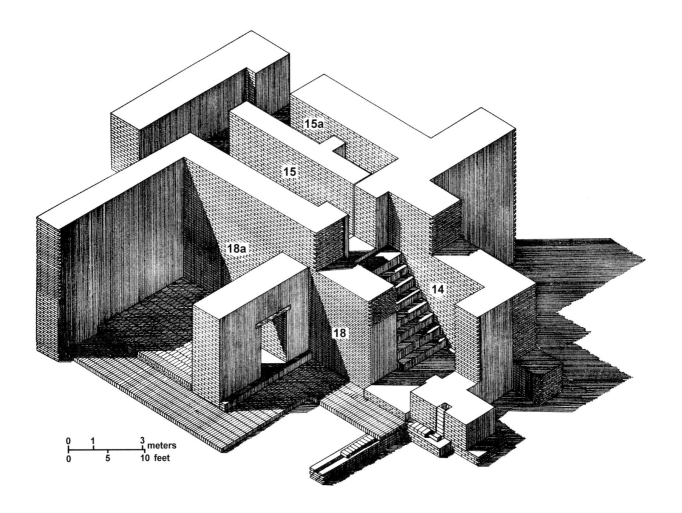

Figure 11.15   Oblique projection of steps in House VIII (after Marshall 1931i)

day family life. Another alternative, one that is probably better than the guest room notion, possibly even the grandmother's room notion, is that this was were the *chowkidar* or some other menial lived. It is on the ground floor and close to the door.

The northern platform in the core structure is of solid brick, very stable and a good protection against floods. Marshall thought that "the idea being to have at least one fair-sized room where the family could find refuge if the rest of the house collapsed."[36]

The upper floor(s) of House VIII were reached via a stairway leading from Courtyard 18 and from a flight of steps at the back door off of an unnamed lane at the northern limit of HR-A (figure 11.15). There is also the set of stairs in a bathing area (space 9). Marshall opines that the first floor above the ground had rooms disposed around the courtyard. This arrangement is eminently reasonable since the hot season at Mohenjo-daro is stifling. The ground floor of the houses in the interior of the city

would be quite uninhabitable if there was not some way for them to have access to air. An open courtyard is the obvious solution to this problem.

Michael Jansen has located the fieldworkers' notebooks for the premodern excavations at Mohenjo-daro, and he published the antiquities register for the finds in HR Area.[37] He informs us that there were more than 200 entries for things found in House VIII.[38] His analysis of them and the layout of the house are interesting.

First, he concludes that the inner courtyard is the focus of the finished building. In the principal settlement level, that is objects recovered from 54.15+15 centimeters above mean sea level, he found a complete absence of ceramics. In most of the other squares at this level there had been an abundance of ceramics. There was a great deal of stone in the courtyard, including one millstone. Complementing this was the recovery of carbonized wheat seeds. One can therefore envision that grain may have been stored here and that the grinding operation took place near storage.

The other thing that Jansen found was that there was a sizable amount of shell in the southwestern corner of the courtyard. Shell made up 61.6 percent of the total finds in this area. This included one complete shell, two partially complete shell bangles, and several other conch shell objects, some of which may have been wasters.

Jansen cautions us that his analysis of objects from House VIII is preliminary and should be taken as an indication that there is potential in this approach. Much of it is dependent on the state of record keeping that the excavators used; however, they did record things in three dimensions. But the association of artifacts in the ground is ultimately related to taphonomic processes, and these are poorly understood at Mohenjo-daro. It could be that the courtyard of House VIII was filled with debris from other abodes in the neighborhood after it had been abandoned. The shells in the southwestern corner may therefore be simply a rich deposit of trash from another place. But work with the collections and field notebooks have the potential to sort out some of these problems, and that is the promise of Jansen's project in House VIII.

House VIII must have been a very fine place in its day. It was well built, with thick sturdy walls, sound stairs, good bathing facilities, all neatly tucked into what seems to have been a congenial neighborhood just off First Street. On the other side of First Street is HR-B, a large complex of buildings and streets about 120 by 100 meters on a side.

HR-B Area

Lane 1 is a good opening into the northern part of HR-B. Taking a left at the end of this lane heads one south on Street 2 and into the back side of an interesting neighborhood, designated Block 2 of HR-B by Marshall. House VIII, room 17, has the remains of one of the few kilns at Mohenjo-daro. This is a very late and very noxious facility. In this same house, room 8 yielded one of the magnificent jewelry hoards found during the first phase of excavation at Mohenjo-daro. The hoard was called "the most important find of the (1925–1926) season" by Sahni, who described it.[39] This large body of material was found just beneath a floor, and it consists of the following:

Two silver vases, originally wrapped in a cotton bag
A copper vase that contained a copper axe and chisels
Four, large hollow, earrings (?)
Two circular ear ornaments of gold
Three fillets or diadems of gold
Thirteen addition fillets, rolled up
Two more broad fillets with hanging beads attached
Three forehead fillets of a pointed shape
Seven hemispheric terminals

One silver bangle broken in two halves
Six silver finger rings
One shell finger ring
A large collection of beads of gold, silver, faience, semi-precious stones, along with pendants, terminals, and spacers that were made up into nine necklaces[40]

The oxidation salts of the two silver vases had preserved the cotton fabric and led to the positive identification of this fiber at Mohenjo-daro.

Block 2 is dominated by House V, which is about 1,000 square meters. This is the place where the HR Area tragedy was found. To give one a sense of just how large this building is, a good-sized American home is about 200 square meters. Getting to House V from Street 2 is either through House IX or across an area that today is a jumble of walls. House V, a structure said to be of the Intermediate Period, is dominated by a large (14 by 19 meters) open courtyard (room 70), which was nicely paved. This is a splendid space, which must have been open to the sky when the building was occupied. To the north of the courtyard is a mass of rooms including an intramural, private well, an elevated house "core" on which the next floor up would have rested, and other spaces. One of these sets House V apart. This is long, narrow room 49, approximately 13.5 by 3.3 meters, immediately distinguished by the fact that the blocked-up doorway in the south wall has a corbelled arch, the only such doorway in Mohenjo-daro as we know it; although there are many smaller corbelled arches.[41] This room is well preserved, with the walls standing over 5 meters high. There are also beam holes for very substantial rafters. The ceiling of room 49 was built to take a very heavy load. When room 49 was cleared, Sahni found a collection of eighteen large ring stones, of the kind that Mackay found in L Area (figure 11.16). These were lying along the north wall of room 49. Sahni has the following to say of the other finds:

Not far from these rings were found two round stone caps with rounded tops (HR 5935, Plate CXXX, 23 and HR 5939, Plate CXXX, 21), which resemble the tops of the so-called "gamesmen" (probably cult-objects) of varying sizes found both at Harappa and Mohenjo-daro. The precise purpose of these stone rings and "gamesmen" is not yet definitely known. Other objects of the same class are the cones of stone, terra-cotta, etc., but without the projecting rim at the top. One cone of this type (height 11 inches) was unearthed by me at Harappa in 1924–25, and I then drew attention to its similarity to the Siva-*linga* and suggested that it might have been fixed in a pedestal (its base was rough dressed) and worshipped in a tiny brick structure found close by it.[42]

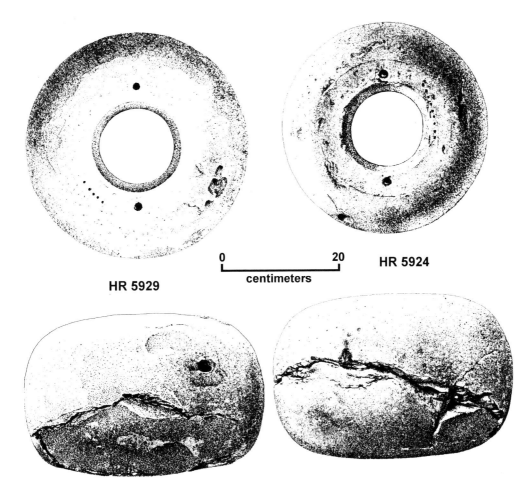

HR 5929   HR 5924

0   20
centimeters

Figure 11.16   Ring stones from Mohenjo-daro (after Marshall 1931i)

A lingum was also found in House V, and it figured in the preliminary report in the same photograph as the objects noted in Sahni's quote.[43] Two limestone capitals were also found in room 49. Others turned up in adjacent rooms; one in 47, the other in 50.[44] These capitals are unique in Mohenjo-daro and tend to strengthen the position documented at Dholavira that the ring stones are column drums.

There are more interesting structures in this neighborhood, including a group of modular structures at the end of Street 3. The direction to head is north, up to Lane 9, then west for 20 meters, up an original flight of stairs with a shortcut through House LV. Room 40 in this house is well paved and the place where the so-called bronze dancing girl of HR Area was found on January 26, 1927, by Daya Ram Sahni.

This shortcut brings us to the southern wall of House L, the building with massive walls discussed previously as one of the structures proposed (wrongly) to have been a temple. It does have well-preserved walls on the order of 1 to 2 meters in thickness. Sahni was of the opinion that this was the basement plinth of a building of the Intermediate Period, the upper portions of which had completely disappeared.[45] The rooms (8, 9, 10) on the western side of this building had been filled with well-laid mud bricks. Sahni makes no mention of rooms 24, 25, and 26. It is the massiveness of this building that sets it apart and makes it comparable to House XXX across Street 3.

House XXX is larger than House L, with a footprint of approximately 24 by 11 meters (figure 8.9). The massive walls are quite apparent and comparable to House L's in thickness. When they were excavated, they stood well over 3 meters in height. There are nine rooms in this building, none with doorways; and at some point in time they were all filled with "sun-dried brick or pure clay."[46] An inner court (room 55) 7 by 5.8 meters is a distinguishing feature of the structure. The southern rooms (56, 57, 58) were paved, and 57 has a well, so at some point they were something other than foundation cells, built to be filled with brick and/or pure clay. The same may have been true for the court; but what we see today appears to be, once again, the basement plinth of a large building of the Intermediate Period, the upper portion of which is no longer extant.

What of the function of House XXX, and its partner L? Sahni says of XXX: "That the building, which stood on such massive foundations, had an exceptional character—probably sacred—can hardly be doubted."[47] There is nothing in the list of finds associated with Houses L and XXX that suggests a function, but more systematic work with the collections might prove interesting.

Between Houses XXX and L is a double row of small quarters that also caught the attention of Wheeler and Piggott (see figure 11.12). There is a total of fifteen spaces here. House XXXII to the north is a single unit. The rest are divided by a central axial space without doors, so the eastern chambers could not communicate directly with those on the west. One of the spaces is a well room. The southernmost pair of rooms has more complicated subdivisions, and they are a bit larger than the others; the one to the west has a second well. The ten modular spaces, those divided by the central axis, and the one opposite the well room, vary in size, but they are similar: 4 by 6 meters, plus or minus about a meter and a half. There is a small room to the rear (approximately 2 by 4 meters) and a larger one in the front (approximately 4 by 4 meters), just twice the size of the back room. The front room has a bathing floor and a drain to the street, which was usually connected to a sump of some kind. The thinness of the walls and the absence of stairs suggest that these were single-story units.

Sahni dealt with this group of buildings as an isolated set, not as an integral part of the neighborhood in association with Houses L and XXX, his sacred building. He refers to them as shops, the front rooms being used as display areas, the back as storage. He even went so far as to suggest that the well room of LXIII was a place where drinking water can be obtained by the glass.

> One corner of this room is occupied by a finely built well with a neat brick paving laid across the rest of the floor. The shallow round pits in the floor near the well were meant to hold pottery jars which were kept filled with water, and by them the attendant to dole out draughts to thirsty persons. The floor was littered with broken pottery goblets with pointed bases. Similar goblets and other jars were also found in the brick-lined pit in the front of the room into which the waste water flowed out.[48]

Sahni has created a wonderful living image here. The association of the scene with the well, standing water jars, and the discarded containers makes a strong case, not necessarily for a public facility, but in a more general way.

Piggott has also described these rooms. He builds on the idea that this part of HR-B was for workers' quarters: "The whole lay-out is so strongly suggestive of ['coolie-lines' of colonial India] that one feels that this is a likely explanation, and this receives confirmation from the more explicit Harappa evidence."[49] The structures at Harappa are on Mound F, to the north. They are associated with a series of husking floors and are discussed in detail as a part of the description of Harappa.

Wheeler sides with Piggott on this, noting that the "coolie-line" analogy and the links to the "workers' quarters" at Harappa would be a fruitful line of inquiry. But there is no small amount of waffling in his position:

> Servile or semi-servile labor is a familiar element in any ancient polity; it is only necessary to recall once more the slave-attendants and craftsmen employed in the Sumerian temples, or the labor cantonments of Egypt, to create an appropriate context for these Mohenjo-daro tenements. If the building in front of them was in fact a temple, their proximity may well have been significant. Alternatively they may have been police-barracks, or even the quarters of a priest-hood. Whatever their precise function, they fit into and enhance our general picture of a disciplined and even regimented civilization.[50]

Wheeler's suggestion is, then, that these modular structures were the abodes of slaves, laborers, police, or priests. This certainly covers a lot of social and institutional ground!

I am not drawn to Piggott's notion that these were workers' quarters, or that they were the places of residence for any category of servile labor. The bathing floors run counter to this, in my mind at least. This leads me to think of them as places where those citizens of the Indus Civilization who were given to use bathing facilities would stay. It just does not make sense to think that these would have been slaves or servile labor, recognizing the fact that *slave* covers a great deal of social space as well. The look of the place, with the relatively thin walls, I take to indicate both a single story and a place of temporary residence; a kind of Mohenjo-daro motel—a place of public accommodation for the "bathing class(es)" of Indus society. The larger units to the north may have been for the permanent caretakers of the complex, or for the accommodation of very special visitors. The rooms to the south around the well would have been for service personnel, since the well implies that the "motel" bathing facilities were provided for from this source. The evidence for standing water pots and the accumulation of pointed-base goblets informs us that the visitors stopped there for drinking water also consumed by the "inn keepers."

VS Area is just to the north, along a modern footpath

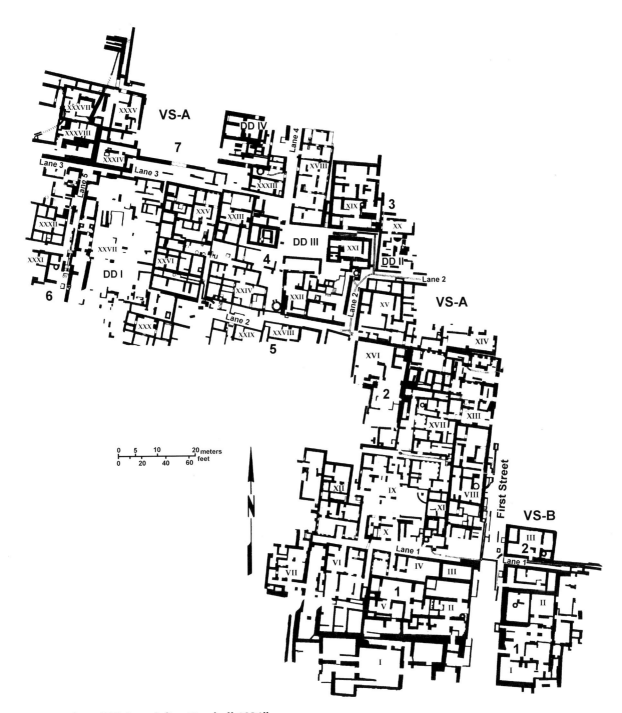

Figure 11.17 Plan of VS Area (after Marshall 1931i)

that approximates the alignment of First Street. It is up and over a hill, down, then up again, in the unexcavated ditch that should be East Street.

VS Area

This area was first opened up by Vats in 1923–1924, the second season of work at Mohenjo-daro. In addition to exposing a substantial amount of architecture there, he confirmed the presence of deeply stratified deposits in the

Lower Town. There are two sections to VS Area: VI-B to the east, and VS-A to the west of First Street (figure 11.17).

VS-B Area

The three houses in VS-B were not described by Sahni in *Mohenjo-daro and the Indus Civilization*. There is no explanation for this—he just left them out. The only description is in the preliminary report for 1926–1927, when they were cleared, and it is perfunctory.[51]

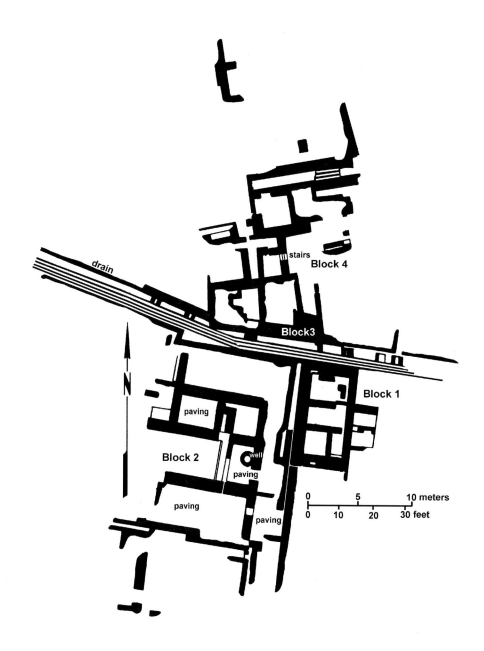

Figure 11.18   Plan of DK-A (after Marshall 1931i)

VS-A Area

VS-A Area is across First Street from VS-B, the lettering being just the reverse of HR Area. The alignment of streets here is relatively poor. Block 4 dominates this part of VS-A. There is something that makes the area not inviting, perhaps it is the concentration of human remains that were found here; the VS Area tragedy being in Block 3, in Lane 4, between Houses XVIII and XXXIII.[52]

To the east of VS Area is the so-called Moneer Area, or Moneer Site, originally DK-I. This is the next place on our tour of the Lower Town of Mohenjo-daro.

The DK Areas

Moneer Area, or DK-I

The first excavation in the Moneer Area was undertaken by Dikshit in 1924–1925. His trench was U-shaped and of no great width, if judged from his plan. There is evidence for lapidary work in semiprecious stones in this area. Puri found a large number of beads, sixteen small weights, and a pair of small copper scale pans together with a fulcrum in a room directly accessible from a lane, suggesting it was a lapidary workshop.[53]

Figure 11.19 Plan of DK-B and DK-C (after Marshall 1931i)

DK-A Area

The principal feature of DK-A is the large east-west street of the Late Period, with its drain (figure 11.18). This may link up with the proposed street at the very southern end of DK-G, an important, unresolved observation bearing on the reality of the grid town plan at Mohenjo-daro. The combined DK-B and DK-C Areas are 100 meters to the north. A modern footpath takes one over the rough terrain.

DK-B Area

DK-B is interesting since all architecture there is of the latest phase of occupation of the city (figure 11.19). DK-B provided the Marshall team with a good deal of information about this phase of city life. The construction here is a counterpoint to practices elsewhere.

> It will be noted in the plan that most of the walls of these houses are comparatively thin. They were also badly built, so much so that some have fallen down, undoubtedly from this cause. The bricks were placed in the queerest positions, some on edge, others showing their flats; joints agape have been left unbroken in many places. This kind of masonry illustrates the great deterioration that had taken place in the art of building since

the preceding period; the difference in style of the masonry of the two periods is at once evident even to the casual eye.[54]

The excavation in DK-B may confirm the presence of Second Street. This was found to be approximately 9 meters wide at this point, very similar to the width of First Street in HR Area. The priest-king statue was found in Block 2, House II, room 2 of HR-B.

DK-C Area

DK-C Area is contiguous to DK-B. It is composed of approximately 7,800 square meters of exposed architecture. Blocks 1, 2, and 3 are to the northern side of the wide, east-west street in this area. The street was well equipped with drains, one of which had a "pent roof."[55] The architecture is not especially interesting, but in room number 2 of Block 16 Dikshit found a hoard of jewelry packed in a silver vase about a meter below ground surface.[56]

Trench E

The first digging at the northern end of Mohenjo-daro was a long, narrow trench designated "E" by Dikshit. It ran east-west and was approximately 400 meters long.

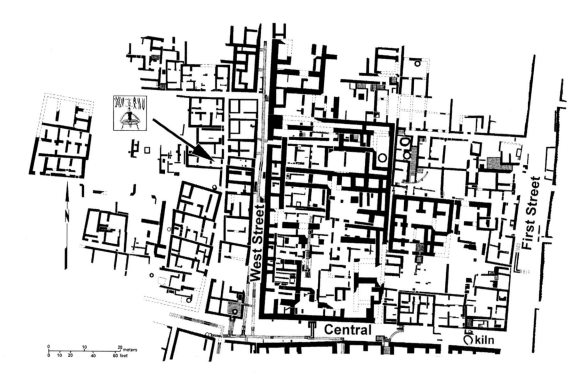

Figure 11.20 Plan of DK-G Northern Portion (after Marshall 1931i)

This trench, and a southern extension, were, for most of their course, about 3 meters wide, having been laterally expanded in two principal places (localities E and M) on account of the exceptional architecture found there.

The building at E is centered on a large courtyard 18.4 meters by 14.4 meters. In the northwest corner of room 1 of House I Dikshit found another hoard of jewelry.[57]

DK-G Area

The exposure of 2.8 hectares of northern Mohenjo-daro was Mackay's principal occupation at the site from 1927 to 1931 (figures 11.20 and 11.21). This work revealed a major east-west road that passed through DK-G Area at about its midpoint. He called this Central Street, and it provided a convenient division of the DK-G Area into Northern and Southern Portions. There is a second large street in DK-G Area Northern Portion that runs parallel to First Street; he dubbed it "West Street."

The total Area of DK-G, both portions, is approximately 28,000 square meters. DK-G South is approximately 16,000 square meters and DK-G North is approximately 12,000 square meters. There is a good deal of difference between the depth of digging in the two portions. Not only is DK-G South larger, but Mackay took many of the blocks well into the Intermediate Period. Virtually all of DK-G North is Late II and I.

First Street Some observations on First Street are in order, since that is the feature that binds this district of Mohenjo-daro together. Mackay discusses it in some detail in his report, which is where the documentation for the following points is found.[58]

Excavation of First Street went down to Mackay's Intermediate III Period. At this time it was approximately 9.5 meters wide. As far as we know, First Street was always provided with street drainage. The roadway was paved during Intermediate II times with a mixture of broken bricks and potsherds in a clay cement. The excavator suspected that the road metal was laid down in wet weather to get a good firm setting, but found no evidence that it had been stamped or rolled. The streets and lanes of Mohenjo-daro were almost never paved. This occurrence in First Street and one at the eastern end of Crooked Lane in Intermediate II are the only good examples of this practice.

DK-G Area, Southern Portion Moving up First Street from VS Area, the first block of DK-G one sees is numbered 3. This is where there may be a street that reaches all the way east to DK-C. The most interesting building in DK-G Southern Portion is Block 1, the Palace.

Block 1 has a large building, approximately 1,750 square meters. Mackay noted that the walls here "must clearly have been a part of some public building, which on the ev-

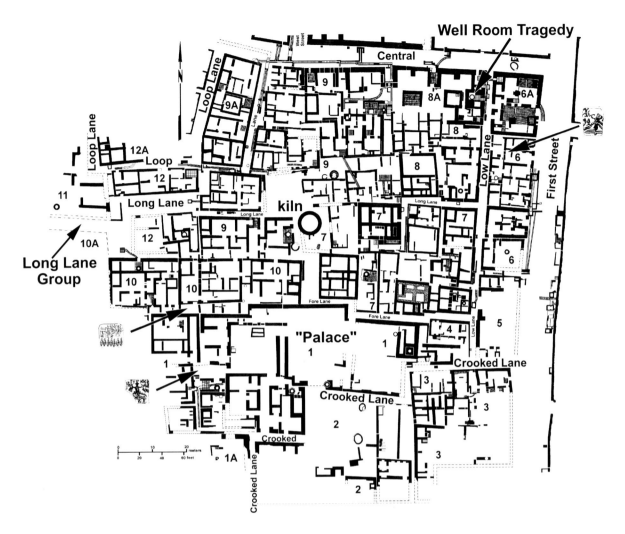

Figure 11.21 Plan of DK-G Southern Portion (after Marshall 1931i)

idence available was almost certainly a palace, not necessarily that of a monarch, but perhaps of a ruler of a province, of which Mohenjo-daro may have been the capital."[59] This may, or may not, be a good guess. Large buildings have functions that go beyond housing political leaders, and size is the only thing that suggests a palace here. There is even some evidence that it is not likely to have been just a residence, at least during the Late Period.

The southern part of the Palace was divided into quite separate suites of rooms by the central corridor already mentioned. Two curious kilns on the eastern side of room 33 of the S. W. wing each measured some 3 feet 3 ins. in diameter at the top, though the flat base of the northern one was 2 feet 10 ins. in diameter and of the other 3 feet 2 ins. Both were 4 feet 3 ins. deep, and paved with brick, and round the inside of each was a 4 inch ledge, but not at the same height (Pl. XXII, 4). The bricks used in their construction were wedge-shaped and laid with mud-mortar, and their walls

had been carefully plastered with mud. Their tops (Pl. XXXV, a) were only slightly above the level of the door-sill east of them.

From the vitrification of the mud-lined walls of these pits, it is evident that they were used to fire objects at a high temperature, the fuel used being either wood or charcoal, of which the white ashes still remained. The ledges mentioned above were probably intended for the support of a crucible, or if we assume that the kilns were used for glazing, a grating may have rested on the circular ledge in each.[60]

Mackay found a neat stack of 8,500 or so bricks against the western wall of the western courtyard.[61] He dates the pile to Intermediate I times. They were the usual sizes (most 27.5 by 13.75 by 5.625 centimeters) and had been robbed from other buildings as demonstrated by the mud plaster adhering to them.

The original description of Block 7 makes interesting

reading. There is good evidence for craft activity, scattered within what is otherwise a domestic environment. The large circle near House IX marks the foundations of a large, unfinished kiln of Late I–II times. House I, below which the deep digging took place, was exceptionally well made and occupied in Late Ib times, so all the building activity near the end of Mohenjo-daro was not slipshod. Mackay suggests that this is another candidate for a temple, or "the house of a deity, rather than of a notable of the city."[62] No one else seems to have taken up this notion. House VII is interesting in that it was built in part (shaded walls) of alternating courses of unbaked and baked bricks.

There are three points that would seem to be appropriate for this short review of the DK-G Area, Southern Portion. The first is that there is an immense amount of change in DK-G South from Intermediate III to Late I times (approximately 200–300 years). There is a constant process of architectural modification that took place in the buildings there, with very significant change in the look and function of this part of Mohenjo-daro over the life of the city in its final centuries. The second point is a contrast to this change. That is, the architectural continuity in terms of building foundation walls. Mackay makes the point time and again that the new buildings rose on the foundations of the walls of their predecessors, at least in terms of the load-bearing walls. Many of these walls are several meters deep. Finally, Mackay's observation that DK-G South had been transformed into a craft/industrial area in Late I–II is important. There were still many "residences," but there is also a great amount of craft activity here during the last centuries of Mohenjo-daro.

DK-G Area, Northern Portion DK-G Northern Portion is bounded on the east by First Street and the south by Central. The northern boundary is not well defined by architecture, and on the west Mackay found the edge of the mounded part of the city, which he explored down to plain level.

Mackay describes Central Street, a major byway of Mohenjo-daro:

> From its junction with First Street as far as the western limit of Block 8A, Central Street a little over 15 feet [4.5 meters] wide. It then gradually widens as it proceeds westwards and at the same time loses its proper alignment on its southern side until West Street is reached, where its width is about 21 feet [6.4 meters]. From this point, Central Street diverges to west-north-west.[63]

There is little change in Central Street between Late II and Late I, the depth to which Mackay's excavations proceeded. It is equipped with a substantial drainage system,

soak pits, and the like. There is a pottery kiln in the street of the Late Period.

Mackay was quite convinced that Central Street led to the river and a gate to the city.

> This very important street between the Northern and Southern Portions of our excavations in the DK Area seems to have been the chief entrance into the city through a north-west gate from the river and the quays that may have existed along its bank, a question which is discussed elsewhere. . . . [The street is] directly aligned to the point at which we have found some evidence of a gateway in what appears to be a portion of the city-wall. Thus Central Street provided direct communication between the river and First Street, one of the main arteries of the city, at right angles to it. There is no evidence in the Late II and I Phases, however, that it crossed First Street and proceeded further east.[64]

Unfortunately, there is no evidence for the presence of a city wall, let alone a gateway into Mohenjo-daro in the northwestern quadrant, or anywhere else, for that matter.

West Street was a major artery in the northern portion of Mohenjo-daro. It narrows from south to north, being 4.8 meters in the south and 3 meters wide in the north. It was also well equipped with drainage.

The blocks to the west of West Street (13, 14, 15, 16, 17, and 29) date mostly to the last phases of the ancient city, Late Ib or Ia. Most of the houses in Block 14 and the southern portions of Blocks 15 and 16 were built on "made ground," taken here to be platforms. Mackay notes that there do not seem to be earlier buildings in these locations, and he believed that this was done to accommodate a growing population in Mohenjo-daro.[65] This might be true, but runs counter to the notion that Mohenjo-daro was a dying urban environment in Late times. It might be that as the city deteriorated generally, DK-G north emerged as one of the neighborhoods that was still functioning, and thus building expansion there ran counter to the general trend.

Mackay's discussion of Block 14 focused on the presence of a possible latrine, and the occurrence of a large hoard of copper–bronze objects.[66] The latter consisted of forty objects found buried in the western side of room 19 in House III. The other objects included two spirals of wire and three more bangles. There was also a delightfully lively copper–bronze figurine of a prancing goat that was found inside a pot, with parallels in Bactria. These fine examples of copper–bronze metalwork were very important in Mackay's last full season of excavation, but there were more. Two other hoards were found across the lane in Block 15.

The western blocks of GK-G North were apparently built late in the life of the city and are distinguishable from other blocks by the flimsy character of their construction. There is also a fair amount of evidence for craft activity late in the life of the city here, as in DK-G South. The hoards inform us that there were still people of substance living there late in the life of the city.

MOHENJO-DARO: THE CITY

We have come to the end of the tour of Mohenjo-daro, a great ancient city whose original name still escapes us. Following Jansen, a strong case can be made that Mohenjo-daro was the quintessential Indus city. This position rests on three observations:

First, Mohenjo-daro seems to have been a founder's city, built within the Transitional Stage, or early in the Mature Harappan. It is therefore reasonable to suggest that it is in some ways a complex reflection of practical day-to-day life and an expression of the ideology of the Mature Harappan.

Second, the planning and investment made in Mohenjo-daro over a protracted period of time (nominally six centuries) informs us that it was no ordinary settlement, nor simply one among several Indus urban environments. Interestingly enough, Mohenjo-daro does not compare well with Harappa or most other Mature Harappan settlements: the very extensive use of baked brick, the Great Bath, site layout, town planning, and the like.

Finally, Mohenjo-daro was a place of wealth, more wealth than is apparent at any other Indus settlement. This wealth is expressed in terms of the continuity of civic planning and investment in urban facilities, in the high quality of the architecture almost to the end, the extensive use of baked bricks, and the rich assemblage of artifacts.

A third Indus city, at Ganweriwala in Cholistan, remains unexcavated. Research is important and could further shape these observations.

What Did Mohenjo-daro Mean during the Indus Age?

Taken together these observations strongly suggest that this city was a kind of embodiment of what it meant to be an Harappan, or whatever the inhabitants called themselves. Urbanization is a defining quality of the Indus Civilization, and Mohenjo-daro is the single best example of this.

Who Lived at Mohenjo-daro?

This interesting, but frequently unasked question has no precise answer. If Mohenjo-daro was the quintessential Mature Harappan city, then we would expect that the citizens of the Indus Civilization who considered themselves to be "good Harappans" would have gravitated there. The city would have been a very special place for them, and the other citizens who lived there would have been the same sort of "true believers" and therefore good neighbors and associates. These are the people who seem to have been the owners and primary residents of the baked-brick residences of Mohenjo-daro.

The Mound of the Great Bath may well have been the abode of elites: individuals we might call leaders, ritual specialists, administrators, and/or overseers. Individuals of this sort may well have resided in the Lower Town as well, and there could have been regular commuters between the two districts of Mohenjo-daro.

The fact that there may have been facilities for travelers and visitors to Mohenjo-daro has been mentioned in connection with the modular buildings in the northwestern quadrant of HR-B Area (see the previous discussion). That these travelers were of the "bathing class" is betrayed by the consistent provisioning of bathing platforms in their rooms, and this suggests an upper-class clientele.

There is thus a case to be made that Mohenjo-daro was home to the upper classes of Harappan society. While Harappa is a different urban environment, it is worth noting here that the individuals in Cemetery R-37 are generally large, well-fed, healthy individuals with few signs of antemortem trauma.[67] This would fit well with the notion that Harappa also had an upper-class population, and they used burial as at least one form of interment.

Not until late in the life of the place is Mohenjo-daro filled with housing that one would immediately think of as "lower-class" dwellings. There are some in the Late I Period that could be assigned to this category, but that is well into the period of transformation of Mohenjo-daro and the Indus Civilization generally. But the lower floors of many of the houses of Mohenjo-daro have small rooms that could have been the abodes of the lower, servant classes. Thus, rather than establishing regular, independent homes, the servant class may have occupied the lower floors of their "employers'" residences—"upstairs–downstairs" may have a long history.

This begs the question of a commuting lower class, living at some distance from the city, at such places as "Spur Number 3" and the "Hasanwahan Road." Since life in such detail is inevitably multifaceted, there may have been some, even much, of this kind of arrangement. But Mohenjo-daro as we know it does not seem to have been a place where different districts had different kinds of housing, districts that would have been the "other side of the tracks," as it were.

Mohenjo-daro does not have the look of a place that was home to large numbers of farmers and herders. The upper class may have included numbers of absentee farmer-pastoralist landlords, but they did not plow the fields themselves. There was probably agricultural activity around the city: gardens, fields, pasture, and the like. Some of the inhabitants may have owned and managed these facilities. Milk and its products, meat, eggs, and vegetables were probably produced relatively close to the city, with food grains being hauled in from greater distances. We know from remains found at Harappa that fish were widely traded, with maritime species reaching there.[68] These exceptions being noted, Mohenjo-daro still does not look like a city that was permanent home to a large number of farmers and pastoralists.

In the Late II–I Periods we know that Mohenjo-daro was a place where a substantial amount of craft activity took place. This is documented best in DK-G Area, especially the Southern Portion as well as on the Mound of the Great Bath.[69] An intensive examination of the surface of Mohenjo-daro informs us of this as well.[70] This substantial amount of craft activity does not seem to have characterized the city in earlier times. Mackay's penetration into the Intermediate levels in DK-G South and observations on the Mound of the Great Bath support this contention better than any other testimony. Thus, we have evidence for an interesting change in the population of Mohenjo-daro. During the founding period of the city, through Late III, Mohenjo-daro may not have been home to a substantial number of craftspeople.

The two site reports on Mohenjo-daro are filled with references to "commercial buildings," "shops," "khans," "storage facilities," "wharves," even "public eating places." These suggestions as to function are in reality based on the form and nature of the buildings, not supported by collateral information on the artifacts associated with them. While it is reasonable for us to believe that there was a rich commercial life in Mohenjo-daro, and this was one of the ways in which the upper classes managed to live in this city, the commercial aspect of Mohenjo-daro does not come though very clearly in the archaeological record. In the end, archaeologists are not sure about what went on inside many of the buildings at Mohenjo-daro, especially places like the Palace in DK-G South and Blocks 18 and 19 in DK-G North.

Why Was Mohenjo-daro Abandoned?

No one knows why Mohenjo-daro was abandoned, but if the Indus Civilization was its ideology, then a failure of that ideology would explain the failure of Mohenjo-daro as the quintessential Indus settlement. By about 1900 B.C., based on radiocarbon dates, the city was no longer a functioning urban center. The changes that engulfed Mohenjo-

daro and the Indus Civilization in general began long before the city was abandoned. Early signs of this are seen with the abandonment of the Great Bath and Warehouse, as well as the changes in Late II-I. A period of civic and social deterioration that was centuries long took place at Mohenjo-daro and elsewhere.

NOTES

1. Sorely 1959: 111.
2. Mackay 1937–38: pl. I.
3. Hussain 1989.
4. Dikshit 1925–26: 100.
5. Marshall 1931j: 127.
6. Wheeler 1968: 44.
7. Marshall 1931c: 24–25.
8. Mackay 1931a: 131.
9. Marshall 1931c: 24; Mackay 1931a: 142.
10. Marshall 1931c: 24, n. 3.
11. Mackay 1948: 43.
12. Mackay 1937–38: 20.
13. Ardeleanu-Jansen, Franke, and Jansen 1983.
14. Wheeler 1968: 127.
15. Marshall 1931i: pl. XXIb.
16. Mackay 1948: 41; Mackay 1937–38: 10.
17. Wheeler 1947: 74–78.
18. Mackay 1937–38: 19–20.
19. Wheeler 1968: 41, 43.
20. Mackay 1931b.
21. Marshall 1931b: 22–24.
22. Mackay 1948: 45.
23. Wheeler 1968: 46.
24. Wheeler 1968: 46.
25. Mackay 1931b: 167.
26. Ardeleanu-Jansen 1993.
27. Dales 1968b; Dales and Kenoyer 1986.
28. Dales 1968b: 59.
29. Dales 1968b: 60.
30. Hargreaves 1931: 179.
31. Marshall 1931b: 17–20.
32. Hargreaves 1931: 182, n. 2.
33. Jansen 1983: 46–47.
34. Marshall 1931c: 18.
35. Marshall 1931b: 19.
36. Marshall 1931b: 19.
37. Jansen and Urban 1985.
38. Jansen 1984: 46.
39. Sahni 1931a: 194.
40. Marshall 1931i: pl. CL; Sahni 1931a: 194; Mackay 1931l: 522–23.
41. Marshall 1931i: pl. LIVb.
42. Sahni 1931a: 191.
43. Sahni 1926–27: pl. XIVa.
44. Marshall 1931i: pl. CXXX, 22.
45. Sahni 1931a: 208.

46. Sahni 1931a: 204.
47. Sahni 1931a: 204.
48. Sahni 1931a: 205.
49. Piggott 1950: 169.
50. Wheeler 1968: 54.
51. Sahni 1926–27: 88.
52. Marshall 1931e: 79, pl. LIX, c.
53. Puri 1936–37: 41.
54. Mackay 1931c: 236.
55. Marshall 1931i: pl. LXX, a.
56. Mackay 1931c: 250.
57. Marshall 1931i: pl. CXIb.
58. Mackay 1937–38: 25–32.
59. Mackay 1937–38: 46.
60. Mackay 1937–38: 49–50, illustrations in *Further Excavations at Mohenjo-daro.*
61. Mackay 1937–38: 53.
62. Mackay 1937–38: 84.
63. Mackay 1937–38: 32.
64. Mackay 1937–38: 32.
65. Mackay 1937–38: 142.
66. Mackay 1937–38: 143–44.
67. Hemphill, Lukacs, and Kennedy 1991.
68. Belcher 1991: 114, 1994.
69. Mackay 1937–38: 6.
70. Tosi, Bondioli, and Vidale 1984.

CHAPTER 12

The Middle Asian Interaction Sphere

INTRODUCTION

The third millennium B.C. was a time of new, unique economic and political configurations in a part of the world that can be called "Middle Asia": the regions between the Indus and the Mediterranean bounded on the north by Bactria and Central Asia and on the south by the Arabian Gulf (figure 12.1).[1] The Middle Asian Interaction Sphere is made manifest in shared artifacts, including objects of trade and exchange as well as artifact styles and design motifs. Mesopotamian sources add written documentation for some of the activities within the Middle Asian Interaction Sphere, especially the maritime trade in the Arabian Gulf.

Maritime activity was a vital component of the Third Millennium Middle Asian Interaction Sphere. This appears to have been founded on a revolution (at least a significant change) in maritime technology and/or knowledge around the middle of the third millennium. Not much is known of this "revolution," but at this time there was a significant change in maritime activity in the Mediterranean and Arabian Seas. This upsurge seems to be based in technology and to have been economically

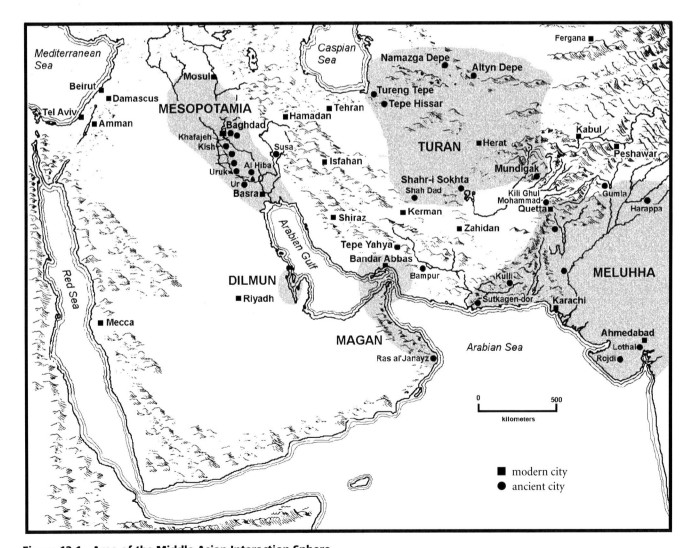

Figure 12.1 Area of the Middle Asian Interaction Sphere

215

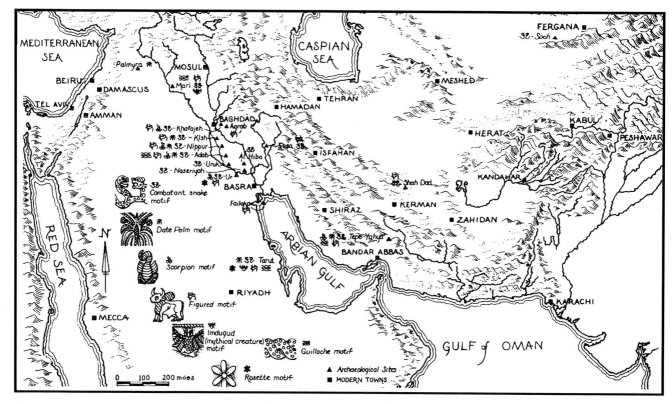

Figure 12.2 Map showing Intercultural-style motifs (after Kohl 1979)

exploited. This relationship to technology leads us back to the Indus ideology. This Harappan participation in the Third Millennium Middle Asian Interaction Sphere has a base in their ideology as well.

The Intercultural Style: A Uniting Ideology?

A series of soft-stone artifacts associated with the Middle Asian Interaction Sphere were carved with a number of stylistically coherent motifs. These include combat snake motifs; humped bulls and other figures; "Umdugud," the lion-headed bird; hut motifs; date palms; and rosettes, along with simpler portrayals such as mats, beveled squares, whirls, and an imbricate design. Since these motifs are widespread within the Middle Asian Interaction Sphere and across a number of ancient cultural regions, it has been called the "Intercultural style."[2] A map of some of these motifs and their distribution is given in figures 12.2 and 12.3. Some of the motifs can be associated with particular regions within the Middle Asian Interaction Sphere. The South Asian zebu is an example of this. Umdugud is a Near Eastern motif, and snakes in this sort of iconography generally bring Central Asia to mind. The hut urns seem best at home in eastern Iran. But, at the broad level, the Intercultural style is a shared set of symbols, brought together in a stylistically coherent set of mo-

tifs, carved on stone that is very much the same wherever it is found.

We know from an analysis of the stone that there were several places where objects of the Intercultural style were made. Tepe Yahya, in southeastern Iran is one, and Tarut Island near Bahrain is another.[3]

The Intercultural style seems to indicate that some of the participants in the Middle Asian Interaction Sphere shared a set of symbols, possibly an ideology. This was a syncretic form of belief that brought together symbols from all over the "intercultural world" of the Middle Asian Interaction Sphere, giving at least some of its participants a shared ideology and a form of unity. The fact that the Intercultural style is documented at the earliest stages of the interaction sphere may be an indication that it played a significant role in its origins (figure 12.4).

Historical Background

It was during the 1920s and 1930s, with the excavations of the Royal Graves at Ur and other sites such as Tell Asmar, Agrab Tepe, Kish, and Susa, that the full richness of Sumerian, Akkadian, and Elamite civilization came to light. During these same decades, but some 1,500 miles to the east, archaeologists unearthed the remains of the contemporary Indus Civilization. It was immediately apparent that the In-

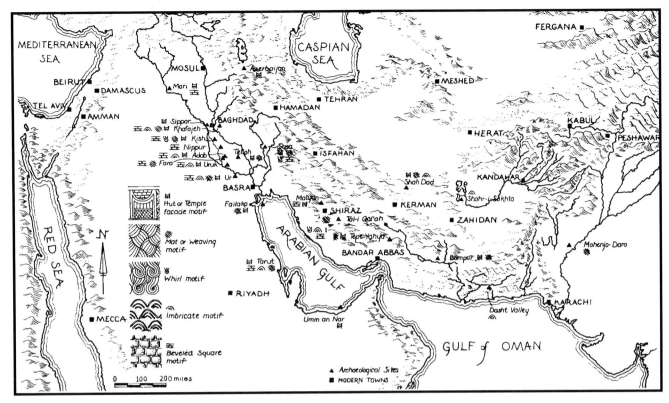

Figure 12.3 Map showing other Intercultural-style motifs (after Kohl 1979)

dus peoples and their Sumerian and Akkadian contemporaries had been in contact with one another since Indus artifacts had been found at a number of Mesopotamian sites.

Other pioneering archaeological work in the gulf, especially on Bahrain and on the Iranian Plateau at sites such as Tepe Sialk and Tepe Hissar, uncovered important new material that was clearly a part of the life of the third millennium in Middle Asia. For example, there were etched carnelian beads and quantities of lapis lazuli at Hissar and proto-Elamite tablets at Sialk, which informed archaeologists of something, but the message was not at all clear.

Renewed archaeological work throughout Middle Asia following the hiatus caused by World War II did much to clarify the early history of this region. The excavation of Altyn Depe and the discovery of the Turanian Bronze Age Civilization brought an important sense of geographic closure to the northern borders of the ancient Middle Asian Interaction Sphere. The urbanization of Turkmenia can now be seen as one more example of the sociocultural vitality of this region in antiquity. What has emerged is a complex mosaic of urban centers and regional polities all seemingly linked by an economic vitality that is both new and impressive.

The publication of A. Leo Oppenheim's "Seafaring Mer-

chants of Ur" in 1954, reviewing tablets from Ur, did much to bring a focus on the Arabian Gulf and third millennium maritime activities between Akkad, Dilmun, Makan, and Meluhha (see figure 12.1). The "Dilmun trade," as it has come to be called, is an extraordinarily important element in the Middle Asian Interaction Sphere.

Figure 12.4 Artifacts of the Intercultural style from Tell Agrab (after Frankfort 1956)

Figure 12.5 Representations of three boats from Mohenjo-daro (after Marshall 1931i and Mackay 1937–38)

Maritime Trade

There are many representations of boats, especially in ancient glyptic art; three come from Mohenjo-daro (figure 12.5). There is also a reconstruction drawing (figure 12.6).

Third millennium maritime trade in the gulf eventually linked ancient India to Mesopotamia and has larger and as yet poorly charted dimensions. In 1952 Carl O. Sauer suggested that the route following the east coast of Africa to Arabia and on to the southern coast of Asia "may be a great lost corridor of mankind."[4] He was looking at the early dispersal of domesticated plants that were moved out of Africa into the economies of Arabia and South Asia at the time. Advances in Arabian archaeology are beginning to give archaeologists good reason to return to Sauer's observation.[5] Of particular importance to this revitalization is the evidence that has been accumulated for the spread of certain millets (sorghum, pearl millet, and finger millet) out of sub-Saharan Africa into Asia. These food grains have been documented at a number of Indian and Pakistani sites within the second and third millennia.[6] Early in the third millennium B.C. sorghum was seemingly well entrenched in the regional economy at

places like Hili 8.[7] The significance of these African millets in terms of the gulf trade is that they help to document the maritime activity in the mid–third millennium.

Luxury Products or Necessities

Many of the materials traded within the Middle Asian Interaction Sphere appear to be luxury products, intended to satisfy the desires of elites and the needs of the Mesopotamian cult system. For the most part, the trade we see directly evidenced in the archaeological record involves semiprecious stones, metals, seals, jewelry, various forms of objets d'art, exotic animals, and the like. Food products, cloth, common building and manufacturing materials, and the material culture of mass consumption (even by Bronze Age standards) are not a part of this record, even in the cuneiform texts. This is classic "long-distance trade in luxury products" that V. G. Childe used as one of his markers of Bronze Age urbanization.[8] It is the trade for aggrandizement, of elites and their cult system, not the common peoples of the Middle Asian Interaction Sphere. The common people may have acquired the products in their raw form and played the central role in manufacturing and transport, but they were not the consumers of these wares.

There is some indication of the common people in the maritime world of the Arabian Gulf in the second half of the third millennium. The important site at Ras al-Junayz, for example, seems to have been a place for fishing and boat repair. The African millets that come to South Asia at this time are foods that were probably not traded, but were acquired in the area of the Horn of Africa, as foodstuffs for the boat crews to consume on their way back home. That these crops proved useful to the monsoon farmers of the Greater Indus region was a by-product of their initial use as food for these crews.

This second level of maritime activity not withstanding, the driving force for the trade we include as a part of the Middle Asian Interaction Sphere was trade for the elites and their cults.[9]

THE DILMUN TRADE

During the Early Dynastic Period, a land known as Meluhha first appears in the Mesopotamian historical record. Another early reference is given by Sargon of Akkad (2334–2279 B.C.) when he described how ships from the lands of Dilmun, Magan, and Meluhha were tied up along the quay of his capital of Akkad.

Where Were Dilmun, Magan, and Meluhha Located?

Dilmun, Magan, and Meluhha were important places in the third and early second millennia B.C. and most archae-

Figure 12.6 Reconstruction drawing of an Indus reed boat (by Jan Fairservis)

ologists are now in general agreement on their locations (figure 12.1).[10]

The Location of Dilmun

There is every reason to believe that Dilmun is the island of Bahrain and the adjacent coast of Arabia. This is based on what we know of the place from cuneiform sources. For example, Dilmun was an island in the Arabian Gulf that could be reached in 30 *beru*, or double hours, a reasonable estimate for sailing time from the northern end of the gulf to Bahrain. The ancient texts also tell us that one could draw fresh water from the sea near Dilmun, and indeed there is a place off the coast of Bahrain where one can do just that, an observation that clinches the case. If the location of Dilmun is virtually certain, the location of Magan is less so.

The Location of Magan

Magan is thought to be to the east of Dilmun. This is based on the consistency of the ordering of place-names in cuneiform texts; either Dilmun, Magan, Meluhha or the reverse. Thus, Oman and/or southeastern Iran are the logical candidates for its location. This would fit well with the fact that in cuneiform texts Magan is said to be rich in copper and Oman has recently produced abundant evidence for third millennium copper mining and smelting.[11] Second, the statues of Naram-Sin and Gudea all mention that the stone used in carving them came from Magan. Modern testing of this material has shown that it comes from the proposed home.[12] Thus, there is good reason for us to assume that Magan was, in the minds of the Mesopotamians, a land beyond Dilmun, which was located on both sides of the Strait of Hormuz.

The Location of Meluhha

The location of Meluhha has proved to be more difficult to determine. This topic has been discussed in many places.[13] Most modern scholars assume it to have been the area we associate with the Indus Civilization, including the Kulli Domain of mountainous southern Baluchistan.[14] The basis for this judgment rests primarily on five historical observations and one implication: (1) Meluhha was a real place as demonstrated by the presence of an Akkadian seal attributed to a translator of the Meluhhan language; (2) Meluhha is beyond Magan, as seen from the regular ordering of place-names; (3) there is Indus material in Mesopotamia, some with the Indus script, and some Mesopotamian material in Indus sites; (4) the presence of Mature Harappan material at Ras al-Junayz in Oman and in the gulf, within a fully maritime environment, supports the notion that the Indus Civilization was in maritime contact with Mesopotamia, as suggested by the written sources; and (5) the products mentioned in the texts said to come from Meluhha do not contradict an association with ancient India. These five observations lead to an implication: If Meluhha was not associated with the Harappan Civilization, then the Indus was apparently not mentioned in cuneiform documents. This would present an awkward historical situation, given the presence of more than trivial amounts of Indus material culture in both Mesopotamia and the gulf.

HISTORICAL SOURCES ON MELUHHA

References to Meluhha are found in texts dealing with the Mesopotamian economy, foreign trade—especially maritime trade—as well as royal inscriptions and literary and lexical texts. A complete corpus of seventy-six Mesopotamian texts from the Early Dynastic period to the reign

Table 12.1   Products mentioned in Mesopotamian texts as coming from Meluhha

Stone and pearls		
	Carnelian	8 attestations
	Lapis lazuli	1 attestation, but in an incantation
	Pearls	1 attestation
Wood and plants		
	Gis-Ab-ba-me-luh-ha	12 attestations
	Mesu wood	7 attestations
	Fresh dates	1 attestation
Animals		
	A bird	8 attestations, but 5 as figurines
	A dog of Meluhha	1 attestation
	A cat of Meluhha	1 attestation
Metal		
	Copper	2 attestations
	Gold	1 attestation
Meluhhan-style objects		
	A ship of Meluhhan style	2 attestations
	Meluhhan-style furniture	3 attestations
	Figurines of Meluhhan birds	5 attestations (see animals above)

of Hammurabi has been published.[15] A summary of these attestations is found in table 12.1.

Ivory is not mentioned as a part of the trade with Meluhha, although it is mentioned in connection with Dilmun. Many of the texts mentioning Meluhhan products occur in a literary context and are therefore difficult to evaluate critically; finally, the number of attestations is small and the references diverse, not the kind of robust data on which sound historical argument can be founded.

THE TEXTUAL REFERENCES AND THE PRODUCTS OF MAGAN AND DILMUN

There are also references to the products that come from Magan and Dilmun. These are so numerous that they have never been systematically tallied, but a partial list, at least, has been assembled in the following sections.

The Land of Magan

Shereen Ratnagar notes seven ancient textual references to the boats of Magan.[16] She also lists, with ancient textual citations, fifteen products associated with Magan, as given in table 12.2. It has already been argued that Magan is now the area we associate with Oman and coastal southeastern Iran, possibly including the region of modern Makran. With this in mind, it appears that Magan was both a place for the ori-

gin of products, especially copper, and an entrepôt. Magan was a place that passed products from Meluhha on to Dilmun and/or Mesopotamia. Gold, carnelian, and ivory are products that most strikingly suggest this.

The Land of Dilmun

More is known of Dilmun than either Magan or Meluhha, and the compilation of a systematic catalogue of textual references to it would be a task of sizable proportions. Ratnagar's book has references to the products in table 12.3 as coming to Ur from Dilmun.

Dilmun has even more the flavor of an entrepôt than does Magan. The first seven items on Ratnagar's list are all attested from either Meluhha and/or Magan and would not be found as a part of the Dilmun landscape. The coral, woods, and dates are, however, things that could have come to Mesopotamia from a number of places, one of which would be Bahrain Island and the adjacent Arabian coast.

In the ancient texts there is mention of Dilmun merchants and, as noted, many references to this place as a commercial center. One gets a sense that Dilmun was the operational nerve center for this early gulf and Arabian Sea trade. It is also worth repeating that none of the texts mention any Mesopotamian products being sent directly

Table 12.2   Products mentioned in Mesopotamian texts as coming from Magan

Copper	Ivory	Timber
Diorite or olivine gabbro	Gold dust	Wood products
Stone vases, some of which are alabaster	Goats	*Gis-mis-makan* or *mesu* wood of Magan
Carnelian and other semiprecious stones	Magan reed	*Gis-ha-lu-ub* or *haluppu* wood
Red ochre	Magan onion	*Gis-gisimmar*, another wood

Note: From Ratnagar (1981: 39–40).

Table 12.3 Products mentioned in Mesopotamian texts as coming from Dilmun

Copper	Lapis lazuli	White coral
Silver	Other semiprecious stones	Various woods
Gold	Ivory and ivory objects	Dates
Carnelian	"Fish eyes" or pearls	

Note: From Ratnagar (1981: 23).

to Meluhha; interesting even in light of the fact that some exports may be "invisible."[17]

INDUS MARITIME INTERESTS

One of the remarkable features of the Indus Civilization is its maritime orientation. It is only after the middle of the second millennium that objects of origin in the Indus Valley make an appearance in Oman and the gulf. While there was a modest presence of Early Harappans near the sea, as at Balakot, for example, the Mature Harappan marks a quantum increase in maritime activity for these ancient peoples. There are four representations of Harappan boats, three from Mohenjo-daro and one from Lothal.[18]

The Indus employment of maritime resources is also documented by their extensive use of shell for bangles, ladles, inlay, and the like.[19] The Indus settlement at Balakot, just removed from Sonmiani Bay in southern Baluchistan, also reveal a surprising and unique dependence on fish for

subsistence. The fish in question is a grunt, found in great quantity in the Indus levels.[20] Large fish vertebrae have been found at some Mature Harappan sites in Kutch.[21] During the Mature Harappan, fish were traded over large distances, probably in salted and/or dried form.[22]

Although it was not necessarily a port, there is evidence at Ras al-Junayz in Oman of Indus sailors. An abundance of Harappan ceramics there are mixed with indigenous wares. Among finds at this maritime way station are pieces of bitumen, which were interpreted as caulking for reed boats.[23]

THE ARCHAEOLOGICAL RECORD OF INDUS CONTACTS WITH MESOPOTAMIA, THE GULF, AND IRAN

The textual record in Mesopotamia is paralleled by a body of material culture that plays a role in the interpretation of Indus–Mesopotamian relations and the identification of Meluhha.

Seals

The most important objects are stamp seals, summarized in table 12.4 and shown in figures 12.7 through 12.23.[24] There is a seal from Tell Brak that has a resemblance to the swastika and has interesting comparisons at Harappa, Lothal, and Tepe Sialk (figure 12.24). More seals have figured in this discussion, from both Iran and Mesopotamia, but they are of doubtful utility for a number of reasons.[25]

Table 12.4 Indus or Indus-like seals from the Near East

Site	Period	Citation	Figure
Tell Umma (?)	Unknown	Scheil 1925	Figure 12.7
Ur	Tomb of the Larsa Period (c. 1900–1700 B.C.)	Gadd 1932, no. 6	Figure 12.8
Ur	Pre-Akkadian (unstratified) (before c. 2280 B.C.)	Gadd 1932, no. 1	Figure 12.9
Ur	Pre-Akkadian or Akkadian (late third millennium)	Gadd 1932, no. 16	Figure 12.10
Tepe Gawra	Late Early Dynastic/Early Akkadian (late third millennium)	Speiser 1935: 163–64, pl. XXXVII, b	Figure 12.11
Tell Asmar	Akkadian house (late third millennium)	Frankfort 1933: 50	Figure 12.12
Tell Asmar	Akkadian house (late third millennium)	Frankfort 1933: 50	Figure 12.13
Kish	Akkadian (late third millennium)	Langdon 1931b: 595	Figure 12.14
Kish	Probably Akkadian (late third millennium?)	Mackay 1925b: 697, pl. X	Figure 12.15
Kish	Probably pre-Akkadian or Akkadian (late third millennium)	Mackay 1931o: 465	Figure 12.16
Tell Suleimeh	Late third millennium	Collon 1996: fig. 8b	Figure 12.17
Tello	Late third millennium	During Caspers 1973	Figure 12.18
Lagash	Larsa Period (c. 1900–1700 B.C.)	de Genouillac 1930: 177	No illustration
Hamma	c. 2000–1750 B.C.	Ingholt 1940: 62, pl. XIX	Figure 12.19
Nippur	Kassite (c. fourteenth century B.C.)	Gibson 1977	Figure 12.20
Susa	Akkadian/Post-Akkadian (c. late third millennium B.C.)	Amiet 1986: 280	Figure 12.21
Susa	Akkadian/Post-Akkadian (c. late third millennium B.C.)	Amiet 1986: 280	Figure 12.22
Shahdad	Cemetery A, 2500–2000 B.C.	Hakimi 1997: 187, object number 0221	Figure 12.23

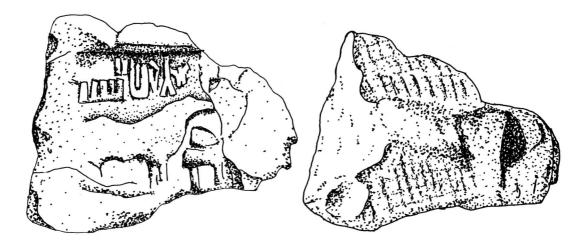

Figure 12.7   Unicorn seal impression from Umma(?) (see Table 12.4 for documentation)

A. Parpola has examined the writing on these seals and the others from the gulf and Altyn Depe.[26] He found a mix of writing systems. Some of them are clearly pure Indus script, as in the two from Kish, and the one from Nippur in table 12.4. Others are probably not Indus writing.

Beads

Beads, especially those of etched carnelian, have been discussed in terms of Indus–Mesopotamian contact.[27] Etched beads in India and the Near East have a long history, beginning with the Indus Civilization. The technique might have been lost at, or shortly after, the Indus transformation, but it is well documented in the mid–first millennium B.C., especially at Taxila. The concerns of this chapter deal only with the initial period of production in the Bronze Age.

Etched Carnelian Beads from Indus Sites

The principal sites of the Indus Civilization that have yielded etched carnelian beads are found in table 12.5.

Figure 12.8   Seal impression from Ur (Gadd No. 6) (see Table 12.4 for documentation)

Etched Carnelian Beads in Mesopotamia

The catalogue of etched carnelian beads from Mesopotamian sites is a substantial one, and there is no advantage to repeating what Reade has presented elsewhere (figure 12.25).[28] The Royal Graves at Ur contained a large num-

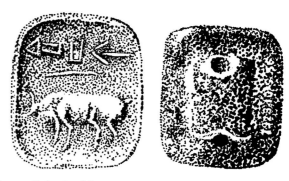

Figure 12.9   Seal from Ur (Gadd No. 1) (see Table 12.4 for documentation)

ber of beads of this general type. Others have been found at Kish and Tell Asmar in Akkadian contexts. There is one Early Dynastic etched bead from Tell Abu Salabikh and another from Nippur from Late Early Dynastic or Early

Table 12.5   Principal Mature Harappan sites with etched carnelian beads

Mohenjo-daro	Marshall 1931i: pl. CXLVI; Mackay 1937–38: pls. CXXXV–CXXXVIII
Harappa	Vats 1940, pls. CXXVIII–CXXXII; Wheeler 1947
Chanhu-daro	Mackay 1943; pl. LXXIX
Kalibangan	*Indian Archaeology, A Review* 1960–61: 32: pl. XLIX B
Lothal	Rao 1985: 601
Rojdi	Possehl and Raval 1989: fig. 84, no. 6

Figure 12.10 Seal from Ur (Gadd No. 16) (see Table 12.4 for documentation)

Figure 12.11 Seal from Tepe Gawra (see Table 12.4 for documentation)

Akkadian times. These occurrences, and others, are all documented.[29]

Etched Carnelian Beads in Iran
There are also etched carnelian beads in Iran (table 12.6).

Other Bead Types
Long barrel-cylinder beads and segmented faience beads have also been found in both the Indus region and the west in the third millennium. Chakrabarti has discussed the occurrence of "long barrel-cylinder" beads in the Indus, Mesopotamia, and Iran.[30] These beads, in a variety of materials (e.g., carnelian, lapis lazuli, terra-cotta) are long (in excess of 5 centimeters) and slender, sometimes with a slight thickening toward the center. Based on their high density at Indus sites and the fact that they have been found in various stages of manufacture at Chanhu-daro,[31] there is little doubt that they are an Indus type. "It may be said that this is a distinct Indus bead type, as distinctive in its own way as etched carnelian beads. And unlike the latter, which are also known to occur in later Indian historic contexts, this bead type died with the Indus civilization."[32]

Sculpture of the Intercultural Style
Philip Kohl has conducted the most significant study of the so-called carved steatite materials from the early Near East and India that has already been noted.[33]

In Mesopotamia, the gulf, and Iran there are a few pieces of the Intercultural style with the zebu. While the natural distribution of *Bos indicus* is not precisely known, it does seem to be indigenous to the Indian Subconti-

Table 12.6 Principal sites in Iran with etched carnelian beads

Site	Period	Citation
Tepe Hissar IIIC	Second half of the third millennium	Schmidt 1937: 229, pl. XXV
Tepe Hissar III	Second half of the third millennium	Schmidt 1937: 438; pl. XLIV, c
Shah Tepe IIA		Arne 1945: pl. XCII, fig. 612, B II S7
Kalleh Nisar	Akkadian cist grave	van den Berghe 1970: 73
Susa	Akkadian grave	de Mecquenem 1943: fig. 84, 7
Tepe Yahya	One surface find, another is in uncertain context, but probably later than 2000 B.C.	During Caspers 1972: 92
Jalalabad	Mid-third millennium	Chakrabarti and Moghadam 1979: 167, fig. 10
Marlik	Late second/early first millennium	Chakrabarti and Moghadam 1979: fig. 10
Shahdad	Late third millennium?	Hakimi 1997: 655, no. Ha. 8

Figure 12.12 Elephant-rhino seal impression from Tell Asmar (see Table 12.4 for documentation)

Figure 12.13 Geometric seal from Tell Asmar (see Table 12.4 for documentation)

Figure 12.14 Unicorn seal impression from Kish (see Table 12.4 for documentation)

nent.[34] Its occurrence as part of the Intercultural style seems to indicate that ancient India was one of the places within which the style itself was shaped.[35]

Figurines

George Dales has brought attention to four male terracotta figurines, three from Nippur and one from Chanhu-daro, that share a number of important, interesting features.[36] These were discussed earlier (see figure 6.13). They were puppets, with arms separately attached at the shoulders, which are well out of proportion to the rest of the body. They are also all fat nudes with prominent buttocks and traces of penises still visible. They may therefore have been ithyphallic. Most of the figurines have prominent holes at the naval and between the buttocks, and there is sometimes evidence for a tail. It has been demonstrated through neutron activation that one of the figurines from Nippur was made in Mesopotamia and the

one from Chanhu-daro was made in the Indus Valley.[37]

Figurines of monkeys from Sumer and Elam are remarkably similar to those of the ancient Indus Valley.[38]

Dice

Dales has discussed cubical dice and their relation to Indus–Mesopotamian interaction.[39] Both cubical and oblong "stick dice" are known from Indus sites. The contemporary Indian games of *chaupar* and *pachisi* (or Parcheesi) seem to be developments out of much simpler games dating back to the third millennium.

Ceramics

Indus ceramics circulated within the Middle Asian Interaction Sphere. "Feeding-cups" and knobbed ware are

Figure 12.15 Seal from Kish (see Table 12.4 for documentation)

Figure 12.16 Seal like the one from Kish in the Baghdad Museum (see Table 12.4 for documentation)

Figure 12.17 Cylinder seal impression from Tell Suleimeh with a unicorn (see Table 12.4 for documentation)

known from Mesopotamia, although in very small numbers. Significant amounts of Indus "common wares" are found at many, perhaps most, of the third millennium sites in the gulf (e.g., Baat, Hili 8, Maysar, Ras al-Junayz, Shimal 6, Tell Abrak, Umm an-Nar).[40] Some sherds have graffiti of the Indus script on them, as at Ras al-Junayz. Sorath Harappan pottery from Gujarat is found in considerable quantity at the third millennium site of Saar on the Island of Bahrain (Dilmun), along with other Indus wares (figure 12.26).[41]

Specialized pottery was a part of the Third Millennium Middle Asian Interaction Sphere as well. Large, pointed-base, black-slipped jars have been found at many Indus sites (e.g., Mohenjo-daro, Harappa, Naushahro, Chanhu-daro, Balakot, Sotkah Koh, Miri Qalat, Dholavira; figure 12.27).[42] Black-slipped jars are also common in the gulf, sometimes represented by hundreds of sherds from individual places (Amlah, Baat, Hili 8, Ras Ghanadha 1, Ras al-Hadd-1, Ras al-Junayz, RJ-2). Examples of this ware were found at Harappa in a potter's workshop, so there is

Figure 12.18 Seal from Tello (see Table 12.4 for documentation)

no doubt about their region of origin.[43] The black-slipped jars inevitably have a short Indus inscription that was scratched on the shoulder of the pot after firing.

These storage/shipping jars are formed with a deep, narrow base, which appears to be a sump for sediment, and look somewhat like a Mediterranean amphora. The constricted sump inhibited the remixing of sediment with the liquids in these jars when they were shipped and jostled about. Viniculture was a part of the Mature Harappan agricultural program, and it is entirely possible that the Indus peoples were shipping wine to the gulf in these interesting containers.

Metal Artifacts

Indus metal implements in Mesopotamian contexts are rare. Copper–bronze blades without a midrib, often

Figure 12.19 Seal from Hamma (see Table 12.4 for documentation)

Figure 12.20 Seal from Nippur (see Table 12.4 for documentation)

Figure 12.21 Impression of a circular seal from Susa (see Table 12.4 for documentation)

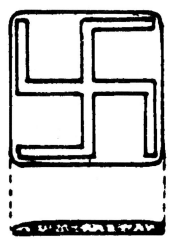

Figure 12.23 Swastika seal from Shahdad (see Table 12.4 for documentation)

thought to have been of Indus affiliation, may have been found at Kish and Tepe Hissar. Spiral-headed pins occur in Mesopotamia, the Indus, and Iran.[44]

Material Miscellany

There is a list of other odds and ends of material culture from the Indus found in Mesopotamia and the gulf. It includes heart-shaped shell or bone inlay from Tell Asmar, a cubical stone weight dating to the Ur III Period found at Ur, shell ladles from Mohenjo-daro duplicated at both Kish and Ur, a limestone tetrahedron from Tell al'Ubaid very much like tetrahedrons from Mohenjo-daro, the Greek cross found in both regions, and well-modeled panther heads found at Mohenjo-daro and Ur. Mackay also notes similarities between a type of terra-cotta "mask" from Mohenjo-daro (a human head with the horns of a bull) and metal examples from Ur.

The copper–bronze mirror with a handle in the form of a human from the Babar Temple is not comparable to the mirror from Mehi in Baluchistan.[45]

Harappan weights have been found in the gulf in some numbers and were one of the Dilmun weight "standards." They were probably accepted there because the Harappans were reliable, high-volume trading partners for the Dilmun merchants.

The significance of the growing corpus of stamp seals from the Greater Gulf is still an area of active, productive research. The classic study of C. J. Gadd, written prior to the notion of the Persian Gulf–type seal, remains an important reference in this area.[46] There is an excellent example of the combined Indus/gulf-style seal from a tomb at Madinat Hamad on Bahrain.[47]

WESTERN MATERIAL IN THE GREATER INDUS VALLEY

The material discussed previously documents the presence of a reasonably substantial amount of Indus material culture in the Arabian Gulf and Mesopotamia. One would think that a comparable amount of Mesopotamian

Figure 12.22 Impression of a cylinder seal from Susa (see Table 12.4 for documentation)

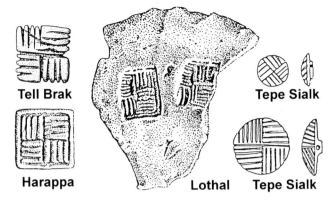

Etched carnelian beads from Susa

Figure 12.25 Etched carnelian beads from Ur and Susa (various sources)

Figure 12.24 Swastika-like seal from Tell Brak, seal impression from Harappa, seal impressions from Lothal, and seals from Tepe Sialk (see Possehl 1996a: 151 for full documentation)

and gulf material would be found in the Greater Indus Valley; but this is not the case. There is actually very little western material in this region, as discussed in the following summary.

Six Persian Gulf seals have been found at Indus sites.[48] There are also six cylinder seals there.[49] Mesopotamian-type "barrel weights" have been found at Mohenjo-daro and Harappa.[50]

There are a few western metal types that have been found in Indus contexts. The toilet set of copper implements comprising an earscoop, piercer, and tweezers from late levels at Harappa has a rather precise parallel at Ur and Kish, with eleven (or twelve) reported sets.[51] This set of implements seems to date to Early Dynastic III and is quite at home in Mesopotamia (figure 12.28).

Animal-headed pins with western parallels have been found at Harappa and Mohenjo-daro.[52]

The copper axe–adzes recovered from Mohenjo-daro some six feet below the surface and one other from Sibri (c. 2000 B.C.) are comparable to other examples from Hissar. Axes of this type are also found in the BMAC graves of northern Afghanistan and farther afield, in Early Minoan II and Troy II.[53]

The stone bust of a male from the site of Dabar Kot has been compared to a head from Khafaje. Other parallels are said to exist at Tell Asmar, Lagash, and Al'Ubaid. There are now four more pieces of sculpture that seem to fit with the Dabar Kot example. Two terra-cotta figurines from Mehrgarh are remarkable for their baldness and the treatment of the eyebrow as a slit. There is an unusual quality to these pieces, which come from Period VII (c. 2800–2500 B.C.), and could recall Near Eastern comparisons. Finally, a terra-cotta head from Lothal with a square-cut beard has been suggested to be the representation of a Mesopotamian.[54]

The well-known Near Eastern "contest scene" between man and animal is also represented in the Indus (see figure 8.6).[55] The Indus motif generally involves a human in combat with two tigers and is found on the stamp seals

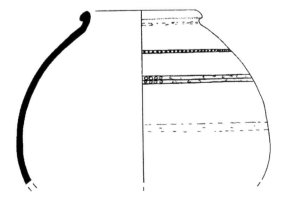

Figure 12.26 A Late Sorath Harappan pot from Saar on Bahrain Island (after Carter *in press*)

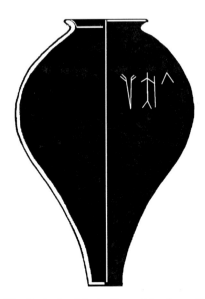

Figure 12.27 An Indus black-slipped jar from Mohenjo-daro, of the type found in the Arabian Gulf (after Mackay 1937–38)

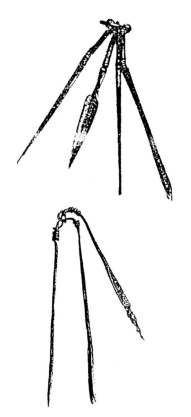

Figure 12.28 Toilet implements from Ur and Harappa (after Woolley 1934 and Vats 1941)

Figure 12.29   Recumbent bull from Lothal (after Rao 1985a)

characteristic of Harappan culture. The motif is thought to be one characteristic of the Near East.

Further comparisons can be made between proto-Elamite glyptic portrayals of the lotus and painted designs on Early Harappan ceramics at Kalibangan dating to circa 3000–2500 B.C.

There is a very fine example of a recumbent bull from Lothal during the Mature Harappan there (figure 12.29).[56] The look and scale of this piece is very much like those from Ur and other Mesopotamian sites.[57] It is close enough to its Mesopotamian counterparts to qualify as one of the few "Mesopotamia" objects from an Harappan site.

B. M. Pande has described four ring-kernoi from Mohenjo-daro and Harappa.[58] Three of these were published for the first time in his paper. This class of ceramic object consists of a ring with small cups attached to the top. The ring is hollow, and the cups have a perforated bottom connecting them to the interior tube of the supporting ring. They appear to be articles at home in the eastern Mediterranean and are found in third millennium contexts in Early Minoan (2500–2100 B.C.) and Pre-Mycenaean (2500–1800 B.C.) sites. Ring-kernoi also appear in much later contexts in the Mediterranean.[59]

This is the only distinctively Minoan or Mycenaean material culture in the Indus Age. The ring-kernoi were used in a festival called the *Kernophoria*, which was associated with the harvest. Their presence in Indus cities would seem to indicate that some residents there (probably Indus peoples) may have enjoyed this rite, which would have come to them as a part of the activity associated with the Third Millennium Middle Asian Interaction Sphere. There might be an association between the ring-kernoi, the *Kernophoria* festival, and the ideology of Intercultural style; however, this is not yet clear.

A Mesopotamian-Type Figurine from Shahr-i Sokhta
There is a very interesting figurine from Shahr-i Sokhta (figure 12.30).[60] The figurine is of a woman with a prominent nose and almond-shaped eyes. Her hair is in a large bun at the back of her head. She is shown carrying a basket or a pot on her head. Her left arm is raised, balancing this object, as though she is walking. Her right arm lays across her lower chest, just below the breasts. The pose of this woman is one with clear Mesopotamian parallels associated with building activity, especially foundation deposits.[61] Such figurines have a long chronology in Mesopotamia from the early third millennium into the second, so the Shahr-i Sokhta figurine is not out of place in this regard. It is interesting, but not out of place, to think that on the eastern end of the Iranian Plateau there may have been people who incorporated ideological aspects of Mesopotamian building practices into their structures.

THE MATERIAL RECORD OF CONTACT BETWEEN MESOPOTAMIA, THE GULF, AND THE INDUS CIVILIZATION: A SUMMARY
There is an uneven quality to the material record of Indus–Mesopotamian contacts. The Mesopotamian archaeological record is far richer in terms of documenting this phenomenon than is the Indus. While there are good ex-

amples of Indus script in the west, the Greater Indus region has yet to produce a convincing example of cuneiform script. A few of the objects in Mesopotamia and the gulf are convincing imports. The Harappan unicorn seal impression from Tell Umma is a good example of this type.[62] But many other things are more debatable: the "cushion" seals from Tell Brak, Tepe Sialk, and Harappa, for example. Some of the material is even derivative, not quite Mesopotamian, nor are they Indus: the cylinder seals from Mohenjo-daro and Kalibangan, for example. This lack of balance is probably best explained by looking to the "invisible" exports (grain, cloth, leather, fish, etc.) that Mesopotamia is known to have traded.[63]

INTERACTION BETWEEN CENTRAL ASIA, BACTRIA, EASTERN IRAN, AND THE INDUS CIVILIZATION

Many of the same products that found their way into the Dilmun trade are a part of a more northern overland trade connection linking the Indus with eastern Iran, Seistan, Afghanistan, and Central Asia. Sites such as Shahr-i Sokhta, Shahdad, Sibri, the Dashli-Sapalli complex, and Altyn Depe all shared with the Indus and Mesopotamia a role in this ancient commerce in luxury goods.[64]

Ancient Turan

Parts of northeastern Iran, Turkmenistan, and western Afghanistan are mentioned in the Zend-Avesta under the geographical term "Turan." M. Tosi has used this term for a region approximately coterminous with the Avestan area that was occupied by peoples who were participants in the Middle Asian Interaction Sphere.[65] Tosi's Turan includes five subregions: (1) southern Turkmenia, (2) the Atrak Valley in the Kopet Dagh Mountains, (3) the eastern Elburz Mountains, (4) the Helmand Valley and Seistan, and (5) Bactria and Margiana (see figure 12.1).

Signs of contact between Turan and the Greater Indus region began to appear in the fourth millennium, when the motifs associated with the well-known Quetta Ware are found in both regions. This proof of contact is complemented by figurines of similar styles found in these places as well.

The Mature Harappan Site of Shortughai

The most distant of the Mature Harappan outlying settlements is Shortughai on the southern side of the Amu Darya, near its confluence with the Kokcha River.[66] Shortughai A, Periods I and II, has a ceramic corpus dominated by Mature Harappan heavy red wares, some decorated in the typical Mature Harappan painted black on red slip style. In addition there are Mature Harappan–style copper–

bronze artifacts, along with an Indus stamp seal with a rhinoceros.

No one is quite sure why there is an Harappan outpost on the Amu Darya. The French excavation team believes that the site was there primarily to give the Harappans access to the lapis lazuli mines of Sar-i Sang, Badakhshan.[67] Jim Shaffer has suggested that the Harappans were there to procure Bactrian camels.[68] I think Shortughai was there as a place of generalized trade and the locus of the "diplomacy" that was needed to promote it between Bactria and Central Asia and the Indus region. Whatever the reason, and no one really knows the answer to this question, Shortughai has an abundance of Mature Harappan material culture, and this seems to be due to direct intervention by the Indus peoples themselves.

Indus Material at Altyn Depe

The well-known proto-urban site of Altyn Depe in Turkmenia has evidence of contact with the Indus Civilization that goes beyond Quetta Ware and figurines. The first two finds of interest are two Indus-style square stamp seals (figure 12.31). These come from different components in the site, and the example with the swastika was found in a context that is probably a bit earlier than the one with the two Indus signs. But they can both be dated to circa 2500–2200 B.C. These two objects were carved in a "provincial" style,

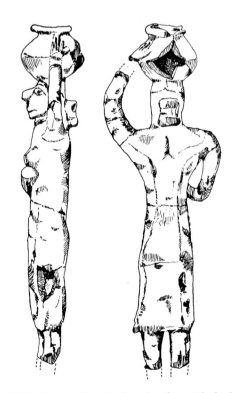

Figure 12.30   Bronze female figurine from Shahr-i Sokhta (after Tosi 1983)

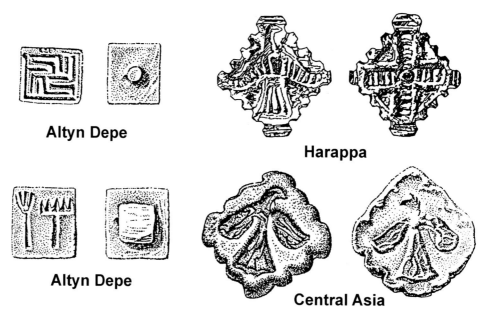

Altyn Depe

Harappa

Altyn Depe

Central Asia

Figure 12.31 Two Indus-style stamp seals from Altyn Depe, the "eagle seal" from Harappa, and a comparable example from Gonur Tepe in Central Asia (after Masson 1988, Vats 1941)

possibly at Altyn Depe itself. The swastika seal comes from the so-called Burial Chamber of Priests, where an Harappan-style gold disk bead and four ivory sticks with Indus parallels were also found (figure 12.32). There is also a flat copper–bronze blade, without a midrib (an Harappan feature), and a frying pan of the same material from Altyn Depe. The blade is a clear Mature Harappan type.[69] The frying pan has a good parallel at Mohenjo-daro.[70] There are also fishing hooks from Altyn Depe, with eyes to take the

line; this is characteristic of Indus hooks and might be the source of another "connection."[71]

Excavations at Gonur Depe in Margiana have produced other objects that recall the Indus Civilization in Namazga V contexts: a bowl with pipal leaves, a bull's head of composite design, and Indus-type stick dice (figure 12.33).[72]

Finally, there is a platform with a "temple" on its summit at Altyn Depe (figure 12.34). There are clear architec-

Altyn Depe

Figure 12.32 Gold disk bead and ivory sticks from Altyn Depe similar to Indus types (after Masson 1988)

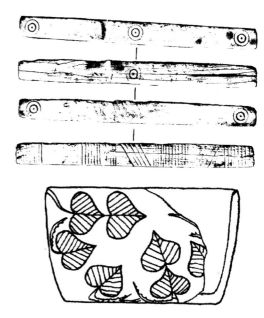

Figure 12.33 Indus-type artifacts from Gonur Depe (after Sarianidi 1998)

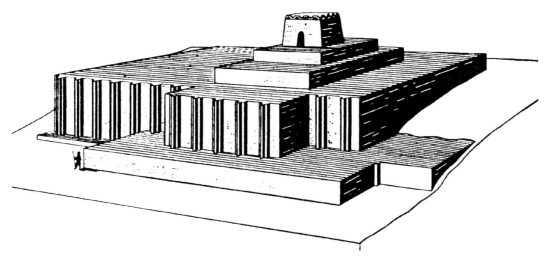

Figure 12.34   Platform with a "temple" from Altyn Depe (after Masson 1988)

tural parallels between this structure and the Temple at Mundigak (Period IV, c. 2700–2300 B.C.).[73]

The Fullol Hoard

There is a hoard from a place called Sai Hazara in northeastern Afghanistan.[74] It was first published as "Kosh Tapa" but is more familiarly known today as "Fullol Tapa." In September 1966 authorities of the Afghan government confiscated five gold and twelve silver vessels, almost all of them fragmentary. No one knows for sure, but the villagers who held the vessels said that they had come from Fullol Tapa. The Fullol hoard consists of the following.

There is one gold vessel and two in silver with the stepped cross motif. Another of the gold vessels has undulating snakes rising from the base, with heads at the rim. A fragment of a small gold bowl has two bulls in procession, one of them is bearded in the Sumerian fashion. A large gold goblet and a small silver bowl have bores in the wild. A large silver bowl has a frieze of romping bulls separated by palm trees, which could be the Mesopotamian tree of life. There is a small silver vessel finely engraved and embossed with two pairs of unhumped bulls confronting each other. The rounded bottom of this vessel is embossed with an eight-armed motif, possibly a stylized star. There is a plain gold vessel and five undecorated silver goblets (figure 12.35).

THE THIRD MILLENNIUM MIDDLE ASIAN INTERACTION SPHERE AND THE BACTRIA-MARGIANA ARCHAEOLOGICAL COMPLEX

At about 2200 B.C., patterns of interaction begin to show themselves in the eastern portions of the interaction sphere. To the north, Margiana is occupied, shifting the center of settlement to the northeast, out of the shadow of the Kopet Dagh. This shift in settlement is accompanied by the development of a new suite of artifacts, which has been called the "Bactria-Margiana Archaeological Complex," or the BMAC (figures 12.36 and 12.37).[75]

By 2000 B.C. the BMAC is a strong presence in Margiana and the Kopet Dagh. The presence of BMAC artifacts in the upper levels of Mohenjo-daro and Chanhu-daro, which date to circa 2000 B.C., seems to indicate the penetration of the BMAC peoples into the Subcontinent. There is also BMAC material in the Quetta Valley, Sibri, and Mehi, extending to Shahdad, Kinneman, and the Khurab, and the cairns near Yahya. There is little if any Indus material in the BMAC homelands (Bactria-Margiana), a shift in the earlier dynamic.

The BMAC emerges in Early Namazga VI times (c. 2000 B.C.) and endures for about 250 years, until circa 1750 B.C.[76] This is a time during which the transformation of the Indus Civilization took place, with the abandonment of Mohenjo-daro and many of the other Mature Harappan sites in Sindh, the "deurbanization" of Harappa, and the emergence of the Cemetery H Culture.

Hiebert's thesis is that the BMAC is a local development, the product of local cultural processes, probably within the large oasis of Margiana.[77] This is best supported by the observation that unfinished artifacts have only been found at Margiana sites. While many of the raw materials were imported, they were fashioned into BMAC-style artifacts only within the oasis. There is even support for the notion that the household, rather than specialized workshops, was the primary locus of production.

There are two phases to the BMAC. The first begins as a kind of architectural revolution in Margiana, with the constriction of towns with massive walls and circular corner bastions. The BMAC-style artifacts first occur in

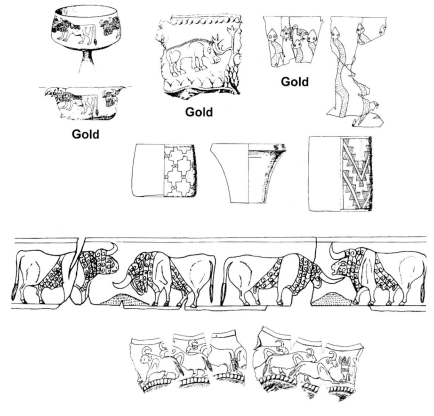

Figure 12.35 Some material from the Follol Hoard (after Tosi and Wardak 1972)

these contexts. Phase 2 is an iconographic revolution, with the elaboration of the artifacts and the introduction of snakes, scorpions, and boars as important new iconographic elements.[78]

Social identity appears to be transformed in Period 2, with the development of the shared BMAC culture. The oasis adaptation spreads to similar deltaic oases in northern Bactria and southern Bactria. The new aspects of Period 2 iconography often relate to the desert environment: snakes, scorpions, boar. Objects such as axes and mace heads, which were used earlier, are transformed into ceremonial objects. Miniature columns, staffs, and mace heads are found in new contexts, indicating perhaps that they are being reinterpreted in the oasis culture. There appears to be an emphasis on the materials of the imported stones, which leads to the deliberate juxtaposition of exotic materials, such as alabaster and steatite.

The new oasis system includes a reorganization of production to craft activities occurring within the qala and the finishing of distinctive objects on exotic materials, such as imported stone and metal. Bullae and cylinder seals are used in Period 2, indicating a sophisticated control of exchange. Sealings on ceramics may indicate control of production as well.[79]

The qala is a sort of manor house, characteristic of medieval Central Asia. Hiebert uses this as a model for the reconstruction of craft production during the BMAC, especially Phase 2.

There is no reason to believe that any of the peoples of the BMAC or their predecessors were speakers of an Indo-European language, let alone Vedic Sanskrit. There is a possibility that some of these peoples spoke a language or languages of this family, but a closely reasoned case let alone proof for this has never been offered. Given the contemporary critique, or deconstruction, of the concept of race, the question of them being Aryans does not arise.[80]

The principal assemblages of BMAC material from the Greater Indus region are discussed in the following sections.

Mohenjo-daro

BMAC materials at Mohenjo-daro are relatively plentiful.[81] There are two animal-headed pins that may be a part of this complex. There is also a small terra-cotta with a bird that has a BMAC "look" to it along with a BMAC socketed axe–adze.

There are a number of heart-shaped objects from Mo-

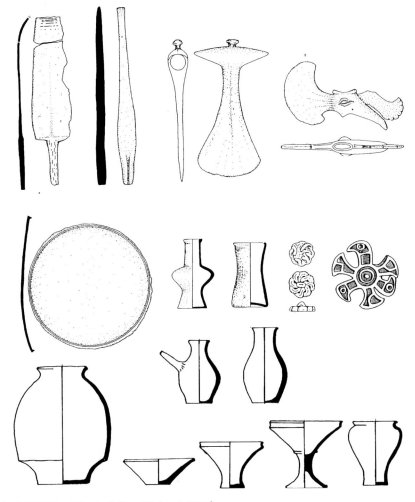

Figure 12.36 Selected BMAC artifacts (after Hiebert 1994)

henjo-daro, including by extension the design on the pectoral with a unicorn bull and a faience plaque. Stepped-cross inlays also occur but may or may not be a part of the complex.[82]

Small "cosmetic bottles" are a part of the BMAC, and Marshall published one from Mohenjo-daro.[83]

There is a silver vase from Bactria with seated men in the upper register.[84] These figures are wearing a distinctive skirt in such a way that it obscures their legs. The Seated Man from L Area on the Mound of the Great Bath at Mohenjo-daro seems to replicate in three dimensions the men on the silver vessel.[85] It would appear that the Seated Man from L Area is a representation of someone in Bactrian dress, possibly a Bactrian himself. Ardeleanu-Jansen has reconstructed the priest-king in this pose, which is a plausible observation.[86]

The BMAC material at Mohenjo-daro is late at the site, at least where it can be documented. This is fully in keeping with the chronology for the BMAC beginning at circa 2000 B.C., and the abandonment of Mohenjo-daro largely complete at circa 1900 B.C. or just a few years later. The same is true for BMAC material at Harappa.

Harappa

The BMAC material at Harappa is more restricted than at Mohenjo-daro.[87] The best piece is a stepped-cross amulet with an eagle on one side. There is also an animal-headed pin. Less definitive are the stepped crosses and heart-shaped objects.

Quetta Treasury

On March 19, 1985, a contractor excavating a pit in connection with the construction of a hotel in Quetta City uncovered a single burial with funerary objects that are a part of the BMAC (figure 12.38).[88] The objects include copper–bronze weapons and tools; alabaster cups and vessels, including one of the well-known circular objects (briefcases) first documented at Tepe Hissar;[89] miniature stone columns, also of the Hissar III type; "scepters" of soft gray stone; "eye" beads of semiprecious stone set in

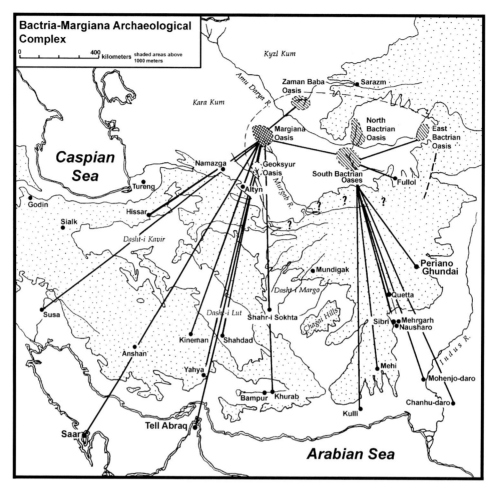

Figure 12.37 Map of sites with BMAC artifacts (after Hiebert 1994)

gold; two small bull figurines or pendants in gold; and a gold cup embossed with running animals (either felid or canid type) above a "rope" design.

As a body of material, this collection of funerary objects is comparable to that from Dashli in northern Afghanistan, Sapalli Depe in southern Uzbekistan, Shahdad in eastern Iran, and the Sibri Cemetery near Mehrgarh at the foot of the Bolan Pass in Pakistan, extending as far east as Tepe Hissar. The gold cup has no close parallels that have been published.

Damb Sadaat

There is some material from Damb Sadaat, also in the Quetta Valley, that may be BMAC in origin.[90] Several of the interesting callipygian figurines were found in Damb Sadaat II and III. This is the figurine type with legs molded together, slightly curved, so the figurine can sit. There are also two compartmented seals in terra-cotta; one with the stepped cross comes from Damb Sadaat III. Masses of Quetta Ware were found as well. No one is sure

who made the callipygian figurines; they just occur in both Central Asia and the Indus.

Other Sites

There is other BMAC material from Sibri on the Kachi Plain, Mehrgarh VIII (South Cemetery), Chanhu-daro, Mehi, and Kulli.

A Hissar III Site in Seistan

Gudar-i Shah is a small mound in Afghan Seistan, on the Gaud-i Zirra.[91] It was visited by G. Dales, whose interest in the site came from the presence of BMAC stone columns and briefcases like those from Hissar III used to trim the Muslim graves there. These had been reported in the nineteenth century by British surveyors settling the Afghan boundary, but this was the first visit by an archaeologist.

The columns and briefcases were clearly in secondary contexts, and Dales was unable to trace the location of the ancient site. But we can be assured that somewhere in the

Figure 12.38 Some key objects from the Quetta Treasury (after Jarrige 1987)

close proximity of Gudar-i Shah there is a Hissar III site, possibly a cemetery, probably with more BMAC material.

Summary

Signs of interaction between the Greater Indus region and Bactria and Central Asia begin to appear with the origins of the Quetta Ware in the fourth millennium B.C. The Quetta Ware connection is expressed in a shared set of pottery motifs. The principal shared motif is the stepped cross and the many variations on this pattern.

During Mature Harappan times, the interaction between the Indus and Central Asia probably intensified. The Indus outpost at Shortughai is evidence for this, as is the presence of Mature Harappan–style seals at Altyn Depe and the other Indus material culture noted previously. There is no evidence at Mature Harappan sites in the Greater Indus region for the presence of Bactrians and Central Asians prior to the BMAC. However, there is Mature Harappan material in these regions prior to circa 2000 B.C.

At 2000 B.C., the BMAC appears in Margiana, as well as in the Greater Indus region. The transformation of the Indus Civilization had already begun. Mohenjo-daro had another hundred years of occupation left, and Harappa probably the same. One might guess that the peoples of

the BMAC sensed a vacuum in the Greater Indus region and moved in to fill it.

NOTES
1. Edens 1993; Hiebert 1994; Lamberg-Karlovsky 1986a, 1986b; Tosi 1986a, 1986b; Possehl 1996c, 1997b; Potts 1990; Mery 2000.
2. Kohl 1975.
3. Kohl 1975: 29–30.
4. Sauer 1952: 36.
5. Tosi 1986b; Potts 1990.
6. Possehl 1986a, 1997b; Weber 1990, 1991.
7. Cleuziou 1982.
8. Childe 1950.
9. Possehl 1997b: 96–97.
10. Possehl 1996c: 136–38, 143.
11. Peake 1928; Weisgerber 1984.
12. Heimpel 1982, 1987; Possehl 1996c: 135–36.
13. See Possehl 1996c: 136 for references.
14. Possehl 1986b.
15. Possehl 1996c: 138–45.
16. Ratnagar 1981: 39.
17. Crawford 1973.
18. See Possehl 1996c: 183–84 for illustrations and documentation.
19. Kenoyer 1984.

20. Meadow 1979: 297.
21. For example, Pabumath, Y. M. Chitalwala, personal communication 1988.
22. Belcher 1991: 114.
23. Cleuziou and Tosi 1994.
24. See Collon 1996 and Possehl 1996c: 148–52 for other reviews.
25. Possehl 1996b: 150–52.
26. Parpola 1994b.
27. Reade 1979.
28. Reade 1979.
29. Reade 1979: 8–23; pls. 9 and 10.
30. Chakrabarti 1982.
31. Mackay 1943: pl. XCIII, no. 14.
32. Chakrabarti 1982: 265.
33. Kohl 1975.
34. See Bokonyi 1985 for a recent discussion.
35. Frankfort 1936: 434, 1956: 19, fig. 9, date based on Reade 2001.
36. Dales 1968a: 19–21; Possehl 1994, 1996c: 164–65.
37. Possehl 1994.
38. Possehl 1996c.
39. Dales 1968a; Possehl 1996c: 167.
40. See Edens 1993: 334–338 for discussion and illustrations.
41. Carter, in press.
42. Blackman, Mery, and Wright 1989
43. Wright 1991: 80.
44. Possehl 1996c: 168–71.
45. Possehl 1996c: 173; Possehl 1986b: Mehi II.I.2a.
46. Gadd 1932; see also Parpola 1994b.
47. Srivastava 1991.
48. Mackay 1937–38: 343, 1943: 148, pl. 15.
49. Possehl 1996c: 176–77.
50. Possehl 1996c: 177.
51. Vats 1940: pl. CXXV, 1; Woolley 1934: pl. 159b; Mackay 1929: 169, pl. XLIII, 1–8.
52. Vats 1940: 390, pl. CXXV, 34, 36; Mackay 1937–38, vol. II, pl. C, 3.
53. Mackay 1937–38: pl. CXX, 27; Santoni 1984: 53; Schmidt 1937: pl. LII, H 2710 and H 3247; Pottier 1984: 149; Wheeler 1947: 80.
54. See Possehl 1996c: 179–80.
55. Parpola 1994a: 246–49; Possehl 1996c: 180–81.
56. Possehl 1996c: 165–66; Rao 1985: 549, fig. 17.
57. Woolley 1934: pl. 141b.
58. Pande 1971.
59. Pande 1971: 314.
60. Tosi 1983.
61. Tosi 1983: 309–16.
62. Scheil 1925.
63. Crawford 1973.
64. Basaglia 1977; Hakimi 1997; Santoni 1984; Gupta 1979: vol. II, 194–204; Masson 1988; Hiebert 1994.
65. Tosi 1977: 47–48.
66. Francfort 1989.
67. Tosi 1988: 66.
68. Shaffer 1987.
69. Masson 1988: pl. XXIX, nos. 1–2.
70. Mackay 1937–38: pl. CXXVIII, no. 15.
71. Masson 1988: 8.
72. Sarianidi 1998: fig. 17, nos. 8, 9, and fig. 21, nos. 6, 7.
73. Casal 1961: fig. 36.
74. Dupree, Gouin, and Omer 1971; Tosi and Wardak 1972.
75. Hiebert 1994.
76. Hiebert 1994.
77. Hiebert 1994: 161–63.
78. Hiebert 1994: 164.
79. Hiebert 1994: 176.
80. Kennedy 1995.
81. Marshall 1931i: pl. CLVIII, no. 1; Mackay 1937–38: pl. C, no. 3; pl. LXXIV, nos. 18–19; pl. CIII, no. 15; pl. CXX, no. 27.
82. Mackay 1937–38: pl. CVI, nos. 3–5; pl. CVII, nos. 5, 15; pl. CXL, no. 35; pl. CXI, no. 59; pl. CXLI, no. 17, pl. CXLII, nos. 29, 130; Marshall 1931i: pl. CLV, nos. 36–47; pl. CLV, nos. 31–33; pl. CLVIII, no. 12;
83. Marshall 1931i: pl. CXL, no. 16.
84. Amiet 1986: fig. 202.
85. Marshall 1931i: pl. C, nos. 1–3.
86. Ardeleanu-Jansen 1991.
87. Vats 1940: XCI, no. 255; pl. CXXV, no. 36; pl. CXXXIV, no. 4; pl. CXXXVII, no. 8; pl. CXXXVIII, nos. 2–4; pl. CXXXIX, no. 84.
88. Jarrige and Hassan 1989.
89. Schmidt 1937: pls. LXI, LXII.
90. Masson and Sarianidi 1972: pls. 26–28; Fairservis 1956: 224, 229.
91. Dales 1977.

CHAPTER 13

The Transformation of the Indus Civilization

INTRODUCTION

The abandonment of Mohenjo-daro and many other sites of the Indus Civilization in the early second millennium is a well-known archaeological observation.[1] This is a time that has come to be called the Posturban Harappan because the focus of change seems to have been centered on urbanization and the other features of the Indus ideology. There is essentially no habitation at Mohenjo-daro between approximately 1900 B.C. and the Kushan Period in the early centuries of the common era, when a Buddhist monastery and stupa were built on the Mound of the Great Bath. Many other Indus sites were abandoned at about 1900 B.C., especially in Sindh, Baluchistan, and Cholistan. The size and complexity of the city of Harappa was reduced at this time. The few people who lived there interred at least some of their dead in the famous Cemetery H. Judged by its small size and lack of signs of internal complexity, Harappa was not a city during Cemetery H times. Ganweriwala, Dholavira, and Rakhigarhi, the other Indus cities, also dissolved as urban centers at the end of the Mature Harappan.

There was an abandonment, or severe depopulation, of a number of important Indus settlements including Chanhu-daro, Kot Diji, Balakot, Allahdino, Kulli, Mehi, Nindowari, Naushéro, Kalibangan, Ropar, Surkotada, Dholavira, Desalpur, and Lothal. There was also a disruption in the Indus economy. The production of a wide range of special materials, many of which seem to have been luxury items, was curtailed (e.g., long barrel-cylinder beads, etched beads generally, inscribed stamp seals). The art of writing was no longer practiced. Long-distance trade was reduced, although the peoples of the BMAC were in evidence in the Greater Indus region.

The distribution of the human population in northwestern India and Pakistan shifted in a significant way. Sindh, the Kulli Domain, and Cholistan were largely abandoned by settled farmers, but there was an increase in the number of settlements in the Punjab, Haryana, western Uttar Pradesh, and northern Rajasthan. The Harappans in Gujarat remained remarkably stable. Posturban times witness a return to a cultural mosaic not unlike the one found during the Early Harappan.

There are a number of theories concerning the transformation of the Indus Civilization. The most important of these are reviewed here.

WHEELER'S ARYAN ARMY

The first coherent "theory" concerning the eclipse of the Indus Civilization was put forward by Wheeler.[2] He held that the Rgveda could be read in part as an historical document and that the conflicts described there were between what he thought of as newly arrived Aryan warriors and the indigenous Indus peoples. This is stated most clearly in Wheeler's report on his 1946 excavations at Harappa:

The Aryan invasion of the Land of the Seven Rivers, the Punjab and its environs, constantly assume the form of an onslaught upon the walled cities of the aborigines. For these cities the term used in the Rgveda is *pur*, meaning a "rampart," "fort" or "stronghold." One is called "broad" (*prithvi*) and "wide" (*urvi*). Sometimes strongholds are referred to metaphorically as "of metal" (*ayasi*). "Autumnal" (*saradi*) forts are also named: "this may refer to the forts in that season being occupied against Aryan attacks or against inundations caused by overflowing rivers" (Macdonell and Keith 1912: vol. 1, p. 538). Forts "with a hundred walls" (*satabhuji*) are mentioned. The citadel may be made of stone (*asmamayi*): alternatively, the use of mud-bricks is perhaps alluded to by the epithet *ama* ("raw," "unbaked," Rgveda, IV, xxx, 20; II, xxxv, 6). Indra, the Aryan war-god, is *puramdara* "fort-destroyer" (Rgveda II, xx, 7; III, liv, 15). He shatters "ninety forts" for his Aryan protégé, Divodasa (Rgveda I, cxxx, 7). The same forts are doubtless referred to where in other hymns he demolishes variously ninety-nine and a hundred "ancient castles" of the aboriginal leader Sambar (Rgveda II, xiv, 6; II, xix, 6; IV, xxvi, 3). In brief, he "rends forts as age consumes a garment" (Rgveda VI, xvi, 13).

Where are—or were—these citadels? It has in the past been supposed that they were mythical, or were merely "places of refuge against attack, ramparts of hardened earth with palisades and a ditch" (Macdonell and Keith 1912: vol. 1, pp. 356, 539). The recent excavation of Harappa may be thought to have changed the picture. Here we have a highly evolved civilization of essentially non-Aryan type (Marshall 1931h: 110–112) now known to have employed massive fortifications, and known also to have dominated the river-system of north-western India at a time not distant from the likely period of the earlier Aryan invasions of that region. What destroyed this firmly-settled civilization? Climatic, economic, political deterioration may have weakened it, but its ultimate extinction is more likely to have been completed by deliberate and large-scale destruction. It may be no mere chance that at a Late Period of Mohenjo-daro men, women and children appear to have been massacred there (Mackay 1937–38: 94–95, 116–117, 172). On circumstantial evidence, Indra stands accused.[3] (original citations included)

Although Wheeler succeeds in presenting the drama of his theory with "Indra stands accused" as its capstone, this theory can be critiqued from a number of perspectives: chronological, cultural, historical. The chronology of the Aryans in South Asia is far from settled.[4] Although Aryans might have entered the Subcontinent well before the composition of the Rgveda, most scholars now date the codification of this liturgical text to about 1000 B.C., almost a millennium after the transformation of the Indus Civilization. Therefore, no one should assume that the Vedic Aryans were on the scene to be active participants in the transformation process examined here. Also, it has been argued here, along with Dales and Kennedy, that the skeletons found in the upper layers of Mohenjo-daro are actually hasty interments, not the remains of massacre victims.[5] Finally, the historical content of the Rgveda has not yet been fully, and convincingly, defined. There is a reasonable supposition that there is important historical information in this liturgical text, but just where within it, and how significant this history might be, is still unsettled.

There is some doubt that this theory is a product of Wheeler's original thinking. Krishna Deva and B. B. Lal have told me that the "Aryan hypothesis" seems to have been developed on information Wheeler took from V. S. Agrawala, a member of the Harappa excavation team in 1946. Agrawala was the tour guide and lecturer for visiting dignitaries and spoke of the Rgveda and references in it to warfare and the conquest of towns and cities, speculating that this might have been a description of the demise of the Indus Civilization.

WEARING OUT THE LANDSCAPE

A second theory on the Indus transformation is ecologically based. The brick kilns of Mohenjo-daro and Harappa have been invoked as a part of a proposal that the peoples of the Mature Harappan were wearing out their landscape. Millions of baked bricks went into the building and rebuilding of Mohenjo-daro. Millions of tons of firewood went into the baking of them. With allowance for the arrival of floating timber from the upper reaches of the Indus, this implies a widespread deforestation of the surrounding region.[6] This notion has been widely critiqued.[7] Four hundred acres of gallery forest is all that would have been needed to rebuild Mohenjo-daro every 140 years.

Other natural causes have been put forward for the eclipse of the ancient cities of the Indus, including the vagaries of the Indus River.

AN AVULSION OF THE INDUS RIVER: THE POSITION OF LAMBRICK AND MUGHAL

The Indus River in Sindh is a mature stream that frequently changes it course. Much river training has been done on the Indus in modern times, so these course shifts are not as apparent today as they were through the nineteenth and early twentieth centuries. But they are a powerful part of the history of Sindh. Two archaeologists have suggested that a dramatic shift in the course of the Indus led to the abandonment of Mohenjo-daro.[8]

An avulsion of the Indus River might explain the abandonment of Mohenjo-daro, but there was a good deal more happening in the Greater Indus region at the turn of the third millennium than the abandonment of this once great metropolis. This leads those who use an avulsion of the Indus and the abandonment of Mohenjo-daro as an element in understanding the transformation of the Indus Civilization to revert to some form of domino effect to account for the eclipse generally: "as Mohenjo-daro went; so went the Indus Civilization."

Mackay also believed that Mohenjo-daro might have been abandoned because of an avulsion of the Indus River, which was noted by his wife, Dorothy, an anthropologist, in another context.[9]

Another theory has a clearer intellectual genealogy, coming from an American hydrologist, R. Raikes, joined by Dales, elaborating an idea first presented by M. Sahni.[10]

THE RAIKES/DALES DAM

The Indus River has reemerged as a dynamic factor in the process of Harappan cultural change, due largely to the work of R. Raikes.[11] He hypothesizes, along with G. Dales, that the waters of the Indus River were impounded by a natural dam in the vicinity of Sehwan (figure 1.2) and that Mohenjo-daro and other sites were so disrupted that it led to, actually "caused," the abandonment of the city and the eclipse of the Indus Civilization. To support this proposition, they claim that the normal behavior of a big river simply cannot account for the evidence of massive flooding at Mohenjo-daro.

There are a number of critiques of this hypothesis.[12] Wasson has noted that the unconsolidated sediments of the Indus floodplain, which would have been the substance of the dam, have very little structural integrity and could not have withstood the static pressure of the impounded Indus River.

This general theory was first proposed by Sahni, who

noted the presence of thick, bedded alluvium at two hillocks south of Hyderabad, Sindh.[13] This alluvium contained freshwater shells, one of which suggested prolonged submergence in fresh water. Sahni thought that this thick alluvium might be accounted for by a dam, perhaps at more than one place, across the Indus.

The forming of a large natural dam across the Indus may at first seem so unusual as to be unrealistic. But in 1819 an earthquake caused the formation of a ridge called the "Allah Bund" in northern Kutch, along the Sindh border, which temporarily dammed the minor eastern courses of the Indus system (figure 1.2). Interestingly, the Allah Bund was breached by the first significant flood against it, sustaining Wasson's thoughts that unconsolidated alluvium is not strong enough to impound the Indus or even its minor extensions.

Another point of disagreement lies in the consideration of historical process. Is it necessary to believe that just because the Indus River was impounded, the Indus Civilization came to an end? It might be a possibility, but it hardly satisfies the "sufficient and necessary" criteria for successful historical explanation. Even if the waters of the Indus River had been impounded, the historical consequences might have been different from those proposed by Raikes and Dales. The impounding of the river would have to be seen as an immediate cause of change that resonated with some deeper, structural aspect of the Mature Harappan sociocultural system. If the Indus Civilization succumbed to new and unpredicted riverine forces, the explanation sought by historians and social scientists lies not directly with geomorphologic matters, but with the internal structure of the Indus way of life. The "flaw" that would have led to such catastrophic sociocultural change is not to be found within the natural world of geomorphology but within the human context of the Indus Civilization, its society, and culture.

NEW DATA FROM THE LOST SARASVATI

Archaeological research along the now largely dry beds of the ancient Sarasvati and Drishadvati Rivers has led to the discovery of a large number of archaeological sites.[14] Mughal's recording of over 170 Indus sites on the Pakistan side of the border represents one of the most impressive archaeological feats of this century in the Subcontinent. When placed within the context of the distribution of Indus sites generally, they lead to a consideration that Cholistan may have been the (or one of the) principal region(s) for Mature Harappan grain production, their "bread basket," as it were. Mughal's findings are the most amenable to quantification at the moment, and a long-term trend in settlement counts

Table 13.1 Site counts, total settled area, and average site size for Cholistan

Period	Site counts	Settled area (hectares)	Average size (hectares)
Early Iron Age (Painted Gray Ware) c. 1000(?)–500 B.C.	14	36	2.6
Posturban Harappan (Cemetery H) c. 1900–1700(?) B.C.	50	255	5.1
Mature Harappan c. 2500–1900 B.C.	174	974	5.6
Early Harappan (Kot Dijian) c. 3200–2600 B.C.	40	256	6.4
Hakra Wares c. 3800–3200 B.C.	99	643	6.5

Note: From Mughal (1997: 40).

can be illustrated by using his materials. The data are given in table 13.1.

The interface between the Cemetery H assemblage and the Painted Gray Ware has not yet been defined in Pakistan. In India, Painted Gray Ware begins at circa 1100 B.C. The interface between this assemblage and the Late Harappan in the Punjab has been documented at such places as Dadheri and Bhagwanpura.[15]

The large number of Mature Harappan sites in Cholistan is due to the presence of a rich inland delta there, which created a large tract of naturally irrigated land for farming and pasture. Sites of the Early Harappan–Mature Harappan Transition, circa 2600–2500 B.C., have not been identified in Cholistan, but they are surely there. The chronology for Mughal's periods is taken from the one used here, not from his 1997 monograph; but there is little difference between them.

The maps of sites from Cholistan seem to give us the broad outlines of the relative strength of flow in the ancient Sarasvati from Hakra Wares times through the Early Iron Age.[16] The relatively high density of Hakra Wares sites may well inform us of a rather strong flow in the river, which diminished in the next period, with the Early Harappan (Kot Dijian) sites being relatively few in number in this area. The very high number of Mature Harappan settlements suggests a resurgence of the river and a rich, well-watered inland delta. Then, in the Cemetery H and Painted Gray Ware periods we see the two-step retreat of the river to the east, eventually with insufficient flow to even reach the old Fort Derawar delta.

The fluvial sequence apparently has little, if anything, to do with broad trends in climatic change, but can be explained by tectonics as outlined in Agrawal and Sood.[17] Over what seems to have been the course of the later third and second millennia B.C., drainage from the Himalayan watershed that fed the Sarasvati was gradually captured by streams that flowed to the east, into the Bay of Bengal, at the expense of the greater Indus system. This process apparently led to the creation of the Yamuna River, a very young stream, and the drying up of the Sarasvati and Drishadvati Rivers.

This is not to propose that stream capture was the direct cause of the eclipse of the ancient cities of the Indus. A sociocultural cause is sought here, but, over the course of the third and second millennia, the Sarasvati dried up, and that seems to have been something that cannot be ignored in a broad consideration of the transformation of the Indus Civilization.

An Indo-French archaeological project has also found many sites along the ancient Sarasvati, but on the Indian side of the border. The team's findings conform to Mughal's data, including a significant number of Kushan Period sites with the well-known, easily recognized red polished ware. They say of the stream capture:

> This shift would have occurred either in the still badly defined Late Harappan period or in the PGW (Painted Gray Ware) period, or gradually during both since Late Harappan (Cemetery H) and PGW sites in the state of Cholistan in Pakistan are found on one of the paleochannels known locally as Hakra. However, the adoption of this "hypothesis" poses an interesting methodological problem. If we accept this hypothesis, we *must* logically accept as well that another tectonic upheaval would have made the rivers revert to the Kushan (Rang Mahal) period since sites from the latter are again found in the region.[18]

This is an important statement that Francfort intends to use to sharpen the problem. It is not certain, however, that Francfort's point is really true. That is, *must* we accept the same explanation for both data sets, the protohistoric and the early historic (Rang Mahal)? Wars and migrations come about for many reasons; the same is surely true for the regeneration of a settlement grid. For example, technologies unavailable, or unused, in prehistoric times might have been part of the Kushan agricultural regime. Facilities like irrigation or the use of bunds for impounding rainwater and soil emerge as important new technological features in western India at about the time of the Kushans. Such agricultural technology could have allowed renewed settlement in northern Rajasthan, independent and unrelated to tectonics.

GURDIP SINGH AND CLIMATIC CHANGE

The work in 1971 of G. Singh and his team at three salt lakes in Rajasthan has already been reviewed.[19] There is evidence for changing salinity in these lakes, but this does not necessarily imply changes in rainfall. An archaeological point can be made in the present context.

The Eastern Domain was well settled in Mature Harappan through Posturban times. This is the area 300 to 400 kilometers to the north of the salt lakes in Rajasthan said to have data for climatic change in the third/second millennia. Premodern agriculture in this area was dependent on rainfall, although some canal irrigation is available today. Site counts go up from 218 during the Mature Harappan to 853 in Posturban times, although there was a dramatic drop in average site size, down from 13.54 to 3.55 hectares. These figures in average site size may also be telling us something important about the kind of "deurbanization" that characterizes the Posturban Harappan. But in the end, these data do not look like those that one would expect if there had been a severe reduction in rainfall as Singh proposed, especially given the fact that it is a dry-cropping region.

THE ALLCHINS' APPROACH

In their most recent book on the archaeology of India, Allchin and Allchin have an important discussion of the transformation of the Indus Civilization.[20] They propose:

> There are several factors that probably contributed to the abandonment of the urban sites. These include economic factors, particularly the decline of Mesopotamian trade, which had been flourishing up to c. 2000 B.C. The reasons for this are unimportant to our discussion, but its decline must have been serious for the Indus cities as, unlike the merchants of Egypt and Mesopotamia, they had no alternative major trading partner to turn to. It would appear that they must have had considerable trade within their own region and its hinterland to fall back on, but this too seems to have been undermined by other causes. In Sindh particularly, and perhaps in other regions to a lesser extent, there was clearly a steady deterioration in the climate and environment. Uplift of the Himalayas due to Plate Tectonics is probably the principal underlying cause of changes in the course of the rivers of the Indus system, as we have outlined in earlier chapters.[21]

The Allchins' approach invokes a series of changes that are coincident and that, working together in some yet to be fully understood way, led to the transformation of the Indus Civilization. This is a sound way to proceed, but has some pitfalls. For example, we are not sure that there was an interruption of foreign trade with Mesopotamia circa 2000 B.C. The trade does seem to trickle off at about 2000 B.C., but it may not have stopped. There are many references to Meluhha, the Indus Civilization, in Mesopotamian texts of the second millennium.[22] The Allchin

Table 13.2 Estimated settlement data for the Mature and Posturban Harappan

Domain	Time	Site count	Average site size (hectares)	Settled area (hectares)
Sindhi Domain				
	Mature Harappan	86	8.0	688
	Jhukar	6	5.6	34
Cholistan Domain				
	Mature Harappan	174	5.6	974
	Cemetery H	41	5.1	209
Kulli Domain				
	Kulli and Quetta	129	5.8	748
	Posturban	0	0	0
Sorath Domain				
	Sorath Harappan	310	5.4	1,674
	Late Sorath Harappan	198	4.3	815
Eastern Domain				
	Mature Harappan	218	13.5	2,943
	Posturban	853	3.5	2,985

proposal also places critical importance on Mesopotamian trade vis-à-vis the Mature Harappan economy. Do we know that it was so important that the termination of trade with the west would have had an impact on the entire civilization? With this proposal also comes the knotty problem of "direction" in causality: Did the secession (or reduction) of trade contribute to the transformation of the Indus Civilization, or did the transformation of the Indus Civilization lead to the secession (or reduction) of the trade? These are serious problems for those interested in the Indus transformation.

In subsequent pages the Allchins draw heavily on natural forces as causes for the eclipse of the Harappan Civilization. They propose that "a reduction of rainfall in Sindh and the immediate hinterland could well have been an added cause for the abandonment of Mohenjo-daro and other urban sites."[23] But Mohenjo-daro today receives less than 12 centimeters of annual rainfall and the ancient city today would be in a desert if it was not for the floods of the Indus. We could take away virtually all of today's rain and still have a viable agropastoral environment.

The Allchins state their case for the interconnection of causes in regional and interregional terms. They deal with the Greater Indus region, which is necessary for a complete understanding of the transformation process.

WHAT HAPPENED?

While there is little doubt that the beginning of the second millennium saw many important changes in the Indus Civilization, there are interesting patterns to the data set that can serve as a starting point to recast the problem. The record of settlement, comparing the Mature with the Posturban Harappan region by region, is summarized in table 13.2 (see also figure 13.1).

The settlement patterns around Harappa are not well enough known at this point for the data at hand to be comparable to other regions. The Pakistan Department of Archaeology and R. Wright are currently engaged in an active program of exploration to rectify this. For now, we know that Harappa shrank in size at the beginning of the second millennium. The archaeological assemblage that succeeds the Mature Harappan is the so-called Cemetery H assemblage. Wheeler found Cemetery H habitation in the western portion of the high AB mound.[24] The U.S. team currently working at the site has found more. Their excavations have also produced the first radiocarbon date for the Cemetery H assemblage at 1730 B.C., nicely within the expected time range.

Documentation for the Posturban in northern Baluchistan, the Northwest Frontier, and Derajat is also not sufficient to make comparative statements with other regions of the Indus Civilization. Moreover, these regions were not securely within the Mature Harappan cultural/political system, if style and politics can be proxied one for the other. There is a lot yet to be learned here. The University of Peshawar and a team from the United Kingdom are currently working in Bannu and Dera Ismail Khan (Rehman Dheri), which should help to overcome this deficiency.

The figures in table 13.2 and the narrative that was developed here indicate that the "eclipse of the Indus Civilization" holds for the Sindhi, Kulli, and possibly the Harappa Domain, but in the Eastern and Sorath Domains, the course of cultural change was different. In these latter areas there were stronger lines of continuity through the early centuries of the second millennium without evidence for the "trauma" that effected Sindh and Baluchistan. The stark image one has for the Kulli Domain in Baluchistan in the second millennium repre-

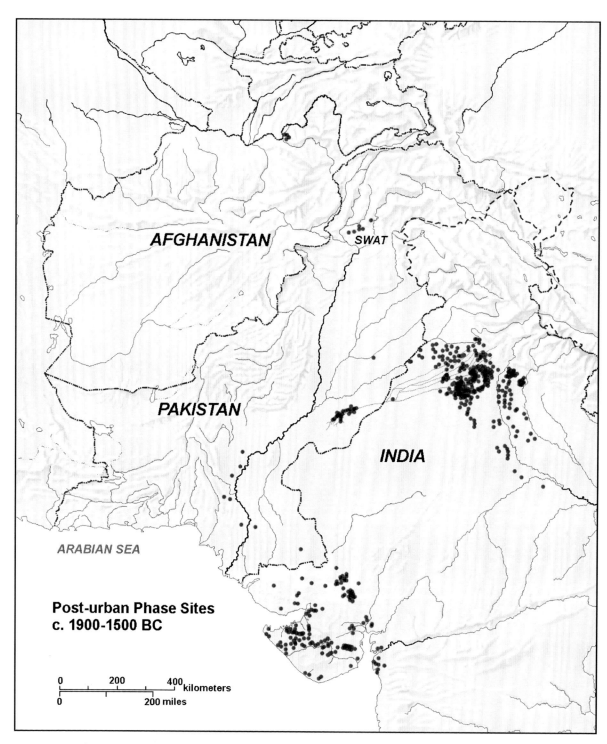

Figure 13.1   Map of sites of the Posturban Indus

sents a clear challenge for field archaeology because it would not seem reasonable to presume that the entire area was deserted at that time. Excavation and exploration are needed to give a more realistic sense of the cultural history at that time.

Archaeological exploration in the Punjab, Haryana, northern Rajasthan, and western Uttar Pradesh has produced good evidence for human habitation in these areas during the opening centuries of the second millennium B.C. These are dry-farming areas, dependent on rainfall. The exploration records indicate a dramatic increase of habitation at this time; yet this is the period of the so-called eclipse of the Indus Civilization and a period proposed to have been "arid" in this region. Lake Lunkaransar, which played a role in the "desiccation hypothesis," is approximately 90 kilometers south of the ancient Sarasvati River and therefore within, or at least on the borders of, this settlement area. The kinds of climatic changes proposed to have taken place around this body of water can be assumed to have pertained to the Punjab, Haryana, the rest of northern Rajasthan, and western Uttar Pradesh. There is an historical awkwardness here on two counts: There is a period of eclipse with a growth of human habitation; and a proposed aridity at a time when archaeological data indicate widespread dry cropping.

Another Interesting Historical Observation from Gujarat

There are other interesting things that happened at the beginning of the second millennium, to the south, in Gujarat. The story there is somewhat different from the one unfolding in the Punjab, Haryana, northern Rajasthan, and western Uttar Pradesh, but the conclusions that are emerging are similar to those reached in this chapter. There is little evidence for climatic change, let alone climatic change that led to cultural change. It is also clear that the history of the Indus Civilization in Sindh and the West Punjab at the beginning of the second millennium is different from that which took place in Gujarat, especially on the peninsula of Saurashtra. There are few signs of collapse or eclipse there, and at some places, such as Rojdi, they were busy with the expansion and rebuilding of their settlements as Mohenjo-daro was being abandoned.[25]

WHAT ACTUALLY HAPPENED IN THE TRANSFORMATION?

What archaeologists see when they examine the Greater Indus region in the early second millennium are abandoned or dysfunctional Indus cities, *wasserluxus* has vanished, and gone is the technological virtuosity of the Indus Civilization. Of the latter, Vidale and Miller note: "An important change occurs during the . . . [Posturban Harappan]. With the end of the Indus way of life, and the extinction of many typical expressions of Indus material culture, many elaborated crafts . . . are extinguished, together with the basic information technology of the urban rulers, writing."[26] The stylistic features of the Indus Civilization that were the signs and symbols of these peoples are also gone, or considerably altered: the painted pottery style, for example, and the stamp seals, writing, the distinctive Indus terra-cotta figurines, amulets, "folkloric" themes like the yogic pose, the human in the pipal tree as in the Seal of Divine Adoration. Some of the ideology was preserved in the Sorath and

Eastern Domains, but in the same attenuated form that was always present in these areas.

A THEORY FOR THE TRANSFORMATION OF THE INDUS CIVILIZATION

From these observations it is clear that the transformation of the Indus Civilization took place at its heart, the ideological core: nihilism, urbanization, *wasserluxus*, technological prowess.

The Great Bath at Mohenjo-daro was abandoned late in the history of the city, but well before the transformation. This is a unique structure elevated above and separated from the vulgar life of the city and is intimately connected with water and the "water ideology" of the Indus peoples. The abandonment of the Great Bath is therefore a moment of considerable importance, since it can be seen as the beginning of the end. Over the next two or three centuries there was a progressive deterioration of urban life and sociocultural complexity at Mohenjo-daro and in the Indus Civilization generally. The symbolic value of water fades away; brick-lined wells, the metropolitan drainage system, and bathing platforms are no longer constructed. The iconographic themes of the ideology of the Indus Civilization are slowly lost: figurines, pottery, seals, and other glyptic items. Technological innovation comes to a virtual end, and much of the Mature Harappan high technology is no longer used: baked-brick architecture, drainage systems, seal cutting, etching carnelian, drilling of long carnelian bead stoneware bangles. Some technological innovations such as bronze and faience survive, but they are in the minority.

The difficulties for nihilism to be completely successful have already been noted. Just as continuities between the Early Harappan and Mature Harappan are present, so, too, is there a legacy of the Indus Civilization in the Subcontinent. This is especially seen in the broad range of adaptations to the natural world: farming, pastoralism, house construction, and so forth. There may also be some philosophical themes that are ultimately rooted in the Indus Civilization, especially yoga and the heaven-male/earth-female duality as it relates to the creation myth of the Vedas.

In spite of these legacies, the successors to the Indus Civilization largely ridded themselves of the memory of a vast enterprise involving millions of peoples who had for several centuries been part of an immensely successful civilization. Since things like this do not happen by accident, or through inattention, I am drawn to the notion that the Indus ideology came to be seen in a terribly negative light. The Indus ideology ultimately had feet of clay. The zealots, the "true believers" of the Indus Civilization ultimately lost, perhaps not everything, but their civilization failed, not as an entire culture but as a complex society.

One of the shortcomings of my 1967 review of the Raikes/Dales hypothesis is that I came far short of offering an alternative explanation for the transformation of the Indus Civilization.[27] I did, however, suggest that the explanation was not likely to be found in natural calamities of any kind, but within the fabric of the Indus sociocultural system. That is, the fatal flaw was centrally, and most importantly, sociocultural in nature; not flood, avulsion, drought, trade, disease, locusts, invasion, or any other of a myriad of "natural" or "outside" forces. A failed Indus ideology is here proposed to be the sociocultural flaw.

Historically, the Mature Harappan is a short-term phenomenon, it lasted a mere 600 years, as opposed to Dynastic Egypt, which encompasses 3,000 years of history, or Chinese civilization, which has survived for at least as long. Because it was a short-term phenomenon from a comparative point of view, the Indus Civilization also emerges as a kind of experiment in sociocultural organization, and one that was not entirely successful.

It would be wrong to imply that the Indus Civilization was a failure from its beginning. The new ideology that these peoples brought forth made them highly successful for 600 years and spread over a vast expanse of the Subcontinent. The Indus peoples built and maintained great urban centers, conducted maritime trade with the gulf and Mesopotamia, and probably reached Africa. They were economically prosperous for their time. They enjoyed the art of writing, were successful technological innovators on a huge scale, and their iconography was integrated into the Intercultural style of the Middle Asian Interaction Sphere. These all tell us of a well-oiled sociocultural system that had created great social harmony in human relationships and with the environment.

This sense that the Indus peoples were part of a well-integrated, well-organized society has been noted before, beginning with Wheeler and his comments on the well-ordered nature of the Mature Harappan settlements, the sameness of it all, the lack of evidence for conflict, let alone warfare.[28] After all, Sir John Marshall's Harappans were peaceful, urban merchant burghers whose beliefs were harbingers of later Indian ideologies. I believe that these observers of the ancient Mature Harappan world were seeing the outcome of the successful Harappan ideology: a well-integrated, harmonic sociocultural system. But it might have been too well adapted for its own good.

One can argue, as J. C. Heesterman has,[29] that sociocultural systems with great time depth, those that have survived for millennia, rather than centuries, are characterized from their inception by an inner conflict, a lack of resolu-

tion of important sociocultural issues. It is these unresolved conflicts that provide the motive force for survival over protracted periods of time, since the peoples are in a constant state of negotiating, resolving, dealing with the maladaptation or lack of harmony in their lives. If the world stood still, the well-integrated, tightly organized sociocultural systems like the Indus Civilization would work pretty well. But the world does not stand still and sociocultural systems of this highly integrated type, which does not require constant negotiation, are vulnerable to changing conditions, both external and internal. It might take 600 years for the system to fail, but eventually the changing world catches up with them. On the other hand, sociocultural systems that lack perfect harmony, that are endowed with Heesterman's "inner conflict," where the peoples find themselves in a constant state of negotiation and the resolution of inconsistencies, even contradictions, are less vulnerable since they are continually dealing with their problems, and a constantly changing world is just one of them.

Robert McC. Adams has dealt with this same sort of sociocultural/historical issue.[30] He thinks of stability as a propensity for systems generally to return to equilibrium after a temporary disturbance. The behavioral qualities that characterize such systems are consistency, integration, and the optimization of performance. Systems of this sort tend toward rigidity and brittleness. Resilience, on the other hand, reflects a primary concern with long-term survival. Behavioral qualities that can be associated with resilient sociocultural systems are an ability to deal effectively with contingencies of many sorts and sufficient lack of integration that a certain level of disequilibrium is always present. Such sociocultural systems survive because they are able to successfully negotiate within a dynamic historical setting, a world that is constantly in flux.

Some perspective is called for at this point. First, no sociocultural system, not even the Indus Civilization, could be perfectly integrated and free of conflict, so I am using this notion in a comparative way. Second, one does not want to live in a world where there is no sociocultural integration, where there is no harmony, where there is only inconsistency and contradiction. But some lack of fit, some internal contradictions, some of Heesterman's "conflict" would seem to be good in the sense that it contributes to long-term survival; however, "too much of a good thing" of this sort can itself be counterproductive, even destructive.

We might begin to think of the Indus ideology as being their "too much of a good thing," too perfect, brought into day-to-day sociocultural reality by true believers who had the answers, at least from their point of view. There was only one good, legitimate way of doing things and that was according to the Indus ideology. This would account for the "tightness" and "sameness" that many researchers on the Indus Civilization have seen. In the end their ideology made the Indus peoples who they were, but it may have proved to be their undoing as well.

NOTES

1. Lahiri 2000 is a book where a number of papers related to this topic have been republished.
2. Wheeler 1947: 78–83.
3. Wheeler 1947: 82.
4. Allchin 1980, 1990.
5. Dales 1964; Kennedy 1982, 1994.
6. Wheeler 1959: 112.
7. Raikes and Dyson 1961: 276; Fairservis 1967: 39.
8. Lambrick 1967; Mughal 1990a.
9. Mackay 1948: 16; Dorothy Mackay 1945.
10. Sahni 1956.
11. Raikes 1964; Raikes and Dales 1986; see Possehl 1997c: 441 for additional bibliography.
12. Lambrick 1967; Possehl 1967; Agrawal 1982: 188–90; Wasson 1984, 1987.
13. Sahni 1956.
14. Stein 1942; Ghosh 1952, 1953a, and 1953b; Mughal 1997.
15. Joshi 1993.
16. Possehl 1997c: figs. 9, 10, 11, 12, 13.
17. Agrawal and Sood 1982.
18. Francfort 1986: 98, original emphasis.
19. Singh 1971; Singh et al. 1974.
20. Allchin and Allchin 1997: 206–22.
21. Allchin and Allchin 1997: 211.
22. Possehl 1996c: 139–44.
23. Allchin and Allchin 1997: 212.
24. Wheeler 1947: 70–74.
25. Possehl 1996b: 450–57.
26. Vidale and Miller 2000: 124–25.
27. Possehl 1967.
28. Wheeler 1950: 29.
29. Heesterman 1985.
30. Adams 1978.

CHAPTER 14

The Indus Civilization: An Overview

INTRODUCTION

This concluding chapter offers an opportunity to bring together some of the disparate threads of ancient India's earliest urbanization, but I am going to begin with an observation not yet made. The Indus Civilization represents the easternmost manifestation of an interregional pattern of third millennium urbanization that encompasses the Nile Valley and the lands from the Mediterranean Sea east across the Iranian Plateau to the Greater Indus region. In today's nomenclature this would be called the "Near East and northwestern South Asia." Beyond the Indus to the east, across the Thar Desert, or south into peninsular India, one enters what can be thought of as "India proper." The peoples of the Indus Civilization had contact with peoples living in these latter regions, but they are not of the Indus Age.

There are a number of themes that were developed in this book. Some of these have to do with the "myths" that have grown up around the Indus Civilization.

MYTHS ABOUT THE INDUS CIVILIZATION THAT NEED TO BE SET ASIDE IF WE ARE TO BETTER UNDERSTAND THESE ANCIENT PEOPLES AND THEIR WAYS OF LIFE

Our interpretation of the remains of the Indus Civilization has gone through two paradigms. The first of these was constructed by Sir John Marshall; the second, by Sir Mortimer Wheeler and his colleague Stuart Piggott. The current generation of archaeologists is in the midst of constructing another paradigm, or possibly several competing paradigms. This book is an effort in that direction.

The parts of the older paradigms are still found in contemporary writing on the Indus Civilization, especially in textbooks, the popular press, and works edited or written by nonexperts. Much in the older paradigms is still valid, but some of this thinking has been replaced.

The Indus Civilization Was Not Ruled by Priest-Kings

We are not certain who ruled the peoples of the Indus Civilization, but there is no reason for us to believe that it was despotic, in the oriental fashion, or that priest-kings held the balance of power. Moreover, the famous image

called the priest-king (figure 6.6) is not necessary an accurate appellation for this piece of art.

The Cities of Mohenjo-daro and Harappa Were Not Twin Capitals of a Vast Empire

Mohenjo-daro and Harappa were important places in the Indus Civilization, and it is not unreasonable to think of them as capitals. Whether there was an "Indus Empire" with an emperor, as in a king of kings, is less certain. Archaeologists are not sure what the political form of the Indus Civilization was, but a corporate form, without kings or emperors, seems reasonable.

Whatever the case, we know that they were not literally twin capitals since Dr. M. R. Mughal has found a third Indus city called Ganweriwala in Cholistan, exactly halfway between Mohenjo-daro and Harappa.[1] We also consider Dholavira and Rakhigarhi Indus cities. There are not just two Indus cities, but five, at least.

The High Mounds at Mohenjo-daro and Harappa, as Well as Other Places, Were Not Citadels

Indus sites often have elevated areas in them: a sort of ancient Indian acropolis. This is true for Mohenjo-daro, Harappa, Kalibangan, Dholavira, and to an extent, Lothal. At some places the entire site is an elevation (e.g., Surkotada). These elevations are not necessarily to the west as at Mohenjo-daro. At Lothal it is in the southeastern quadrant of the site. There is no consistency in the Indus town planner's use of elevation as a part of civic design.

Citadels are places of defense and refuge in times of conflict. The elevated area at Mohenjo-daro was not fortified so much as it was constructed with a retaining wall to contain the earth used to create an elevated symbolic landscape to raise the Great Bath, Warehouse, and other large buildings built atop it.

The Indus Cities Did Not Have Civic Granaries

Whatever the buildings often called "granaries" at Mohenjo-daro and Harappa may have been, there is no evidence that they were actually grain-storage facilities. The building on the Mound of the Great Bath at Mohenjo-daro seems to have been a Warehouse. The use of the one at Harappa is more obscure, but it, too, could have been a warehouse.

The Indus Cities Were Not Planned with a Grid Layout

Close inspection of the Mohenjo-daro grid town plan is presented in chapter 5 of this book. It demonstrates that there is so much missing and contradictory information about this feature of the city that it is impossible to say for sure that it was laid out in a grid fashion. There is no evidence for a grid town plan at Harappa, Chanhu-daro, Banawali, and almost all other Indus sites.

The Indus Was Not a Civilization of Brick Cities

In fact, Mohenjo-daro is the only city of baked brick within the Indus Civilization. There is a fair amount of baked brick at Harappa, but it may not be the predominant building material. Chanhu-daro, too, has much baked brick, but it is much smaller than Mohenjo-daro. There is literally no baked brick at many sites, and trivial amounts at others. Some of the sites that would fit this description are prominent places such as Dholavira, Lothal, Surkotada, Allahdino, Bala Kot, Sutkagen-dor, Rojdi, Amri, Banawali.

The Remains of the Indus Peoples Are Not Boring and Monotonous

One of the most successful and important successes of the "new archaeology" of the Indus Civilization has been putting to rest that notion that the remains of the Indus peoples were monotonous and boring, the same wherever they are found. In fact, there is a rich variety of Indus material and a diversity of peoples who made them. The notion of domains is a result of the efforts to document the diversity of the Indus Civilization.

The Peoples of the Indus Civilization Were Not Necessarily All Dark-Skinned Dravidians

We do not know the skin color of the Indus peoples, or the Vedic Aryans, for that matter. That some of them may have been dark skinned is possible, given the hot tropical environment and the protection that dark skin offers from the sun. But there was probably a mix of skin colors, along with head shape, hair texture, and other phenotypic features of human biology.

The Indus Peoples Did Not Necessarily Speak a Proto-Dravidian Language, and That Is Not Necessarily the Language of Its Writing System

We do not know which language families were represented among the Indus peoples, let alone the specific languages that they spoke. Archaeology unaided by texts makes an assessment of this issue very difficult. The inference concerning the ethnic complexity of the Indus peoples is supported by the diversity of archaeological remains and indicators from physical anthropology. That many peoples would have spoken many languages is a reasonable inference.

One or more of the languages spoken by the peoples of the Indus Age may have been some early form of a Dravidian language. This makes good sense since the modern Dravidian languages are so close to the Greater Indus region. Brahui, in fact, is within it.

There are other choices for languages as well. One or more of the languages of the peoples of the Indus Age could have been from a very ancient language family called "Proto-Elamo-Dravidian."[2] Early forms of languages like Munda or the Altaic group might also fit as possible languages spoken by the peoples of the Indus Age. Of course, we have to also admit that one or more of the languages of the peoples of the Indus Age are long lost to the modern world, dead as the individuals who would have spoken them.

The real point is that we just do not know the languages of the peoples of the Indus Age. And equally important, it is, in my opinion, a virtual impossibility that there was only one language; surely there were many, and probably from different language families. And given the historical dynamics of the Indus Age, the languages spoken within the Greater Indus region changed, from season to season, year to year, century to century. There was much movement of peoples and ideas during the Indus Age and that would have meant that the language dimension of history was dynamic as well.

There may have been a lingua franca for the peoples of the Indus Age to give common ground to daily life, commerce, politics, and the like. If the script of the Indus peoples turns out to render one language into written form, this language would be a good candidate for the lingua franca, a tongue that was common among the diversity of Indus peoples, helping to unite their diverse cultures on at least this dimension.

The Indus Writing System Has Not Been Deciphered

In spite of many claims to the contrary, the Indus writing system has not yet been proved to be deciphered.[3] While one should be hopeful about eventually reading the Indus script, there are many problems to be surmounted, and the job will not be easy. The three most significant of these problems are (1) we do not know the language, or even the language family of the script; (2) the inscriptions are very short, about five characters on the average. Such short messages make decipherment inherently difficult; (3) there is no agreed-upon sign list, so the task of deciding just what should be deciphered has not yet been settled.

Invading Indo-Europeans Did Not Destroy the Indus Civilization

I believe from linguistic evidence that the homeland of the Indo-European peoples was somewhere in the temperate forest regions of Eurasia, so they came to the Subcontinent from somewhere else. When the speakers of an Indo-European language(s) first came to the Subcontinent is not known. They first appear in the Near East just after 2000 B.C., but this is from linguistic evidence and they could have been there much before this, as would be the case for the Subcontinent. I am in agreement with F. Allchin that there could have been Indo-European–speaking peoples in the Greater Indus region at the time of the Indus Civilization. It is unlikely that they were speakers of Vedic Sanskrit, and it is therefore also doubtful that they were Aryans, since that is what the speakers of Vedic Sanskrit called themselves. When the speakers of Vedic Sanskrit came to the Subcontinent is also obscure, but their great book, the Rgveda, dates to about 1000 B.C.

The sometimes vivid description of life in the Punjab given in the Rgveda at about 1000 B.C. informs us of people who were organized in lineages (tribes), with leaders, ritual specialists, and the common people. They were cattle pastoralists who undertook some cultivation, mostly of barley. The Rgveda includes many battles. Early interpreters of these events thought that they could be taken as evidence for a military invasion of the Subcontinent, using the bodies in the upper strata of Mohenjo-daro as archaeological evidence that they sacked the Indus Civilization. But this is incorrect. The battles were simply a part of life in the ancient Punjab during the Early Iron Age, almost a millennium after the transformation of the Indus Civilization. Moreover, Sindh is a distant land in Rgveda, not the central region it was in Indus times.

In fact, the Rgveda does not contain the story (or even a hint) of the Aryan journey to the Punjab. No one knows for sure when the Indo-Europeans who spoke Vedic Sanskrit came to the Subcontinent, or how they got there. Speakers of other Indo-European languages were in the Near East early in the second millennium, and this may approximate the date of the Aryans into the Subcontinent. But there is no evidence for an invasion, and most contemporary scholars who deal with this issue think more in terms of the movement that characterizes cattle pastoralists because of their need for pastureland, than military conquest. Moreover, the Aryans may have come to the Punjab over a long period of time (a matter of centuries), not in a great rush, as an invasion would suggest.

DEEP HISTORY OF "INDEPENDENT" FOOD PRODUCTION

The Indus Civilization rests on a deep history of food production, now well documented at Mehrgarh. The old idea about the food production "revolution" held that diffusion across the Iranian Plateau was the mechanism that brought farming and pastoralism to the Subcontinent. The new ideas on the beginning of food production there rest on the observations that all of the early domesticates found at Mehrgarh, except for wheat, are found in their wild state in Pakistani Baluchistan and adjacent uplands. Costantini and Biasini make the important point that this environment shares important features with the old "Neolithic nuclear zone" of the Near East.[4] While wild wheat has not been documented there, there has been a good deal of environmental degradation over the past 10,000 years, and there is good, if speculative, thought that this missing plant was a part of the ancient environment. This position is bolstered by quite certain observations that domestication of animals took place in the Indus region.

THE BEGINNINGS OF URBANIZATION AND THE INDUS IDEOLOGY

The Indus Civilization, as well as Mesopotamia and Dynastic Egypt, were made possible because of the productive vigor of sheep, goats, cattle, wheat, and barley. There is at least 5,000 years of cultural development that separates the Indus Civilization from the beginnings of farming and herding in the Greater Indus region. This period of gestation is characterized by gradualist change, except at two points. The first is the time that marks the beginnings of Mehrgarh III, the Togau Phase, which is a period of considerable technological change and may mark the introduction of one or more new human populations into the Mehrgarh gene pool. The next moment of punctuated equilibrium in the history of the Indus Civilization is in the middle of the third millennium, with the Early Harappan–Mature Harappan Transition.

Many of the archaeologists working on the Indus Civilization have recognized that the Mature Harappan is preceded by a relatively short period of rapid cultural change. This is what I have come to call the Early Harappan–Mature Harappan Transition, first defined at Amri by Jean-Marie Casal in 1964.[5] It is a tribute to him to have made this important observation before so many other of the archaeologists working on the Indus Civilization. The Early Harappan–Mature Harappan Transition was the period during which the features of the Indus Civilization that most clearly define it, the Indus ideology, were developed from the four regional "cultures" of the Early Harappan. This is the "fusion" that Shaffer and Lichtenstein speak.[6] Based on the stratigraphy of Amri and Naushaco, as well as the radiocarbon dates available, this transition was on the order of 100 to 150 years. From the perspective of an archaeological chronology, this would be quite short, within the standard deviation of many radiocarbon dates. But it is still three or four generations, and that is not "instantaneous."

Wheeler used a suite of artifacts to define the Indus Civilization.[7] This included the S-form jar, pointed-base goblet, beaker, knobbed ware, and the like. While this definition was a reasonable one for its time, I have attempted to define the Indus Civilization in terms of its ideology proxied by urbanization, nihilism, technology and technological innovation, and water in terms of symbolic and physical cleanliness.

I think of Mohenjo-daro as a representation of this ideology, par excellence. This city was where the Indus ideology was epitomized. Some other centers with very strong expressions of Indus ideology would be Harappa, Chanhu-daro, Kalibangan, and probably Naushaco and Dholavira. The Mature Harappan sites in the Cholistan Domain are also probably included here, but we will have to await excavation there to know for sure. The Indus ideology is expressed in some form at all of the 1,052 Mature Harappan sites.[8] But there are differences among them, as with the Kullis, for example. There is an attenuation of the Indus ideology as one moves from Sindh into Saurashtra and the South Gujarat coast, away from the strong, clear expression at Mohenjo-daro. The peoples of the Sorath Harappan were involved with the Indus ideology, but in their own way, somewhat differently, attenuated if measured against the scale of Sindh. They have their own character, possibly even their own ideology, a syncretic blend of the Indus and their own view of the world. The same quality of Indus ideology characterizes the peoples of the Eastern Domain. The syncretic expression is clearly different from the Sorath Harappan, but the peoples of the Eastern Domain are not "mainline" Harappans out of the Mohenjo-daro mold. They participated in the Indus ideology, but in their own way, with local traditions brought in as a part of their way of life.

There are even peoples contemporary with the Mature Harappans who preserved the material culture of the Kot Dijian Early Harappan. These are the so-called Late Kot Dijians of the Derajat and Potwar Plateau. They seem to represent peoples who did not buy into the Indus ideology and stayed with the older lifeways of Kot Dijian times.

THE TRANSFORMATION OF THE INDUS CIVILIZATION

The transformation of the Indus Civilization took place at the heart of the ideology. It is clearest at the urban sites and had less of an impact on the lives of the farmers and herders in the countryside, especially the Eastern and Sorath Domains, those domains most removed from the ideological centers.

J. P. Joshi's explorations of the Indian Punjab and his excavations at Bhagwanpura and Dadheri have demonstrated that the peoples of the Posturban Stage in this area persist to just before 1000 B.C., and he can document the development of the Painted Gray Ware out of the Bronze Age ceramic technology. He calls this period of change an "overlap."[9] So, in the Indian Punjab we have a complete cultural historical sequence that documents the times during which the Indus Civilization flourished on to the Early Iron Age, represented by the Painted Gray Ware, into historical India. There are both Cemetery H and Painted Gray Ware sites in Cholistan. Well-conceived and -conducted fieldwork might provide us with the same story there.

The Sorath Domain presents us with a gap between the end of the Indus cultural tradition and the Early Iron Age beginnings of history. The end of the Late Sorath Harappan sequence is associated with Lustrous Red Ware, which disappears at about 1500 B.C. There are no sites that are known between this point and the appearance of Northern Black Polished Ware in the second or third century B.C. Having worked in this area, I believe there are sites that fill this gap and have one or two good candidate sites in mind for excavation. But, once again, the proof is in the excavation, and this problem presents younger archaeologists with an opportunity to undertake sound, productive fieldwork.

The descendents of the Indus Civilization in northern India flow gracefully into the peoples of the Early Historic there. And there are important continuities in the life of the peoples of historical India that can be traced back to the Indus Civilization, even earlier. Much of the subsistence system, including the "second revolution" in farming made possible by the large-scale use of millets and double cropping, has very deep roots. Elements of architecture, settlement planning, and location are also based on concepts that began during the Indus Age. There are other potentially important observations as well. For example, the form of ritual discipline we now know as yoga may be represented in an early form in the Indus Civilization.[10] The most famous of these is the so-called Proto-Siva seal. Allchin has also pointed to a seal from Chanhu-daro that seems to represent the theme of male-heaven and female-earth (Mother India) as related to the creation myth found in Vedic literature.[11]

This brings us face to face with one of the great challenges of South Asian archaeology: understanding the Vedic literature and the rise of the second urbanization in the Subcontinent. Unlike the Indus Civilization, ancient India saw the creation of an enduring configuration of human organization. This is represented in many ways: social organization, a complex interweaving of philosophy and practical knowledge, concepts of history, kingship, politics, and power. It is this distinct configuration of social organization, philosophy, and values that gives ancient India and Pakistan their place in human history and makes them worthy of our understanding.

NOTES

1. Mughal 1990b.
2. McAlpin 1981.
3. Possehl 1996b has a review of this material.
4. Costantini and Biasini 1985: 16–17.
5. Casal 1964: 39–43.
6. Shaffer and Lichtenstein 1989: 123.
7. Wheeler 1968: 63.
8. Possehl 1999b: 727–835.
9. Joshi 1993.
10. McEvilley 1981.
11. Allchin 1985.

References

Adams, R. M. 1978. Strategies of maximization, stability and resilience in Mesopotamian society, settlement and agriculture. *Proceedings of the American Philosophical Society* 122(5):329–35.

———. 1992. Ideologies: Unity and diversity. In *Ideology and pre-Columbian civilizations*, edited by A. A. Demarest and G. W. Conrad, pp. 205–21. School of American Research Press, Santa Fe.

Agrawal, D. P. 1982. *The archaeology of India.* Scandinavian Institute of Asian Studies Monograph Series No. 46, Copenhagen.

———. 2000. *Ancient metal technology and archaeology of South Asia: A pan-Asian perspective.* Aryan Books International, Delhi.

Agrawal, D. P. and R. K. Sood. 1982. Ecological factors and the Harappan Civilization. In *Harappan Civilization: A contemporary perspective*, edited by G. L. Possehl, pp. 223–31. Oxford & IBH and the American Institute of Indian Studies, Delhi.

Aitken, E. H. 1907. *Gazetteer of the province of Sind.* Government of Bombay, Karachi.

Allchin, B. and F. R. Allchin. 1982. *The rise of civilization in India and Pakistan.* Cambridge University Press, Cambridge.

———. 1997. *Origins of a civilization: The prehistory and early archaeology of South Asia.* Viking, New Delhi.

Allchin, F. R. 1980. Archaeological and language historical evidence for the movement of Indo-Aryan-speaking peoples into India and Pakistan. *Journal of the K. R. Cama Oriental Institute* 48:68–102.

———. 1985. The interpretation of a seal from Chanhu-daro and its significance for the religion of the Indus Valley. In *South Asian archaeology 1983*, edited by J. Schotsmans and M. Taddei, pp. 369–84. Instituto Universitario Orientale, Dipartimento di Studi Asiatici, Series Minor 23, Naples.

———. 1990. Indo-Aryan and Aryan: Language, culture and ethnicity. *Ancient Ceylon* 10:13–23.

———. 1992. An Indus ram: A hitherto unrecorded stone sculpture from the Indus Civilization. *South Asian Studies* 8:53–54.

Allchin, F. R. and R. Knox. 1981. Preliminary report on the excavations at Lewan, 1977–78. In *South Asian archaeology 1979*, edited by H. Hartel, pp. 241–44. Dietrich Reimer Verlag, Berlin.

Allchin, F. R., B. Allchin, F. A. Durrani, and M. F. Khan. 1986. *Lewan and the Bannu basin: Excavation and survey of sites and environments in northwest Pakistan.* British Archaeological Reports, International Series, no. 310.

Amiet, P. 1974. Antiquites du desert de Lut, I: A propos d'objets de la collection Foroughi. *Revue d'Assyriologie et d'Archeologie Orientale* 68(2):97–110.

———. 1986. *L'Age Des Exchanges Interiraniens, 3500–1700 avant J.-C.* Notes et Documents des Musées de France, Paris.

Ardeleanu-Jansen, A. 1984. Stone sculptures from Mohenjo-daro. In *Reports on field work carried out at Mohenjo-daro, Pakistan 1982–83 by the IsMEO–Aachen University Mission*, edited by M. Jansen and G. Urban, pp. 139–57. Interim Reports, vol. 1. RWTH/IsMEO, Aachen/Rome.

———. 1987. The theriomorphic stone sculpture from Mohenjo-daro reconsidered. *Reports on field work carried out at Mohenjo-daro, Pakistan, 1983–84.* ed. M. Jansen and G. Urban, pp. 59–68. RWTH/IsMEO, Aachen/Rome.

———. 1991. The sculptural art of the Harappa culture. In *Forgotten cities on the Indus: Early civilization in Pakistan from the 8th to the 2nd millennium B.C.*, edited by M. Jansen, M. Mulloy, and G. Urban, pp. 167–78. Verlag Philipp von Zabern, Mainz.

———. 1993. Who fell in the well? Digging up a well in Mohenjo-daro. In *South Asian archaeology 1991*, edited by A. J. Gail and G. J. R. Mevissen, pp. 1–15. Franz Steiner Verlag, Stuttgart.

Ardeleanu-Jansen, A., U. Franke, and M. Jansen. 1983. An approach toward the replacement of artifacts into the architectural context of the Great Bath at Mohenjo-daro. In *Forschungsprojekt DFG Mohenjodaro*, edited by G. Urban and M. Jansen, pp. 43–69. Reinische-Westfalischen Technischen Hockschule, Aachen.

Arne, T. J. 1945. *Excavations at Shah Tepe, Iran.* Sino-Swedish Expedition Publication, 27, VII, 5, Stockholm.

Atre, S. 1987. *The archetypical mother: A systematic approach to Harappan religion.* Ravish Publishers, Pune.

Balfour, E., ed. 1885. *The cyclopaedia of India: And of Eastern and Southern Asia, commercial, industrial and scientific.* Bernard Quaritch, London.

Barth, F. 1969. *Ethnic groups and boundaries: The social organization of cultural differences.* Little Brown, Boston.

Bar-Yosef, O. and A. Belfer-Cohen. 1989. The origins of sedentism and farming communities in the Levant. *Journal of World Prehistory* 3(4):447–98.

Bar-Yosef, O. and R. H. Meadow. 1995. The origins of agriculture in the Near East. In *Last hunters, first farmers: New perspectives on the prehistoric transition to agriculture*, edited by T. D. Price and A. B. Gebauer, pp. 39–95. School of American Research, Santa Fe.

Basaglia, P. 1977. *La Città Bruciata del Deserto Salato.* Erizzo, Venezia.

Basham, A. L. 1967. *The wonder that was India.* 3d ed. Taplinger Publishing Company, New York.

Belcher, W. R. 1991. Fish resources in an early urban context at Harappa. In *Harappa excavations 1986–1990: A multidisciplinary approach to third millennium urbanization*, edited by

R. H. Meadow, pp. 107–20. Prehistory Press, Monographs in World Archaeology, no. 3, Madison.

———. 1994. Riverine fisheries and habitat exploitation of the Indus Valley tradition: An example from Harappa, Pakistan. In *South Asian archaeology 1993*, edited by A. Parpola and P. Koskikallio, pp. 71–80. Annales Academiae Scientiarum Fennicae, series B, vol. 271, 2 vols, Helsinki.

Bhan, S. 1975. *Excavation at Mitathal (1968) and other explorations in the Sutlej-Yamuna Divide*. Kurukshetra University, Kurukshetra, India.

Bhan, K. K. and J. M. Kenoyer. 1984. Nageswara: A Mature Harappan shell working site on the Gulf of Kutch. *Journal of the Oriental Institute, Maharaja Sayajirao University of Baroda* 341–2:67–80.

Bisht, R. S. 1982. Excavations at Banawali: 1974–77. In *Harappan Civilization: A contemporary perspective*, edited by G. L. Possehl, pp. 113–24. Oxford & IBH and the American Institute of Indian Studies, Delhi.

———. 1991. Dholavira: A new horizon of the Indus Civilization. *Puratattva* 20:71–82.

———. 1999. Dholavira and Banawali: Two different paradigms of the Harappan urbis forma. *Puratattva* 29:14–37.

Blackman, J. M. and M. Vidale. 1992. The production and distribution of stoneware bangles at Mohenjo-daro and Harappa as monitored by chemical characterization studies. In *South Asian archaeology 1989*, edited by C. Jarrige, pp. 37–44. Prehistory Press, Monographs in World Archaeology, no. 14, Madison.

Blackman, J. M., S. Mery, and R. Wright. 1989. Production and exchange of ceramics on the Oman Peninsula from the perspective of Hili. *Journal of Field Archaeology* 16:61–77.

Blanton, R. E., G. Feinman, S. A. Kowalewski, and P. N. Peregrin. 1996. A dual-processual theory for the evolution of Mesoamerican civilization. *Current Anthropology* 37:1–14.

Bokonyi, S. 1985. Preliminary results of a thorough evaluation of the mammal bone material from Shahr-i Sokhta. *East and West* 35(4):426–29.

———. 1997 Horse remains from the prehistoric site of Surkotada, Kutch, late 3rd millennium B.C. *South Asian Studies* 13:297–307.

Braidwood, R. J. 1975. *Prehistoric men*. 8th ed. Scott-Foresman and Company, New York.

Carter, R. A. In press. Saar and its external relations: New evidence for interaction between Bahrain and Gujarat in the early 2nd millennium B.C. *Arabian Art and Archaeology* 12(1).

Casal, J.-M. 1961. *Fouilles de Mundigak*. Memoires de la Delegation Archaeologique Français en Afghanistan, tome 17, 2 vols. Paris.

———. 1964. *Fouilles d'Amri*. 2 vols. Publications de la Commission des Fouilles Archaeologiques, Fouilles du Pakistan, Paris.

Chakrabarti, D. K. 1978. Reserved slip ware in the Harappan context. *Puratattva* 8:158–64.

———. 1982. "Long barrel-cylinder" beads and the issue of pre-Sargonic contact between the Harappan Civilization and Mesopotamia. In *Harappan Civilization: A contemporary perspective*, edited by G. L. Possehl, pp. 265–70. Oxford & IBH and the American Institute of Indian Studies, Delhi.

———. 1988. *A history of Indian archaeology: From the beginning to 1947*. Munshiram Manoharlal, Delhi.

Chakrabarti, D. K. and P. Moghadam 1977. Some unpublished Indus beads from Iran. *Iran* 15:192–94.

Chakravarty, K. K., V. S. Wakankar, and M. D. Khare. 1989. *Dangawada excavations*. Commissioner of Archaeology and Museums, Bhopal.

Childe, V. G. 1934. *New light on the most ancient East: The Oriental prelude to European prehistory*. Kegan Paul, Trench, Trubner & Company, London.

———. 1950. The urban revolution. *Town Planning Review* 21:3–17.

———. 1953. *New light on the most ancient East*. Frederick A. Praeger, American printing of the 3d ed. New York.

Claessen, H. J. M. and J. G. Oosten. 1996a. Introduction. In *Ideology and the formation of early states*, edited by H. J. M. Claessen and J. G. Oosten, pp. 1–23. Studies in Human Society, vol. 11. E. J. Brill, Leiden.

———, eds., 1996b. *Ideology and the formation of early states*. E. J. Brill, Leiden.

Cleuziou, S. 1982. Hili and the beginnings of oasis life in eastern Arabia. *Proceedings of the Seminar for Arabian Studies* 12:15–22.

———. 1986. Dilmun and Makkan during the third and early second millennia B.C. In *Bahrain through the ages, the archaeology*, edited by S. H. A. A. Khalifa and M. Rice, pp. 143–58. KPI Limited, New York.

Cleuziou, S. and M. Tosi. 1994. Black boats of Magan: Some thoughts on Bronze Age water transport in Oman and beyond from the impressed bitumen slabs of Ras al-Junayz. In *South Asian archaeology 1993*, edited by A. Parpola and P. Koskikallio, pp. 745–61. Annales Academiae Scientiarum Fennicae, series B, vol. 271, 2 vols. Helsinki.

Collon, D. 1996. Mesopotamia and the Indus: The evidence of the seals. In *The Indian Ocean in antiquity*, edited by J. Reade, pp. 209–25. Kegan Paul International in association with the British Museum, London.

Cooke, S. B. and S. E. Aschenbrenner. 1975. The occurrence of metallic iron in ancient copper. *Journal of Field Archaeology* 2(3):251–66.

Costantini, L. and L. C. Biasini. 1985. Agriculture in Baluchistan between the 7th and 3rd millennium B.C. *Newsletter of Baluchistan Studies* 2:16–30.

Crawford, H. E. W. 1973. Mesopotamia's invisible trade in the third millennium B.C. *World Archaeology* 5(2):232–41.

Cucarzi, M. 1984. Geophysical investigations at Moenjo-daro. In *Reports on field work carried out at Mohenjo-daro, Pakistan 1982–83 by the IsMEO–Aachen University Mission*, edited by

M. Jansen and G. Urban, pp. 191–200. Interim Reports, vol. 1. RWTH/IsMEO, Aachen/Rome.

———. 1987. A model of morphogenesis for Mohenjo-daro. In *Reports on field work carried out at Mohenjo-daro, Pakistan, 1983–84*, edited by M. Jansen and G. Urban, pp. 79–90. Interim Reports, vol. 2. RWTH/IsMEO, Aachen/Rome.

Cunningham, A. 1875. Harappa. *Annual Report of the Archaeological Survey of India* 5:105–8.

Dales, G. F. 1964. The mythical massacre at Mohenjo-daro. *Expedition* 6(3):36–43.

———. 1968a. Of dice and men. In *Essays in memory of E. A. Speiser*, edited by W. W. Hallo. *Journal of the American Oriental Society* 88(1):14–23.

———. 1968b. Mohenjodaro. *Pakistan Archaeology* 5:56–62.

———. 1977. Hissar III objects in Afghan Seistan. *Mountains and lowlands: Essays in the archaeology of greater Mesopotamia*, ed. L. Levine and T. C. Young, pp. 17–27. Undena Publications, Malibu.

———. 1979. The Balakot project: Summary of four years of excavations in Pakistan. *Man and Environment* 3:45–53.

———. 1982. Mohenjodaro miscellany: Some unpublished, forgotten or misinterpreted features. *Harappan Civilization: A contemporary perspective*, ed. Gregory L. Possehl, pp. 97–106. Oxford & IBH and the American Institute of Indian Studies, Delhi.

Dales, G. F. and J. M. Kenoyer. 1986. *Excavations at Mohenjo-Daro, Pakistan: The pottery*. The University Museum, University of Pennsylvania, Philadelphia.

Dales, G. F. and C. P. Lipo. 1992. *Explorations on the Makran coast, Pakistan: A search for paradise*. Contributions of the Archaeological Research Faculty, University of California, no. 50, Berkeley.

Dales, G. F., J. M. Kenoyer, and staff. 1991. Summaries of five seasons of research at Harappa (District Sahiwal, Punjab, Pakistan), 1986–1990. In *Harappa excavations 1986–1990: A multidisciplinary approach to third millennium urbanism*, edited by R. H. Meadow, pp. 185–262. Prehistory Press, Monographs in World Archaeology, no. 3, Madison.

Dames, M. L. 1886. Old seals found at Harappa. *The Indian Antiquary* 15:1.

Dani, A. H. 1950. Hariyupiya in the Rigveda. *Varendra Research Society Monographs* 8:17–24.

———. 1963. *Indian palaeography*. At the Clarendon Press, Oxford.

———. 1970–71. Excavations in the Gomal Valley. *Ancient Pakistan* 5:1–177.

Datta, A. 1998. Iron technology at the Chalcolithic Phase of West Bengal. In *Archaeometallurgy in India*, edited by V. Tirpathi, pp. 36–43. Sharada Publishing House, Delhi.

de Genouillac, H. 1930. Rapport sur les traveaux de la mission de Tello (IIè campagne 1929–30). *Revue D'assyriologie et D'archéologie Orientale* 27(4):169–86.

Demarest, A. A. 1992. Archaeology, ideology and pre-Columbian cultural evolution: The search for an approach. In *Ideology and pre-Columbian civilizations*, edited by A. A. Demarest and G. W. Conrad, pp. 1–14. School of American Research Press, Santa Fe.

Demarest, A. A. and G. W. Conrad, eds. 1992. *Ideology and pre-Columbian civilizations*. School of American Research Press, Santa Fe.

de Mecquenem, R. 1943. *Fouilles de Suse, 1933–1939: Suse, Tepe Bouhallan, Tepe Zohab*. Mémoires de la Delegation Archéologique Française en Perse, 29, Paris.

Dikshit, K. N. 1924–25. Explorations, Western Circle, Sind, Mohenjo-daro. *Annual Report of the Archaeological Survey of India, 1924–25*, pp. 63–73.

———. 1925–26. Exploration, Western Circle, Upper Sind Frontier district. *Annual Report of the Archaeological Survey of India, 1925–26*, pp. 98–100.

———. 1984. The Harappan levels at Hulas. *Man and Environment* 8:99–102.

Dupree, L., ed. 1972. Prehistoric research in Afghanistan (1959–1966). *Transactions of the American Philosophical Society* 62(4).

Dupree, L., P. Gouin, and N. Omer. 1971. The Kosh Tapa hoard from north Afghanistan. *Afghanistan* 24(1):44–54.

During Caspers, E. C. L. 1972. *Etched Carnelian Beads*. Bulletin no. 10, Institute of Archaeology, University College, London.

———. 1973a. De handelsbetrekkingen van de Indus-beschaving in de 'Perzische Golf' in het IIIe mill. v. Chr. *Phoenix* 19:214–66.

———. 1973b. Sumer and Kulli meet at Dilmun in the Arabian Gulf. *Archiv Für Orientforschung* 24:128–32.

———. 1987. Was the dancing girl from Moenjo-daro a Nubian? *Annali dell'Instituto Orientale di Napoli* 47(1):99–105.

Durrani, F. A. 1988. Excavations in the Gomal Valley: Rehman Dheri excavation report, no. 1. *Ancient Pakistan* 6:1–204.

Dutta, P. C. 1983. *The Bronze Age Harappans: A bio-anthropological study of the skeletons discovered at Harappa*. Anthropological Survey of India, Calcutta.

Edens, C. 1993. Indus-Arabian interaction during the Bronze Age: A review of the evidence. In *Harappan Civilization: A recent perspective*, 2d ed., edited by G. L. Possehl, pp. 335–63. Oxford & IBH and the American Institute of Indian Studies, Delhi.

Ehrenriech, R. M., C. M. Crumley, and J. Levy, eds. 1995. *Heterarchy and the analysis of complex societies*. American Anthropological Association, Arlington.

Fairservis, W. A. 1956. *Excavations in the Quetta Valley, West Pakistan*. Anthropological Papers of the American Museum of Natural History, New York, 45(2).

———. 1959. *Archaeological surveys in the Zhob and Loralai districts, West Pakistan*. Anthropological Papers of the American Museum of Natural History, New York, 47(2).

———. 1961. The Harappan Civilization: New evidence and more theory. *Novitates*, no. 2055.

———. 1967. The origin, character and decline of an early civilization. *Novitates*, no. 2302.

———. 1975. *Roots of ancient India.* 2d ed. University of Chicago Press, Chicago.

———. 1976. *Excavations at the Harappan site of Allahdino: The seals and other inscribed material.* Papers of the Allahdino Expedition, no. 1, New York.

———. 1986. Cattle and the Harappan chiefdoms of the Indus Valley. *Expedition* 28(2):43–50.

———. 1992. *The Harappan Civilization and its writing: A model for the decipherment of the Indus script.* Oxford & IBH, Delhi.

Flam, L. 1981. *The Palaeogeography and prehistoric settlement patterns in Sind, Pakistan (4000–2000 B.C.).* PhD. diss., University of Pennsylvania, Philadelphia.

———. 1984. Palaeogeography and prehistoric settlement patterns of the lower Indus Valley, Sind, Pakistan. In *Studies in the archaeology and palaeoanthropology of South Asia,* edited by K. A. R. Kennedy and G. L. Possehl, pp. 77–87. Oxford & IBH and the American Institute of Indian Studies, Delhi.

———. 1993. Excavations at Ghazi Shah, Sindh, Pakistan. In *Harappan Civilization: A recent perspective,* 2d ed., edited by G. L. Possehl, pp. 457–67. Oxford & IBH and the American Institute of Indian Studies, Delhi.

———. 1999. Ecology and population mobility in the prehistoric settlement of the lower Indus Valley, Sindh, Pakistan. In *The Indus River: Biodiversity, resources, humankind,* edited by A. Meadows and P. S. Meadows, pp. 313–23. Oxford University Press, Karachi.

Flannery, K. V. 1995. Prehistoric social evolution. In *Research frontiers in anthropology,* pp. 1–26. Prentice Hall, Englewood Cliffs, N.J.

Fleet, J. F. 1912. Seals from Harappa. *Journal of the Royal Asiatic Society of Great Britain and Ireland,* pp. 698–701.

Francfort, H.-P. 1986. Preliminary report (1983–1984): Archaeological and environmental researches in the Ghaggar (Saraswati) Plains. *Man and Environment* 10:97–100.

———. 1989. *Fouilles de Shortughai: Recherches sur l'Asie Centrale Protohistorique.* 2 vols. Diffusion de Boccard, Paris.

Franke-Vogt, U. 1989. Inscribed bangles: An inquiry into their relevance. In *South Asian archaeology 1985,* edited by K. Frifelt and P. Sorensen, pp. 237–46. Curzon Press, Scandinavian Institute of Asian Studies, Occasional Papers no. 4, London.

———. 1991. *Die Glyptik Aus Mohenjo-Daro: Uniformitat und Variabilitat in der Induskultur, Untersuchungen zur Typologie, Ikonographie und raumlichen Verteilung.* 2 vols. Verlag Philipp von Zabern, Mainz.

———. 1992. Inscribed objects from Mohenjo-daro: Some remarks on stylistic variability and distribution patterns. In *South Asian archaeology 1989,* edited by C. Jarrige, pp. 103–12. Prehistory Press, Monographs in World Archaeology, no. 14, Madison.

Frankfort, H. 1933. *Tell Asmar, Khafaje and Khorsabad: Second preliminary report of the Iraq expedition.* The Oriental Institute of the University of Chicago, Studies in Ancient Oriental Civilization, no. 16, Chicago.

———. 1936. A new site in Mesopotamia: Tell Agrab, temples deserted 5000 years ago and a wealth of art relics, including fresh proof of Indo-Sumerian cultural association. *Illustrated London News,* September 12, pp. 432–36.

———. 1956. *The art and architecture of the ancient Orient.* Penguin History of Art, Baltimore.

Gadd, C. J. 1931. Sign-list of early Indus script: Part I. Some external features of writing. In *Mohenjo-daro and the Indus Civilization,* edited by J. Marshall, pp. 406–14. 3 vols. Arthur Probsthain, London.

———. 1932. Seals of ancient Indian style found at Ur. *Proceedings of the British Academy* 18:191–210.

Geddes, D. S. 1983. Neolithic transhumance in the Mediterranean Pyrenees. *World Archaeology* 15(1):51–66.

Ghosh, A. 1952. The Rajputana desert: Its archaeological aspect. *Bulletin of the National Institute of Sciences in India* 1:37–42.

———. 1953a. Exploration in Bikanir. *East and West* 4(1):31–34.

———. 1953b. Fifty years of the Archaeological Survey of India. *Ancient India* 9:29–52.

———. 1962. The archaeological background. In *Human skeletal remains from Harappa,* edited by P. Gupta, P. C. Dutta, and A. Basu, pp. 1–5. *Memoirs of the Anthropological Survey of India,* no. 9, Calcutta.

———. 1965. The Indus Civilization: Its origins, authors, extent and chronology. In *Indian prehistory: 1964,* edited by V. N. Misra and M. S. Mate, pp. 113–24. Deccan College Postgraduate and Research Institute, Poona.

Gibson, M. 1977. An Indus Valley stamp seal from Nippur, Iraq. *Man and Environment* 1:67.

Godley, A. D., trans., 1926. *Herodotus.* Rev. ed., 4 vols. Harvard University Press, Loeb Classical Library, Cambridge.

Goody, J. 1978. *Literacy in traditional society.* Cambridge University Press, Cambridge.

Government of India. 1884. *Gazetteer of the Gujranwala district, 1883–84.* Punjab Government, Lahore.

Griffith, R. T. H., trans. 1896. *The hymns of the Rigveda.* 2d ed. 2 vols. 1987 reprint. Munshiram Manoharlal, Delhi.

Grigson, C. 1984. Some thoughts on unicorns and other cattle depicted at Mohenjo-daro and Harappa. In *South Asian archaeology 1981,* edited by B. Allchin, pp. 166–69. Cambridge University Press, Cambridge.

Guha, B. S. and P. C. Basu. 1938. Report on the human remains excavated at Mohenjo-Daro in 1928–29. In *Further excavations at Mohenjo-Daro,* edited by E. J. H. Mackay, pp. 613–38. Government of India, Delhi.

Gupta, P., P. C. Dutta, and A. Basu. 1962. *Human skeletal remains from Harappa. Memoirs of the Anthropological Survey of India,* no. 9, Calcutta.

Gupta, S. P. 1978. Origin of the form of Harappa culture: A new proposition. *Puratattva* 8:141–46.

———. 1979. *Archaeology of Soviet Central Asia and the Indian borderlands.* 2 vols. B. R. Publishing Corporation, Delhi.

———, ed. 1989. *An archaeological tour along the Ghaggar-Hakra River.* Kusumanjali Prakashan, Meerut, India.

Hakimi, A. 1997. *Shahdad.* IsMEO, Roma.

Halim, M. A. 1972a. Excavation at Sarai Khola, part I. *Pakistan Archaeology* 7:23–89.

———. 1972b. Excavations at Sarai Khola, part II. *Pakistan Archaeology* 8:1–112.

Halim, M. A. and M. Vidale. 1984. Kilns, bangles and coated vessels. In *Reports on field work carried out at Mohenjo-daro, Pakistan 1982–83 by the IsMEO–Aachen University Mission*, edited by M. Jansen and G. Urban, pp. 63–97. Interim Reports, vol. 1. RWTH/IsMEO, Aachen/Rome.

Hargreaves, H. 1929. Excavations in Baluchistan 1925, Sampur Mound, Mastung and Sohr Damb, Nal. *Memoirs of the Archaeological Survey of India*, no 35.

———. 1931. HR area. In *Mohenjo-daro and the Indus Civilization*, edited by J. Marshall, pp. 176–86. 3 vols. Arthur Probsthain, London.

Harlan, J. R. 1971. Agricultural origins: centers and noncenters. *Science* 174:468–74.

———. 1977. The origins of cereal agriculture in the Old World. In *Origins of agriculture*, edited by C. A. Reed, pp. 357–83. Mouton, The Hague.

Harvey, M. D. and S. A. Schumm. 1999. Indus River dynamics and the abandonment of Mohenjo-daro. In *The Indus River: Biodiversity, resources, humankind*, edited by A. Meadows and P. S. Meadows, pp. 333–48. Oxford University Press, Karachi.

Hawkes, J. 1982. *Adventurer in archaeology: The biography of Sir Mortimer Wheeler*. St. Martin's, New York.

Heesterman, J. C. 1985. *The inner conflict of tradition*. University of Chicago Press, Chicago.

Heimpel, W. 1982. A first step in the diorite question. *Revue D'assyriologie et Archéologie Orientale* 76(1):65–67.

———. 1987. Das Untere Meer. *Zeitschrift für Assyriologie* 77:22–91.

Hemphill, B. E., J. R. Lukacs, and K. A. R. Kennedy. 1991. Biological adaptations and affinities of Bronze Age Harappans. In *Harappa excavations 1986–1990: A multidisciplinary approach to third millennium urbanization*, edited by R. H. Meadow, pp. 137–82. Prehistory Press, Monographs in World Archaeology, no. 3, Madison.

Hiebert, F. T. 1994. *Origins of the Bronze Age oasis civilization in Central Asia*. Peabody Museum of Archaeology and Ethnology, American School of Prehistoric Research, Bulletin no. 42, Cambridge.

Hiltebeitl, A. 1978. The Indus Valley "Proto-Siva," reexamined through reflections on the goddess, the buffalo, and the symbolism of vahanas. *Anthropos* 73:767–97.

Holmes, D. A. 1968. The recent history of the Indus. *Geographical Journal* 134(3):367–82.

Hunter, G. R. 1932. Mohenjo daro—Indus epigraphy. *Journal of the Royal Asiatic Society of Great Britain and Ireland*, pp. 466–503.

———. 1934. *The script of Harappa and Mohenjo-daro and its connection with other scripts*. Kegan Paul, London.

Huntington, S. L. 1985. *The art of ancient India*. Weatherhill, New York.

Hussain, M. 1989. Salvage excavation at Moenjodaro. *Journal of the Pakistan Historical Society* 37(1):89–98.

Indian Archaeology, A review. *1960–61. Excavations at Kalibangan*, pp. 31–32, Archaeological Survey of India, Delhi.

Indian Archaeology, A review. *1961–62. Excavations at Burzahom*, pp. 17–21, Archaeological Survey of India, Delhi.

Indian Archaeology, A review. *1964–65. Excavations at Burzahom*, p. 13, Archaeological Survey of India, Delhi.

Indian Archaeology, A review. *1986–87. Palaeobotanical and pollen analytical investigations, Hulas*, pp. 46–50, Archaeological Survey of India, Delhi.

Ingholt, H. 1940. *Rapport Préleminaire sur Sept Campaignes de Fouilles à Hamma en Syrie (1932–38)*. Archaeologiskkunsthistoriske Meddelelser, III, 1. Det Kgl. Danske Videnskabernes Selskab, Copenhagen.

Jansen, M. 1983. Preliminary results of three years' documentation at Mohenjo-daro. In *Forschungsprojekt DFG Mohenjo-daro*, edited by G. Urban and M. Jansen, pp. 21–35. Veroffentlichung des Geogatischen Instituts der Reinisch-Westfalischen Technischen Hochschule, nr. 34, Aachen.

———. 1984. Theoretical aspects of structural analysis for Mohenjo-daro. In *Reports on field work carried out at Mohenjo-daro, Pakistan 1982–83 by the IsMEO–Aachen University Mission*, edited by M. Jansen and G. Urban, pp. 39–62. Interim Reports, vol. 1. RWTH/IsMEO, Aachen/Rome.

———. 1985. Mohenjo-daro HR-A, house I, a temple? Analysis of an architectural structure. In *South Asian archaeology 1983*, edited by J. Schotsmans and M. Taddei, pp. 157–206. Instituto Universitario Orientale, Dipartimento di Studi Asiatici, Series Minor 23, Naples.

———. 1986. *Die Indus Zivilization: Wiederentdeckung Einer Fruhen Hochkultur*. DuMont Buchverlag, Koln.

———. 1987. Preliminary results on the "forma urbis" research at Mohenjo-Daro. In *Reports on field work carried out at Mohenjo-daro, Pakistan, 1983–84*, edited by M. Jansen and G. Urban, pp. 9–22. Interim Reports, vol. 2. RWTH/IsMEO, Aachen/Rome.

———. 1989a. Early cities: A comparative study of urban development. *Lahore Museum Journal* 2(1):5–14.

———. 1989b. Some problems regarding the forma urbis Mohenjo-Daro. In *South Asian archaeology 1985*, edited by K. Frifelt and P. Sorensen, pp. 247–56. Curzon Press, Scandinavian Institute of Asian Studies, Occasional Papers no. 4, London.

———. 1993a. *Mohenjo-daro: Stadt der brunnen und kanale (City of wells and drains), Wasserlexus vor 4500 jharan (Water splendor 4500 years ago)*. Frontinus-Gesellschafte. V., Dual German–English text. Bergisch Gladbach.

———. 1993b. Mohenjo-daro: Type site of the earliest urbanization process in South Asia. In *Urban form and meaning in South Asia*, edited by H. Spodek and D. M. Srinivasan, pp. 33–51. National Gallery of Art. Studies in the History of Art, 31. Center for Advanced Study in the Visual Arts Symposium Papers 15, Washington, D.C.

———. 1994. Mohenjo-daro, type site of the earliest urbanization process in South Asia: Ten years of research at Mohenjo-daro, Pakistan, and an attempt at synopsis. In *South Asian Archaeology 1993*, 2 vols., ed. A. Parpola and P. Koskikallio. pp. 263–80. Annales Academiae Scientiarum Fennicae, Series B, vol. 271. Helsinki.

Jansen, M. and G. Urban. 1985. *Mohenjo Daro: Report of the Aachen University Mission 1979–1985. Section one: Data collection. volume one: Catalogue and concordance of the field registers, 1924–38. Part one: The HR-area field register, 1925–27.* E. J. Brill, Leiden.

Jansen, M., M. Mulloy, and G. Urban. 1991. *Forgotten cities on the Indus: Early civilization in Pakistan from the 8th to the 2nd millennium B.C.* Verlag Philipp von Zabern, Mainz.

Jarrige, C. 1984. Terracotta human figurines from Nindowari. In *South Asian archaeology 1981*, edited by B. Allchin, pp. 129–34. Cambridge University Press, Cambridge.

———. 1991. The terracotta figurines from Mehrgarh. In *Forgotten cities on the Indus: Early civilization in Pakistan from the 8th to the 2nd millennium B.C.*, edited by M. Jansen, M. Mulloy, and G. Urban, pp. 87–94. Verlag Philipp von Zabern, Mainz.

Jarrige, C., J.-F. Jarrige, R. H. Meadow, and G. Quivron. 1995. *Mehrgarh: Field reports 1974–1985, from Neolithic times to the Indus Civilization.* Department of Culture and Tourism of Sindh, Pakistan, Department of Archaeology and Museums, French Ministry of Foreign Affairs, Karachi.

Jarrige, J.-F. 1985. Continuity and change in the north Kachi plain (Baluchistan, Pakistan) at the beginning of the second millennium B.C. In *South Asian archaeology 1983*, edited by J. Schotsmans and M. Taddei, pp. 35–68. Instituto Universitario Orientale, Dipartimento di Studi Asiatici, Series Minor 23, Naples.

———. 1988. Excavation at Naushari. *Pakistan Archaeology* 23:149–203.

———. 1989. Excavation at Naushari, 1987–88. *Pakistan Archaeology* 24:21–68.

———. 1995. Introduction. In *Mehrgarh: Field reports 1974–1985, from Neolithic times to the Indus Civilization*, edited by C. Jarrige, J.-F. Jarrige, R. H. Meadow, and G. Quivron, pp. 51–103. Department of Culture and Tourism of Sindh, Department of Archaeology and Museums, French Ministry of Foreign Affairs, Karachi.

Jarrige, J.-F. and M. U. Hassan. 1989. Funerary complexes in Baluchistan at the end of the third millennium in the light of recent discoveries at Mehrgarh and Quetta. In *South Asian archaeology 1985*, edited by K. Frifelt and P. Sorensen, pp. 150–66. Scandinavian Institute of Asian Studies, Occasional Papers no. 4.

Joshi, J. P. 1984. Harappa culture: Emergence of a new picture. *Puratattva* 13–14:51–54.

———. 1986. Settlement patterns in the third, second and first millennia in India—with special reference to recent discoveries in Punjab. *Rtambhara: Studies in Indology*, pp. 134–39. Society for Indic Studies, Ghaziabad, India.

———. 1993. Excavation at Bhagwanpura 1975–76 and other explorations and excavations 1975–81 in Haryana, Jammu & Kashmir and Punjab. *Memoirs of the Archaeological Survey of India*, no. 89, Delhi.

Joshi, J. P. and A. Parpola. 1987. *Corpus of Indus seals and inscriptions.* vol. 1, *Collections in India.* Suomalainen Tiedeakatemia, Suomalaisen Tiedeakatemian Toimituksia Annales Academiae Scientiarum Fennicae, Sarja, series B, NIDE, tome 239, Helsinki.

Joshi, R. V. 1978. *Stone Age cultures of central India.* Deccan College Postgraduate and Research Institute, Poona, India.

Kennedy, K. A. R. 1977. A reassessment of the theories of the racial origins of the people of the Indus Valley Civilization from recent anthropological and archaeological data. (Paper read at the 6th University of Wisconsin South Asia Conference, Madison, November 4–6).

———. 1982. Skulls, Aryans and flowing drains: The interface of archaeology and skeletal biology in the study of the Harappan Civilization. In *Harappan Civilization: A contemporary perspective*, edited by G. L. Possehl, pp. 289–95. Oxford & IBH and the American Institute of Indian Studies, Delhi.

———. 1984. Trauma and disease in the ancient Harappans. In *Frontiers of the Indus Civilization*, edited by B. B. Lal and S. P. Gupta, pp. 425–36. Books and Books, Delhi.

———. 1990. Reconstruction of trauma, disease, and lifeways of prehistoric peoples of South Asia from the skeletal record. In *South Asian archaeology 1987*, edited by M. Taddei, pp. 61–77. Instituto Italiano per il Medio ed Estremo Oriente, Serie Orientale Roma, 66(1), Roma.

———. 1994. Identification of sacrificial and massacre victims in archaeological sites: The skeletal evidence. *Man and Environment* 19(1–2):247–51.

———. 1995. Have Aryans been identified in the prehistoric skeletal record from South Asia? Biological anthropology and concepts of ancient races. In *The Indo-Aryans of ancient South Asia: Language, material culture and ethnicity*, edited by G. Erdosy, pp. 32–66. Walter de Gruyter, Berlin.

———. 2000. *God-apes and fossil men: Paleoanthropology of South Asia.* University of Michigan Press, Ann Arbor.

Kennedy, K. A. R. and P. C. Caldwell. 1984. South Asian prehistoric human skeletal remains and burial practices. In *The people of South Asia: The biological anthropology of India, Pakistan and Nepal*, edited by J. R. Lukacs, pp. 159–97. Plenum Press, New York.

Kennedy, K. A. R., J. R. Lukacs, and B. Hemphill. In press. *The people of Harappa.*

Kennedy, K. A. R., J. Chiment, T. Disotell, and D. Meyers. 1984. Principal-components analysis of prehistoric South Asian crania. *American Journal of Physical Anthropology* 64(2):105–18.

Kenoyer, J. M. 1984. Shell working industries of the Indus Civilization: A summary. *Paleorient* 10(1):49–63.

———. 1991. The Indus tradition of Pakistan and western India. *Journal of World Prehistory* 5(4):331–85.

———. 1992. Harappan craft specialization and the question of urban segregation and stratification. *Eastern Anthropologist* 45(1–2):39–54.

———. 1993. Lithic studies. In *Harappan Civilization: A recent perspective,* 2d ed., ed. Gregory L. Possehl, p. 512. Oxford & IBH and the American Institute of Indian Studies, Delhi.

———. 1998. *Ancient cities of the Indus Valley Civilization.* Oxford University Press, Karachi.

Kenoyer, J. M. and R. H. Meadow. 2000. The Ravi Phase: A new cultural manifestation at Harappa Pakistan. In *South Asian Archaeology, 1997,* ed. M. Taddei and G. De Marco, pp. 55–76. Instituto Italiano per l'Africa e l'Oriente and Instituto Universitario Orientale, Roma.

Kenoyer, J. M. and H. M.-L. Miller. 1999. Metal technologies of the Indus Valley tradition in Pakistan and western India. In *The archaeometallurgy of the Asian Old World,* edited by V. C. Pigott, pp. 107–51. University Museum Monograph 89, MASCA Research Papers in Science and Archaeology, vol. 16. University Museum, University of Pennsylvania, Philadelphia.

Khan, F. A. 1965. Excavations at Kot Diji. *Pakistan Archaeology* 2:11–85.

Khan, F., J. R. Knox, and K. D. Thomas. 1991. *Explorations and excavations in Bannu District, North-west Frontier province, Pakistan, 1985–88.* British Museum, Department of Oriental Antiquities, Occasional Paper no. 50, London.

———. 2000. The Bannu Archaeological Project: Archaeological explorations and excavations in Bannu Division, Northwest Frontier Province, Pakistan, 1985–2000. *Journal of Central Asian Civilizations* 23(2):1–6.

Khatri, J. S. and M. Acharya. 1995. Kunal: A new Indus-Saraswati site. *Puratattva* 25:84–86.

———. In press. Kunal. In *South Asian archaeology, an encyclopaedia,* edited by G. L. Possehl and B. M. Pande. Oxford & IBH, Delhi.

Kohl, P. L. 1975. Carved chlorite vessels: A trade in finished commodities in the mid-third millennium. *Expedition* 18(1):18–31.

Koskenniemi, K. and A. Parpola. 1982. *A concordance to the texts in the Indus script.* Research Reports no. 3. Department of Asian and African Studies, University of Helsinki, Helsinki.

Koskenniemi, S., A. Parpola, and S. Parpola. 1973. *Materials for the study of the Indus script, I: A concordance to the Indus inscriptions.* Acta Academiae Scientarium Fennicae B 185, Helsinki.

Lahiri, N., ed. 2000. *The decline and fall of the Indus Civilization.* Permanent Black, Delhi.

Lal, B. B. 1970–71. Perhaps the earliest ploughed field so far excavated anywhere in the world. *Puratattva* 4:1–3.

———. 1979. Kalibangan and Indus Civilization. In *Essays in Indian protohistory,* edited by D. P. Agrawal and D. Chakrabarti, pp. 65–97. B. R. Publishing Corporation, Delhi.

———. 1981. Some reflections on the structural remains at Kalibangan. In *Indus Civilization: New perspectives,* edited

by A. H. Dani, pp. 47–54. Quaid-i-Azam University, Islamabad.

———. 1989. Faience. In *An encyclopaedia of Indian archaeology,* edited by A. Ghosh, pp. 321. vol. 1. Munshiram Manoharlal, Delhi.

———. 1992. Antecedents of the signs used in the Indus script: A discussion. In *South Asian archaeology studies,* edited by G. L. Possehl, pp. 54–56. Oxford & IBH, Delhi.

Lamberg-Karlovsky, C. C. 1975. Third millennium modes of exchange and modes of production. In *Ancient civilization and trade,* edited by C. C. Lamberg-Karlovsky and J. A. Sabloff, pp. 341–68. School of American Research/University of New Mexico Press, Albuquerque.

———. 1986a. Death in Dilmun. In *Bahrain through the ages, the archaeology,* edited by S. H. A. A. Khalifa, and M. Rice, pp. 157–64. KPI Limited, New York.

———. 1986b. Third millennium structure and process: From the Euphrates to the Indus and the Oxus to the Indian Ocean. *Oriens Antiquus* 25(3–4):189–219.

———. 1996. *Beyond the Tigris and Euphrates: Bronze Age civilizations.* Studies by the Department of Bible and Ancient Near East, vol. 9. Ben-Gurion University of the Negev, Beer-Sheva.

Lamberg-Karlovsky, C. C. and M. Tosi. 1973. Shahr-i Sokhta and Tepe Yahya: Tracks on the earliest history of the Iranian plateau. *East and West* 23(1–2):21–57.

Lambrick, H. T. 1964. Sind: A general introduction. *History of Sind series,* vol. 1. Sindhi Adabi Board, Hyderabad, Pakistan.

———. 1967. The Indus flood-plain and the "Indus Civilization." *Geographical Journal* 133:483–94.

Langdon, S. H. 1931a. The Indus script. In *Mohenjo-daro and the Indus Civilization,* edited by J. Marshall, pp. 423–55. 3 vols. Arthur Probsthain, London.

———. 1931b. A new factor in the problem of Sumerian origins. *Journal of the Royal Asiatic Society of Great Britain and Ireland,* pp. 593–96.

Lechevallier, M. 1984. Flint industry of Mehrgarh. In *South Asian archaeology 1981,* edited by B. Allchin, pp. 41–51. Cambridge University Press, Cambridge.

Leshnik, L. S. 1968. Prehistoric explorations in North Gujarat and parts of Rajasthan. *East and West* 18(3–4):295–310.

Lukacs, J. R. 1982. Dental disease, dietary patterns and subsistence at Harappa and Mohenjodaro. In *Harappan Civilization: A contemporary perspective,* edited by G. L. Possehl, pp. 301–7. Oxford & IBH and the American Institute of Indian Studies, Delhi.

———. 1985. Dental pathology and tooth size at Mehrgarh: An anthropological assessment. In *South Asian archaeology 1983,* edited by J. Schotsmans and M. Taddei, pp. 121–50. Instituto Universitario Orientale, Dipartimento di Studi Asiatici, Series Minor 23, Naples.

———. 1989. Biological affinities from dental morphology: The evidence from Neolithic Mehrgarh. In *Old problems and new perspectives in the archaeology of South Asia,* edited by J. M. Kenoyer, pp. 75–88. Wisconsin Archaeological Reports, no. 2, Madison.

——. 1990. On hunter-gatherers and their neighbors in prehistoric India: Contact and pathology. *Current Anthropology* 31(2):183–86.

Mackay, D. 1945. Ancient river beds and dead cities. *Antiquity* 19:135–44.

Mackay, E. J. H. 1925a. Report on the excavations of the "A" cemetery at Kish, Mesopotamia. Part 1. Field Museum of Natural History, *Anthropology Memoirs*, 1(1), Chicago.

——. 1925b. Sumerian connections with ancient India. *Journal of the Royal Asiatic Society of Great Britain and Ireland*, pp. 697–701.

——. 1925–26. Exploration, Western Circle, Mohenjo-daro (area DK). *Annual Report of the Archaeological Survey of India, 1925–26*: 87–93.

——. 1928–29. Excavations at Mohenjo-daro. *Annual Report of the Archaeological Survey of India, 1928–29*:67–75.

——. 1929. A Sumerian palace and the "A" cemetery at Kish, Mesopotamia. Part II. Field Museum of Natural History, *Anthropology Memoirs*, 1(2), Chicago.

——. 1930–34. Excavations at Mohenjo-daro. *Annual Reports of the Archaeological Survey of India for the Years 1930–31, 1931–32, 1932–33, and 1933–34*. Part One: 51–71.

——. 1931a. SD area: The Great Bath and adjacent buildings. In *Mohenjo-daro and the Indus Civilization*, edited by J. Marshall, pp. 131–50. 3 vols. Arthur Probsthain, London.

——. 1931b. L area. In *Mohenjo-daro and the Indus Civilization*, edited by J. Marshall, pp. 151–75. 3 vols. Arthur Probsthain, London.

——. 1931c. DK area. In *Mohenjo-daro and the Indus Civilization*, edited by J. Marshall, pp. 233–61. 3 vols. Arthur Probsthain, London.

——. 1931d. Architecture and masonry. In *Mohenjo-daro and the Indus Civilization*, edited by J. Marshall, pp. 262–86. 3 vols. Arthur Probsthain, London.

——. 1931e. Plain and painted pottery with tabulation. In *Mohenjo-daro and the Indus Civilization*, edited by J. Marshall, pp. 287–337. 3 vols. Arthur Probsthain, London.

——. 1931f. Figurines and model animals. In *Mohenjo-daro and the Indus Civilization*, edited by J. Marshall, pp. 338–55. 3 vols. Arthur Probsthain, London.

——. 1931g. Statuary. In *Mohenjo-daro and the Indus Civilization*, edited by J. Marshall, pp. 356–64. 3 vols. Arthur Probsthain, London.

——. 1931h. Faience and stone vessels. In *Mohenjo-daro and the Indus Civilization*, edited by J. Marshall, pp. 365–69. 3 vols. Arthur Probsthain, London.

——. 1931i. Seals, seal impressions and copper tablets, with tabulation. In *Mohenjo-daro and the Indus Civilization*, edited by J. Marshall, pp. 370–405. 3 vols. Arthur Probsthain, London.

——. 1931j. Household objects, tools and implements. In *Mohenjo-daro and the Indus Civilization*, edited by J. Marshall, pp. 456–80. 3 vols. Arthur Probsthain, London.

——. 1931k. Copper and bronze utensils and other objects: Technique and description of metal vessels, tools, implements and other objects. In *Mohenjo-daro and the Indus Civilization*, edited by J. Marshall, pp. 488–508. 3 vols. Arthur Probsthain, London.

——. 1931l. Personal ornaments. In *Mohenjo-daro and the Indus Civilization*, edited by J. Marshall, pp. 509–48. 3 vols. Arthur Probsthain, London.

——. 1931m. Games and toys. In *Mohenjo-daro and the Indus Civilization*, edited by J. Marshall, pp. 549–61. 3 vols. Arthur Probsthain, London.

——. 1931n. Ivory, shell, faience and other objects of technical interest. In *Mohenjo-daro and the Indus Civilization*, edited by J. Marshall, pp. 562–88. 3 vols. Arthur Probsthain, London.

——. 1931o. Further links between ancient Sind, Sumer and elsewhere. *Antiquity* 5(20):459–73.

——. 1933. India: Technology. Decorated carnelian beads. *Man* 33:143–46.

——. 1937. Bead making in ancient Sind. *Journal of the American Oriental Society* 57:1–15.

——. 1937–38. *Further excavations at Mohenjo-daro*. 2 vols. Government of India, Delhi.

——. 1943. *Chanhu-daro excavations 1935–36*. Vol. 20. American Oriental Society, American Oriental Series, New Haven, Conn.

——. 1948. *Early Indus Civilizations*. 2d ed. Revised by Dorothy Mackay. Luzac & Co., London.

Mahadevan, I. 1977. The Indus script: Texts, concordance and tables. *Memoirs of the Archaeological Survey of India*, no. 77.

Majumdar, N. G. 1934. Explorations in Sind. *Memoirs of the Archaeological Survey of India*, no. 48, Delhi.

Marshall, J. 1922. The monuments of ancient India. In *The Cambridge history of India*, edited by E. J. Rapson, pp. 612–49. Cambridge University Press, Cambridge.

——. 1923–24. Exploration and research, Harappa and Mohenjo-daro. *Annual Report of the Archaeological Survey of India, 1923–24*: 47–51.

——. 1924. First light on a long forgotten civilization. *Illustrated London News*, September 20, pp. 528–32, 548.

——. 1925–26. Exploration, Western Circle, Mohenjo-daro. *Annual Report of the Archaeological Survey of India, 1925–26*:72–98.

——. 1926–27. The Indus culture. *Annual Report of the Archaeological Survey of India, 1926–27*: 51–60.

——. 1931a. The country, climate and rivers. In *Mohenjo-daro and the Indus Civilization*, edited by J. Marshall, pp. 1–7. 3 vols. Arthur Probsthain, London.

——. 1931b. The site and its excavation. In *Mohenjo-daro and the Indus Civilization*, edited by J. Marshall, pp. 8–14. 3 vols. Arthur Probsthain, London.

——. 1931c. The buildings. In *Mohenjo-daro and the Indus Civilization*, edited by J. Marshall, pp. 15–26. 3 vols. Arthur Probsthain, London.

——. 1931d. Other antiquities and art. In *Mohenjo-daro and the Indus Civilization*, edited by J. Marshall, pp. 27–47. 3 vols. Arthur Probsthain, London.

———. 1931e. Religion. In *Mohenjo-daro and the Indus Civilization*, edited by J. Marshall, pp. 48–78. 3 vols. Arthur Probsthain, London.

———. 1931f. Disposal of the dead. In *Mohenjo-daro and the Indus Civilization*, edited by J. Marshall, pp. 79–90. 3 vols. Arthur Probsthain, London.

———. 1931g. Extent of the Indus Civilization. In *Mohenjo-daro and the Indus Civilization*, edited by J. Marshall, pp. 91–101. 3 vols. Arthur Probsthain, London.

———. 1931h. The age and authors of the Indus Civilization. In *Mohenjo-daro and the Indus Civilization*, edited by J. Marshall, pp. 102–12. 3 vols. Arthur Probsthain, London.

———, ed. 1931i. *Mohenjo-Daro and the Indus Civilization.* 3 vols. Arthur Probsthain, London.

———. 1931j. The Stupa area. In *Mohenjo-daro and the Indus Civilization,* ed. J. Marshall, 3 vols., pp. 113–30. Arthur Probsthain, London.

Masson, V. M. 1988. *Altyn Depe.* Translated by Henry Michael. University Museum, Philadelphia.

Masson, V. M. and V. I. Sarianidi 1972. *Central Asia: Turkmenia before the Achaemenids.* Praeger, New York.

McAlpin, D. W. 1981. Proto-Elamo-Dravidian: The evidence and its implications. *Transactions of the American Philosophical Society* 71(3).

McCrindle, J. W. 1882. *Ancient India as described by Ktesias the Knidian.* Trubner & Co., London.

McEvilley, T. 1981. An archaeology of yoga. *Res* 1:44–77.

Meadow, R. H. 1979. Prehistoric subsistence at Balakot: Initial consideration of the faunal remains. In *South Asian archaeology 1977*, edited by M. Taddei, pp. 275–315. Instituto Universitario Orientale, Seminario di Studi Asiatici, Series Minor 6, Naples.

———. 1984. Notes on the faunal remains from Mehrgarh with a focus on cattle (Bos). In *South Asian archaeology 1981*, edited by B. Allchin, pp. 34–40. Cambridge University Press, Cambridge.

———. 1993. Animal domestication in the Middle East: a revised view from the eastern margin. In *Harappan Civilization: A recent perspective*, 2d ed., edited by G. L. Possehl, pp. 295–320. Oxford & IBH and the American Institute of Indian Studies, Delhi.

———. 1998. Pre- and Proto-historic agricultural and pastoral transformations in northwestern South Asia. *Review of Archaeology* 192:12–21.

———, ed. 1991. *Harappa excavations 1986–1990: A multidisciplinary approach to third millennium urbanism.* Prehistory Press, Monographs in World Archaeology, 3, Madison.

Meadow, R. H. and K. J. Mark 2000. The "tiny steatite seals" (incised steatite tablets) of Harappa: Some observations on their context and dating. In *South Asian archaeology 1997*, edited by M. Taddei and G. de Marco, pp. 321–40. Instituto Italiano per l'Africa e l'Oriente and Instituto Universitario Orientale, Roma.

Meadow, R. H. and A. Patel. 1997. A comment on "Horse remains from the prehistoric site of Surkotada, Kutch, late 3rd millennium B.C." by Sandor Bokonyi. *South Asian Studies* 13:308–15.

Meadow, R. H., J. M. Kenoyer, and R. P. Wright. 1996. *Harappa Archaeological Research Project: Harappa excavations 1996.* Peabody Museum, Cambridge.

Mehta, R. N., K. N. Momin, and D. R. Shah. 1980. *Excavation at Kanewal.* Maharaja Sayajirao University, Archaeology Series, no. 17, Baroda.

Mery, S. 2000. *Les Ceramiques d'Oman et l'Asie Moyenne: Une archeologii des exchanges à l'Age du Bronze.* CRA Monographies 23. CNRS Editions, Paris.

Miller, Heather M.-L. 1997. Pottery firing structures (kilns) of the Indus Civilization during the third millennium B.C. In *Prehistory and history of ceramic kilns*, edited by P. M. Rice and D. W. Kingery, pp. 41–71. *Ceramics and Civilization*, vol. VII. American Ceramic Society, Columbus.

———. 2000. Reassessing the urban structure of Harappa: Evidence from craft production distribution. In *South Asian archaeology 1997*, edited by M. Taddei and G. de Marco, pp. 77–100. Instituto Italiano per l'Africa e l'Oriente and Instituto Universitario Orientale, Roma.

Miller, Heidi. 2000. A functional typology of metal objects from Chanhu-daro. In *South Asian archaeology 1997*, edited by M. Taddei and G. de Marco, pp. 301–20. Instituto Italiano per l'Africa e l'Oriente and Instituto Universitario Orientale, Roma.

Misra, V. N. 1973. Bagor: A late Mesolithic settlement in northwest India. *World Archaeology* 5(1):92–100.

———. 1984. Climate, a factor in the rise and fall of the Indus Civilization—evidence from Rajasthan and beyond. In *Frontiers of the Indus Civilization*, edited by B. B. Lal and S. P. Gupta, pp. 461–89. Books and Books, Delhi.

Mockler, E. and Major. 1877. On ruins in Makran. *Journal of the Royal Asiatic Society of Great Britain and Ireland* 9:121–34.

Mughal, M. R. 1968. Excavations: Harappa, 1966 (Cemetery R-37). *Pakistan Archaeology* 5:63 68.

———. 1970. *The Early Harappan period in the Greater Indus Valley and Baluchistan.* PhD. diss., Department of Anthropology, University of Pennsylvania.

———. 1972. Excavation at Jalilpur. *Pakistan Archaeology* 8:117–24.

———. 1990a. The decline of the Indus Civilization and the Late Harappan period in the Indus Valley. *Lahore Museum Journal* 3(2):1–22.

———. 1990b. The Harappan "twin capitals" and reality. *Journal of Central Asia* 13(1):155–62.

———. 1997. *Ancient Cholistan: Archaeology and architecture.* Ferozsons, Lahore.

Nath, A. 1998. Rakhigarhi: A Harappan metropolis in the Sarasvati-Drishadvati divide. *Puratattva* 28:39–45.

———. 1999. Further excavations at Rakhigarhi. *Puratattva* 29:46–49.

Noetling, F. W. 1899. *Uber eine prahistorische neiderlassungen in Baluchistan.* Berliner Gesellschaft fur Anthropologie Ethnologie und Urgeschichte, 31, Zeitschrift Fur Ethnologie.

O'Flaherty, W. D. 1973. *Asceticism and eroticism in the mythology of Siva.* Penguin Books, London.

Oppenheim, A. L. 1954. Seafaring merchants of Ur. *Journal of the American Oriental Society* 74:6–17.

Pande, B. M. 1971. A note on the Harappan ring-kernoi. *K. A. Nilakanta Sastri Felicitation Volume,* pp. 231–33. Professor Nilakanta Sastri Felicitation Committee, Madras.

———. 1973. Inscribed copper tablets from Mohenjo-daro: A preliminary analysis. In *Radiocarbon and Indian archaeology,* edited by D. P. Agrawal and A. Ghosh, pp. 305–22. Tata Institute of Fundamental Research, Bombay.

———. 1974. On the origin of the Harappan sign. *Puratattva* 7:25–33.

———. 1985. On the origin of certain Harappan signs. In *Indus Valley to Mekong Delta: Explorations in epigraphy,* edited by N. Karashima, pp. 205–13. New Era Publications, Madras.

Parpola, A. 1984. New correspondences between Harappan and Near Eastern glyptic art. In *South Asian archaeology 1981,* edited by B. Allchin, pp. 176–95. Cambridge University Press, Cambridge.

———. 1985a. The Harappan priest-king's robe and the Vedic tarpya garment: Their interrelation and symbolism (astral and procreative). In *South Asian archaeology 1983,* edited by J. Schotsmans and M. Taddei, pp. 385–404. Instituto Universitario Orientale, Dipartimento di Studi Asiatici, Series Minor 23, Naples.

———. 1985b. The Sky-Garment: A study of the Harappan religion and its relation to the Mesopotamian and later India religion. *Studia Orientalia* 57:8–216.

———. 1990. Bangles, sacred trees and fertility—interpretation of the Indus script relating to the cult of Skandra-Kumara. In *South Asian archaeology 1987,* edited by M. Taddei, pp. 263–84. Instituto Italiano per il Medio ed Estremo Oriente, Serie Orientale Roma, 66(1), Roma.

———. 1992. The "fig deity seal" from Mohenjo-daro: Its iconography and inscription. In *South Asian archaeology 1989,* edited by C. Jarrige, pp. 227–36. Prehistory Press, Monographs in World Archaeology, no. 14, Madison.

———. 1994a. *Deciphering the Indus script.* Cambridge University Press, Cambridge.

———. 1994b. Harappan inscriptions: An analytical catalogue of the Indus inscriptions from the Near East. In *Qalat al-Bahrain, volume 1: The northern city wall and Islamic fortress,* edited by F. Hojlund and H. A. H, pp. 304–492. Jutland Archaeological Society Publications, 30(1), Aarhus.

Parpola, A., S. Koskenniemi, S. Parpola, and P. Aalto. 1969. *Decipherment of the proto-Dravidian inscriptions of the Indus Civilization: A first announcement.* Scandinavian Institute of Asian Studies, Special Publications, no. 1, Copenhagen.

Peake, R. H. 1928. The copper mountain of Magan. *Antiquity* 2:452–54.

Pedde, F. 1993. Pottery from northern Baluchistan—the Noetling Collection in the Museum of Indian Art, Berlin. In *South Asian archaeology 1991,* edited by A. J. Gail and G. J. R. Mevissen, pp. 215–30. Franz Steiner Verlag, Stuttgart.

Piggott, S. 1950. *Prehistoric India to 1000 B.C.* Penguin Books, Baltimore.

Piperno, M. 1973. Micro-drilling at Shahr-i Sokhta: The making and use of lithic drill-heads. In *South Asian Archaeology,* edited by N. Hammond, pp. 119–29. Noyes Press, Park Ridge.

———. 1983. Bead making and boring techniques in 3rd millennium Indo-Iran. Prehistoric Sistan, 1. In M. Tosi, pp. 319–26. Italiano per il Medio ed Estremo Oriente, Roma.

Pittman, H. 1984. *Art of the Bronze Age: Southeastern Iran, western central Asia and the Indus Valley.* Metropolitan Museum of Art, New York.

Possehl, G. L. 1967. The Mohenjo-daro floods: A reply. *American Anthropologist* 69(1):32–40.

———. 1975. The chronology of gabarbands and palas in western South Asia. *Expedition* 17(2):33–37.

———. 1976. Lothal: A gateway settlement of the Harappan Civilization. In *Ecological backgrounds of South Asian prehistory,* edited by K. A. R. Kennedy and G. L. Possehl, pp. 118–31. Cornell University South Asia Program, Occasional Papers and Theses, no. 4, Ithaca, N.Y.

———. 1979. Pastoral nomadism in the Indus Civilization: An hypothesis. In *South Asian archaeology 1977,* edited by M. Taddei, pp. 537–51. Instituto Universitario Orientale, Seminario di Studi Asiatici, Series Minor 6, Naples.

———. 1980. *Indus Civilization in Saurashtra.* B. R. Publishing Corporation, Delhi.

———. 1982. The Harappan Civilization: A contemporary perspective. In *Harappan Civilization: A contemporary perspective,* edited by G. L. Possehl, pp. 15–28. Oxford & IBH and the American Institute of Indian Studies, Delhi.

———. 1986a. African millets in South Asian prehistory. In *Studies in the archaeology of India and Pakistan,* edited by J. Jacobson, pp. 237–56. Oxford & IBH and the American Institute of Indian Studies, Delhi.

———. 1986b. *Kulli: An exploration of ancient civilization in South Asia.* Carolina Academic Press, Durham, N.C.

———. 1990. Revolution in the urban revolution: The emergence of Indus urbanization. *Annual Review of Anthropology* 19:261–82.

———. 1992. The Harappan cultural mosaic: Ecology revisited. In *South Asian archaeology 1989,* edited by C. Jarrige, pp. 237–44. Prehistory Press, Monographs in World Archaeology, no. 14, Madison.

———. 1993. The date of Indus urbanization: A proposed chronology for the Pre-urban and Urban Harappan Phases. In *South Asian archaeology 1991,* edited by A. J. Gail and G. R. Mevissen, pp. 231–49. Franz Steiner Verlag, Stuttgart.

———. 1994. Of men. In *From Sumer to Meluhha: Contributions to the archaeology of South and West Asia in memory of George F. Dales, Jr.,* edited by J. M. Kenoyer, pp. 179–86. Wisconsin Archaeological Reports 3, Madison.

———. 1996a. Climate and the eclipse of the ancient cities of the Indus. In *Third millennium B.C. climate change and Old*

World collapse, edited by H. N. Dalfes, G. Kukla, and H. Weiss, pp. 193–244. Vol. 49. Global Environmental Change, Berlin, NATO ASI, series I.

———. 1996b. *Indus Age: The writing system.* University of Pennsylvania Press, Philadelphia.

———. 1996c. Meluhha. In *The Indian Ocean in antiquity*, edited by J. E. Reade, pp. 133–208. Kegan Paul International in Association with the British Museum, London.

———. 1997a. The date of the Surkotada cemetery: A reassessment in light of recent archaeological work in Gujarat. In *Facets of Indian civilization—recent perspectives (Essays in honor of Professor B. B. Lal)*, edited by J. P. Joshi, pp. 81–87. Aryan Books International, Delhi.

———. 1997b. Seafaring merchants of Meluhha. In *South Asian archaeology 1995*, edited by B. Allchin, pp. 87–100. Oxford & IBH, Delhi.

———. 1997c. The transformation of the Indus Civilization. *Journal of World Prehistory* 11(4):425–72.

———. 1998. Sociocultural complexity without the state: The Indus Civilization. In *The archaic state*, edited by G. M. Feinman and J. Marcus, pp. 261–91. School of American Research, Santa Fe.

———. 1999a. An Harappan outpost on the Amu Darya: Shortughai, why was it there? *Indologica Taurinensia* 23–24:57–70.

———. 1999b. *Indus Age: The beginnings.* University of Pennsylvania Press, Philadelphia.

Possehl, G. L. and P. Gullapalli 1999. The Early Iron Age in South Asia. In *The Archaeometallurgy of the Asian Old World*, ed. V. Pigott, pp. 153–75. University Museum, University of Pennsylvania, Philadelphia.

Possehl, G. L. and C. F. Herman. 1990. The Sorath Harappan: A new regional manifestation of the Indus Urban Phase. In *South Asian archaeology 1987*, edited by M. Taddei, pp. 295–320. Instituto Italiano per il Medio ed Estremo Oriente, Serie Orientale Roma, 66(1), Roma.

Possehl, G. L. and K. A. R. Kennedy. 1979. Hunter-gatherer/agriculturalist exchange in prehistory: An Indian example. *Current Anthropology* 20(3):592–93.

Possehl, G. L. and M. H. Raval. 1989. *Harappan Civilization and Rojdi.* Oxford & IBH and the American Institute of Indian Studies, Delhi.

Possehl, G. L. and P. C. Rissman. 1992. The chronology of prehistoric India: From earliest times to the Iron Age. In *Chronologies in Old World archaeology*, 3d ed., edited by R. W. Ehrich, pp. 447–74, 465–90. 2 vols. University of Chicago Press, Chicago.

Pottier, M.-H. 1984. *Materiel Funeraire de la Bactriane Meridionale de L'age du Bronze.* Editions Recherche sur les Civilizations, Mèmoire no. 36, Paris.

Potts, D. T. 1990. *The Arabian Gulf in antiquity.* 2 vols. Clarendon Press, Oxford.

———. 1994. South and Central Asian elements at Tell Abraq (emirate of Umm al-Qaiwain, United Arab Emirates), c. 2200 B.C.–A.D. 400. In *South Asian archaeology 1993*, edited

by A. Parpola and P. Koskikallio, pp. 616–28. Annales Academiae Scientiarum Fennicae, series B, vol. 271, 2 vols., Helsinki.

Puri, K. N. 1936–37. Excavations at Mohenjo-daro. *Annual Report of the Archaeological Survey of India, 1936–37*, pp. 41.

Puskas, I. 1984. Society and religion in the Indus Valley Civilization. In *South Asian archaeology 1981*, edited by B. Allchin, pp. 162–65. Cambridge University Press, Cambridge.

Raikes, R. L. 1964. The end of the ancient cities of the Indus. *American Anthropologist* 66(2):284–99.

———. 1968. Kalibangan: Death from natural causes. *Antiquity* 42:286–91.

Raikes, R. L. and G. F. Dales. 1986. Reposte to Wasson's sedimentological basis of the Mohenjo-Daro flood hypothesis. *Man and Environment* 10:33–44.

Raikes, R. L. and R. H. J. Dyson. 1961. The prehistoric climate of Baluchistan and the Indus Valley. *American Anthropologist* 63:265–81.

Rao, S. R. 1963a. Excavations at Rangpur and other explorations in Gujarat. *Ancient India* 18–19:5–207.

———. 1963b. A "Persian Gulf" seal from Lothal. *Antiquity* 37:96–99.

———. 1973. *Lothal and the Indus Civilization.* Asia Publishing House, Bombay.

———. 1979. Lothal: A Harappan port town, 1955–62. *Memoirs of the Archaeological Survey of India* 1(78).

———. 1985. Lothal: A Harappan port town, 1955–62. *Memoirs of the Archaeological Survey of India* 2(78).

Ratnagar, S. 1981. *Encounters: The westerly trade of the Harappan Civilization.* Oxford University Press, Delhi.

———. 1996. Ideology and the nature of political consolidation and expansion: An archaeological case. In *Ideology and the formation of early states*, edited by H. J. M. Claessen and J. G. Oosten, pp. 170–86. *Studies in Human Society*, vol. 11. E. J. Brill, Leiden.

Reade, J. E. 1979. *Early etched beads and the Indus-Mesopotamia trade.* British Museum, Department of Western Asiatic Antiquities, no. 1, London.

———. 2001. Assyrian king-lists, the royal tombs of Ur and Indus origins. *Journal of Near Eastern Studies* 60(1):1–29.

Rhodes, D. 1981. *Kilns: Design, Construction and Operation.* Chilton Publishers, Radnor.

Rissman, P. C. 1989. The organization of seal production in the Harappan Civilization. In *Old problems and new perspectives in the archaeology of South Asia*, edited by J. M. Kenoyer, pp. 159–70. Wisconsin Archaeological Reports, no. 2, Madison.

Roy, T. N. 1961. *The story of Indian archaeology: 1784–1947.* Government of India, Delhi.

Sahni, D. R. 1920–21. Exploration, Hindu and Buddhist monuments, Punjab, Harappa. *Annual Report of the Archaeological Survey of India, 1920–21*, pp. 15–17.

———. 1926–27. Mohenjo-daro. *Annual Report of the Archaeological Survey of India, 1926–27*, pp. 60–88.

———. 1931a. HR area (continued) Section B. In *Mohenjo-daro and the Indus Civilization*, edited by J. Marshall, pp. 187–213. 3 vols. Arthur Probsthain, London.

———. 1931b. VS area. In *Mohenjo-daro and the Indus Civilization*, edited by J. Marshall, pp. 214–32. 3 vols. Arthur Probsthain, London.

Sahni, M. R. 1956. Biological evidence bearing on the decline of the Indus Valley Civilization. *Journal of the Palaeontological Society of India* 1(1):101–7.

Samzun, A. and P. Sellier. 1985. First anthropological and cultural evidences for the funerary practices of the Chalcolithic population of Mehrgarh, Pakistan. In *South Asian archaeology 1983*, edited by J. Schotsmans and M. Taddei, pp. 91–120. Instituto Universitario Orientale, Dipartimento di Studi Asiatici, Series Minor 23, Naples.

Sankalia, H. D. 1974. *The prehistory and protohistory of India and Pakistan*. 2d ed. Deccan College Postgraduate and Research Institute, Poona.

———. 1978. *Born for Archaeology: An autobiography*. B. R. Publishers, Delhi.

Sankalia, H. D., S. B. Deo, and Z. D. Ansari. 1971. *Chalcolithic Navdatoli: The excavations at Navdatoli 1957–59*. Deccan College Postgraduate and Research Institute/Maharaja Sayajiro University Publication no. 2, Poona/Baroda.

Santoni, M. 1984. Sibri and the south cemetery of Mehrgarh: 3rd millennium connections between the northern Kachi Plain (Pakistan) and Central Asia. In *South Asian archaeology 1981*, edited by B. Allchin, pp. 52–60. Cambridge University Press, Cambridge.

Sarcina, A. 1978–79. A statistical assessment of house patterns at Mohenjo-daro. *Mesopotamia* 13–14:155–99.

———. 1979. The private house at Mohenjo-daro. In *South Asian archaeology 1977*, edited by M. Taddei, pp. 433–62. Instituto Universitario Orientale, Seminario di Studi Asiatici, Series Minor 6, Naples.

Sarianidi, V. I. 1998. *Margiana and Protozoroastrism*. Kapon Editions, Athens.

Sarkar, S. S. 1985. Human skeletal remains from Lothal. In *Lothal: A Harappan port town, 1955–62*, edited by S. R. Rao, pp. 269–304. *Memoirs of the Archaeological Survey of India* 2(78).

Sastri, K. N. 1957. *New light on the Indus Civilization*. Vol. 1. Atma Ram & Sons, Delhi.

———. 1965. *New light on the Indus Civilization*. Vol. 2. Atma Ram & Sons, Delhi.

Sauer, C. O. 1952. *Agricultural origins and dispersals*. American Geographical Society, New York.

Sayce, A. H. 1924. Remarkable discoveries in India. *Illustrated London News*, September 27, p. 566.

Scheil, V. E. 1925. Un nouveau sceau Hindon pseudo-Sumerian. *Revue d'Assyriologie et d'Archéologie Orientale* 22(2):55–66.

Schimmel, A. 1976. *Pain and grace: A study of two mystical writers of eighteenth century medieval India*. E. J. Brill, Leiden.

———. 1999. The Indus—river of poetry. In *The Indus River: Biodiversity, resources, humankind*, edited by A. Meadows and P. S. Meadows, pp. 409–15. Oxford University Press, Karachi.

Schmandt-Besserat, D. 1933. Tepe Hissar Excavations, 1931. *The Museum Journal* 23(4):323–483.

———. 1979. Reckoning before writing. *Archaeology* 32(3):22–31.

Schmidt, E. F. 1937. *Excavations at Tepe Hissar, Damghan*. University Museum, Philadelphia.

Sewell, R. B. S. and B. S. Guha. 1931. Zoological remains. In *Mohenjo-daro and the Indus Civilization*, edited by J. Marshall, pp. 649–73. 3 vols. Arthur Probsthain, London.

Shaffer, J. G. 1982. Harappan culture: A reconsideration. In *Harappan Civilization: A contemporary perspective*, edited by G. L. Possehl, pp. 41–50. Oxford & IBH and the American Institute of Indian Studies, Delhi.

———. 1984. Bronze Age iron from Afghanistan: Its implications for South Asian protohistory. In *Studies in the archaeology and palaeoanthropology of South Asia*, edited by K. A. R. Kennedy and G. L. Possehl, pp. 41–62. Oxford & IBH and the American Institute of Indian Studies, Delhi.

———. 1987. One hump or two: The impact of the camel on Harappan society. In *Orientalia Josephi Tucci Memoriae Dicata*, edited by E. Curaverunt, G. Gnoli, and L. Lanciotti, pp. 1315–28. Istituto Italiano per il Medo ed Estremo Oriente, Serie Orientale Roma, 56(2), vol. 3, Roma.

———. 1992. The Indus Valley, Baluchistan and Helmand traditions: Neolithic through Bronze Age. In *Chronologies in Old World archaeology*, 3d ed., edited by R. W. Ehrich, pp. 441–64, 425–46. 2 vols. University of Chicago Press, Chicago.

Shaffer, J. G. and D. A. Lichtenstein. 1989. Ethnicity and change in the Indus Valley cultural tradition. In *Old problems and new perspectives in South Asian archaeology*, edited by J. M. Kenoyer, pp. 117–26. Wisconsin Archaeological Reports, 2, Madison.

———. 1999. Migration, philology and South Asian archaeology. In *Aryan and non-Aryan in South Asia: Evidence, interpretation and ideology*, edited by J. Bronkhorst and M. Deshpande, pp. 239–60. Harvard Oriental Series, Opera Minor, vol. 3. Harvard University, Cambridge.

Shah, S. G. M. and A. Parpola. 1991. *Corpus of Indus seals and inscriptions*. Vol. 2. Collections in Pakistan. Suomalainen Tiedeakatemia, Suomalaisen Tiedeakatemian Toimituksia Annales Academiae Scientiarum Fennicae, Sarja, series B, NIDE, tome 240, Helsinki.

Shar, G. M. and M. Vidale. 1985. Surface evidence of craft activity at Chanhu-daro, March 1984. *Annali dell'Instituto Universitario Orientale* 45:585–98.

Sharma, A. K. 1974. Evidence of horse from the Harappan settlement at Surkotada. *Puratattva* 7:75–76.

———. 1982. The Harappan cemetery at Kalibangan: A study. In *Harappan Civilization: A contemporary perspective*, edited by G. L. Possehl, pp. 297–91. Oxford & IBH and the American Institute of Indian Studies, Delhi.

———. 1999. *The departed Harappans of Kalibangan.* Sundeep Prakashan, Delhi.

Shinde, V. 1991. A horn-headed human figure on a Harappan jar from Padri, Gujarat. *Man and Environment* 16(2):87–89.

———. 1992. Padri and the Indus Civilization. *South Asian Studies* 8:55–66.

Shinde, V., E. T. Thomas, and G. L. Possehl, eds. 2002. *The Sorath Harappan: A regional perspective on the Indus Civilization.* Oxford & IBH, Delhi.

Singh, G. 1971. The Indus Valley culture seen in the context of post-glacial climatic and ecological studies in northwest India. *Archaeology and Physical Anthropology in Oceania* 6(2):177–89.

Singh, G., R. J. Wasson, and D. P. Agrawal. 1990. Vegetational and seasonal climatic changes since the last full glacial in the Thar Desert, northwestern India. *Review of Palaeobotany and Palynology* 64:351–58.

Singh, G., R. D. Joshi, S. K. Chopra, and A. B. Singh. 1974. Late Quaternary history of vegetation and climate of the Rajasthan Desert, India. *Philosophical Transactions of the Royal Society of London, B, Biological Sciences* 267(889):467–501.

Singh, P. 1991. *The Neolithic origins.* Agam Kala Prakashan, Delhi.

Smith, G. 1997. Political units of the Mature period Harappan Civilization. Master's thesis, Department of Anthropology, University of Pittsburgh.

Sorley, H. T. 1959. The former province of Sind including Khairpur State. *Gazetteer of West Pakistan.* Government of West Pakistan, Karachi.

Sorre, M. 1962. The concept of genre de vie. In *Readings in cultural geography,* edited by P. L. Wagner and M. W. Mikesell, pp. 399–415. University of Chicago Press, Chicago.

Southworth, F. C. 1990. The reconstruction of prehistoric South Asian language contact. In *The uses of linguistics,* edited by E. H. Benedict. Annals of the New York Academy of Sciences, 583, New York.

———. 1992. Linguistics and archaeology: Prehistoric implications of some South Asian plant names. In *South Asian archaeology studies,* edited by G. L. Possehl, pp. 81–86. Oxford & IBH, Delhi.

Speiser, E. A. 1935. *Excavations of Tepe Gawra.* Vol. 1. American School of Oriental Research, Philadelphia.

Srinivasan, D. 1975–76. The so-called proto-Siva seal from Mohenjo-daro: An iconographical assessment. *Archives of Asian Art* 29:47–58.

———. 1984. Unhinging Siva from the Indus Civilization. *Journal of the Royal Asiatic Society of Great Britain and Ireland,* pp. 77–89.

Srivastava, K. M. 1991. *Madinat Hamad burial mounds—1984–85.* Bahrain National Museum, Manama.

Stein, A. 1905. *Report on Archaeological Survey work in the North-West Frontier province and Baluchistan for the period from January 2nd, 1904 to March 31st, 1905.* North-West Frontier Province Government Press for the Archaeological Survey of India, Peshawar.

———. 1929. An archaeological tour in Waziristan and northern Baluchistan. *Memoirs of the Archaeological Survey of India,* no. 37, Delhi.

———. 1930. An archaeological tour in Upper Swat and adjacent hill tracts. *Memoirs of the Archaeological Survey of India,* no. 42, Delhi.

———. 1931. An archaeological tour in Gedrosia. *Memoirs of the Archaeological Survey of India,* no. 43, Delhi.

———. 1942. A survey of ancient sites along the "lost" Sarasvati River. *Geographical Journal* 99:173–82.

———. 1943a. On Alexander's route into Gedrosia: An archaeological tour in Las Bela. *Geographical Journal* 102(5–6):193–227.

———. 1943b. An archaeological tour along the Ghaggar-Hakra River, 1940–42. *American Documentation Institute Microfilm,* no. ADI-4861.

Sullivan, H. P. 1964. A re-examination of the religion of the Indus Civilization. *History of Religions* 4:115–25.

Tessitori, L. P. 1918–19. Exploration, Bikaner. *Annual Report of the Archaeological Survey of India, 1918–19,* pp. 22–23.

Thapar, B. K. 1973. New traits of the Indus Civilization at Kalibangan: An appraisal. In *South Asian archaeology,* edited by N. Hammond, pp. 85–104. Noyes Press, Park Ridge.

———. 1975. Kalibangan: A Harappan metropolis beyond the Indus Valley. *Expedition* 17(2):19–32.

———. 1989. Kalibangan, -1 and -2. In *An encyclopaedia of Indian archaeology,* edited by A. Ghosh, pp. 194–96. Vol. 2. Munshiram Manoharlal, Delhi.

Thomas, K. D. and F. R. Allchin. 1986. Radiocarbon dating some early sites in N. W. Pakistan. *South Asian Studies* 2:37–44.

Tod, J. 1829–32. *Annals and antiquities of Rajasthan: Or the central and western Rajput states of India.* 2 vols. Routledge & Kegan Paul, London.

Tosi, M. 1977. The archaeological evidence for protostate structures in eastern Iran and central Asia at the end of the 3rd mill. B.C. In *Le Plateau Iranien et l'Asie Centrale des Origins à la Conquete Islamique,* pp. 45–66. Colloques Internationaux du C. N. R. S., no. 567, Paris.

———. 1983. A bronze female statuette from Shahr-i Sokhta: Chronological problems and stylistic connections. In *Prehistoric Sistan, 1,* edited by M. Tosi, pp. 303–18. Istituto Italiano per il Medio ed Estremo Oriente, Roma.

———. 1986a. Early maritime cultures of the Arab Gulf and the Indian Ocean. In *Bahrain through the ages, the archaeology,* edited by S. H. A. A. Khalifa and M. Rice, pp. 94–107. KPI Limited, New York.

———. 1986b. The emerging picture of prehistoric Arabia. *Annual Review of Anthropology* 15:461–90.

———. 1988. The origins of early Bactrian civilization. In *Bactria: An ancient oasis civilization from the sands of Afghanistan,* edited by G. Ligabue and S. Salvatori, pp. 41–66, 70–72. Erizzo and the Centro Studi Ricerche Ligabue, Venice, Roma.

Tosi, M. and R. Wardak. 1972. The Fullol Hoard: A new find from Bronze-Age Afghanistan. *East and West* 22(1–2):9–17.

Tosi, M., L. Bondioli, and M. Vidale. 1984. Craft activity areas and surface survey at Moenjodaro. In *Reports on field work carried out at Mohenjo-daro, Pakistan 1982–83 by the Is-MEO–Aachen University Mission*, edited by M. Jansen and G. Urban, pp. 9–38. Interim Reports, vol. 1. RWTH/IsMEO, Aachen/Rome.

van den Berghe, L. 1970. La necropole de Kalleh Nisar. *Archeologia* 32:64–73.

Vandiver, P. 1995. The production technology of early pottery at Mehrgarh. In *Mehrgarh: Field reports 1974–1985, from Neolithic times to the Indus Civilization*, edited by C. Jarrige, J.-F. Jarrige, R. Meadow, and G. Quivron, pp. 648–61. Department of Culture and Tourism, Government of Sindh, Pakistan, in Collaboration with the French Ministry of Foreign Affairs, Karachi.

van Lohuizen-de-Leeuw, J. 1974. Moenjo Daro—A cause of common concern. In *South Asian archaeology 1973*, edited by J. van Lohuizen-de-Leeuw and J. Ubaghs, pp. 1–11. E. J. Brill, Leiden.

Varma, S. 1990. Changing settlement patterns in Kathiawar. *Studies in History* 62:137–61.

Vats, M. S. 1928–29. Excavations at Harappa. *Annual Report of the Archaeological Survey of India, 1928–29*:76–85.

———. 1930–34a. The Chalcolithic site at Chak Purbane Sayal. *Annual Reports of the Archaeological Survey of India for the Years 1930–31, 1931–32, 1932–33, and 1933–34*, part one: 106–7.

———. 1930–34b. Excavations at Harappa: Excavations during 1933–34, brick platform in the southern slope of Mound F. *Annual Reports of the Archaeological Survey of India for the Years 1930–31, 1931–32, 1932–33, and 1933–34*, part one: 89–90.

———. 1940. *Excavations at Harappa*. 2 vols. Government of India, Delhi.

Vavilov, N. I. 1949–50. *The origin, variation, immunity and breeding of cultivated plants*. Translated by K. Starr Chester. *Chronica Botanica*, 16(1–6).

Vidale, M. and H. M.-L. Miller. 2000. On the development of Indus technological virtuosity and its relation to social structure. In *South Asian archaeology 1997*, edited by M. Taddei and G. de Marco, pp. 115–32. Instituto Italiano per l'Africa e l'Oriente and Instituto Universitario Orientale, Roma.

Vinogradov, A. V. 1979. Studies of Stone Age sites in northern Afghanistan (in Russian). *Ancient Bactria* 2:7–62.

von Meriggi, P. 1934. Zur Indus-schrift. *Zeitschrift Der Deutschen Morgenlandischen Gesellschaft* 87 (NF 12):198–241.

Waldbaum, J. C. 1980. The first archaeological appearance of iron and the transition to the Iron Age. In *The coming of the age of Iron*, edited by T. A. Wertime and J. D. Muhly, pp. 69–98. Yale University Press, New Haven, Conn.

Walker, B. 1968. *Hindu world: An encyclopedic survey of Hinduism*. George Allen & Unwin, London.

Wasson, R. J. 1984. The sedimentological basis of the Mohenjo-daro flood hypothesis. *Man and Environment* 8:88–90.

———. 1987. The sedimentological basis of the Mohenjo-daro flood hypothesis—a further comment. *Man and Environment* 11:122–23.

Weber, S. A. 1990. Millets in South Asia: Rojdi as a case study. In *South Asian archaeology 1987*, edited by M. Taddei, pp. 333–48. Instituto Italiano per il Medio ed Estremo Oriente, Serie Orientale Roma, 66(1), Roma.

———. 1991. *Plants and Harappan subsistence: An example of stability and change from Rojdi*. Oxford & IBH and the American Institute of Indian Studies, Delhi.

Weisgerber, G. 1984. Makan and Meluhha—third millennium B.C. copper production in Oman and the evidence of contact with the Indus Valley. In *South Asian archaeology 1981*, edited by B. Allchin, pp. 196–201. Cambridge University Press, Cambridge.

Wheeler, M. 1947. Harappa 1946: The defenses and cemetery R-37. *Ancient India* 3:58–130.

———. 1950. *Five thousand years of Pakistan: An archaeological outline*. Royal India & Pakistan Society, London.

———. 1953. *The Indus Civilization*. 1st ed. Supplementary volume to the Cambridge History of India. University Press, Cambridge.

———. 1955. *Still digging*. E. P. Dutton, New York.

———. 1959. *Early India and Pakistan: To Ashoka*. Frederick A. Praeger, New York.

———. 1966. *Civilizations of the Indus Valley and beyond*. McGraw-Hill, New York.

———. 1968. *The Indus Civilization*. 3d ed. Supplementary volume to the Cambridge History of India. University Press, Cambridge.

Willcox, G. H. 1992. Some differences between crops of Near Eastern origin and those from the tropics. In *South Asian archaeology 1989*, edited by C. Jarrige, pp. 291–99. Prehistory Press, Monographs in World Archaeology, no. 14, Madison.

Woolley, C. L. 1932. Excavations at Ur, 1931–32. *Antiquaries Journal* 12(4):355–92.

———. 1934. The royal cemetery. In *Ur Excavations*, vol. 2. 2 vols. British Museum/University Museum, London/Philadelphia.

Wright, R. P. 1985. Technology and style in ancient ceramics. In *Ceramics and civilization: Ancient technology to modern science*, vol. 1, edited by W. D. Kingery, pp. 5–25. American Ceramic Society.

———. 1986. The boundaries of technology and stylistic change. In *Technology and style: Ancient technology to modern science*, vol. 2, edited by W. D. Kingery and E. Lense, pp. 1–20. American Ceramic Society.

———. 1991. Patterns of technology and the organization of production at Harappa. In *Harappa excavations 1986–1990: A multidisciplinary approach to third millennium urbanization*, edited by R. H. Meadow, pp. 71–88. Prehistory Press, Monographs in World Archaeology, 3, Madison.

Zohary, D. 1970. Centers of diversity and centers of origin. In *Genetic resources in plants—their exploitation and conservation*, edited by D. H. Frankel and E. Bennett, pp. 33–42. International Biological Programmes, London.

Zohary, D. and M. Hopf. 1988. *Domestication of plants in the Old World: The origin and spread of cultivated plants in West Asia, Europe and the Nile Valley*. Clarendon Press, Oxford.

Zvelebil, K. V. 1970. *Comparative Dravidian phonology*. Mouton, The Hague.

———. 1990. *Dravidian linguistics: An introduction*. Pondicherry Institute of Linguistics and Culture, Pondicherry, India.

Index

Italicized numbers refer to figures.

acropolis, 80, 99, 100, 247
Adamgarh Cave, 34
Adams, Robert, 244
Afghanistan, 24, 227, 229, 231, 234
Agrawala, V. S., 238
agriculture, 1–2, 19, 23. *See also* farming; pastoralism; seasons
Aitken, E. H., 64
alabaster, 232
Alexander the Great, 3, 7–8, 10, 11
Allah Bund, 239
Allahdino site, 31, 123, 131, 237
Allchin, B., 146, 240–41
Allchin, F. R., 146–48, *147*, 154, 240, 249
alluvium: deep, 25, 239; fertility of, 7, 64; old, 9, 36, 43; use of, 103, 104
Altyn Depe site, 217, 229–31, *230, 231*, 235
American Institute of Indian Studies, 17
Amri-Nal Phase, 40–42, *42*, 43–44
Amri site, 10; disruption of, 47; excavations at, 40; Transitional Stage and, 48, 50
Amu Darya site, 24, 229
Ancient India, 18
animals, 4; on artifacts, 9, 82, 227, 232, 233; domestication of, 15, 23–24, 27–28, 32, 56, 63, 83; and plants in art, 120–22, *122*; tools and, 33; wild, 27, 32, 83. *See also* zoolatry
Anjira site, 35
anthropology, 3, 118, 174–75
Aq Kupruk I. *See* Snake Cave
Aq Kupruk II. *See* Horse Cave
Arabian Gulf, 221–26, *227*, 228–29
Aravamuthan, T. G., 10
Archaeological Survey of India. *See* ASI
archaeology, 4, 13, 15; anthropological, 30; history of Indian, 20n24; partition, independence and, 19–20; of Subcontinent, 16, 17, 34
archaeozoologists, 24
architecture: bricks and, 14, 51, 58; Period I and II, 31; permanent, 32; privacy and, 61; public, 46; religious, 57, 148–52; residential, 107–9; sophisti-

cation of, 89. *See also* buildings; cities; houses; *specific sites*; towns
Ardeleanu-Jansen, A., 115, 120, 233
art, 15, 61, 124; animals/plants in, 120–22, *122*; Bactrian, *116*, 117; maritime trade and, 218, *218*; religious, 142. *See also* sculpture
artifacts, 4–5, 55, 56, 250; funerary, 233–34; Intercultural style, *217*; metal, 27, 84, 93, *94*, 210, 225–27, *228*, 229, 232; of priests, *230*; types of, 34, 91, 203, 232, 233; unfinished, 231. *See* animals; graffiti; *specific sites*; taphonomic processes
Aryans: invasions by, 157, 160, 164–65, 237–38; language and, 16; Vedas and, 154
Ashmolean prism, 144
ASI (Archaeological Survey of India), 9, 10, 17–18. *See also* field schools
Asia, Central, 1, 5, 229–31, 235

Bactria-Margiana Archaeological Complex. *See* BMAC (Bactria-Margiana Archaeological Complex)
Bagor site, 32–34, 168
Bahrain, Island of, 225, 226, *227*
Baines, J., 135
Balakot site, 47, 49, 221, 237
Balfour, Edward, 96
Balkh River, 24
Baluchistan region, 6; Amri-Nal Phase of, 40; Amri wares in, 42; Bronze age and, 15; history of, 9, 10, 237; Indus lowlands and, 4; Posturban Harappan and, 241; trade and, 25, 35. *See also* Kullis; Quetta Valley
Banawali site, 130, 154
Banerji, Rakal Das, 12
Bannu, 241
barley, 63; v. wheat, 35, 65; wild/domesticated, 23, 27–29
Barth, F., 120
Barua, B. M., 137
baskets, 27, 31, 90

bathing facilities, 51, 204; description of, 106, *106*, 198–99; evidence of, 57–58, 80–81
bathrooms, 74
bead(s): Bronze Age and, 222; maritime trade and, 222–23, *223*; material for, 34, 35, 38, 82, 95, *96*; technology, 51, 58, 95–97; types of, 27, 223, *230*; workshops/factories, 16, 74, *76*, 82. *See also* carnelian; faience; *specific countries*; *specific sites*; steatite
Belt and Hotu Caves, 30
Bhadar River, 82
Bhandarkar, Devadatta Ramkrisna, 12
Bisht, R. S., 20, 67
bitumen, 27, 189, 221
Blackman, J. M., 97–98
Blanton, R., 57
BMAC (Bactria-Margiana Archaeological Complex), 117, 229–31; artifact sites for, *234*; materials from, *116*, 117, 231–32, 233, *233*; Middle Asian Interaction Sphere and, 231–35
boats, 218, *219*, 221. *See also* bitumen
Bolan River, 25
Borrow, Thomas, 17
boustrophedon, 134, 136
Brahuis, 14, 17
Braidwood, Robert, 23, 24, 29
bricks, 26; architecture and, 14, 51, 58; baked, 14, 15, 58, 72, 81, 99, 107–8, 248; manufacture of, 93; mud, 68, 74, 107; robbing, 10, 12, 14; uses for, 15, 25, 31; wedge-shaped, 51
bronze, 32, 51, 58
Bronze Age: Baluchistan and, 15; beads and, 222; ceramics and, 250; civilization of, 3, 12; site chronology for, 85; Turanian, 217. *See also* Mohenjo-daro
Brown, W. Norman, *16*, 16–17
Buddhists, 12, 103, 149, 193, 237
buffalo: cult, 143–44; motifs, 73, *74*, *123*, 142–43, *143*

economy, 4, 53, 56, 237, 241
Egypt, 3, 19, 148
Ehrenreich, R., 57
Elam, 224
Eliade, M., 148
elites, 175, 211; buildings for, 56, 58, 107; trade and, 218, 229
Emeneau, Murray B., 17
engineering, 89
epistemology, 16
ethnographic analogy, 19, 122, *123*
etymological dictionary, 17
Evans, Arthur, 10, 15
excavations: by American-Pakistani team, 65; methods of, 10, 12, 17, 20, 35; training, 18. *See specific sites*
exchange systems, 4, 5, 232
exports, invisible, 229

faience, 91
Fairservis, W. A.: on ethnicity, 120, *121*; on seals, 128, 131, 137, 138
famine, 7
farming, 43, 56, 85, 250; communities, 23, 25, 30, 34, 42; dry, 240, 242–43; hunter-gatherers v., 174
field schools, 20
figurines, 180–81; animal, 35, 74, 177, 210, *228*; callipygian, 234; clay, 27, 82; ethnicity and, 120; female/male, 177–83, *178*, 179, *179*, 228, *229*; goddess, *117*, 141, *182*, *183*; horned, 58, *59*; human, 74, *117*, 117–18, *118*; ithyphallic, *119*, 119–20, 224; puppet, 61, 124. *See also specific countries; specific sites*
fire(s), *43*, *48–50*, 73, *108*; altars, 72, 76, 152, 153. *See also* hearths
fish, and fishing, 27, 64, 84, 221, 230
Flam, L., 64
Fleet, J. F., 10–11
floods, 7, 51, 101, 103–4, 185
floors, types of, 25
food, 27, 85
food production, 1, 3, 6, *25*, 46; chronology of, *24*, 249; documentation of, 24, 30–31; harvest and, 228; health and, 175; revolution of, 5, 15, 20, 23. *See also* Early Food-Producing Aspect; tools
Fort Derawar, 9, 239
fortification: evidence of, 43, 68–69, 74, 76; reasons for, 103–4, 237
Franke-Vogt, U., 128–30, 138
Fullol Hoard. *See* Sai Hazara site

funerals, 152, 233–34. *See also* cemeteries; human remains; *specific sites*
furnace, 74, *76*, 85
furniture, 108–9

Gadd, C. J., 12, 134, 226
Gandhara, 3
Ganga-Yamuna Doab, 6
Ganweriwala site, 56, 65, 237, 247
"Gazetteer of Settlements of the Indus Age," 43
Gedrosia, 77
gender, 181, 182–83. *See also* figurines
geographical expansion, 34, 40
Ghaggar-Hakra. *See* Sarasvati River
Ghaggar River, 8
Ghosh, A., 51, 174
gifts, 4
glass, 32. *See also* faience
goats, 24, 27, 28
goddess: fertility, 179–80; figurines, *117*, 141, *182*, *183*
godown, 48
gods, 16, 19. *See also* deity; figurines; goddess; Mahisha; Proto-Siva
gold, 35; artifacts, 230, *230*, 234; vessels, 231, *232*
Gonur Depe site, 230, *230*
government, centralized, 57
graffiti, 72, 84, *87*, 225
granaries, 19, 101, 247–48. *See also specific sites*; warehouses
graves, 28, 35, *173*
Great Bath, 13, 14, 15, 89; chronology for, 191; description of, 187, 189–91; importance of, 57, 61, 243; plans of, *189*, *190*; platforms at, 99, 103; purpose of, 19, 58, 107, 147, 148–49, 152, 193
Great Bath, Mound of, *188*; Blocks 6 and 10, 193; excavations of, 149; L Area, 194, *196*; Pillared Hall at, 194–95, *197*; purpose of, 185, 195–96; stupa and, 185. *See also* Buddhists; College of Priests; warehouse
Grigson, C., 131
growth, 1, 34, 40
Gudar-i Shah site, 234–35
Gufkral site, 36–38, *38*
Guha, B. S., 157, 162
Gujarat, 6, 10, 20, 40, 43, *44*
Gumla site, 30, 47, 48, 62. *See also* Dera Ismail Khan
Gupta, S. P., 49, 51
Gurnikalan One site, 63

Hajji Firuz site, 30
Hakra River, 8
Hakra Wares Phase, 34, *38*; regionalism and, 35–36; river flow and, 63, 239; sites of, *37*
hammam (sauna), 114
Harappa site, 1, 3, 56; BMAC and, 233; cemeteries at, *168*, 168–71, 237; citadels at, 18, 19, 66; description of, 10, 66; excavations of, 11, 14–15, 17–18; finds at, 15, 35; granaries at, 15, 66, *67*; human remains from, 168–71, *169*; Mohenjo-daro site v., 15, 211, 247; mounds at, 18, 66; occupation at, *66*; plan of, *11*; sculpture from, 111, *111*, 112, *112*, 117, 123–24, 182, *182*, *183*; seals from, 10–11, *11*, 20, 221, *227*, 229; as urban center, 2, 231, 241
Harappan, Early: chronology of, 40; cultures of, 249–50; graph of settlement size, 47, *48*; Kot Diji and, 20, 239; sites of, *41*; transition to Mature Harappan, 30, 46, 50–53, 249–50
Harappan, Mature, 6; Early Harappan transition to, 30, 46, 50–53, 249–50; as Indus Civilization, 1, 244; Kot Dijian assemblage and, 20; Mesopotamian sequence and, 29; renewal and, 50; settlement data and, *47*, 240, *241*; sites, *63*; water and, 9, 63. *See also* BMAC (Bactria-Margiana Archaeological Complex); Period II; Shortughai site
Harappan(s): Civilization, 1, 20, 20n24; Posturban, 237, 240, *241*; script, 69, *70*; Sindhi and Punjabi, 85. *See also* Sorath Harappans
harbors, 80
Hargreaves, H., 162
Harvey, J., 10
Haryana, 6, 10, 237, 242
Hasanpur Two site, 63
health, 62, 169–70, 174–75. *See also* disease
hearths, 25–26, 36, 108
Heesterman, J. C., 244
Helmand Traditions, 30
Hemphill, B. E., 35
herders, 35, 85
Herodotus, 62
heterarchies, 57
Heyerdahl, Thor, 80
Hiebert, F. T., 231–32
hierarchies, 4, 5, 57
Hiltebeitel, A., 142

Mahisha, 142, *143*
Majumdar, N. G., 14, 17, 40, 74
Makran, survey in, 79
manufacturing, 81, 85
Margiana, 231, 235. *See also* BMAC
    (Bactria-Margiana Archaeological
    Complex)
maritime activities, 64, 80; evidence of,
    84; Indus, 221; during Middle Asian
    Interaction Sphere, 215; sophistica-
    tion of, 89. *See also* Dilmun site, Ma-
    gan site, Meluhha site;
    Mesopotamia; Middle Asian Interac-
    tion Sphere; technology; trade
Marshall, John, 1, *10*, 16, 17, 19; on archi-
    tecture, 106, 107, 108; ASI and, 9–10,
    13; Indo-Sumerian Civilization and,
    5; on language, 135; at Mohenjo-
    daro and Harappa, 3, 11, 12, 61, 103,
    162; religion and, 141–43; on sculp-
    ture, 112, 114
masks, *118*, 118–19, 226
massacres, 157, 160, 163, 238
Masson, Charles, 10
McAlpin, D., 135
McEvilley, T., 141, 144
Meadow, Richard, 27–28, 32–33
Mehi site, 78, 231, 237
Mehrgarh site, 24–25; animal/plant
    domestication and, 29; dwellings at,
    25–26, *27*; excavations at, 25–28;
    findings from, 35, *177*, 177–80, *178*,
    179, 227; paleobotany of, 27; Period
    II/III, 30–31, 35; plan of, *26*; Togau
    Phase at, 34–35, 177
Meluhha site, 218–21, *220*, 240
menials, 200, 201. *See also chowkidar*
Mesolithic Aspect, sites of, 31
Mesopotamia, 3, 119, 148; archaeology of,
    13; seals in, 3, 5, 29, 131; texts on Ma-
    gan, Dilmun, and Meluhha, 219–21,
    220, 221; themes and iconography,
    122, 146, *147*, 231; trade and, 1, 218,
    221–26, 228–29, 240; writing in, 134.
    See also Middle Asian Interaction
    Sphere; pictographs
metallurgy, 35, 93–95
metal(s), 15, 40, 51, 69; artifacts, 27, 84,
    93, *94*, 210, 225–27, *228*, 229, 232
microliths, 31–32, 35
Middle Asian Interaction Sphere, 117,
    215, *215*, 229. *See also* BMAC (Bac-
    tria-Margiana Archaeological Com-
    plex); Dilmun site; Intercultural
    style; Magan site; Meluhha site

Miller, H., 60, 89, 93, 243
mirrors, 226
Mitathal site, 154
Mockler, E., 79
models, 6, 16, 28, 41–42, 53
Mohenjo-daro, 3, 11–12, 60, 185;
    abandonment of, 165, 212, 231, 237;
    architecture at, 99, 107–9, *110*;
    Assembly Hall at, 14; Block 11, DK-
    G Area, 150, *151*; Block 8A, DK-G
    Area, 150–51, *152*; BMAC and,
    232–33; Buddhists and, 12, 103, 149,
    237; chronology for, 29; DK Areas,
    206, 206–11, *207*, *208*, *209*; drainage
    system at, 9, 105, *106*; excavations of,
    12–14, 65–66; financial problems at,
    14; findings from, 12, 13–14, 40, 202;
    as founder's city, 56, 101, 185, 211;
    granaries at, 103; v. Harappa site, 15,
    211, 247; houses at, 149–50, *150*,
    151, 197–204, *199*, *200*, *201*; HR
    Area, 149–50, *150*, *151*, 196–204,
    198; human remains from, 157, *159*,
    160, *160*, *161*, 162–66, *164*, *165*, *166*;
    Indus River and, 7; maritime trade
    and, 218, *218*; people of, 211–12;
    plans of, *13*, *100*, 100–103, *102*, *186*,
    187, *188*; religion and, 12, 62,
    149–52; sculpture from, 14, *113*,
    113–18, *114*, *115*, *116*, *117*, 120,
    123–24, 181–82; seals from, 3, 12, 58,
    60, 229; structures from, *187*; VS
    Area, 204–6, *205*; wells at, 103–4,
    104. *See also* College of Priests; Great
    Bath; houses; sculpture; warehouses
Mohenjo-daro: City of Wells and Drains,
    Water Splendor 4000 Years Ago
    (Jansen), 58
Mohenjo-daro and the Indus Civilization
    (Marshall), 15, 205
monsoons, 36, 64
Moti Pipli site, 40
motifs: animal, 76, 78, 120, *122*, *124*, 131,
    146, *228*, 231, *232*; buffalo, 73, *74*,
    123, 142–43, *143*; centaur, 122, *123*;
    human/tree, 58, *59*; Intercultural
    style, 216, *216*, *217*; man/animal,
    147, 227–28; plants/animals as reli-
    gious, 144–45, *144*; pottery, 56, 62;
    proto-Elamite, 228
mounds, 97; as citadels, 18, 247; double,
    77; layout of, 12; railway and brick,
    10. *See also* Great Bath, Mound of;
    specific sites
Mughal, M. R., 35–36, 50, 67, 239, 247

Mundigak, 44, 231, *231*
museums: Baghdad, 224; British, 10–11;
    of Fine Arts in Boston, 16; site, 12
myths, 247–49, 250–51

Nagoor site, 63
Nagwada site, 40
nais, 43
Nal site, 40, 42, *43*. *See also* Amri-Nal Phase
Namazga VI, Early, 231
Natufians, 24
natural resources, 40, 81–82
Nausharo site: abandonment of, 47, 48,
    237; figurines from, 180–81; ID pot-
    tery, 51, *52*
Nawanbans site, 45
Neolithic, 24; Northern, 36–40, *38*, *39*;
    sites, 20, 23
Niai Buthi site, 77
nihilism, 55–56, 61, 185, 243
Nindowari site, 60, 77, 78, 118, 237
Nippur site, 74, *119*, 119–20, 222, 224
nomads, 4, 65
Northwest Frontier, 4, 6, 241

oasis, 232
observations, historical and ethnographic,
    16
O'Connor, T. A., 10
ornaments, 15
ovens, 25–26

Padri site, 40, 143, *143*
Pakistan, 1, 5, 19; animal domestication
    in, 28; artifacts from, 234; Early Iron
    Age in, 3, 170
Pakistan Department of Archaeology, 20,
    241
palaces, 6, 18, 209
paleobotanical remains, 83
paleochannels, 7
Pande, B. M., 134, 228
paradigms, 18–19, 40, 103–4, 247
Parpola, A., 115, 131, 144, 222
pastoralism, 1–2; agriculture and, 23, 65;
    evidence of, 32, 36, 83; migration of,
    4, 41–43
Pathans, 5
peoples, 2, 4–5; age/sex of, *170*; Indus, 3,
    61, 87n9, 248. *See also specific coun-*
    tries; typology
period(s): I and II, 31, 34, 40–42, *43*, 48,
    50; aceramic, 25, 27; Akkadian, 29;
    architecture and, 31; Early
    Harappan, 48; of Indus Age, 1–2, 3;

Kushan, 240; Vedic, 16. See *also* Harappan, Early; Harappan, Mature; Transitional Stage

Persian Gulf, 226

Peshawar, University of, 241

pestles, 35

Petrie, Flinders, 14

phase(s), 29–30; Amri-Nal, 40, *42*; Burj Basket-marked, 30, 31, *32*; Damb Sadaat site and, 40, 44; of Early Harappan, 40; Painted Gray Ware, 63; Posturban, 16, 63, 91; Togau, 34–35, 177. *See also* Hakra Wares Phase; Kechi Beg Phase; Sothi-Siswal Phase

Philibangan. *See* Kalibangan

pictographs, 131, *132*, 132–33, *133*, 137–38

Piggot, Stuart, *18*; on Indus peoples, 87n9, 114; subregions and, 6; on technology, 89; on town planning, 101, 204. *See also* paradigms

plants, 65; and animals in art, 120–22, *122*; domestication of, 23–24, 27–28, 64

platforms: bathing, *106*, 243; with temple, 231, *231*; use of, 99, 101–4, 191

political organization, 5–6, 57

pollen cores, 9

population: distribution of, 23, 32, 46, 237; pathologies of, 174; stability of, 175

Possehl, G. L., 134

potter's wheel, 34, 90

pottery, 3, 23, 34, 92; cemeteries and, *170*; decoration of, 15, 25, 30, 40, 91; Kulli, 78, *79*; Northern Neolithic, 36; painted, 15, 61, 91, 122–23, *124*; trade and, 32; Transition Stage, 51, *52*; types of, 35, 39, 90, *230*. *See also* ceramics; graffiti; motifs; *specific sites*; wares

Potwar Plateau, *41*, 62

Prehistoric India (Piggot), 19

pre-Mauryan epoch, 11

Pre-Pottery Neolithic A (PPNA), 24

Pre-Pottery Neolithic B (PPNB), 24

priest-king(s): artifacts of, *114*, *115*, 230, *230*, 233; at Mohenjo-daro, 13, 193; rule by, 19, 247; statue, 207; of Sumer, 18

principal components analysis, 171

privies, 106–7, *107*, *151*, 198

Priyanka, B., 137

problem orientation, 18

Proto-Siva: as religious symbol, 141–44; seals, 58, *59*, 114, 250

Punjab(s), 1, 242: movement from Baluchistan to, 35; Pakistani and Indian, 6; people of, 5, 10, 15, 237

Puskas, I., 142

pyrotechnology, 3, 58, 89–95

Quetta Valley, 30, 44, 231

race, 114, 248. *See also* Aryans; Brahuis; Dravidians; Pathans; Punjabs; Sindhis

radiocarbon dating: chronology and, 29, 30, 32, 40, 85, 250; problems with, 67. *See also specific sites*

Raikes, R., 238–39, 244

railway, 10, 12, 14

rain, 6, 9, 15; drainage systems and, 105, 106; dry-farming and, 240–41, 242–43

Rajasthan, 6, 9, 242; population of, 10, 237, 240

Rakhigarhi site, 56, 237, 247; ceramics from, *72*; excavation at, 20, 71–72; plan of, *71*

Rang Mahal, 240

Rangpur site, 19–20

Rao, S. R., 19–20, 80

Ratnagar, Shereen, 220

Ravi River, 1, 10, 66

recording, types of, 4, 17, 18, 30

red ocher, 35

Red Sea, 1

Region(s), 6, 35–36, 40, 56; Afghan-Baluch, 23, 28. *See also* Domains

religion(s), 16, 19, 141; architecture and, 57, 148–52; diversity of, 62, 153; evidence of, 6, 62; funerals and, 152; Harappan, 148. *See also* deity; devil; figurines; fires; Great Bath; Hinduism; Mahayogi; Mohenjo-daro; motifs; Proto-Siva; Rgveda; Shaktism; *specific sites*; temples; traditions; water; yoga; zoolatry

research: on script, 135–37, 139n49; on subsistence system, 74, 83–84, 86; types of, 9, 24, 28, 83–84

reservoirs, 69

Rgveda: rivers in, 6–8, 145–46; text of, 10, 154, 237–38, 249

ring-kernoi, 228

Rissman, P., 128

rituals. *See* figurines; fires; Great Bath; religions

rivers, 6; changes in, 240; fossils and, 9; navigation of, 15. *See also* floods; *specific rivers*

Rohri Hills, 7, 9, 43

Rojdi site, 60, *82*; architecture and, 82, *83*, *84*, *85*, *86*; excavations at, 82–86; plants in, 65

roofs, 26, 36, 108

Ropar site, 237

Saar site, 225, *227*

Sahni, D. R.: Harappa and, 11, 12, 112; Mohenjo-daro and, 14, 113, 203–4, 205, 238–39

Sai Hazara site, 231, *232*

sand dunes, 9

Sankalia, H. D., 16–17, *17*, 18

Sankarananda, Swami, 137

Sanskrit, 16, 62, 135, 249

Santhli site, 40, 43

Sarab site, 30

Sarai Khola site, 20, 36

Sarasvati River, 6, 8–9, 239–40; Early/Mature Harappan and, 20; flow of, 63; sites along, 45, 74, 77

Sarcina, A., 109, *110*

Sargon of Akkad, 218

Sastri, K. N., 15, 169

sati, 167

Sauer, Carl O., 218

Saurashtra site, 6, 15, 82; chronology of, 85; nihilism and, 60; settlement history of, 50, 63. *See also* Sorath Harappans

Sayce, A. H., 3, 12

script, 52, 133–34; deciphering, 16, 17, 127, 131, 132, 134, 138–39; Dholavira and Harappan, 69, *70*; length of, 132, *133*; location of, 127, *127*; logosyllabic, 132, 136; materials and, 127, *127*, 135, 138; Proto-Elamite, 16, 131, 136; research on, 135–37, 139n49. *See also* boustrophedon; pictographs; seals, stamp

sculpture, 6; Bearded Man, *113*, 116, 149; Bronze Dancing Girls, *113*, 113–14, 123, *124*, 181, 182, 203; Dancing Siva, 112; Gray Stone Torso of a Dancer, 112, *112*, *113*, 124; Intercultural style, 223–24, 227; Lady of L Area, 14; The Man from DK-B, *113*, 116; Priest-King, *113*, *114*, 114–15, *115*; Red Jasper Male Torso, 111, *111*, 123, 124, 182; Sad Man, 149, 197; Seated Man, *113*, 116–17, 233; The Stern Man, *113*, 117. *See also* figurines

seafarers, 55, 60. *See also* maritime activities

toys, 74, 124. *See also* figurines
trade, 5, 237, 241; agriculture and, 19; artifact distribution and, 4; ceramics and, 224–25, 229; evidence of, 32; long-distance, 1, 28, 61; maritime, 218, *218*, 221; in Quetta Valley, 44; raw materials and, 231. *See also* communication; Dilmun site; Magan site; maritime activities; Meluhha site; Mesopotamia; seals, stamp
traditions, 3, 30, 34, 62, 153–54
Transitional Stage, 62–63; Amri Period II as, 40–43, 48, 50; burning and, 49; chronology of, 50–53; nihilism and, 56
triangles, 32
Turan, 217, 229
Turkmenia, 229
turquoise, 73
type fossil, 30
typology, 31, 131, *132*, 157

Ullah, Mohammad Sana, 95
ulus, 37
unicorn: motifs, 76, 131; seals, 72, 78, *162*, *222*, *224*, 229
University of Peshawar, 241
Upper Paleolithic occupation, 24
Ur: maritime trade and, 222, 226, *227*; Royal Graves of, 29, 216; seals from, *222*, *223*
urbanization, 1; as ideology, 55, 56–57, 243, 249–51; rise/fall of, 5, 10, 20, 23, 237. *See also* deurbanization
Uttar Pradesh, 10, 237, 242
Uzbekistan, 234

variables, independent v. dependent, 30
vase, Bactrian, *116*, 117

Vats, M. S.: on faience, 91; at Mohenjo-daro, 14–15, 108, 205; sculpture and, 111, 112; on seals, 134
Vavilov, N., 23
Vedas: Aryans and, 154, 165; ethnic diversity and, 62; holy river in, 8; ideology and, 3, 147–48, 243. *See also* myths; periods; Proto-Siva; Rgveda; Sanskrit
vehicles, 15, 51, 82
Vidale, M., 60, 89, 97–98, 243
villages, 9, 23, 25, 36, 85
viniculture, 35, 225
Vinogradov, A., 24
Volchok, B., 142

Walker, B., 144
walls, 31, 103. *See also* circumvallation
warehouse(s), 80; function of, 103–4, 187, 191–92, 193, 247; plans, *192*, *193*, *194*
ware(s): Ahar, 122; Amri, 42; Banas, 71; common, 225; Faiz Mohammad Grey, 45; Hakra, 35–36, *38*; Nal, 42; Northern Black Polished, 250; Painted Gray, 239, 240, 250; Quetta, 44–45, 90, *91*, 229, 234, 235; red, 229, 240; Reserved Slipped, 91; soft, 30; Togau, 35. *See also* Hakra Wares Phase; Painted Gray Ware Phase; stoneware
warfare, 6, 19, 49, 238
wasserluxus: at Dholavira, 69, 71; as ideology, 55, 57–58, 185, 243
Wasson, 238, 239
wasters, 84
water, 80; ideology and, 55, 57–58, 107, 146–47, 149, 153, 243; management system, 20, 69, 71, 104–7. *See also* dams; Great Bath; *wasserluxus*

Wavell, Archibald, 17
wealth, 56, 211
weather, 201
weaving, 31
weights, 84, 226
wells, 99, 103–5, 243; circular, 51, 57, 58; deaths in, 163, *166*; quantity of, 89, 102. *See also* bricks; *specific sites*
wheat, 35, 65; absence of wild, 23–24; domestication of, 27–29
Wheeler, Mortimer, 17–18, *17*; on Aryan invasion, 237–38; on climatic change, 9; on Indus peoples, 87n9; on religion, 154; subregions and, 6; on town planning, 101, 149; training by, 17, 18, 20; on Transition Stage, 50–51. *See also* paradigms
windows, 108
World War II, 17, 18, 217
Wright, R., 90, 241
writing, 1, 15, 222, 244; beginnings of, 51–52, 72; change/direction of, 134, 136; deciphering, 248–49; language and, 248; purpose of, 127; quality of, 61. *See also* boustrophedon; language; script; seals, stamp

Yahya, 231
Yamuna River, 9, 240
yoga, 58, 144, 145, 243, 250. *See also* Proto-Siva
Yoga Sutra (Patanjali), 144

Zagros Mountains, 28
zebu: as domesticated cattle, 27, 28, 83; motifs, *40*, 76, *112*, 144, 223
Zend-Avesta, 229
zoolatry, 146
Zvelebil, K., 136

Gregory L. Possehl is a professor of anthropology at the University of Pennsylvania and curator of the Asian Collections at the University of Pennsylvania Museum of Archaeology and Anthropology. He has been engaged in archaeological research in India and Pakistan since 1964, when he first visited the great ancient city of Mohenjo-daro with his mentor Professor Walter A. Fairservis.

Professor Possehl has been associated with excavations at many sites in the subcontinent, from Iron Age megaliths to Mesolithic encampments. Most of his research has been on the villages and towns of the Indus Civilization. He directed the excavations at Rojdi in Gujarat for seven seasons and is now engaged in investigating Gilund in southern Rajasthan, an important site on the eastern borderlands of the Indus Civilization.

Possehl has written and edited a number of books on the Indus Civilization and related topics. His most recent works are titled *Indus Age: The Beginnings* and *Indus Age: The Writing System.* These books chart the early history of the ancient cities of the Indus and investigate their undeciphered writing system.